The Anti-Group

The 'anti-group' has been described as an ideological and historical breakthrough. It is a concept which challenges the conventional optimism of group psychotherapy. The disruptive elements it comprises place a burden on the therapist and threaten the integrity of the group. Nevertheless, understanding the 'anti-group' offers therapists new perspectives on the nature of group relationships and alternative strategies for managing destructive behaviour.

Theories of group psychotherapy tend to polarise creative and destructive aspects. Morris Nitsun offers critical evaluations of the contributions made by S.H. Foulkes and Wilfred Bion, and demonstrates how, in practice, these forces interact and even complement each other. The 'anti-group', which manifests itself in a variety of ways ranging from demoralisation to excessive dropping out, expresses the frustration and anger that patients often experience. These feelings are invoked in intense ways during group sessions. Recognising the anti-group offers the therapist alternative coping strategies, helps to liberate the creative processes and strengthens the theoretical base of group psychotherapy.

Taking a wider view of the subject, Morris Nitsun places the 'anti-group' in the context of universal ambivalence about groups, which is evident in social settings such as the family, the workplace and the culture at large.

Morris Nitsun is Head of Psychology, Psychotherapy and Counselling Services, Redbridge Health Care NHS Trust, and a member of the teaching staff at the Institute of Group Analysis, London.

The International Library of Group Psychotherapy and Group Process

General Editor: Dr Malcolm Pines
Institute of Group Analysis, London, and formerly of the Tavistock Clinic, London

The International Library of Group Psychotherapy and Group Process reflects the group-analytic approach to psychotherapy from both practical and theoretical viewpoints. It takes into account developments in related areas and includes important works in translation.

Other titles in the series

Basic Aspects of Psychoanalytic Group Therapy
Peter Kutter
Bion and Group Psychotherapy
Edited by Malcolm Pines
The Evolution of Group Analysis
Edited by Malcolm Pines
Jacob Levy Moreno 1889–1974: Father of Psychodrama, Sociometry and Group Psychotherapy
Rene F. Marineau
Memorial Candles: Children of the Holocaust
Dina Wardi
Object Relations, the Self and the Group: A Conceptual Paradigm
Charles Ashbach and Victor L. Schermer
Personal Transformation in Small Groups: A Jungian Perspective
Robert D. Boyd
The Practice of Group Analysis
Edited by Jeff Roberts and Malcolm Pines
The Psyche and the Social World: Developments in Group-Analytic Theory
Edited by Dennis Brown and Louis Zinkin
Psychoanalytic Therapy in the Hospital Setting
Paul Janssen
The Sexual Relationship: An Object Relations View of Sex and the Family
David E. Scharff
Using Groups to Help People
Dorothy Whitaker
A Work Book of Group-Analytic Interventions
David Kennard, Jeff Roberts and David Winter
Ring of Fire: Primitive Affects and Object Relations in Group Psychotherapy
Edited by Victor L. Schermer and Malcolm Pines
The Third Eye: Supervision of Analytic Groups
Edited by Meg Sharpe

The Anti-Group

Destructive forces in the group and their creative potential

Morris Nitsun

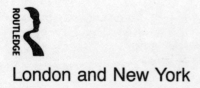

London and New York

First published 1996
by Routledge
11 New Fetter Lane, London EC4P 4EE

Simultaneously published in the USA and Canada
by Routledge
29 West 35th Street, New York, NY 10001

© 1996 Morris Nitsun

Extract from *Choruses from 'The Rock'* (1934) by T.S. Eliot
in *Collected Poems 1909–1962*, © Faber and Faber Ltd,
with permission

Typeset in Times by Intype London Ltd
Printed and bound in Great Britain by
Clays Ltd, St Ives PLC

All rights reserved. No part of this book may be reprinted
or reproduced or utilised in any form or by any electronic,
mechanical, or other means, now known or hereafter
invented, including photocopying and recording, or in any
information storage or retrieval system, without permission
in writing from the publishers.

British Library Cataloguing in Publication Data
A catalogue record for this book is available from the British Library

Library of Congress Cataloguing in Publication Data
A catalogue record for this book has been requested

ISBN 0–415–10210–3 (hbk)
ISBN 0–415–10211–1 (pbk)

*To Tony, whose belief in me and
my work made this book possible*

Contents

Foreword	ix
Saul Tuttman	
Preface and acknowledgements	xii
Prologue	xvi
1 Introduction	1
2 Foulkes' contribution: a critical appreciation	17
3 The concept of the anti-group	42
4 Clinical illustrations of the anti-group	75
5 Determinants of the anti-group I: regression, survival anxiety, failures of communication, projective identification, envy	106
6 Determinants of the anti-group II: interpersonal disturbance, the primal scene, aggression and hatred, the death instinct	133
7 Technical considerations in dealing with the anti-group	153
8 The role of the conductor	174
9 The transformational potential of the anti-group	197
10 'Nippets and Imps': the transformational process in a psychotherapy group	216
11 The anti-group in the wider social sphere	232
12 Conclusion: towards an integrative theory of group analysis	272
References	292
Name index	307
Subject index	311

Foreword

Saul Tuttman

Morris Nitsun's first paper about the anti-group was published in *Group Analysis* in 1991. That report and this new volume examine anger in group members expressed by the 'acting out' of destructive impulses and affects towards the group. I welcome and applaud this new appreciation of the role of aggression and hostility within groups by a British group analyst. In my commentary on Nitsun's original paper, I referred to the anti-group as an historical and ideological breakthrough. In this book, the concept of the anti-group emerges more fully as an original and important contribution to the overall field of group psychotherapy.

For many years several American group therapists have been concerned about the importance of group members venting aggressive and destructive impulses and affects in group treatment situations. In England and elsewhere, Kleinian psychoanalysts and group therapists, including Wilfred Bion, have expressed similar concerns.

I have admired Foulkes and his English group-analytic colleagues (including James Anthony, Malcolm Pines and Robin Skynner); nonetheless, as the years have gone by, I have become increasingly concerned about what appeared to me to be a neglect of the crucial role of aggression and hostility in the Foulkesian view of the therapeutic group. Unless we identify, experience and acknowledge the role of aggression and destructive forces and feelings at work in groups, we ignore an important part of human relationships and thereby endanger ourselves and limit our capacity to help 'work through' crucial issues. I greatly value Nitsun's determination to do just this.

Nitsun offers perhaps the first systematic critique of the work of S.H. Foulkes, giving due weight to the strengths of the approach while at the same time challenging the gaps and weaknesses in group-analytic theory. He compares Foulkes' contribution to that of Bion, arguing that they be seen not as contradictory, which is the general view in the UK, but as complementary: Foulkes emphasised the positive aspect of groups, Bion the regressive and destructive. Instead of these representing polar opposites, Nitsun suggests a dialectical view which embraces both in a mutually generating cycle.

There is an additional issue to which Nitsun refers but which I would like to emphasise. This is the important and productive role which aggression plays in healthy emotional developmental processes. This role of aggression has been discussed by, among others, Edith Jacobson, Donald Winnicott and myself. I consider this important since an appreciation of this aspect may help us to avoid 'splitting off' or utilising denial in attempting to counteract rage, anger or violence. We can only hope to support the further development of our 'true selves' by responding to the whole of our experiences.

In addition to the need to understand aggression as reflected in the anti-group, it is important to consider the role of aggression as a *pro-group* factor. Nitsun himself several times uses this term as a contrast to the anti-group. In the United States in the 1950s and 1960s, Edith Jacobson, applying an ego–psychological–object relations developmental approach, described in children an aggressive assertion towards self-sufficiency on behalf of emotional growth. This helps not only to establish their own identity but to strengthen their differentiation in the family group.

Nitsun makes substantial use of object relations theory to support his arguments, particularly the work of Donald Winnicott. The sequence described in Winnicott's late paper 'The use of an object...' is so important that I wish to highlight it here: 1) the developing child experiences the wish to destroy an object in fantasy and becomes aware of that wish, and 2) the child recognises that the object survives the destructive impulse in fantasy. Only after learning the sequence can the youngster begin to grasp the vitally important notion that there is an external reality outside the realm of one's fantasies. There are 'real' objects as well as fantasies and impulses. Through such processes, it becomes clear, after repetition during phase-specific experiences, that aggressive fantasies need not be dangerous and that there are real differences between feelings and actions. Guilt feelings and dread of retaliation abate as reality testing improves when the child learns to distinguish feelings from actions involving aggression and hostility.

In *Ring of Fire*, in my chapter on the therapeutic response to the expression of aggression by group members, I make a related point – the group provides an opportunity for experimentation, including the chance to express and release anger or to contain it as a recipient, and *survive* in either case: a learning experience of the utmost significance.

Throughout the book, Nitsun emphasises the transformational potential of the anti-group (see particularly Chapter 9). Not only is this offered as a theoretical possibility, but crucial technical considerations in dealing with the anti-group, which must be of interest to any group psychotherapist, are given a separate focus in Chapter 7. In Chapter 8, he discusses the all-important role of the conductor in addressing and modifying the impact of the anti-group.

In the very challenging final sections of this book, Nitsun moves from group treatment to broader social issues in life. He examines contemporary processes in three major contexts – the family, the workplace and the culture in its entirety. In each, the concept of the anti-group deepens our perspective of the drift in social cohesion. He is understandably concerned about our increasingly technologically complex environment in which we are in danger of becoming victims of the anti-group in a climate of profound alienation and self-destructiveness.

Can an enhanced appreciation of this destructive potential and increased effort to recognise, appreciate and deal clinically and socially with the anti-group help us cope with these most challenging problems? Nitsun's writing offers an invaluable perspective which is realistically pessimistic and yet offers some hopeful potential in a dynamic, generative and inspirational manner.

Saul Tuttman is President of the American Group Psychotherapy Association, clinical Professor of Psychiatry at the Albert Einstein College of Medicine, Department of Psychiatry, New York and Adjunct Professor of Psychiatry at New York Medical College, Valhalla, New York where he is also Training and Supervising Psychoanalyst at the Psychoanalytic Institute.

Preface and acknowledgements

The origin of this book goes back to my training as a group analyst, when I conceived the notion of the anti-group. It was first presented as a theoretical paper on the qualifying course at the Institute of Group Analysis (Nitsun 1991). It was subsequently published in *Group Analysis* (Nitsun 1991), accompanied by an appreciation by Kennard (1991) and, later that year, a commentary by Saul Tuttman (1991), President of the American Group Psychotherapy Association.

I would like to thank those people who recognised the paper and valued the challenge it made to group analysis in terms of Foulkes' limited appreciation of group-destructive forces. In general, the concept was taken up with interest – at times ambivalent – by members of the Institute of Group Analysis. It is this recognition that encouraged me to write this book, creating an opportunity to explore the concept of the anti-group in greater depth, to examine aspects that I had barely touched on in the original paper, and to consider its application beyond the therapy group.

The fact that the concept of the anti-group was received in the way it was at the Institute of Group Analysis is a measure of the openness of the Institute: a capacity to remain loyal to Foulkes' model while showing curiosity about new and divergent ideas.

I particularly wish to thank Malcolm Pines. As editor of the International Library of Group Psychotherapy and Group Process at Routledge, he was from the beginning supportive of the book and facilitated its progress through the various stages of publication. His erudition and guidance were important to me in structuring the text and relating it to the wider literature.

I also wish to thank John Schlapobersky for his support on several levels: as a critic who read an early draft of the book and gave me valuable advice; as a colleague who presented a clear and committed view of group analysis; and as a friend whose generosity and warmth made the difficult times easier. Among other friends at the Institute I wish to thank for their support are Geraldine Festenstein, Graham Fuller, Eva Gottesman, Sylvia Hutchinson, and Gabrielle Rifkind.

I also wish to thank my secretaries, Sandra Bendall and Karen Rogers, who typed the manuscript in their own time, for their hard work, patience, and humour.

It has been gratifying that in my teaching at the Institute of Group Analysis, the students on the qualifying course have been so open to my ideas. They carry forward the traditions of the past and mould them to fit new times and contexts. That they saw in the concept of the anti-group something useful, not only in terms of the destructive potential in groups but as the link to the creative power of the group, has been especially rewarding.

Since I started writing this book, there appears to have been an increasing recognition of the importance of disruptive and destructive processes in groups. Victor Schermer (1994) suggested that we might now find a consensus that 'disorganisation, chaos, death, aggression and unknowing are important and hitherto neglected aspects of groups as of all living systems' (p. 31). There has also been a growing number of references to the concept of the anti-group in the group psychotherapeutic literature. A recent paper by Craib (1996) focuses entirely on the anti-group and offers some important new insights. I hope this book will provide a further stimulus to those who are interested in the 'dark hour' in the group and its potential for transformation into light.

AN OUTLINE OF THE BOOK

Chapter 1 addresses the lack of theoretical coherence in group psychotherapy, including group analysis. It examines the interpretation of group destructive forces in this matrix. Chapter 2 looks specifically and critically at S.H. Foulkes' contribution. The strengths of the group-analytic model, its openness and creative possibilities, are considered alongside its weaknesses, its vague, idealising tendency, and its lack of an adequate recognition of the destructive component of groups. Aspects of Foulkes' biography are linked to his theoretical approach. Chapter 3 introduces the anti-group as a critical principle which challenges some of the underlying assumptions of group psychotherapy. It examines the paradoxical characteristics of analytic therapy groups and considers how these evoke anxiety and ambivalence about the group experience. The work of Bion is evaluated in this context, viewed as representing the opposite pole of Foulkes' optimism about groups. This split is considered as creating an unnecessary polarisation in the group field. Chapter 4 provides a wide range of clinical illustrations of the anti-group. Focusing on problems arising in psychotherapy groups, it also considers staff support groups and experiential training groups. The chapter emphasises the variability of the anti-group in different groups and different contexts.

Chapters 5 and 6 deal with the determinants of the anti-group. A notion of circular rather than linear causality is presented. Within this framework, insights gained from object relations theory and self psychology are utilised. The combined understanding locates the anti-group in deep-rooted, developmentally early fantasies and conflicts about relationships, including the clash between self or individual and group needs, the complex interplay of transference and counter-transference phenomena in the group, and the influence of primitive perceptual and defence mechanisms.

Chapters 7 and 8 address the question of managing the anti-group. In Chapter 7, basic technical concerns such as the setting, selection, and drop-outs are explored, highlighting both existing contributions in the literature that are useful in dealing with disruptive group forces and the gaps in our knowledge that create technical ambiguities. Chapter 8 considers the role of the conductor in more detail. Clinical interventions that may be helpful in dealing with the anti-group are suggested, while emphasis is placed on the conductor's counter-transference in these difficult situations.

The creative and transformational potential of the anti-group forms the theme of Chapters 9 and 10. In the former, key concepts of transformation from philosophy, psychoanalysis, and group analysis are outlined, setting the anti-group in the framework of the 'logics of change'. Chapter 10 gives a detailed description of the transformational process in a particular group, symbolised in the theme of the 'Nippets and Imps'.

Chapter 11 considers the application of the anti-group concept to the wider social sphere. Three contexts are examined – the family, organisations, and our culture at large – suggesting that a deep ambivalence about groups is both generated and reflected in the socio-cultural domain.

Chapter 12 concludes by attempting to reconcile not just the different strands of the book but some of the theoretical and ideological splits that have fragmented the field of group psychotherapy. Three integrative perspectives are presented – the dialectical perspective, the ecological perspective, and the aesthetic perspective.

Prologue
'Michael's[1] curtains': an anecdote

S.H. Foulkes, the founder of group analysis, died suddenly in 1976 while running a group. Perhaps the suddenness and recency of his death have made it difficult to stand back and examine the man as a man and link personal history to theoretical development. Yet, the occasional story offers a glimmer of insight.

Foulkes went one day to Liberty's department store in London with his wife, Elizabeth, to buy curtains for his consulting room in the Group-Analytic Practice at Montagu Mansions. He chose a set of curtains with an antique Persian motif. Elizabeth Foulkes later recalled, 'Michael didn't have his glasses on and he didn't really look at the detail of the design, he just liked the colours and general effect. He had no idea that it contained these rather ghoulish scenes' (E. Foulkes 1990b, p. 38).

Scrutiny of the curtains reveals, among the patterned motif, scenes of aggression and violence – Persian soldiers in their turbans and tunics capturing, tying up, striking and beheading their captive prisoners. Yet, at first glance the overall impression of the curtains is a pleasing one of colour and harmony. The whole is more than the sum of its parts.

There is an irony and humanity in this story which make one reluctant to read deeper meaning into it. Yet, the curtains are like a projection screen, inviting speculation on Foulkes' apparent blindness to their aggressive and destructive content (the absence of his glasses notwithstanding). Does the incident symbolise Foulkes' predilection for seeing the group as a creative whole, colourful and attractively patterned, even while there is aggression lurking just beneath the surface and erupting into

---

[1] S.H. Foulkes was known to family and friends as Michael.

violence? Are the curtains themselves symbols of a boundary drawn between the dark forces (night) and the light forces (day), perhaps representing some anxiety about the interaction of the two – good and evil, creative and destructive? Or are the curtains the protective cover of the unconscious, hiding the feared primitive impulses that threaten to break out of control?

Woven into these symbols and referents are the elements of a history and the contributions of a man, Foulkes, who left Nazi Germany to create a new home in England and a new psychotherapeutic form in group analysis. The well-springs of denial, destruction, and reparation are all here, themes that will recur through the pages of this book.

Foulkes' curtains were later taken over by Robin Skynner for his consulting room at the Group-Analytic Practice. When Skynner left the practice, the curtains found their way to the Institute of Group Analysis in Daleham Gardens, London NW3, where they now hang in the front group room, which is used for institute business and training purposes. They hang there rather too heavily for the relatively small room, as if bearing some incongruous weight.

In the dark hour you cannot call on goods and chattels to save you, or old ski trails or the paths to streams. You must find something greater. And the mind in which the forces of contumely and destruction seem greater than the forces of creativity. Creativity is there, but it seems, in relation to the forces of destruction, like a nipple on a balloon.

John Cheever (1991)
The Journals

But God, it has been said, dwells in the details.

Yosef Yerushalmi (1991)
Freud's Moses

What life have you if you have not life together?

T.S. Eliot (1934)
Choruses from 'The Rock'

Chapter 1

Introduction

Group remains one of the most mysterious, elusive, and controversial concepts in the domain of psychological understanding. What is the group? Does it exist? Is it an illusion, as Bion (1961) and Anzieu (1984) have suggested? This book reflects my own struggles to make sense of the complex phenomena of the group. It is a struggle that both led to and begins with the concept of the anti-group.

In the course of my training and practice as a group analyst, I found it necessary to evolve a way of understanding the negative and destructive processes in groups that seemed to me more pronounced and more perplexing than had commonly been recognised in the clinical literature on groups. In essence, this is the anti-group. The concept made it possible to understand the otherwise inexplicable flux in groups and the tendency for some groups to turn in on themselves in self-destructive ways.

The concept of the anti-group runs the risk of itself being vague and confounding rather than facilitating our understanding, and so I begin with a definition.

The anti-group is a construct by which I describe and understand destructive processes that threaten the functioning of the group. These processes appear to have several sources. One is an underlying fear, anxiety, and distrust of the group process. This is often confirmed by actual adverse experience in the group, as if the anticipatory anxiety becomes a self-fulfilling prophecy. A second source is the frustration of narcissistic needs, so that instead of providing an empathic mirror for the individual, the group is experienced as neglectful, depriving, and undermining. Exposure in the group is felt to be shameful and humiliating. A third source is aggression activated between members of the group. This may be expressed directly in hostile confrontation or indirectly in envy, rivalry, and destructive competition. Where the group fails to contain and constructively resolve these feelings, the group itself is experienced as the dangerous agent. 'It is the fault of the group; it is unsafe, threatening, exposing.' The group as object becomes impregnated with the hostile projections of the membership. The attitude to the group takes on a negative valence that may undermine the cohesiveness required to sustain and strengthen it.

My interest in anti-group processes arose in my training as a group analyst and in my observation of phenomena in group psychotherapy. In turn, it became apparent to me that similar processes occurred in groups outside the clinical setting and that the psychotherapy group, as it so often is, was a microcosmic reflection of more universal phenomena. This book traces the development of my thinking about the anti-group from its clinical origins to its wider applications. In so doing, the question emerges about what purpose it will serve to explore the anti-group in greater detail. On the practical side, I would suggest that recognising and understanding the anti-group will empower the group facilitator and the participants. It will help to contain and limit the destructive potential of the group, to harness the aggression involved, and to facilitate the transformation of the group into a therapeutic entity. It will help to differentiate between aggression that supports the development of the group, akin to what Winnicott called 'creative destruction', and aggression that is destructive in a pathological and disintegratory way.

On the theoretical side, I suggest that the concept of the anti-group fills a significant gap. Except for Bion's seminal contribution, there has been insufficient attention paid to destructive processes in groups, particularly those directed at the group itself. The group-analytic tradition to which I belong has dealt with these phenomena inadequately, emphasising constructive group forces to the neglect of the destructive. Further, while Bion's observations are crucial, they are, as a number of writers have pointed out (Brown 1985; Ashbach and Schermer 1987), theoretically unbalanced in their emphasis on group regression. A further aim of this book is to attempt a reconciliation between the approaches of S.H. Foulkes and those of Bion. I suggest that the anti-group is an intermediary concept that can help to establish a creative middle-ground and thereby strengthen both theory and practice in group psychotherapy and its applications in the non-clinical sphere. But, first, the present-day situation in group psychotherapy is considered, as this represents a starting-point for the formulation of the anti-group.

THE STATUS OF GROUP PSYCHOTHERAPY

Group psychotherapy occupies a major place in the contemporary field of psychotherapeutic endeavour. Together with individual therapy, family therapy, and to a lesser extent couple therapy, it defines the full scope of psychological help provided in the public and private spheres. There are even suggestions that the balance may be shifting towards group therapy. With the increasing demand for psychological assistance, the pressure on financial resources, and the renewed interest in more socially oriented therapies – much of which characterises mental health services in the late twentieth century – group psychotherapy emerges as the approach that may hold out the greatest promise for an equitable and socially relevant form of therapy. Yet, of all the approaches mentioned, it is the least developed in terms of its theoretical and practical base. The field abounds with confusion, ambiguity, and conflict.

It is instructive to compare comments made by leading practitioners in the field about fifteen years apart. The first is by Skynner (1983), speaking in the British context in the late 1970s. Comparing group psychotherapy with other therapeutic approaches, he describes it as

> still in a much more primitive, confused, conflicted, vague, and ill-defined state, even when attempts have been made to map some of the territory involved, containing, moreover, much disagreement and contention between its different practitioners.
>
> (Skynner 1983, p. 328)

The second observation comes from Dies. In a major review of the state of the art based on the publication in the *American Journal of Group Psychotherapy* of ten contemporary group psychotherapy models, Dies highlights

> confusion in the realm of theoretical conceptualisation of group interventions, limitations in the empirical understanding

of group process and outcome, and inadequate interface between research and practice.

(Dies 1992, p. 265)

Dies' comments suggest that little has changed in the intervening years since Skynner's statement – a worrying conclusion given the proliferation of literature in the field, containing some brilliant and original contributions, and paralleled by the ever-widening practice of group therapeutic methods. Added to this, I suggest, is a curious ambiguity in the status of group therapy in the overall psychotherapeutic milieu. Groups are both revered and despised, sought-after and feared. Therapeutic groups are ubiquitous, they are run in all sorts of settings, in the public and private domains, and yet the recognition of their contribution is highly ambivalent. In the minds of many, both patients and staff, they occupy a second-best position relative to individual psychotherapy. Many people run groups but questions of their qualifications to do so and the theoretical underpinning and rationale of the groups in question are often disregarded. Few clinicians would claim expertise in individual psychotherapy without a specialist training, whereas many run psychodynamically oriented groups without training, as if a smattering of clinical skills, generally deriving from an individual model, is sufficient to be a group analyst.

This is a minimising, even devaluing attitude towards group therapy and its particular characteristics and needs that I see as part of a more fundamentally ambivalent view of groups. This ambivalence has elements of anxiety, mistrust, and misunderstanding that I believe are reflections of an 'anti-group' attitude, an attitude I see as influencing reactions *within*, *between*, and *towards* groups.

The lack of theoretical coherence in group psychotherapy invites further comment. What accounts for the lack? Does it have to do with the shorter history of group therapy as a discipline relative to individual therapy? Psychoanalysis and the individual therapies took root in the late nineteenth century, whereas group therapy was more clearly a product of the twentieth century. The individual analytic approaches have had time to assert their identity, to be questioned and challenged, to face deconstructive trends, to deal with criticism, respond, and survive, but the field of group psychotherapy is in various respects undeveloped and unchallenged, and, as I suggested, widely but loosely anchored in the clinical arena.

This statement needs qualification. Of course, the wider matrix of group therapies contains some outstanding formulations and theories that have at least a degree of coherence. Further, we cannot imagine, or even desire, a state of absolute coherence in any psychotherapeutic field, or indeed any complex human discipline, but the fragmentation in the field of group psychotherapy nevertheless remains a striking phenomenon.

The postmodernist trends of our age continually challenge our assumptions about coherence and meaning. In one respect, the group therapy field already appears deconstructed. Brown and Zinkin, in a recent overview of theoretical perspectives in group analysis, to some extent use this as an argument to justify the great diversity and inconsistency they observe:

> Group analysis takes its place among the generally recognised category of human sciences, as distinct from natural science. In this respect, it follows the trend of postmodernist culture, where the search is not for some absolute compendious total system, nor the establishment of a standard text setting out the received wisdom of the experts in the field. This is neither possible nor desirable. Instead, there is a great value in partial and provisional insights.
> (Brown and Zinkin 1994, p. 251)

Inviting as this argument might be, it runs the risk of denying the need for greater theoretical coherence, of perpetuating the plethora of viewpoints that characterise the field. It also shrinks from the task of exploring why the absence of coherence came about in the first place. In this regard, the question of deconstruction applies at a more fundamental level of theory building. What is needed is an examination of the group itself as an entity and the way its underlying characteristics are seen to be reflected in the complex tangle of conceptual and technical systems.

Complexity is a key consideration. It is generally agreed that the complexity of the group process, which incorporates individuals, sub-groups, and the group-as-a-whole, while operating within the span of intrapsychic to systemic determinants, makes it very difficult to establish a sound conceptual base. Skynner (1983), comparing group therapy to a number of other different forms of therapy, from individual to family, concluded that the group is the *'most complex of all'*. Foulkes (1964) proposed four levels of group functioning – the current level, the transference level, the projective level, and the primordial level. This is one of his most integrative accounts of group life, but it reveals none the less the great complexity of interacting phenomena. Undoubtedly, the group's complexity is a major factor in the genesis of the theoretical confusion pervading group therapy.

But does this account sufficiently for the splits and divergences which seem to occupy the theoretical positions so virulently and which result in a fragmented body of theory, practice, and research? Could it be suggested that this reflects at a meta-theoretical level underlying tensions and contradictions in group life itself, that ambivalent, antagonistic processes that are an integral part of group development are themselves reflected in our intellectual systems, and that these are mirrored rather than transmuted in our theories of group psychotherapy? If this is the case, something akin to an anti-group phenomenon would seem to operate isomorphically at different levels of discourse about the group – a negative, disruptive, or disorganising process which infiltrates not only the group as a living process, but also the conceptual order of group psychotherapy.

THE ANTI-GROUP PERSPECTIVE

My ideas for the concept of the anti-group arose from the difficulties I encountered in running analytic groups and applying the method in non-clinical settings such as staff support groups. These difficulties emerged in the setting up and composition of groups, where I discovered considerable anxiety and distrust of groups, and in the conduct of groups, where antagonistic group processes threatened to undermine the integrative and therapeutic aims of the group. In most groups, constructive development supplanted the destructive, but not without a substantial struggle. The volatility and unpredictability of groups quite often left me – and the group – puzzled and disturbed.

These observations originated in my training as a group analyst, where I observed other students experiencing similar difficulties, though not always admitting to them openly. To some extent, I connected this with the group-analytic model and the framework of training it provided, believing that I had been prepared for the growth and development in groups, but insufficiently for the resistance, regression, and aggression. There is probably an element of truth in this, but my wider knowledge of groups increasingly suggested that the difficulty was not vested in group analysis *per se*: rather, it reflected underlying tensions and paradoxes in group life that were inadequately recognised in the group therapy field as a whole. I believe that this has limited the development of group psychotherapy as a coherent discipline. I believe that it has also limited the extent to which knowledge gained from therapy groups could be applied to the universe of groups outside the consulting room, such as the family, organisational, and social groups, and that it may also have impeded the reverse process, i.e. applying our knowledge of groups at large to the understanding of group therapy process.

Linking the psychotherapy group to wider social issues has particular relevance in so far as the therapeutic group itself is a form of social group. Unlike the fixed dyadic form of individual psychotherapy, the therapeutic group approximates a social group, which Jacobson (1989) has termed a 'small temporary society'. In some respects, this is the advantage of group therapy – it draws on the ordinary language of shared conversational experience in social groups in which people struggle with meaning (Schlapobersky 1995). But the members of a therapy group have generally had failed group experiences in one way or another, so the new group must offer them something different, something healing. In order to release this healing potential, the therapy group depends largely on its cohesive and constructive properties. In principle, this would distinguish it from groups in the surrounding culture, such as family and work groups, which are not uncommonly prone to disruption and breakdown, and which may have provided the flawed container that led the individual to seek psychotherapeutic help in the first place. The therapeutic group, therefore, needs to be defined as a different sort of group, a group that transcends the problems and limitations of other groups.

This, I believe, has led to an over-optimistic stance in the group therapy literature. Optimism is a necessary part of the therapeutic endeavour, but there is a danger that in excess it becomes idealisation. Optimism needs to take account of the darker, disruptive side of human behaviour, since without this there is a failure of differentiation, and, without differentiation, there can be no integration (Agazarian 1989, 1994). The group therapy literature tends strongly to emphasise the constructive and therapeutic potential of groups and to neglect or underemphasise destructive group processes. The emphasis is on how groups help people with problems without a corresponding recognition of the problems that groups create – a perspective that is more commonly found in the non-clinical small group literature (Smith and Berg 1988).

The overall body of writing in the field is of course complex, and it would be wrong to over-generalise, but this dual tendency – to maximise the positive and to minimise the negative – links a number of writers in different contexts. Another tendency, perhaps an even more serious one, is to split the constructive components of the group into one body of theory and the destructive into another. This sets up ideologies in which the search for objectivity, so elusive anyway, is eclipsed by the politics of institutions. These politics themselves replicate and obscure many of the dynamic group issues that urgently need addressing and understanding. This is nowhere truer than in the work of Foulkes and Bion, to which I briefly turn in anticipation of a fuller consideration in Chapter 2.

THE IDEOLOGICAL SPLIT

Group analysis was originated by S.H. Foulkes, a German psychoanalyst, in England in the early 1940s and has become the pre-eminent model of in-depth group psychotherapy in this country. Its influence has extended to many other parts of the world, particularly Europe. Its accessibility and applicability as a mode of group therapy make it all the more important to recognise both its strengths and its weaknesses.

In evolving group analysis as a separate discipline from psychoanalysis, Foulkes created a powerful vision of the group. His ability to conceive of the group as a rich source of therapeutic growth, essentially through the processes of dialogue and mirroring, was a contribution which seems to grow stronger with the passage of time. But, at the same time, he created an idealised vision of the group. There is a paradox in this, in that, from his writing, Foulkes appears to have been deeply aware of destructive and self-destructive forces in human nature (see pp. 30–31). But this awareness is inadequately integrated in his group-analytic model. His vision is rarely counterbalanced by a sense of the oppositional forces in groups, of the pull of regressive and destructive impulses. This leaves the group-analytic approach strangely ungrounded and incomplete, as if lacking gravitas.

Foulkes' (1964) greatest theoretical contribution is almost certainly his concept of the group matrix, 'the hypothetical web of communication and relationship in a given group, the common shared ground which ultimately determines the meaning and significance of all events and upon which all communication, verbal and non-verbal, rests'. The matrix is a highly generative concept and probably the single group-analytic concept that has stimulated the most debate. The tone of the debate tends towards an ever-expanding notion of the group matrix as a universal whole, increasingly taken out of the consulting room and into a cosmos which embraces phenomena such as quantum physics and holomovement (Powell 1993; Dicks 1993). Fascinating as these ideas are, they do little to operationalize the matrix as a dynamic entity in the therapy group. If anything, they add to the idealising vein running through group analysis.

There have been some important recent attempts to differentiate the group matrix that add an element of balance, particularly Roberts' notion of benign and malignant matrices (Roberts 1993), Prodgers' formulation of the dual nature of the matrix (Prodgers 1990), and Cortesao's concept of negative elaboration (Cortesao 1991). Hopefully, recognition of these contributions will help to correct the over-optimistic tendency of group analysis. But in the meantime the edifice of group analysis remains largely unchallenged from within and without, and in the next chapter a critical appreciation of Foulkes' contribution aims to explore this point in greater depth.

As suggested above, the significance of psychotherapeutic theory is closely related to its value in clinical practice. The successful implementation of a therapeutic model requires sound conceptual tools, and there are concerns that the theory–practice link in group analysis is a weak one (Skynner 1983). A more recent publication by Kennard *et al.* (1993) helps to clarify the nature of group-analytic interventions, but also reveals the enormous diversity of possible responses, the effect of which is at once exhilarating and perplexing.

The same is true of the application of group analysis in non-clinical settings. There is a growing interest in the application of the model to organisations and the wider social sphere. But this, too, suffers from confusion, from a problem of rooting technique and practice in firm conceptual ground. I suggest this relates to the global, undifferentiated nature of group analysis in general, remarkably open and flexible in some respects, but inadequately attuned to the power of destructive forces and the problem of reconciling these with the creative potential of the group.

Foulkes is not alone. In the USA, for example, the group psychotherapy culture is to some extent dominated by the work of Yalom (1975). This approach makes no pretensions at being psychoanalytically based, but it also manages to present a deceptively optimistic picture of group psychotherapy. Yalom is perhaps best known for his categorisation of the 'curative factors in group psychotherapy'. These factors –

> instillation of hope, universality, imparting of information, altruism, the corrective recapitulation of the primary family group, the development of socialising techniques, imitative behaviour, interpersonal learning, cohesiveness, and existential factors –

are usefully culled from the group therapy literature, but whether they can be called 'curative' is another matter. We tend no longer to associate the notion of cure with psychotherapy, seeing the process more in terms of growth and development. Yet, Yalom's epithet 'curative' continues to be widely accepted and quoted in the field. The term 'curative' is probably meant more in its broad, metaphorical sense than its literal and prescriptive sense. But, interestingly, the term has stuck, when, by contrast, we might find a list of curative factors in individual or family therapy reductionist and misplaced.

Where the group therapy literature deviates from this largely optimistic framework, it tends to swing in a diametrically opposite direction. This is epitomised in the work of Bion. One of the most influential of group theorists, Bion emphasised regression above all else. His theory of the basic assumptions (dependency, flight–fight, pairing) essentially concerns group-destructive processes in so far as it portrays the group task as undermined by the impact of primitive fantasies and behaviour. In this model, there is little, if any, room for optimism, for a constructive view of group relationships. The group is doomed to play out, in a continuing cycle, archaic patterns of relating that maintain an illusion of a working group while subverting its potential power and efficacy. This approach has not become part of mainstream group psychotherapy, and research has indicated that its application in the clinical setting yields unsatisfactory outcomes (Malan *et al.* 1976). But, if Bion's approach deals with destructive forces in too extreme a way, this leaves the group therapeutic endeavour without ballast, lacking a realistic and balanced method of understanding and containing the destructive processes that emerge in groups. Also, although its value in therapeutic group work is doubtful, Bion's approach has had a strongly generative impact on organisational theory and research, deeply influencing the Tavistock movement and suggesting that it has a relevance which can in no way be dismissed.

The growing impression is of a group field polarised between optimism and pessimism. Ideological rifts continue to drive the split. Skynner (1983), reviewing the situation in the 1970s, was led to lament 'a failure to examine actively the possibilities of integration'. He commented on how articles on Bion's work, in both England and the USA, gave the impression that Foulkes never existed, although he believed the acknowledgement to be fairer the other way round. Brown (1985) also made a strong and wise plea for a reconciliation between the two approaches. But it seems fair to say that no such reconciliation has taken place. In a recent critique of Bion's work from within the Tavistock mould, Hoggett (1992) expressed regret at the lack of 'a positive, creative and constructive force' in Bion's accounts of group life (and more generally the traditional psychoanalytic view of groups), but made no mention whatever of Foulkes and the group-analytic contribution. This even prompted a reviewer of Hoggett's book in the *International Journal of Psycho-Analysis* to comment pointedly on the omission (Barnett 1993).

THE LARGE GROUP – ALTERNATIVE VIEWS

A group-analytic perspective that is close to the views presented in this book comes not from the domain of small-group psychotherapy but from that of the large group. De Maré *et al.* (1991) have presented a model of the genesis of hatred in the large group and its transformation into what he calls 'koinonia' or impersonal fellowship. They see the large group as creating considerable frustration largely through its size (up to several hundred participants), and the alienating and fragmenting effect this has on the individual member. This frustration generates hate.

However, the 'structured' large group provides opportunities for dialogue which enable the hatred to be transmuted, leading to a spirit of kinship in the group.

This thesis is similar to my notion of the anti-group and its creative and transformational potential, as explored more fully in later chapters. However, there are a few distinguishing and critical points that I need to make. The first is that de Maré *et al.* focus on hatred *in* the group (between members) rather than hatred *towards* the group, which is more specifically my concern. This is a surprising omission in view of the great ambivalence that large-group participants frequently express towards the group (an observation based on my participation over several years in large groups). If anything, anti-group phenomena are exacerbated in the large group, partly through the intense anxiety and discomfort generated and partly through a process of amplification linked to the greater number of participants. A second point is that the sequence de Maré *et al.* describe from hate to dialogue to transformation in the large group is achieved to a very variable degree. I have experienced a strong sense of community developing in some groups, but also states of impasse, escalating rather than diminishing anger, and even mass withdrawal in others. Ultimately, de Maré *et al.*'s vision suffers from similar flaws to that of Foulkes: idealisation of the group, overvaluation of the process of verbal communication, and a seeming lack of attention to discrepancies that challenge the substance of the theory. However, this is a significant contribution that provides a useful parallel to the thesis I am developing in relation to the small group.

THE ANTAGONISM OF PSYCHOANALYSIS

In a trenchant commentary entitled 'Psychoanalysis and the fear of the group', Hoggett (1992) draws attention to the psychoanalytic tradition of group psychology originated by Freud. This is a view of groups, in Hoggett's opinion, as a product of primitive intra-psychic phenomena that render the group a highly disturbed and disturbing container. Contrasting Freud's *Group Psychology and the Analysis of the Ego* (1921) with more contemporary psychoanalytic views about groups as represented by Chasseguet-Smirgel (1985a, 1985b), Hoggett highlights how, in spite of differences between the two,

> each account essentially posits the group as a dangerous phenomenon from which psychoanalysis offers a form of consolation through its conception of a mature individualism.... Groups bring out the worst in us. What solace there is ... must be wrung by settling accounts with oneself. To turn outwards through action on and within the social world is almost inevitably an attempt to deny, through action, painful inner reality: politics is the last refuge of the scoundrel.
>
> (Hoggett 1992, p. 143)

If this is the psychoanalytic view of the group, it is not surprising that a common attitude towards group psychotherapy in conventional individual psychotherapy, particularly psychoanalytic, circles is one of doubt and hostility. This is by no means universal – there are numerous practitioners who are both individual and group therapists or analysts, others who are only individual analysts but value group methods highly, and occasions for considerable mutual respect between representatives of the two approaches. Nevertheless, a vein of scepticism and suspicion can be discerned in relation to group psychotherapy in general and the notion of analytic work in groups in particular.

E. James Anthony, himself a psychoanalyst, group analyst, and close collaborator of Foulkes, remarked:

> it is quite difficult to understand why we should be confronted with a dilemma of two cultures – the individual therapeutic culture and the small and large group culture. It almost seemed as if the 'pure' psychoanalysts equated an interest in group psychotherapy with suspicion and sometimes downright hostility. Foulkes experienced some of this and many creative psychoanalysts in the United States also suffered from what James Joyce once referred to as being nailed to a 'crucifiction', and it is indeed a cruel fiction with very little bearing on the realities of group analysis. The mischievous and mistaken segregation of two-body and many-body therapies has led to prejudice and demeaning attitudes: the individual approach was looked upon as 'deeper', intrapsychic, metapsychologically based and technically tied to the extraordinary phenomenon of transference and the transference neurosis during which an artificial illness was generated and 'cured' during the treatment. The group approach, by comparison, was seen as somewhat shallow, inter-personal and transpersonal, lacking in

metapsychological under-pinning, relatively ahistorical and diluting all its therapeutic efforts by concentrating on too many individuals at one and the same time.

(Anthony 1983, pp. 36–7)

As Anthony points out, Foulkes himself encountered considerable hostility to group analysis from British psychoanalysts, a matter which I believe had a strong influence on the way he presented group analysis and to which I will return in the next chapter. Seen from Hoggett's and Anthony's perspectives, the opposition to group psychotherapy, perhaps group analysis in particular, begins to assume meaning as a form of anti-group in itself. The supposition that psychotherapy can legitimately be conducted in groups, leading to powerful individual change, is met with scorn and derision. But, underlying this, there appears to be a deeper fear and hostility towards the group itself. If anti-group attitudes are to some extent part of our culture, as I will suggest, reflecting ambivalence and anxiety about belonging and participating in groups, this is as true of the psychoanalytic establishment as of anyone else, perhaps even more so, given the vested interest in protecting the territory of individual analysis and preserving the sanctity of the one-to-one transference relationship. Here, an anti-group process can be seen to operate at two levels – an ideological level in which the notion of psychotherapy in a group is rejected on intellectual grounds, and a deeper, perhaps unconscious level, in which fears of group experience predominate.

COMMENT

What emerges from the foregoing observations is the emotive power of the group, its capacity to generate fear, terror, and mistrust, as well as creativity, hope, and inspiration. What also emerges is its deep complexity, its multi-faceted origins and consequences, its intricate link to history and future, and its confused metapsychological status. It is perhaps for these reasons that so much theory about groups and group psychotherapy has become polarised, since polarisation offers the illusion of simplicity and certainty. Thus, we find in the metapsychology of group therapy a series of dichotomies that often present themselves in rigid opposition – the individual vs. the group, group analysis vs.

psychoanalysis, Foulkes vs. Bion, constructive vs. destructive forces, the deification of the group vs. the denigration of the group. That these poles represent different aspects of the same whole, that they are complementary perspectives of a many-sided phenomenon is at one level clear, but they remain very difficult to integrate into a coherent, working model of group psychotherapy.

When I first conceived of the phenomenon of the anti-group, my sights were narrowly set. My mind was focused on the clinical problems of composing and running therapy groups. But, as time has gone by, the concept has seemed to key into some of the fundamental questions about the theory of group development as well as the potential space that links the therapy group to the wider culture of groups. My hope is that the extended use of the concept will achieve several objectives: it will serve as a critical principle that challenges our assumptions about group therapy; act as a possible bridge between Foulkesian group analysis and the Bion tradition; and, more ambitiously, it will bring group analysis closer to the political sphere.

The point about the political arena is that, since group analysis has established itself more or less securely in the clinical field, questions have begun to be asked about its political perspective. The general impression is that this is lacking. In my own view, Foulkes' vision of aggression as located in the individual rather than the group and his conservative ideas about a normal society, both of which will be examined more closely in later chapters, diminish the potential application of group analysis to the political sphere. Richards (1989), in a commentary on the link between psychoanalysis and politics, suggests that 'Psychoanalysis is ... a source of opposition to the disintegrative tendencies in modern culture: its explicit purpose of repairing the fabric of individual experience has implications for a number of political agendas ... in the work of reconstituting and enriching the public sphere' (pp. 6–21). A similar claim, at the least, could be made for group analysis, since its aims are so close to social and cultural consciousness, but further development as a discipline is needed in order to realise this considerable potential.

To some extent, my experience of bringing forth the concept of the anti-group has felt to me to have a political dimension, this time political with a small p rather than a big P. It is one of the first attempts to challenge Foulkes' theory from within the ranks of group analysis. Although the original concept was received with considerable interest and enthusiasm by some, in others I detected a *frisson* of surprise, even anger. I felt that, in their eyes, I was a betrayer. Espousing a notion of the anti-group seemed to be equated with an anti-group position on my part, as a brazen attack on the integrity of Foulkesian theory. In the next chapters, I present what I believe is a balanced appreciation of Foulkes' contribution, its strengths and weaknesses. And, as the book proceeds, I hope to show that aggression and destructiveness in the group and towards the group are linked to its creative roots, that the anti-group is close to the sources of reparation and transformation, and that the concept may ultimately reinforce the group-analytic approach rather than diminish it.

Chapter 2
Foulkes' contribution
A critical appreciation

The purpose of this chapter is to examine aspects of Foulkes' life and work in order to tease out the phenomena that influenced his particular group-analytic vision, with specific reference to the problem of aggression and destructive conflict. It is suggested that he made an immensely creative but deeply flawed contribution and that this reflected, in part, his response to the unique set of social and professional circumstances that formed the context of his life's work.

There has so far been little serious biographical study of Foulkes and the link between the man and the development of his theory. Stories, impressions, and anecdotes abound (e.g. Anthony 1983; Skynner 1983). There also are several excellent accounts of the intellectual and wider historical influences on his thinking (Pines 1983a, b; Rothe 1989; Gfäller 1993). But in many ways Foulkes the man remains a mystery. The relative recency of his death (in 1976) may explain this, since in some respects he is still very much alive for the generation of group analysts who knew him. But this link regrettably will fade and a new generation will want to know more about Foulkes. The need for biographical study deepens in relation to Foulkes' own insistence on the influence of personal, social, and cultural history on the formation of the individual – 'the colossal forces of society that permeate the individual to the core' – and, connected with this, the way the individual adapts in an organismic sense to his total environment, inner and outer, a view Foulkes acquired from one of his great teachers, the neurologist, Kurt Goldstein.

A detailed biography is beyond the scope of this book, but a biographical slant is adopted here as a focus for exploring Foulkes' tendency to idealise groups and group analysis, and his difficulty in integrating into his model the destructive aspects of individual and group behaviour that he was himself only too aware of (Foulkes 1964a).

Before proceeding, however, it is necessary to raise a qualification about this approach. A theory, such as group analysis, must be judged on its own merits. The biographical slant may illuminate the origins of the theory but represents a different order of discourse. Hence, I attempt to set Foulkes' contribution in the context of his life, but also evaluate the theory, its strengths and weaknesses, in its own right.

THE BIOGRAPHICAL PERSPECTIVE

Contemplating Foulkes' body of work almost 100 years after his birth in 1898, there is a dawning sense of a visionary (Roberts and Pines 1992). Foulkes took a bold, impassioned, and far-seeking position in relation to the group-psychotherapeutic endeavour. He was a psychoanalyst who made a radical departure from psychoanalysis by originating group analysis. He also incorporated into group analysis a rich panoply of intellectual traditions, particularly Goldstein's neuropsychological approach, Gestalt psychology, and the teachings of the Frankfurt School. Yet, he remained committed to psychoanalysis and straddled the complex terrain between individual and group analysis.

Foulkes was a German Jewish psychoanalyst who left his native Germany suddenly in 1933 to come to London with his family. The Nazis were rapidly gaining power, the Jews were in peril, and the integrity of psychoanalysis was under attack. Foulkes responded to an invitation from Ernest Jones to move to England. There are few recorded details of the circumstances surrounding his departure – compare this to our dense knowledge of Freud's move to London a few years later. Although Foulkes left earlier than some other analysts, including Freud, so avoiding the rapid escalation of hostilities in pre-war Germany, it is difficult not to imagine that he faced at least elements of considerable uncertainty and threat in this major life change. Some of the questions we might seek to ask of any informed biography are: how did he deal with the separation from his mother country? how did he adjust personally to his immigrant status in a new and highly competitive environment? how did he feel about being a survivor of the war? how did the Holocaust affect him and his family?

and how did the reality of a world war impact on him as a person and a thinker?

The overall impression is that Foulkes adjusted very successfully to the change. He obtained a British medical qualification and relatively soon became a member of the Institute of Psycho-Analysis in London. He became actively involved with the Institute, later becoming a training analyst, and, in the words of his third wife, Elizabeth, remained a psychoanalyst of 'a strictly Freudian persuasion' until the end (E. Foulkes 1990b). In parallel to this, he began to experiment with group analysis, was a key figure in the Northfield Military Experiment in the 1940s – which established a brilliant tradition of group work in England – and produced his first book, *Introduction to Group-Analytic Psychotherapy*, in 1948.

Reading Foulkes' work, it is sometimes difficult to know where his strongest allegiance lay – to psychoanalysis or group analysis. Certainly, his most original contribution was as a group analyst, but this dual allegiance sometimes creates an ambiguous, even ambivalent impression in his writing. The roots of group analysis in psychoanalysis are ever-present in his work, sometimes clearly stated, but often conveying the impression of an uncomfortable position mid-way between the individual and group orientations. He made numerous references to this link, and the following, quoted by E.J. Anthony (1983, p. 37), is an example:

> I myself have not ever maintained that the interest in group analysis goes at the expense of that in psychoanalysis; as I have so often explained, group analysis is both less than psychoanalysis as well as more. Looking at it solely from a psychoanalytic point of view, it is not more than application of psychoanalytic insight, thinking and attitude to psychotherapy in the group. From the point of view of psychotherapy as a whole and the study of human beings it has contributions to make which exceed those of psychoanalysis although in no way replaces them.

Anthony (1983) describes this as 'a very balanced statement that did not detract or subtract from one or the other'. But the text betrays a sense of strain in holding together two very different models of psychotherapy. Although group analysis is in most respects a distinct mode of psychotherapy, there is a sense in which it never emerged fully as separate from psychoanalysis, in spite of Foulkes' inclusion of theoretical approaches that were unrelated to psychoanalysis in any direct way. In spite also of various attempts Foulkes made at clarity, the place of a number of key psychoanalytic principles in group analysis, e.g. regression, interpretation, and transference, remains confused. Ultimately, the two approaches may not be fully separable, but the problem of separation/differentiation may be a factor in the overall lack of theoretical clarity and identity in the group-analytic approach.

Another aspect of Foulkes' changed context was the psychoanalytic establishment he encountered in England. This was a turbulent period in the history of the British Psycho-Analytic Society, dominated by the Freud–Klein controversies which led to deep divisions in the society (King and Steiner 1990). Within this hostile and competitive environment, Foulkes appears to have made limited impact as a psychoanalyst. Phyllis Grosskurth (1989), in her biography of Melanie Klein, describes Foulkes as one of the 'continental males' (including Hoffer and Walter Schmideberg) who were 'not very effective'. If this was the case for Foulkes the psychoanalyst, how much more so would it have applied to Foulkes the creator of group analysis? In general, psychoanalysis in Britain at that time did not welcome or support the excursion into group analysis. Bion's involvement with groups was intense but brief, probably also reflecting the pressure to return to 'pure' psychoanalysis. Although Foulkes started practising group work outside London, in Exeter, away from the tense, unwelcoming atmosphere of the psychoanalytic milieu, he did so in an overall climate of hostility.

Several biographically related questions suggest themselves here. How much did Foulkes' struggle to differentiate psychoanalysis from group analysis parallel his problems of transition from one country to another? How much were the problems of theoretical separation between disciplines connected with issues of emotional separation in his life? To what extent did the hostility he encountered at the Institute of Psycho-Analysis influence the idealised way in which he presented group analysis? – a point that will be pursued more fully in the next section. And what happened to aggression and destructiveness in groups in all this – how did these phenomena manage to fall through the conceptual net? Was aggression projectively identified with the world war raging outside? And, further, how was it possible to maintain awareness of the war and at the same time evolve such an optimistic vision of human groups?

We cannot answer these questions satisfactorily without access to more substantial biographical data, but it is difficult to avoid the impression that a particular dynamic was at work: denial. This could tie in with Foulkes' status as refugee and, later, immigrant, requiring a radical readjustment at a time of considerable personal stress. Some available facts are, to an extent, corroboratory. Foulkes became a British citizen in 1938. At the same time, he changed his name from Fuchs to Foulkes. He also referred to himself by his initials, S.H., rather than by his full first names, Siegmund Heinrich, and later became known as *Michael Foulkes*. We can only guess at what was possibly being avoided here: his German or his Jewish identity, or both. Identity shifts of this sort were not uncommon in the great turmoil in Europe at this time but suggest in Foulkes at least a degree of discomfort, possibly threat, associated with his core identity and recent past.

A further aspect of the missing biography is information and understanding of the development of Foulkes the man and his work over the course of time. Most of the data available concern events and influences in Foulkes' relatively early adulthood: it is difficult to get a sense of periods of development through his life and how these were reflected in his group-analytic thinking. And what of his death? We know that he died very suddenly in 1976 while running a group and that the group consisted of the next generation of group analysts. We know something of the shock and disarray this caused (Sharpe 1991) but little of the implications it had for the further development of group analysis. We will return to this point in a later section, but it is necessary first to give an account of Foulkes' creative contribution as a group analyst.

FOULKES' CREATIVE VISION

Foulkes' contribution was creative both in the sense of his productivity as a psychotherapist and thinker and in his vision of the powerfully creative potential of the group. At the centre of his vision was the group matrix, which Foulkes saw as the 'hypothetical web of communication' that draws on the past, present, and future lives of the individual members, conscious and unconscious, verbal and non-verbal, to become the dynamic core of group development.

The matrix has the properties of a container, symbolically linked to the mother, or specifically to the womb, through its generative capacity (Foulkes 1948). It provides a context for transformation of both the individual and the group (Roberts 1983). This aspect has been associated with Winnicott's notion of the transitional space (Winnicott 1953), in which the space within the group circle becomes a projective screen, a practising ground for early interactions, an intermediate area of play and discovery, and a place for everyday creativity (Anthony 1983; Garland 1982; Schlachet 1986). Foulkes' emphasis on these group properties has linked our understanding of human communication in groups with a large body of art and science that deals with creation and transformation (Roberts and Pines 1992; Powell 1994; Rance 1992).

Connected with the concept of the matrix was Foulkes' vision of the network. This was not so much an original contribution as a synthesis of a long tradition of European and American thought emphasising the crucial place of the individual in the psychosocial sphere and the profound influences that permeate through culture to society, family, and the individual. In Foulkes' view, the individual was an abstraction: social preceded psychological, the group before the individual. Foulkes' genius was to link this perspective to the therapy group, not only expanding our understanding of the social context in which group members functioned, but adding a stronger interpersonal dimension to the intra-psychic focus of psychoanalysis and thereby evolving a more radical form of psychotherapy. This social-contextual point of view has become familiar to us in present-day systemic thinking (Blackwell 1994), but in Foulkes' time it was relatively new and he pioneered its application in the psychotherapeutic setting.

A further step was for Foulkes to encourage direct therapeutic intervention with families (Foulkes 1964). Although he himself did not develop this to any great extent, his conceptual approach to family networks foreshadowed family therapy as we know it today (Skynner 1987). His work at Northfield Hospital, in conjunction with Tom Main and Harold Bridger, led to the concept of the therapeutic community (Main 1977), widely influencing hospital psychiatry in the succeeding years. Linked to this, the emphasis he placed on context and his awareness of the interrelationship between small and large groups laid the basis for the application of group-analytic principles to non-clinical settings, notably in the organisational field (Rance 1989). Further applications include the development of transcultural group analysis (Brown 1992) and group-analytic anthropological studies (Bosse 1985; Knauss 1987).

The medium through which all these relationships came together in the therapy group was *communication*. An oft-quoted statement of Foulkes is 'Working towards an ever more articulate form of communication is identical to the therapeutic process itself.' Although, in itself, the emphasis on communication is fairly obvious – without it, how can human beings relate in any way? – Foulkes' contribution lay in his particular view of communication and the methods he applied to unblocking and enhancing communication in the group.

The essential concepts include:

- *mirroring*: the patient sees aspects of him or herself reflected in the image of another member or members of the group. This provides opportunities to confront various aspects of the self, including social, psychological, and bodily concerns, that may otherwise be repressed or dissociated. Foulkes described the group as a 'hall of mirrors'. The recognition and potential acceptance of the projected part of the self in the other may represent an important therapeutic gain (Foulkes 1964a; Pines 1982).
- *exchange*: Foulkes (1948, 1964a) used this term to describe sharing by members of the group at different levels of depth, including the most emotionally sensitive issues concerning relationship to self and other. This contributed to the supportive and socialising functions of the group.
- *free-floating discussion*: this is the group equivalent of free association in psychoanalysis. Since various members of the group contribute spontaneously to this process, the associative pattern in a group can build up in particularly rich, imaginative ways, releasing unconscious imagery and emotional expressiveness that lead to insight and understanding (Schlapobersky 1994). Dream material particularly lends itself to this process in the group, often in highly generative ways.
- *resonance*: this refers to the echoing of themes and feelings through the group, creating identifications from one member

to another. This can be far-reaching in that it awakens and heightens emotional awareness and leads to social bonding through a spirit of communality. Through this process is often attained the sense of universality described by Yalom (1975) as a 'curative' factor in group therapy.
- *translation*: this is the group equivalent of making the unconscious conscious. It differs from individual analysis in so far as the translation occurs across the group and not only between therapist and patient. This enables participants to move from less articulate, primitive forms of expression to a greater articulacy. 'The language of the symptom', described by Foulkes and Anthony (1965) as 'autistic', is given a social meaning. 'The group has to go downwards and to deepen its understanding of the lower levels of the mind by broadening and deepening its vocabulary until every group member also understands these levels' (Foulkes and Anthony 1965, p. 263).

As a psychoanalyst, Foulkes adhered to the classical Freudian approach as well as the ego psychology of Anna Freud. He was less convinced by the post-Freudian developments, particularly object relations theory. However, his intuitive grasp of a wide range of psychological experience, as suggested in the above concepts, brought group analysis close to important contemporary sources of developmental theory and research, notably the work of Daniel Stern (1985) on attunement, Kohut (1971, 1977) on empathy, and Bowlby (1977, 1988) on attachment. The broad experiential and intellectual base of group analysis provides the framework for an integrative psychotherapeutic approach of the kind that has become influential and popular in the late twentieth century (Norcross and Goldfried 1992).

Last but by no means least was Foulkes' perspective on leadership in the group. He used the word 'conductor' deliberately to suggest that running a therapy group was more akin to conducting an orchestra than leading in the conventional, directive sense. This was associated with a democratic view of the group process, in which the vertical emphasis of psychoanalysis (including the hierarchies of past to present and analyst to patient) gave way to the horizontal emphasis in group analysis (in which transference, communication, and therapy itself occurred across the group). Another well-known saying of Foulkes was 'therapy of the group by the group, including the conductor'. Above all, as Roberts and

Pines (1992) have pointed out, Foulkes was a facilitator, and his style of leadership has had an important influence on group work and psychotherapy in general.

Foulkes not only generated a far-reaching vision of group analysis but provided a working model of the group that was at once playful and profound – what Anthony (1983) has referred to affectionately as 'the magic circle'. In terms of his own leadership qualities and his talents as a teacher, Foulkes drew around himself a large, vibrant circle of colleagues who were profoundly influenced by his teachings and who carried the group-analytic tradition forward into all the fields, clinical and applied, mentioned above. Among these, Malcolm Pines and Robin Skynner perhaps stand out both for their creative and far-reaching contributions and for the debt of gratitude to Foulkes they freely acknowledge in their many writings.

The problem was that Foulkes' greatest strengths were in some ways also his weaknesses and in the next section a more critical view is cast on some of his contributions.

FOULKES' FLAWED VISION

Foulkes displays in much of his writing an overriding tendency to emphasise wholeness: he frequently speaks of the 'total situation', the 'whole person', the 'group as a whole'. This is particularly evident in a paper in which he criticises object relations theory (Foulkes 1975b), arguing against the part-objects implied in object relations theory on the grounds that the theory denies the essential wholeness of the person. This ties in directly with some of his most positive contributions, such as the group matrix and the network of communications, both of which are very much conceived as wholes. In many ways it was Foulkes' search for wholes that shaped his vision and most important contributions.

Foulkes linked this clearly to the influence of the neuropsychiatrist, Kurt Goldstein: 'From training and insight acquired in neurobiology... I held a conviction that the situation in which one works, the situation as a whole really decided all part processes and their meaning.... Naturally in a group the total situation is a group situation' (Foulkes 1973, p. 73).

Without question, Foulkes subscribed to the notion that 'the whole is more than the sum of its parts', the Gestalt principle that has become a commonplace but that continues to inform our understanding of groups. There is an appeal in wholes. They point towards integration and transformation and they counteract the fragmentation implicit in so much psychological and psychopathological theorising. In the case of group analysis, they bring the theory in line with current psychotherapeutic approaches, particularly self-psychology (Harwood 1992). The emphasis on wholeness is also supported strongly by group analysts of a Jungian persuasion. Zinkin (1994) stresses that the aim of all psychotherapy is the pursuit of wholeness as expressed by Jung in his idea of individuation. He also suggests that this is clearer in group analysis than in individual analysis, as the individuation of the group member is easily seen as depending on the individuation of the group-as-a-whole. Powell (1993, 1994) goes several steps further, to relate the group to cosmic states of interconnectedness, viewed in the framework of a psychophysical matrix, and suggesting the achievement of a transcendent religious dimension.

The negative aspect of wholes is that, if taken to the extreme, this perspective obscures and obfuscates details in a way that leads to confusion and lack of clarity. In this sense, Foulkes' great emphasis on the 'total situation' is, paradoxically, both a strength and a weakness. The concept of the group matrix, for example, a generative concept which contains a wealth of implicit detail and is meant to be the core of group development, tends to be used in a global way that obscures rather than illuminates the dynamics of the group. Group analysts who are at a loss to explain group phenomena, I find, often tend to fall back on the maxim 'it's in the matrix': a generalisation that is comforting but not necessarily illuminating.

I suggest that the emphasis on wholes in Foulkes' approach accounts, in part, for the inadequacy of his theory, the vagueness and tendency to over-generalisation. A complete psychological theory requires both wholes *and* parts. Without the whole, the detail becomes fragmentary and meaningless, but, without details, wholes become empty and diffuse.

Skynner (1983), in an important state-of-the-art review of group analysis about a decade ago, reveals that it took him some considerable time to realise the lack of theoretical coherence in group analysis. Until then, he believed it was his own difficulty in understanding and communicating the way groups worked. He refers to an 'Emperor's new clothes' phenomenon, whereby it was not just that an adequate theory of group psychotherapy was missing, but that he and others all *believed* that it existed. He suggests that this places a great burden on students, who may attribute their lack of clarity about group functioning and therapeutic intervention to their own deficiencies. 'Often it is not,' Skynner says. 'It is due to the fact that, in addition to not having a clear and comprehensive theory to teach them, we are behaving as if we have' (p. 341). Perhaps the ultimate danger of wholes is that they can be misleading and deceiving.

Skynner ends on an encouraging note, pointing out the vital strengths of Foulkes' contribution that he feels were *not* adequately conveyed in his writing, and proposes that it is 'our task to fashion for the Emperor the clothes that he deserves' (p. 343). My own view is that the requirement is not in the first instance for further theory construction: rather it is for deconstruction. This is precisely the aspect of Foulkes' work that requires a deconstructionist counter-perspective. The wholes need, at least provisionally, to be dismantled and dissected, so that the components can be identified and understood more clearly – and, ultimately, so that the wholes themselves can be reassembled and strengthened.

Pines, who has done a great deal to elucidate and refine Foulkes' concepts, adopts as a core psychotherapeutic position the notion of coherence (Pines 1986, 1994a). This he defines as representing 'the meaningful organisation of parts that make a whole', underlying concepts such as identity, integration, and unification. This usage of coherence implies the need for greater differentiation – as a basis for integration – in the way I am suggesting. Also, I believe that in actual clinical practice most group analysts, with their attention to figure–ground reversals and their emphasis on the individual within the group, adopt an approach that is compatible with this notion. However, this is inadequately reflected in the theory, which I see as to a large extent dominated by the conception of the whole.

The overemphasis on wholes, I believe, is associated with what I have already referred to several times as 'Foulkes' idealising tendency'. This idealisation appears in various ways. On the broadest scale, Foulkes had highly ambitious and optimistic views about the potential of group analysis as a school of psychotherapy. He wrote:

> I am convinced that this work is the best method to make the

revolutionary discoveries of psycho-analysis effective on a broader front both in therapy and in teaching. Moreover, the study of mental processes in their interaction inside the group-analytic situation will teach us much that is new and help to solve theoretical, conceptual problems which are self-perpetuating in the psycho-analytical situation. Therapeutic group analysis is the foundation upon which a new science of psychotherapy can rest.

(Foulkes 1964a, p. 14)

This statement highlights, perhaps exaggerates, some of the characteristics of Foulkes' approach: a global, idealising tone; a somewhat omnipotent view of group analysis as spreading the influence of psychoanalysis and, in a sense, surpassing it; the assumption that it will help to solve theoretical problems when in some respects it has *created* more theoretical problems than it has solved; and the attribution to group analysis of a scientific status which, in view of all that has so far been said, is, at best, premature.

Similarly, when Foulkes came to describe the therapeutic effectiveness of group analysis *per se*, he made extravagant claims:

The therapeutic impact is quite considerable, intensive, and immediate in operation. By and large, the group situation would appear to be the most powerful therapeutic agency known to us.

(Foulkes 1964a, p. 76)

Statements of this sort appear with an uncomfortable frequency in Foulkes' writing. There is seldom sufficient evidence to justify his claims – his writing provides disappointingly little in the way of clinical illustration – and there is an absence of a clear awareness of counterbalancing and antagonistic forces in group analysis. Even James Anthony, Foulkes' close associate and co-author, disassociated himself from this degree of idealisation. 'The claim is large but the evidence is by no means large and depends more on personal conviction' (Anthony 1983, p. 42). In the same article, Anthony draws interesting contrasts between Foulkes and Freud:

Foulkes, like Freud, was forever fighting the good fight for his own created form of therapy, but, unlike Freud, he tended to overestimate what the group could do. As Freud became older, his interest in psychoanalysis as providing an incomparable instrument for the investigation of the individual mind grew stronger and his belief in its therapeutic power became gradually weaker.

(Anthony 1983, p. 46)

Anthony goes on to provide a balancing statement about group psychotherapy. He suggests that 'anti-therapeutic processes' are more inclined to operate in groups than in individual therapy because the counter-transference of the therapist is greater and the sadism and envy of the group members are not constrained by any analytic considerations. Anthony also questions the claim that these 'anti-therapeutic' measures eventually become therapeutic, since groups often contain very vulnerable members with markedly fragile self-esteem and disturbed sensitivities who may be hurt rather than healed by the process.

Anthony's statement contains the germ of an anti-group perspective. Reflective statements of this sort concerning the limitations and dangers of group analysis are almost if not entirely absent from Foulkes' writing. The result is a strikingly one-sided view of group therapy, lacking the openness to doubt and dialectical tension that is intrinsic not only to the psychotherapeutic endeavour but to emotional development in its general sense, with its progressions and regressions, and its alternating expression of love and hate.

Instead of the recognition we may need when in doubt, there is Foulkes' well-known exhortation to 'trust the group'. The idea behind this is that deep down the group has a creativity, integrity, and healing power that transcends the limits of technique and therapeutic doubt. A similar note is struck in the principle that group analysis is an 'act of faith'. These maxims have been adopted by a continuing line of group analysts. I believe they reflect Foulkes' idealised, even religious vision of the therapy group conceived in global terms. Although they provide the sometimes necessary encouragement in the complex and often baffling task of running a psychotherapy group, they reinforce an unscientific, uncritical position which has done little to advance group analysis as a discipline. They make it difficult to identify and get to grips with the negative aspects of group functioning, such as fear and hostility towards the group, attacks on the group, evidence of group malfunctioning such as drop-outs and acting out, and group disintegration.

My own experience of trusting the group is that in a carefully composed group with fairly sound intellectual and emotional resources, meeting in a controlled, protected setting, the maxim 'trust the group' is certainly supportable and that the group usually fulfils the belief in its intrinsic potential. But many group therapists run groups in less than perfect situations, in which they are not able to select patients according to established principles: the membership of the group may be highly disturbed, volatile, and prone to acting out; there is a large degree of ambivalence about attending group therapy; and the setting itself is unpredictable, even hostile, such as in some out-patient clinics or hospital departments. Regrettably, this is often the reality we work in, and we may ask: which is the true test of the power of group-analytic psychotherapy – the problematic or the ideal setting? If the former, there are serious questions to be asked about the application of the model with more disturbed populations, what modifications in theory and technique may be required in these circumstances, and whether a theory is sufficient if it relates to only a segment of the population.

The crucial point emerging from this discussion is the need for theoretical balance. Neither unqualified optimism nor unremitting pessimism is satisfactory. The problem, and the challenge, is to reconcile the two. Anthony comes closer to this than Foulkes. The article referred to above, in which he makes his 'disclaimer', is in fact a paean of praise to Foulkes and his work, an elegiac tribute to his friend and colleague who had died a few years previously. But this does not stop Anthony from voicing doubts about the method he himself helped to develop. To hold this form of ambivalence is an achievement.

FOULKES' VIEW OF AGGRESSION IN GROUPS

If I have given the impression that Foulkes was unaware of aggressive and destructive forces, this must be corrected. The problem was not his unawareness: it was his difficulty in integrating his awareness into his model of group analysis.

In a paper recalling his one visit to Freud in 1936, Foulkes (1969) describes an episode in which Freud asked his opinion about the Nazi situation in Germany and the possibility of war. He then asked Foulkes how old he was. When Foulkes said 38, Freud commented, *'Was Sie noch alles schreckliches erleben konnen'* – 'What terrible things you have yet to experience'. From this remark, Foulkes says about Freud, 'I got a good impression of his pessimism and, strange as it might sound, of his conviction of the death instinct.' And Foulkes adds, *'Both of these I happen to share and believe I understand'* (Foulkes 1969, p. 24, italics mine).

In a paper originally delivered as Chairman's Address to the Medical Section of the British Psychological Society in 1961, he endorsed his belief in some form of death instinct:

> Personally I have become more and more aware in the course of years of the truth and usefulness of the concept of a primary self-destructive force. *Nothing is more certain than the ubiquity of destruction – a fact difficult to accept.*
>
> (Foulkes 1964a, pp. 138–9: italics mine)

A late paper by Foulkes (1974) on his philosophy in psychotherapy contains the question: 'Why do we fail?' He proposes two main factors: the enormous resistance people have to change, to learning or unlearning, and 'the need for self-damage, self-destruction'. He continues, 'This is also universal, and one could say that it is the amount and nature of unnecessary suffering that people add to that inevitable suffering which is part of life' (Foulkes 1974, p. 275).

It would appear that his belief in a self-destructive force remained a constant throughout Foulkes' career, and the tone of his statement above conveys a sense of regret and sadness about it: it is 'a fact difficult to accept'. Also, this late paper demonstrates more openly his lack of confidence in the psychotherapeutic method: Foulkes' pessimistic side.

Recognising the significance of destructive and self-destructive forces, Foulkes in fact attempted to give these a major focus in his view of group relationships. He saw the neurotic or psychotic individual as an isolated part of his social group and related this to destructive tendencies in the individual:

> The particular form which the neurotic position assumes is in its very nature highly individualistic. It is group disruptive in essence because it is genetically the result of an incompatibility between the individual and his original group. *It is at the same time an expression of aggressive and destructive tendencies.*
>
> (Foulkes 1964a, p. 89: italics mine)

Pines (1983a), commenting on Foulkes' statement, clarified it further by adding that what was for the healthier individual a social situation, where he or she represents a nodal point in an openly communicative social system, becomes for the neurotic individual a focal point for aggressive and destructive tendencies. This was thought to originate in the family group and to spread to relationships within the wider social network.

Foulkes had positive and optimistic views about the transformation in group therapy of aggression and destructiveness into healthy forms of aggressiveness and assertiveness:

> This disruptive, anti-social, destructive aspect to neurotic behaviour is forced to come out into the open and does not receive the sanction of the group ... the individual in his neurotic aspects is set upon by the others, a process in which he participates actively in his turn, when he attacks the other man's neurotic defences, and thus, by the way, his own.
>
> (Foulkes 1964a, p. 89)

A process follows whereby aggressive tendencies in the individual are used to attack and shift the neuroses of other members while constructive tendencies are used to support each other and build up the group: 'In a word, one could say that disruptive forces are consumed in mutual analysis, constructive ones utilised for the synthesis of the individual and the integration of the group as a whole' (Foulkes 1964a, p. 90). This view links with Foulkes' sociobiological orientation in so far as the constructive tendencies, once liberated, are seen as slowly leading the group towards the norms of the community of which it is part. Foulkes laid great emphasis on the socialising function of the group, but essentially within the norms of external society.

I see this as a worthy but limited and essentially misguided attempt to relate aggression to the core of group-analytic psychotherapy. I question it on several counts:

1 Aggression, as described here by Foulkes, is essentially located in the individual: it is the individual's destructive tendencies which make him or her a deviant in an otherwise healthy social group. Not only is the individual categorised and labelled – as neurotic, psychotic, or destructive – so simplifying the complexities of psychopathology, but there is no sense that the group itself, or the community, may be deviant or destructive

– in fact, that the group can adversely influence the individual, rather than the other way round. This is ironic, indeed contradictory, in view of Foulkes' consistent emphasis on the social context of the group. It also represents, in my view, the loss of an important opportunity to relate group analysis to wider social pathology – a crucial concern in applying the model to organisational and political concerns.

2 The attempt to equate aggressive energies in groups with analysis and constructive energies with synthesis is an oversimplification. It attempts to reduce complicated issues to a mechanical formula. The resolution and integration which Foulkes suggests this produces in the group appear facile (and inconsistent with the troubled, depressive tone of his statement about destructive and self-destructive forces).

3 Foulkes' sociobiological orientation has an optimistic but naive ring. The notion of the deviant therapy group moving slowly towards the norms of its community assumes both a stability within social norms and a form of ethical superiority over the therapy group: both assumptions are questionable. The contemporary history of social and family groups – and this is a significant feature of the twentieth century – is that of frequent disruption and destabilisation of norms. Equally, conservatively held norms (to which the group might move) may be expressions of social resistance and regression, or even oppression, rather than axiomatic standards to which we should all aspire. In either event, the relationship between our therapy groups and wider society is a complex one, not easily accounted for by a unipolar sociobiological perspective.

It is surprising that Foulkes' sociobiological theory has been as widely accepted by group analysts as it has. Even writers who normally reserve judgement about some fundamental Foulkesian premises seem to have regard for this view. Skynner, for example, notes: 'the group as a whole is far more normal than the individuals contained within it, forming a consensus which is a reliable guide to the outside world and thus permitting constant resocialisation and re-education in more healthy and helpful values and forms of interaction' (Skynner 1983, p. 339). Here, not only are the norms of the outside world regarded as the unquestioned criteria for individual development but the group's success may be measured against the achievement of these criteria.

That the group as a collective represents a consciousness which is greater than its individual members', and that there are opportunities in this for transcendence, is an encouraging point of view, but that this of necessity acts as a mirror of conventional society is debatable.

Only Karterud (1992), to my knowledge, challenges this view. He questions the notion of the group as a mirror of societal norms, suggesting that this is a 'dogma' which requires re-evaluation. He believes it does not take into account the impact of 'collective self-deceptions' in society; also, that it does not fit with groups which are composed of severely disturbed patients, which seems to be increasingly the case in clinical settings (it could be argued that this in itself reflects features of contemporary society and its tendency towards fragmentation and alienation – a different view of societal norms).

Returning to Foulkes, I am led to the conclusion that his failure to elucidate the power of destructive processes in groups was linked to his search for an idealised conception of groups and the wider community. The impression, rather as Foulkes himself suggested in the passage cited earlier, is that 'the ubiquity of destruction' was difficult for him to accept, that it did not fit into an idealistic view of groups, and that he made a partial but unsuccessful attempt at including it in his theory, thereby leaving a crucial area of group analysis underdeveloped and unresolved.

FOULKES AND INSTITUTIONS

Freud's questions to Foulkes about the Nazi regime in Germany and the possibility of war (see above) are surprisingly relevant in the present context. They take on a prophetic meaning when we consider that Foulkes started group analysis in England in the early 1940s. This was approximately ten years after he had left Hitler's Germany and at a time when World War II had engulfed Europe in a wave of violence. Foulkes developed his approach in parallel to the unfolding events of the war – the relentless destruction, the demonic behaviour of groups, the revelations of the Holocaust with all its atrocities, and beyond that, the killing fields of Nagasaki and Hiroshima. How do we explain the genesis of an optimistic model of human behaviour in the context of such destruction? This can be contrasted with Freud, whose experiences at roughly the same time, in roughly the same place, contributed a deep pessimism to his view of human conduct, a theme crystallised in *Civilization and its Discontents* (Freud 1930). What accounts, in Foulkes' case, for the disparity between the events of external reality and his trusting vision of the therapeutic potential of the group? I have already touched on the issue of denial, but there are other considerations.

Perhaps an explanation, in part, is that Foulkes was fighting his own private war in England. It is clear that he felt alienated from the British psychoanalytic establishment on the issue of group analysis: 'The idea of a psychology or psychotherapy based fundamentally upon the group is anathema to the psychoanalysts ... the vast majority of psychoanalysts today ignore or belittle group psychotherapy' (Foulkes 1964a, p. 230). This and other statements reveal that Foulkes felt he was fighting, if not losing, a lone battle against the psychoanalytic (and to some extent psychiatric) establishment. Not surprisingly, he felt compelled to argue the merits of group analysis forcefully: 'You say that I advocate my own approach. But what else can I do? If I did not think it the right one, I would not adopt it' (Foulkes 1964a, p. 121).

We can sympathise with these statements, but none the less note that these difficult circumstances appear to have led Foulkes to evolve a largely one-sided model. Ironically, what was missing was a convincing account of aggression in groups – exactly what Foulkes was facing in his hostile encounter with the psychoanalytic establishment. One also wonders whether the sometimes defensive idealisation helped or hindered the cause. After all, what Foulkes was picking up was essentially 'anti-group' reactions. In my original paper on the anti-group, I noted:

> The objection of the orthodox psychoanalytic establishment to group analysis was no doubt an intolerant reaction to the deviation from the sacred transferential context of individual psychoanalysis, but how much did it also reflect anxiety about the power of group processes, about the transposition of the therapeutic focus from the cosy privacy of the one-to-one relationship to the group arena, with its potential for explosive aggression, rivalry, and alienation? I feel that had Foulkes been able to explore these aspects more openly and more fully, rather than emphatically optimising the process and outcome

of group analysis at all costs, he might have made a more convincing impact on his critics.

(Nitsun 1991, p. 11)

Of course, if the group setting was anathema to some psychoanalysts, to Foulkes it was probably home. Very possibly, Foulkes' powerful investment in group was a way of finding himself and of establishing and building his identity in a new country. Viewed in a positive light, his optimism about group therapy and his emphasis on wholes and networks could be seen not so much as a denial of group hatred and war but as a way of balancing the destruction and suffering that he was only too aware of, of evolving a reparative vision of society and psychotherapy, of generating hope.

This leads into the last theme in this section – the institutionalisation of Foulkes' model and how the group-analytic milieu enshrined his legacy, in both its positive and negative aspects. Karterud (1992) makes some trenchant points about this. He emphasises not so much Foulkes' idealisation of groups but the institutionalised idealisation of Foulkes in the Group Analytic Society. This he suggests serves as a crucial cohesive factor which strengthens the international group-analytical community against the threat of internal conflict and disintegration – almost as if pre-empting an internal anti-group. The problem is that the force for cohesion is also an expression of weakness, a sign of immaturity. It produces an ideology, a term which Karterud defines as 'the systematic distortion of communication by the hidden exercise of force'. Various writers, notably Schwartz (1990), have noted the pressures to conform in organisations, the aim being to strengthen the narcissistic ideal of the organisation rather than the progress of the organisation. Karterud warns against this as an impediment to progress in both theory and research.

I would argue that these two circumstances – Foulkes' idealisation of groups and the idealisation of Foulkes – are intimately linked, representing a mirror between the theoretical and institutional domains and combining to maintain the status quo in group analysis.

FOULKES AND PSYCHOANALYSIS

The convergence between Foulkes and Freud, as people and psychoanalysts, has already been touched on in a previous section. In this section, some further comparisons of their intellectual value systems are made, highlighting the conceptual nature of group analysis. The relationship between group-analytic theory and classical psychoanalysis and the later objects relations theory is also explored, with particular reference to the role of aggression in development.

Freud's pessimism about wider social issues was evident in *Civilization and its Discontents* (Freud 1930). In one of his last papers, 'Analysis terminable and interminable' (Freud 1937), he revealed considerable pessimism about psychoanalysis itself, questioning its therapeutic efficacy and its power to prevent the recurrence of emotional breakdown after the termination of treatment. This paper has been the subject of a scholarly review by Thompson (1991). Her observations, in combination with Freud's own paper, provide a useful framework for assessing important aspects of Foulkes' model.

'Analysis terminable and interminable' is a courageous expression of Freud's doubts about the fruits of a lifetime's work. He unflinchingly confronts the disappointing and ambiguous outcomes of psychoanalytic treatment, offering a set of theoretical explanations for this. Here, the death instinct takes centre stage. Freud's view is that the regressive and self-destructive aspects of the death instinct are in fundamental opposition to the curative aims of psychoanalysis. The concept of the death instinct as a concrete force in human life and a causative agent in psychoanalysis has been one of Freud's most controversial contributions, not widely accepted in the psychoanalytic community (Ricoeur 1970; Brenner 1971; Hamilton 1976; Berenstein 1987). Thompson points out, however, that the concept has significance not so much as a concrete belief, but as an abstract principle that counteracts the overriding optimism in psychoanalysis. The optimistic view, which remains largely central to psychoanalytic thinking, is that psychoanalytic treatment leads to increasing structure, integration, and progress. Freud challenges this in various ways, pointing out that the ego is limited in its organising and integrating capacity, that it can be weakened by the force of instinctual demands and conflicts, and that developmental trends may lead to disintegration rather than integration.

Linked to this view of development, Freud also questions the unity of the psychoanalytic process itself, especially the notions of transference, transference neurosis, and the resolution of transference, notions which have also been idealised in the psychoanalytic culture and that, in the words of Bergmann (1988), have become a 'psychoanalytic article of faith' – an interesting corollary to the aforementioned principle that group analysis is an 'act of faith' (see above). In Freud's view, these 'articles' are only approximations of psychic reality and cannot be expected to be dealt with completely in psychoanalysis. In this sense, the psychoanalytic process itself is incomplete, at times even disintegrated.

Thompson suggests that Freud's pessimism should be seen not as absolute but as a form of 'corrective pessimism'. His paper did not end on a note of final pessimism and his aim was not to eradicate psychoanalytic belief but to restore theoretical balance to the overemphasis on optimism. In the terms of Bakhtin (1981), who focuses on dialogue as vital to the process of development, Freud sought to re-establish a dialogue between integration and disintegration, regression and progress; to give voice to a side that is easily submerged and silenced by optimism, a side he felt had to be maintained in constant dialogue with the other. 'This counterbalancing is no easy task, even today', writes Thompson (1991, p. 166), and she goes on to point out the resistance that Freud's paper elicited at the time of publication and in a continuing way. She also sees it as a tribute to Freud's greatness as a thinker and as a writer that at the end of his life he was able to take this stance towards his own creation.

The impetus to give voice to the side representing pessimism, disintegration, and regression in Freud's work closely resembles the postmodernist stance of deconstructionism. In this, the limits of a theoretical system are subjected to close scrutiny and the structures which imply integration and progress are challenged, dissected, and possibly dissolved.

These observations are of considerable importance in assessing the work of Foulkes. They tie in directly with the thesis I have been developing so far, which is that group-analytic theory is marked by an overemphasis on the optimistic aspects of the individual–group encounter, that it lacks a coherent account of destructive and disintegratory group processes, and that, for all its openness as a method of therapy and inquiry, it lacks reversibility and conceptual balance. Like Freud, Foulkes believed in the death instinct, or at least in the universality of destructive and self-destructive processes, but, unlike Freud, he did not incorporate this view in his theoretical model, either as an actual component of group functioning or as a critical principle in the domain of discourse and debate.

Foulkes' position is further clarified – and challenged – by relating to group analysis one of the central theses of Freud's thinking – the duality of Eros (the life instinct) and Thanatos (the death instinct). Foulkes inherited the dual instinct theory from Freud and there are indications that he strongly valued it (Foulkes 1957). But the group-analytic model would appear to subscribe only to Eros – indeed, it is interesting to see the very great extent to which it is suffused by Eros, when the two great forces are examined in greater detail.

Attributing the origin of the notion of a life and death instinct to the philosopher Empedocles, Freud notes, 'Of these two powers ("love" and "strife") ... the one strives to agglomerate the primal particles of the four elements into a single unit, while the other, on the contrary, seeks to undo all these fusions and to separate the primal particles of the elements from one another' (1937, p. 246).

Many of the characteristics of Foulkes' vision of the analytic group resonate with this description of Eros. The striving to combine particles into a single unity is an excellent metaphor for Foulkes' view of the group matrix, supporting his overwhelming emphasis on wholes. This impression is reinforced by noting Laplanche's characterisation of Eros: 'the life drive contains within it a mixture of the optimism borne by the ideology of progress or evolution: Eros is the gatherer and tends to form perpetually richer and more complex entities, initially on the biological level, then on the psychological and social one' (1970). The trajectory described here from biological through psychological to social fits with Foulkes' view of development as well as his conception of the group as facilitating progress from the isolated individual state to a shared existence in a social network. But the modifying, counterbalancing force of Thanatos, the death instinct, is absent from Foulkes' model – and, even without the pessimism inhering in it, group analysis is deprived of the levelling – and ultimately strengthening – force of this construct as a critical standpoint.

If Foulkes adhered in principle to classical psychoanalysis, although without incorporating some of its dialectical strengths, he showed a distinct reluctance to take on board the later developments in object relations theory.

In a late paper, 'Concerning criticism of inner-object theory' (Foulkes 1975b), he rejects object relations theory largely on the grounds of its intra-psychic emphasis, objecting to the 'objects' as 'personifications' of a mechanistic sort that are projected into the human mind, without reference to their interpersonal origins. In some respects, this is a relevant criticism for a group analyst to make, but Foulkes' rejection is a sweeping one, incorporating a degree of exaggeration and over-simplification – 'they go back rather to a theory that corresponds to exorcism or penitence' (p. 282) – and he fails to entertain some of the most powerful aspects of the theory, including the understanding of aggressive and destructive impulses as mobilising forces in interpersonal relationships. For example, Melanie Klein's views on the defence mechanisms of projection, splitting, and projective identification as arising from the struggle to deal with primitive aggression and envy are important for understanding aspects of group life. Fairbairn's theory of the anti-libidinal object also has much to offer to understanding the projections onto the group itself of a frustrating, depriving, even punishing object. Bion (1961), of course, applies Klein's concepts directly to the study of groups, and his views, together with those of Klein and Fairbairn, will be explored more fully in later sections. Group analysis does not necessarily exclude use of these concepts, and indeed they are assumed by many writers, suggesting that in fact they are more relevant than Foulkes admitted, but their conceptual origins tend to be denied and there remain in group analysis pockets of intense resistance to object relations theory.

Powell (1993), among others, has noted that Foulkes' conceptual thinking about groups came to an impasse. I agree with this: almost two decades since Foulkes' death, it is clear that there has been an atrophying of some of his basic concepts. The notions of communication, translation, and resonance, among others, have become so commonplace as to lose their theoretical distinctiveness and vitality. I also agree with Powell's observation that Foulkes' leaning towards the whole accounts for this impasse in that it, to some extent, disorganised his psychoanalytic inheritance. But, whereas Powell implies that Foulkesian theory might have developed more had he had the conceptual tools to elaborate further on the whole, such as in the work of Jung and the present-day transpersonal psychologists, my own view is that the emphasis on the whole, generative as it was in some ways, obscured important aspects of the group.

I have some sense of wholeness in the link between history and ideology in Foulkes' development: that his experience of leaving Germany on the eve of World War II, the very fact of the war, and his struggle to establish group analysis as a respected method of psychotherapy in England are not coincidental. All probably contributed in different ways to his striving to create a powerful nexus for group analysts in an ambitious, highly positive way. This has been reinforced by the idealisation of Foulkes and his work in the international group-analytic community, resulting in the spread of his influence but also in the dangers of reification and institutionalisation.

Even if we exclude the biographical parallels, we are left with an incomplete, theoretically biased conception of the group. Viewed in a positive light, however, the very incompleteness of Foulkes' theory and his open-systems approach as a theorist and therapist leave the way open for developments, which include a deeper appreciation of the role of aggression and disintegration in group life.

Chapter 3
The concept of the anti-group

The previous chapter highlighted the lack of theoretical balance in the group-analytic approach arising from its markedly optimistic view of the psychotherapy group. This was seen as consistent with the overall trend in the group therapy culture towards a determinedly optimistic stance. In this chapter, the concept of the anti-group is introduced more fully, both as an explanatory paradigm for group-destructive forces and as an abstract principle to challenge the optimistic view and to inform debate about creative and destructive forces in groups.

The chapter describes the origin of the concept in the clinical setting of group psychotherapy. It also outlines the manifestations and development of the anti-group, although detailed illustrations are left until the following and subsequent chapters. Here, the emphasis is more on concepts, structures, and theoretical antecedents. Part of this is an attempt to deconstruct the therapy group in order to identify the characteristics of groups that lend themselves to destructive and disintegratory forces. In this context, the work of group theorists outside the group-analytic framework becomes important, particularly that of Bion, but also the contributions of other writers who have wrestled conceptually with the powerful forces that challenge the growth and development of the therapy group.

THE CONCEPT AND ITS BACKGROUND

The concept of the anti-group grew out of the discrepancy I perceived between expectations based on the group psychotherapy literature and the actual experience of running analytic groups. The predominant areas of dissonance I encountered were

1) resistance to participation in groups linked to fear and dislike of groups, 2) hostility and anger arising in the group that could not only threaten interpersonal cohesion in the group but be directed destructively at the group itself, and 3) spiralling destructive processes in the group that could not be contained by the usual clinical management. These phenomena seemed to me to occur in a circular fashion, so that underlying resistance to the group would lead to negatively perceived experience in the group, which in turn would reinforce resistance and aversion to group participation. If occurring in a group with weak cohesion and/or excessive conflict, this cycle could result in an escalation of destructive processes that could threaten the continuity of the group. This is not to ignore the great constructive potential of groups, but to suggest that creative group developments are frequently counterbalanced by the oppositional forces of the anti-group, in individuals, sub-groups, or the group-as-a-whole. I have seen groups flounder badly in training and clinical practice, groups break down, end abruptly, or linger on in states of tense, negativistic impasse. In teaching situations, where I have frequently presented the principles of group work, I have found the most commonly voiced anxiety to be that groups can be destructive. Usually, there is at least one student who reports a destructive experience in a group, often a staff sensitivity group. In the different domain of organisational and work groups – which I deal with more fully in Chapter 11 – I have seen parallel difficulties leading to crises within and between groups, sometimes generating severely disruptive group relationships with destructive outcomes. In numerous ways, I have witnessed and been confronted by anti-group phenomena.

It was difficult to find in the literature a sufficient description and explanation of these phenomena, indeed even a recognition that there was a problem and a gap to be filled. In recent years, writers from different schools of group psychotherapy have begun to show a greater concern about the issue. Ormont (1984) notes that 'a reader, skimming through the indices of volume after volume, may find only desultory references to aggression, usually under "anger" or "hostility"'. Hawkins (1986) observes the substantial body of writing on group cohesion but the paucity of work on groups during periods of instability or disruption. I would add to these comments the observation that such descriptions as there are of group aggression are generally confined to aggression *in* the group in the form of anger, hostility, or rivalry between members; what is particularly missing in the literature is a notion of aggression *towards* the group. It is generally assumed that the psychotherapy group is a safe, good place to be and that any problems about it reside in individual participants rather than that the group itself creates a problematic setting which can trigger withdrawal or destructive activity and that this can ultimately undermine the group.

Where concepts are invoked to consider the sorts of phenomena described above, these are usually borrowed from the individual psychoanalytic or psychotherapeutic literature, concepts such as negative transference, negative therapeutic reaction, acting out, and so on. Useful and relevant as these concepts are, they do not provide the group perspective that is necessary to explain processes that are specific to group therapy. I could find no conceptual language within which to consider and explore the particular forms of group aggression that concerned me. The work of Bion comes close in some respects, and his contribution will be reviewed in a later section of this chapter; however, problems of emphasis and theoretical imbalance in his work leave the situation polarised and unresolved. I was particularly interested in how constructive and destructive forces could coexist in the group and what sort of dialectical relationship they could co-evolve. This led me to formulate the concept of the anti-group.

The following is my original description of the concept:

> [The anti-group] is a broad term describing the destructive aspect of groups that threatens the integrity of the group and its therapeutic development. It does not describe a static 'thing', that occurs in all groups in the same way, but a set of attitudes and impulses, conscious and unconscious, that manifest themselves differently in different groups. I believe that most, if not all, groups contain an anti-group, but that whereas in some groups it is resolved with relative ease, in others it can undermine and destroy the foundations of the group. Because of this, I consider it important – if not essential – to be able to understand its origins. I also believe that the successful handling of the anti-group represents a turning point in the development of the group. By helping the group to contain its particular anti-group, not only are the chances of destructive

acting out reduced, but the group is strengthened, its survival reinforced and its creative power liberated.

(Nitsun 1991, pp. 7–8)

The emphasis on the creative potential of the group in the last part of the quote is essential. The anti-group is not conceived as a monolithic force that inevitably destroys the group. Rather, it is seen in a complementary relationship with creative group processes, but requiring recognition and handling in order that the constructive development of the group can proceed without serious obstruction. The conflict between creative and destructive is itself seen as generative: it heightens and illuminates the paradoxical nature not only of the group but of human life in general and its containment and recognition is strengthening. In this sense, the concept of the anti-group remains true to the tradition of Foulkes, who valued the group and saw its inherent potential as a therapeutic medium, and it differs from that of Bion, who viewed regression in groups as occurring within a destructive closed system.

Before embarking on a further explanation of the various manifestations of the anti-group, it is necessary to make a brief digression. This is to examine more closely the characteristics of therapy groups that are conducive to anti-group reactions. This is done within a framework that emphasises the paradoxical nature of the group and its contradictory demands on participants.

THE PARADOX OF THE GROUP: GROUP CHARACTERISTICS RELATED TO THE ANTI-GROUP

A psychotherapy group is a highly specific form of group that captures some of the essential characteristics of group life in general while adding some unique features of its own. Smith and Berg (1988), commenting on a wide range of groups, suggest that group life is inherently paradoxical. They argue that it is impossible to have a group without certain types of conflict and that contradictory processes of progression and regression, individuality and belonging, attachment and alienation, occur in most groups. Yet, they point out that 'there is a tendency to forget or ignore the problems *created* by groups while attending to the problems that will be *alleviated* by them' (p. 4). They suggest that this in itself presents us with a paradox, since remembering what we know about groups is both enabling and disabling: 'Attention to the difficult and problematic aspects of life in groups makes it possible to manage them more effectively, but the memories generated by this attention may dissuade us altogether from connecting with groups' (Smith and Berg 1988, p. 4).

The psychotherapy group in various ways heightens the paradox of group life. Not only does it contain the contradictions that are common to groups in general, but it offers this paradoxical setting as the context for psychotherapy. It is also designed for people whose psychological problems involve at least a measure of social alienation, in which group membership is likely to have suffered owing to underlying difficulties in the capacity for social relationships (remember Foulkes' assertion that the neurotic and psychotic condition is in essence 'group disruptive'). The paradox deepens when we consider that it is these individuals who are required to create and build up the psychotherapy group. In the analytic group, the development of the group is essentially determined by its participants and the group as an object is a product of the creative and destructive projections onto it. We have a situation then which is layered by paradox: the group as an entity is inherently paradoxical; the psychotherapy group exaggerates some of these paradoxes; group members bring to the group their background of difficulties in group life; yet they are the creators of the group and determine its destiny.

The group as a concept is not only paradoxical: it is elusive. Since groups vary so much in terms of size, form, content, context, duration, and purpose, there is no single conception of 'group' that holds true for all (Hargie *et al.* 1991). More than that, there are questions about the very existence of the group and the extent to which it constitutes a real entity. Some writers question whether an entity such as 'group' exists at all, since there is no physical body to the group other than as a collection of individuals who together constitute the group and no psychological group entity other than in the minds of its participants. Smith and Berg (1988) state, 'There can be no group unless people belong to it.' Bion (1961) describes the group as an illusion: 'The belief that a group exists, as distinct from an aggregate of individuals, is an essential part of this regression, as are also the characteristics with which the supposed group is endowed by the individual' (p. 142). Brown (1985) contests this assertion, largely on the basis that the group matrix provides a living momentum to the group. But the matrix itself is a hypothetical construct, 'an invisible web of communications', and the reality of the group therefore remains ambiguous.

These difficult and challenging aspects may create unease in those who work with groups. They also question the rather easy assumptions made in the group psychotherapy literature, in which the concepts of group and group therapy appear to be axiomatic and indivisible. This may explain the preoccupation in group psychotherapy with cohesion. Group cohesion is indeed necessary for the survival and development of the group, and for the fulfilment of its therapeutic aims, but the overriding emphasis on cohesion, often to the exclusion of other group characteristics, such as coherence (Pines 1986), may reflect underlying anxiety about group existence vs. non-existence and the need to counter this with a vision of the group that emphasises the integrity and durability of the group.

These characteristics have a direct bearing on the anti-group. The psychological challenge of belonging to a group may be greater than is commonly recognised (notwithstanding the positive attractions and benefits of group belonging), participation in a psychotherapy group all the more so. Bion (1961) maintained that, for an adult, membership of a group may be as difficult and complex as the relationship to the breast is for the infant. But the psychotherapy group is different from most other groups in at least one crucial aspect: the opportunity it affords for awareness and reflection. This means that much of the difficulty of group belonging is open to recognition and understanding. With this in mind, it is useful to have as clear as possible a picture of the complex and paradoxical demands of the group: what follows is an attempt to identify those characteristics that are most likely to create conflicts about group belonging but, at the same time, are available for self- and group reflection. This is similar to the deconstructionist approach I previously suggested in which the group-as-a-whole is disaggregated in order to achieve a more coherent understanding of its parts, thus providing the possibility of strengthened re-integration.

Some of the characteristics described here are obvious and incontrovertible, but they may contain hidden paradoxical elements. Others are less obvious and need articulation. I suggest the following ten characteristics of psychotherapy groups:

- The group is a collection of strangers
- The group is unstructured
- The group is created by its members
- The group is a public arena
- The group is a plural entity
- The group is a complex experience
- The group creates interpersonal tensions
- The group is unpredictable
- The group fluctuates in its progress
- The group is an incomplete experience

Each characteristic is examined here in greater detail. Since these are the aspects of group therapy that worry participants, they not uncommonly elicit comments from prospective or actual group members and some of these comments are quoted below.

The group is a collection of strangers

'I can't imagine talking in front of a group of strangers. How will I know whom I can trust? The thought terrifies me.'

Stranger composition is a *sine qua non* of the psychotherapy group, allowing for the creation of a group entity that is new to participants and that, hopefully, will not repeat the distortions and failures of previous relationships. But it is also a major source of anxiety for members, confronting them with the very problems of interpersonal difference and unfamiliarity that may have brought them to the group in the first place. Even in ordinary life, stranger anxiety is common: this is intensified in group psychotherapy. The therapy group paradoxically requires participation and involvement in a setting that re-evokes and re-creates often feared interpersonal situations.

The group is unstructured

'I can't see the point of being in this group. We have no guidance or direction. Anything could happen.'

The analytic psychotherapy group, although firmly held within a boundary of space and time, is none the less unstructured in relation to task. There is no agenda or programme. The value of this is that it invites projections into the group space, mobilising the group matrix and constructing the therapeutic arena. But the absence of structure frustrates dependency needs and can arouse considerable confusion and anxiety in participants, potentiating an aversive effect in the group membership. Further, potential for aggressive conflict, and the fear of aggression, is particularly evident in an unstructured group setting. Kernberg (1980) notes, 'Aggression emerges much more directly and much more intensely when group processes are relatively unstructured.'

The group is created by its members

> 'It's up to us to make of the group what we can. But how do we know? We all have such problems – it's like the blind leading the blind.'

The group is a construction of the psychological efforts and projections of its participants. In a paradoxical sense, the group depends for its survival and growth on the members. Pines writes:

> The group is dependable only in as much as the patients contribute to its dependability. The needs of (his) child-self are rewarded through the combined efforts of all the patients and therapist to create a dependable object and situation, the group. The patient is therefore at one time simultaneously both child in the family, dependent on and supported by his parents but he is also the parent who has to give his time, his attention, his economic and social efforts to maintain the situation of the group akin to the boundary of a family within which emotional growth can take place.
>
> (Pines 1978, p. 124)

The degree of participants' responsibility for the group implied here may be a hidden factor in the ambivalence about group membership: patients want their treatment to be responsible for them, not the other way round. Hostility arising from frustration in this area may lead to negative projections onto the group and the failure of some groups to develop as therapeutic entities.

The group is a public arena

'I hate the thought of talking in a group, with all those people watching me. I need to talk about my problems in private.'

The eventual aim of the therapy group is intimate sharing in an atmosphere of trust and safety, but the route to this is tortuous. One aspect of the problem is that the group is often experienced as a public rather than private space. This arouses fears of exposure, humiliation, and attack. It is not unusually felt by patients to lack the essential requirements of containment and protection. Fears of a breach of confidentiality and exposure in the wider community outside the group exacerbate anxiety and suspiciousness.

The group is a plural entity

'I can't handle so many people at once. I won't know how to talk to them. I would much rather have a therapist of my own.'

The multiple membership of the group is another *sine qua non*, constituting a source of rich diversity and potential therapeutic gain. It provides an opportunity for externalising and exploring the 'group inside the individual' and for constructive relating in a situation of real encounter with others. Thyssen (1992) argues that diversity is fundamental in providing the stimulus that eventually leads to coherence: this embodies differentiation as opposed to cohesion, with its potentially stultifying sense of sameness. But plurality – and diversity – are often perceived as threats. The necessity of relating to a number of different people, as opposed to one therapist, particularly in an unstructured psychodynamic group, can be extremely testing of participants' capacity to encompass otherness, difference, and sharing. It creates an interpersonal field of great complexity and variability, when often what is being searched for by members is simplicity, unity, and oneness. The plurality of the group stimulates regressive projections and a fragmented sense of self and others. Brigham (1992) has described the disintegratory effects that multiple group membership may have on the intra-psychic experience of being in a

The group is a complex experience

'I find the group difficult because there are so many opinions and I end up very confused.'

Although there are times when a group is dominated by a single theme or preoccupation, there is usually a great deal happening psychologically at any one time, verbally and non-verbally, consciously and unconsciously. Even apparently simple situations or periods of silence may hide considerable complexity. This links with the plurality of the group in so far as the combination of several personal histories in the foundation matrix (Foulkes' term for what is brought to the group by members), amplified by the dynamic matrix (the changing constellation of dynamics in the group), is bound to be very complex. The group also functions on several levels of communication. Foulkes (1948, 1964a) spoke of the current level, the projective level, the transference level, and the primordial level. Although this is all part of the richness of the group experience it can be highly confusing, even baffling, creating a 'Tower of Babel' effect which is disturbing to participants.

The group creates interpersonal tensions

'I'm worried about what could happen to me in a group, whether I'll get on with the others. Say I'm attacked? Or I could really hurt someone else.'

Yalom (1975) described interpersonal learning as probably the core 'curative factor' in group psychotherapy. But with the opportunity for interpersonal learning also comes interpersonal threat and the latter may outweigh the former. Characteristic interpersonal tensions in group therapy concern competition, rivalry, envy, dominance, submission, criticism, rejection, group pressure, scapegoating, and hostility in general. The tensions can trigger sudden and violent explosions in the group, in which the stability of the group may be disrupted, or the tensions may be hidden and submerged, leading to an uncomfortable impasse in group development. Whatever the case, they add to a sense of danger in the group.

The group is unpredictable

'The group is different each week because different people come and you can't ever get a handle on it.'

The number of participants in a group and the various levels of interaction and communication noted above combine to create a situation that can be filled with surprise, both welcome and unwelcome. Participants are often worried by the prospect of unforeseen events and emotional upheavals in the group and their fears are not uncommonly confirmed. This is also linked to the unstructured nature of the therapy group, in which the lack of direction opens the way for spontaneous, unpredictable, and irrational group behaviour. Linked to this is the irregularity of attendance at the group. Even in a well-established group, the pattern of attendance may vary from session to session. This is likely to worsen in a less well-established, uncohesive group, reinforcing the lack of safe predictability that participants may need in order to risk self-disclosure and interpersonal engagement.

The group fluctuates in its progress

'It seems to me that people in the group are worse than they were earlier on. We keep going over the same material and everyone seems so stuck.'

The therapy group rarely assumes a form of linear progress. Linked to the above point about unpredictability, the group tends to oscillate between periods of progress, stasis, and regression. An overall developmental sequence can usually be discerned in terms that approximate the different models of group-stage development proposed by various writers (see Agazarian 1994; Ashbach and Schermer 1987; Beck 1983; Tuckman 1966). But this is seldom as smooth or as linear as the theories of group development might hold. Dell and Goolishan (1981) have suggested that, even in cohesive groups, disequilibrium and fluctuating change are a natural part of group life. Hawkins (1986) has described the considerable sensitivity of the therapy group to events such as breaks and losses and the disruptive effect these can have on group progress. This aspect both reflects and reinforces the complexity and unpredictability of the group.

The group is an incomplete experience

'I don't feel I'm really getting to grips with my problem in this group. There just isn't the chance to sort some of my own things out.'

The group can only deal with so much material at any one time and the individual participant is likely to have a limited opportunity to express his or her thoughts and feelings. Individual contributions have to be curtailed for the sake of the group as a whole. Although the notion of group psychotherapy assumes that members ultimately benefit from overall involvement in the group, through identification and assimilation of the wider group experience, participants not uncommonly express frustration at their inability to deal adequately with their own problems. Complex or deep-seated problems may be difficult to voice in the group, and not only individual but interpersonal and group needs may be frustrated. Interpersonal tensions or longings, transference and counter-transference reactions, may all be difficult to explore or resolve in any detail or depth.

Garland (1982) argued that the 'alternative system' created in the group constitutes its therapeutic effect. Participants' absorption in the 'group problem' – to them, the 'non-problem' – counteracts their absorption in their own problems, providing a simulated reality which promotes psychological growth. This is a useful perspective on the therapeutic group but perhaps overstates the extent to which the non-problem can replace the problem. There are usually participants who end up feeling frustrated and resentful at the lack of attention to their own personal problems.

Thompson (1991) pointed out Freud's honesty in recognising the incompleteness of psychoanalysis in 'Analysis terminable and interminable' (1937). It is possible that group analysis is even more prone to this dilemma.

The group characteristics described above all interconnect in various ways, combining to illustrate how the constructive potential of the therapy group is opposed by its fragility, its precarious and paradoxical core. These characteristics are given insufficient weight in most of the group therapy literature. They warrant a sharper focus in their own right. Within this framework, the importance of the anti-group – manifested as an adverse response to the group – becomes clearer, both as a reaction to the threats and challenges of group life and as a threat itself to the continuity and productivity of the group. The characteristics described have deeper links with both the intra-psychic and the social realms, which will be explored more fully in Chapters 5, 6, and 11. But for the present, further observations about the basic manifestations and development of the anti-group are required, starting with the origins of my thinking about the phenomenon in the psychiatric setting.

THE ANTI-GROUP IN THE CLINICAL SETTING

A theme that runs through this book concerns the importance of context in triggering and maintaining anti-group tendencies. It is not surprising, therefore, that my first thoughts about the phenomenon arose in my work setting, where I encountered difficulties in the implementation of the group-analytic approach. Most of my work as a clinical psychologist over a period of twenty-five years has been in the setting of a National Health Service psychiatric hospital in England. At the time of writing, the hospital faced possible closure, but it had functioned for decades as the predominant psychiatric facility in a local setting. As Kernberg (1980) pointed out, there are powerful regressive pressures in institutions of this sort. The level of psychopathology among patients is considerable and communication within patient, staff and staff–patient groups can be highly problematic. A complex mirroring of destructive processes can be discerned at different levels of the organisation, and positive group aims and purposes are not uncommonly subverted by negative group processes.

These observations touch on the wider issue of the anti-group as occurring in the larger organisational context, a theme to which Chapter 11 is addressed. But here the organisation serves more as a background to the clinical application of group analysis, in which the chief concern is the setting up and running of analytic psychotherapy groups. Most of the work I am referring to occurred within the out-patient service of a psychology department based in the psychiatric hospital. It is likely that the external context had its influence, but the present focus is on the specific processes I observed in the running of psychotherapy groups *per se*.

Anti-group attitudes appeared at the very start. This happened in the recruitment of group participants, well before they actually joined the group. I found that many patients referred did not want group therapy. They wanted individual therapy. The suggestion of a group was often met with surprise, anxiety, and suspicion. This was particularly the case with analytic groups, where the long-term, open-ended, and unstructured nature of the group, once described to patients, tended to arouse more anxiety and resistance than did the offer of a short-term, focused group. Numerous patients rejected the offer of a place in a psychotherapy group. Others could be persuaded to join, but tended to do so reluctantly. Patients who actually came asking for group therapy were, in my experience, the minority.

When the group starts, there appears, for several months at least, prevailing mistrust *in* the group and *of* the group. Often, this takes the form of attacks on the group: it is not good enough; it is second best; it is because the National Health Service is overstretched and provides so little help; it is directionless; there is no guidance; the presence of others with problems is a liability rather than an asset; it is an artificial situation; it gives too little time to the individual; it feels unsafe. Many of these comments echo the quotes I cited previously when describing therapy group characteristics. Some of these are familiar strains to anyone who has run groups in a similar setting, but they seem to me too often glossed over as inevitable frustrations that will be modified in time. As I see it, these complaints form the elements of the anti-group and should be recognised and addressed as such. (Technical approaches to these problems will be considered in Chapters 7 and 8.)

Still in the early phase of the group, drop-outs begin to occur. Drop-outs, in my view, are symptomatic of an anti-group process, not just in the individual drop-out, but in the group-as-a-whole, which may unconsciously select a member to enact the rejection of the group. Drop-outs tend to have a disturbing and demoralising effect on the group and can produce a chain reaction. If this happens, it can lead to anxiety, even despair, about the group surviving. In my experience, most groups do survive, but not all do. Even in fragile groups of this kind that continue, the impact of early traumas on the group's development may be so profound that the group never quite recovers. Communication may be extremely difficult or disordered and the group continues, but in a state of severe impasse.

Even in well-functioning groups, underlying anti-group attitudes, possibly not previously addressed, may suddenly flare up. A new member joins, an emotional conflict or clash erupts, or some other change occurs, and the group suddenly becomes very negativistic or fragmented. Breaks, I find, have a particularly strong effect on groups, and in my experience can produce an anti-group backlash both before and after the break. Often, this is a way of denying the value of the group and so avoiding painful feelings of separation.

The anti-group tends to evoke considerable despair and feelings of failure in the conductor. He or she readily feels to blame for the group not working properly. A sense of hopelessness in the conductor may in fact be an important signal of an anti-group at work. Of course, such a situation will also trigger the conductor's own anti-group tendencies – and in turn his or her ability to tolerate and deal with anti-group phenomena will influence the way in which the anti-group is or is not resolved. The conductor's position in relation to the anti-group is crucial in determining the outcome of the group: it is examined in greater detail in Chapter 8 on the role of the conductor.

Difficulties in running out-patient groups are paralleled in my experience by the problems of running in-patient groups and staff groups in the psychiatric setting. Unless a group milieu is already established, the attempt to develop such a culture can be fraught with difficulty. I had an early experience of consulting to a psychiatric unit which was attempting to set up patient and staff groups on an admission ward. The consultant psychiatrist had already made some frustrated efforts in this direction. The patient group had started operating but there was such a degree of misunderstanding and consequent acting out in one of the groups that a cohort of patients refused to return to the group and for a period instigated an anti-group culture on the ward. The staff group (intended to be a sensitivity-type group) had still not got off the ground. Efforts to establish a time and a place for the group to meet were continually sabotaged. When individual staff were questioned about their reactions to this, it appeared that there was considerable fear of the entire staff group coming together. The threat of angry challenge and confrontation, of a humiliating sense of difference in hierarchical relations, and of unwanted personal exposure appeared to outweigh in people's minds the potential benefits of greater understanding and co-operation that might be a product of such a venture. Anxiety about attending staff sensitivity groups is of course heightened by the fact that members are colleagues and not strangers; their proximity in the work setting makes personal exposure and confrontation all the more risky. The absence of safe boundaries and concerns about confidentiality exacerbate anti-group reactions in this setting. In various ways, staff sensitivity or 'support' groups, as will be illustrated further in Chapter 4, intensify the negative reactions observed in therapy groups.

THE COURSE AND DEVELOPMENT OF THE ANTI-GROUP

The anti-group is not a unitary phenomenon that occurs in all psychotherapy groups in the same way. Rather, it is a part of a process that varies considerably in its expression from one group to another or at different times in the same group. Recognising and dealing with the anti-group, therefore, requires an awareness of these different manifestations and how they are influenced by variables in the group process. Several dimensions of the anti-group are examined here: the degree of overt vs. covert expression of such tendencies in the group; the influence of the stage of group development on the anti-group; indirect and symbolic expressions of the anti-group; and the transformation of the anti-group into a positive, constructive group force. All of these dimensions, particularly the transformational and reparative aspects, will be explored more fully in later chapters (5, 6, 9, and 10), but are briefly introduced here.

Overt vs. covert expression

This question can be conceived in terms that are familiar in psychodynamic thinking, i.e. manifest and latent. This is the dual construct that Freud originally used to describe both dream content and analytic material in general. It has since been applied to a number of different clinical phenomena. In relation to the anti-group, it is a useful way of differentiating direct, discernible from indirect or submerged manifestations of the process.

The manifest level may be divided into two parts, 1) a fear or dislike of groups, often expressed directly by an individual member or members of the group. This is not infrequently consciously linked in participants' minds to previous adverse group experiences and tends to be associated with a conviction about the destructive potential of the group. In the psychotherapy group this often takes the form of direct attacks on the group, or it may be expressed in other forms of devaluing and undermining the group, such as an excessive drop-out rate, highly irregular attendance, and dwindling group morale and cohesiveness, 2) actual adverse experience in the present group which confirms existing anxiety, doubt, and mistrust of the group and leads to further withdrawal or attacks on the group. This can occur at all levels of the group system, i.e. individual, sub-group, and group-as-a-whole. As previously suggested, the individual or sub-group may be carrying the anti-group for the rest of the group.

The latent anti-group consists of the underlying constellation of anti-group attitudes and expectations shared by the group membership. These attitudes are more submerged than those of the manifest anti-group: they may be unconscious or preconscious and relate to early intra-psychic or interpersonal experiences, often in the family of origin, which creates the original mistrust of groups. A latent anti-group can exist in an individual member or sub-group but is more likely to gain force as part of a common pool of fantasies and attitudes towards the group. The latent anti-group may remain concealed in the group until such time as an event or situation in the group triggers its overt expression. It may also not become manifest in the group at all, either remaining contained at a latent level, or finding some expression in the group but without constituting a major challenge to the group.

A circular relationship tends to exist between covert and overt levels of the anti-group. The latent anti-group feeds into the manifest anti-group, by prompting anxious and adverse reactions to the group and stimulating disruptive group behavour. This in turn reinforces underlying or latent anti-group fantasies, the strength of the cycle determining the extent to which actual destructive processes erode the therapeutic culture of the group.

The therapeutic goal is to break the vicious circle of negativity or at least to diminish its rigidity and intensity. This usually happens through positive or 'corrective' experiences in the group which disconfirm negative fantasies and expectations and lead to an increased belief in the safe, containing aspects of the group and its capacity for growth and restoration. In a previous publication (Nitsun 1990), I described some of the constructive processes in groups; see also Chapter 10 of this book for a detailed illustration of the creative and transformational process in a group. In most cases, the therapeutic transition occurs naturally in the course of group development, with the support and facilitation of the group conductor. But, as will be illustrated throughout this book, the danger of a self-reinforcing destructive pattern in the group, leading potentially to the disintegration of the group, cannot be ignored. This requires active recognition, understanding, and intervention on the part of the conductor (explored more fully in Chapter 8).

Developmental stages and the anti-group

It is widely agreed in the group psychotherapy literature that the stage of group development strongly influences the pattern of dynamic processes in the group (Agazarian 1989, 1994; Ashbach and Schermer 1987; Beck 1981, 1983). Much of this book is devoted to an exploration of the developmental implications and consequences of the anti-group. These gain complexity in the group-analytic framework with its slow-open character and gradual fluctuating development. But, for present purposes, a generalised perspective on group developmental stages is required. This categorises group development into an early stage, a middle stage, and a mature stage, and is based on a schema described by Gans (1989).

The early stage is crucial in determining the form and future of anti-group developments. It is likely to be marked by possibly the most intense evocation of the anti-group, at both manifest and latent levels, at any time in the group's development. The vulnerability of members in the new and unfamiliar situation and the vulnerability of the group, itself a fledgling entity, render the setting a particularly anxiety-provoking one (Nitsun 1988). Fears of exclusion, of attack, of hostile prejudice, of loss of control, of shameful exposure, and of narcissistic injury are likely to be uppermost at this stage. Participants' heightened sensitivity and anxiety contribute to a tense, highly charged atmosphere in which a word or a sentence may have a dramatic impact. Doubts and anxieties about the group that members had at the outset are likely to be reinforced in this atmosphere. Particularly if there is a marked latent anti-group to start with, reflecting a deeper level of shared anxiety and hostility towards the group, a culture may be established early on in which distrust and lack of safety predominate and in which the anti-group strongly takes root.

The middle stage can be seen as the stage of control in so far as issues of dominance, power, and rivalry are likely to be uppermost. There may be sharp clashes between members, unleashing hurt and hostility, anger and defiance, and this atmosphere of conflict may threaten the stability of the group. The group itself is not uncommonly blamed for provoking such conflict, as if it were the setting rather than the members themselves which generated the problem. The group becomes impregnated with the bad associations of the anti-group. Even if some early cohesion and safety had been achieved in the group, anti-group attitudes are likely to flare up again in the volatile atmosphere of the middle stage.

The mature stage is likely to see a lessened expression of the anti-group, since, by definition, the group's maturity implies some resolution or reduction of destructive group tendencies. This is usually the phase of greatest trust and intimacy. However, even this mature stage can hold surprises for the group, with the greater openness creating further threats of exposure and confrontation, potentially rekindling anti-group attitudes. The mature stage is also likely to culminate in the ending of the group. Ambivalence about this may produce an anti-group backlash, fears of separation and group disintegration re-arousing early anxieties about abandonment (Kauff 1977). The group may become destabilised, making the separation a fraught, piecemeal process rather than a coherent working through.

The notion of stages of group development, as noted above, is complicated in the setting of the 'slow-open' group which is characteristic of group-analytic psychotherapy. As old members leave and new members join the group, there may be a conflation of developmental stages in a way that influences the expression of the anti-group. A new member joining may precipitate a return to an earlier developmental stage, partly through members of the group identifying with the new participant. If this is an unwelcome entry, resentment and hostility may disorganise the gains achieved in the group, and an anti-group atmosphere may be provoked. Sudden drop-outs are likely to demoralise the group and the departure of a valued member, even if planned, may leave the group feeling empty and deprived, throwing it back on its own resources in a way that rekindles anti-group reactions. The slow-open group is prone to greater vicissitudes than more structured, time-limited groups, and the ensuing uncertainties and ambivalence can feed the anti-group process.

The anti-group as a developmental phenomenon

A further perspective views the anti-group itself as a developmental phenomenon. In this interpretation, the anti-group represents a part of the group process that is charged with handling and mitigating destructive group phenomena so that constructive processes may proceed. This suggests not only that the anti-group is a natural part of group development but that it has a developmental function which ultimately serves to support and strengthen the group (assuming that the destructive aspects do not get out of hand). This applies at several levels of the group – individual, sub-group, and group-as-a-whole. It is a common situation in groups that a particular member or a small cluster of members adopt contrary or non-conformist group positions, often in a hostile, defiant way, relative to the rest of the group. This can cause considerable unease and friction in the group, and may be especially difficult for the conductor to handle, since he or she may also be targeted for criticism and blame. But if these individual or sub-group positions are seen as reflecting the developmental pressure in the group-as-a-whole to deal with anti-group forces, these apparently negative contributions to the group may be viewed in a more constructive light. If the projections onto these elements can be recognised and owned by the rest of the group, this may be therapeutically helpful to all.

This view accords with the systems-oriented approach of Agazarian (1994), which seeks to find coherence between different levels of group-system functioning and to integrate splits that commonly occur in groups. Although the approach in this book is predominantly group-analytic and psychoanalytic, much of the thinking is consistent with the systemic approach. The systemic function of the anti-group at various levels of organisation will be demonstrated throughout the text. Here, a link between the developmental and the systemic perspectives is suggested.

Indirect expressions of the anti-group

It was noted above that drop-outs may reflect an anti-group constellation, not only in the individual drop-out but in the group-as-a-whole which chooses a member to represent and enact the anti-group. The investment of the anti-group in a particular member or members is consistent with the systemic viewpoint described above and is an illustration of how the expression of the anti-group can be shifted to different levels of the system.

A similar process may apply to scapegoating. Here, an individual member has to bear the brunt of group criticism and exclusion, creating a negative focus in the group, which feels uncomfortable to most of the membership, particularly the scapegoat, but which is very difficult to modify or resolve. One consequence of this process is that the scapegoat is left with heightened anxiety and resentment about the group, often to the point of breaking down under the strain or withdrawing in hurt and anger. These are anti-group reactions. In a similar fashion to the drop-out, the scapegoat may be carrying anti-group reactions that are disowned and projected by the rest of the group in a state of self-righteous condemnation. Of course, there are other aspects to the dynamics of scapegoating. But in this and other problematic group situations, which are otherwise difficult to explain or resolve, an anti-group process is likely to be interwoven in the group dynamic. An illustration of this process is given in Chapter 9 (p. 206).

The anti-group and reparation

Manifestations of the anti-group so far described indicate the potentially noxious effects of the process if not recognised or contained. However, they also suggest that the germ of reparation or transformation exists in the process itself and that group development may be facilitated by recognising the close connection between constructive and destructive forces. The therapeutic potential of the anti-group is a complex subject that will be explored in detail in Chapters 9 and 10, but here some preliminary hypotheses are suggested.

The underlying principle of transformation is that the group's capacity to survive the destructive threat of the anti-group is itself transformational in that it attests to the strength of the group and the greater power of constructive group tendencies. Where members are able to recognise their part in the formation of the anti-group, with all its destructive potential, there will emerge a heightened sense of responsibility for the well-being and development of the group. The realisation by members that they create the group, for better or for worse, has a developmental component in that it secures the group in the sphere of shared responsibility. This encourages the creative and reparative efforts of the group. In Chapter 9, it is suggested that the conflict between constructive and destructive forces may produce a group crisis which is akin to the depressive position in Melanie Klein's terminology. As in the depressive position, the confrontation with anxiety about destructiveness and loss tends, in sufficiently favourable conditions, to awaken and strengthen the urge to repair.

On a more fundamental level, the containment, if not resolution, of the anti-group relieves participants of the anxious preoccupations engendered by a destructive group process. This paves the way for a freer use of imagination, thought, and feeling, and, in particular, the exercise of play, in both a symbolic and an actual sense. The group becomes a transitional object in the Winnicottian sense (James 1982), and there is a creative use of the transitional group space (Schlachet 1986; Jacobson 1989). Winnicott himself (1974b) noted that play leads to group relationships, but, as will be shown in later examples, the containment of destructive tendencies is necessary in order for the group to play.

At an existential level, the paradoxical interplay of destructive and creative forces in the group deepens the awareness and acceptance of the natural flux of life with its inevitable frustrations and contradictions and reduces the belief in idealised and unitary solutions. The overall impact of this process is to crystallise the value of the group as a therapeutic medium. In Winnicott's terms the capacity of the object to withstand destructive attacks leads to the greater 'use of the object' (Winnicott 1968).

THE ANTI-GROUP AND OTHER THEORETICAL LINKS

I have argued that the group-analytic tradition fails to pay sufficient attention to destructive forces in groups and that this reflects a more general gap in the group psychotherapy field. But there are theoretical approaches that relate more closely to the concept of the anti-group. Of these, the most powerful is the work of Bion, who made a very different contribution from that of Foulkes to our understanding of group process, and it is necessary now to turn our attention to Bion. Alongside this will be considered the views of other writers in the USA and the UK, particularly those who interpret the group as symbolising a maternal figure with good and bad associations. The aim here is not so much a blanket review of these approaches but a means of finding theoretical coherence in the complex subject of group-destructive forces, ideally within a framework that also recognises the creative potential of the group and supports its growth and maturation.

Bion

The work of Bion and Foulkes is usually viewed as sharply dissimilar and in many respects this holds true. However, there is one point on which they converge: the inseparability of individual and group and the ongoing interpenetration between the two. But, whereas Foulkes saw this as a problematic interaction for neurotic or psychotic individuals whose disturbance is 'group-disruptive in essence', Bion (1961) regarded the individual–group constellation as universally problematic: 'The individual is a group animal at war, not simply with the group, but with himself for being a group animal and with those aspects of his personality that constitute his groupishness' (p. 131). Most of Bion's work on groups concerned this conflict about group belonging, showing how it undermined the group task: as such, it is directly relevant to the concept of the anti-group.

In his classic text on groups, *Experiences in Groups* (1961), Bion introduced a number of seminal concepts of group functioning. One was the notion of group mentality. This emphasises the pool of primitive unconscious contributions each member makes to the group, determined largely by disavowed hostile impulses.

Bion refers to these as 'anonymous contributions' and describes the group mentality as expressing and gratifying these impulses without the individual having to take responsibility for them.

Bion saw the basic assumptions, his most important theoretical contribution, as products of group mentality. In brief, the basic assumptions represent primitive stages of group functioning that constitute faulty, regressive attempts to reconcile the conflicting pulls of individuality and group membership. They aim at one level to preserve the group but, in so doing, undermine the purpose of the group. Bion named three basic assumptions: 1) dependence, in which problems are believed to be resolvable only by an idealised leader or counterpart; 2) flight–fight, in which problems (or those who represent them) are handled by attacking or fleeing from them; and 3) pairing, in which solutions are expected to be generated by the interaction of two people, whom the rest of the members watch.

Bion formulated the concept of the 'proto-mental' to further explain the origin of the basic assumptions. This describes a psychological state, deriving from early infancy, in which body and mind are undifferentiated. The basic assumption groups trigger a regression to these primitive psychological states, which Bion sees as having a potentially noxious effect: 'It is these proto-mental levels that provide the matrix of group diseases' (p. 102). Both psychological and physical distress are seen as emanating from basic assumption functioning. Bion suggests that, although the 'diseases' manifest themselves in the individual, 'it is the group rather than the individual that is stricken' (p. 102).

The notion of the proto-mental ties up with some of Bion's later work, subsequent to *Experiences in Groups* (Bion 1967, 1970). Central to this work is the notion of the container–contained. Linked to the mother–infant relationship, the concept describes the dynamic relation between experience that is projected, the contained, and an object which absorbs the experience, the container. In favourable development, this relationship is a constructive one: the container helps to transform chaotic and fragmented experience into meaningful awareness. But, in adverse development, the relationship between container and contained is mutually spoiling and destructive. Factors such as envy and greed (Bion's notion of –k) impede the communicative relationship so that experience remains unprocessed and incoherent. Thinking, intellectual discovery, and emotional development are thereby all rendered impossible. Bion speaks of a 'hatred of learning', which is based on omnipotence and denial of intrapsychic and external reality and militates against the achievement of learning in the group.

Bion's observations are highly relevant to group psychotherapy in general and the anti-group concept in particular. Overall, his appreciation of paradox in the group gives sharp definition to the contradictory processes that underlie group functioning. Picking up on his later work, the notion of the container–contained is a valuable paradigm for understanding the holding and transformational functions of the group. Within this framework, the anti-group can be seen as representing a failure of the container–contained relationship. Through projective identification, the failed group becomes impregnated with the chaotic and persecutory elements of the uncontained, leaving the membership floundering in a morass of unprocessed and unresolved experience. In this situation learning is impossible. The connectedness and meaning that is aimed for in group therapy fails to materialise. The group becomes an empty, aversive experience. A compelling recent account of the group seen from this perspective is given by Gordon (1994). He describes an impasse in the group that he interpreted in terms of Bion's notion of –k and how his own subjective responses served as a reflection of the painful group process and a pointer towards its understanding and resolution.

Utilising Bion's earlier conceptualisations, the anti-group can be seen as an expression of group mentality. In a parallel way to the spoiled relationship of the container–contained, the anti-group draws on the disowned hostility of the participants, creating a destructive group atmosphere for which individual members may deny responsibility. Similarly, the anti-group is tinged by the primitive properties of the proto-mental state. Bion's notion of the matrix of 'group diseases' is relevant here, since the anti-group creates a distorted experience in which healing fails to take place and in which the group itself, to use Bion's term, is 'stricken'.

But it is the theory of the basic assumptions that is most directly relevant to the anti-group. I would suggest that basic assumption groups are fundamentally anti-groups. In so far as the work group or 'pro-group' represents the purpose of fulfilling a task – in the case of therapy, the development of a coherent framework in which group members can learn to understand and overcome their problems – the basic assumptions undermine the capacity of the group to achieve its purpose. The group is preserved – or there is an attempt to do so – but at the expense of personal and group development. In promising gratification in the form of fantasied or magical solutions, the basic assumptions destroy the group's capacity to generate realistic solutions. In fact, the preservation of the group is an illusion: the group is rendered more vulnerable by its failure to address the creative task and to build on the mature resources of its membership. What is preserved is the shell of a group, with the inner unconscious core still riven by anxiety and aggression. Paradoxically, the fantasy of preserving the group leads to its weakening and possible destruction.

The anti-group is implicit in the organisation and structure of basic assumption groups since this reveals the absence of actual group formation in the sense of coherent intra-group relatedness. Basic assumption groups do not function as groups. In the dependency assumption, the group is strongly organised around the leader, creating virtually a dyadic relationship of group as a single, undifferentiated mass to the leader. In the flight–fight assumption, the group may either disperse or disappear in the flight phase and split into sub-groups through faction fighting in the fight phase, again disintegrating the group. In the pairing group, the emphasis is on the couple in a magically tinged, sexually toned dyadic relationship, with the rest of the group looking on as observers. All these groups avoid true group inter-relatedness. In this sense, they are anti-groups. The anti-group aspect of the basic assumptions is deeply implicit in Bion's theory.

Bion's work has been the subject of as much criticism as it has been of approbation. One point of criticism is his emphasis on the group at the expense of the individual (Brown 1985). Rather than representing an active agent who helps to mould the development of the group, the individual in Bion's schema appears lost in the generalised regressive pull of the basic assumptions. This belief leads not only to a theoretical imbalance, but to an overemphasis in technical interventions on the group-as-a-whole, leaving the individual unrecognised and marginalised (Malan *et al.* 1976). The concept of the anti-group differs in that dynamic contributions to the group are seen as occurring at all levels – individual, sub-group, and whole group. These levels are seen as interactive, not exclusive, which is more in keeping with the underlying Foulkesian philosophy of the individual as a nodal point in the social network. In Chapters 5 and 6, where theories of the dynamic origins of the anti-group will be explored, the place of the individual in the group will be further emphasised.

But by far the most serious criticism of Bion's work is its overwhelmingly negative emphasis – the group is doomed to play out an unending cycle of regression and destructiveness. As Schermer (1985) suggests, 'There is a particular denial of Eros in Bion's group psychology, as he portrays the group forever enmeshed in the ba states, à la the repetition compulsion or the death instinct' (p. 144). This makes for an interesting comparison with Foulkes, whose work I have previously described as dominated by Eros and the life instinct, seemingly to the exclusion of Thanatos, in spite of Foulkes' own assertions to the contrary (see p. 31). What we have then are two major approaches to the group that represent polar opposites. Brown (1985) has argued for an integration of the two. The concept of the anti-group does not purport to be a complete theory of group behaviour in itself, but its aim is to strike a balance between constructive and destructive forces in groups. The caution and pessimism inhering in the concept of the anti-group have an affinity with Bion's work, but this is counterbalanced by a belief in the creative potential of the group and its capacity to deal with reality, which belongs to the Foulkesian tradition.

THE GROUP AS MOTHER

An important strand of thinking in relation to therapy groups, and one which deals more directly with the duality of creative and destructive forces, is linked to the metaphor of the group as mother. There appears to be a unanimous recognition of the group as symbolising the mother figure, this being another point on which Bion and Foulkes converge. Foulkes described the group as 'the all embracing mother who embodies the whole world'. Bion (1961) believed that the well-spring of anxiety in the group is related to primitive fantasies about the mother. Much of his analysis of the group, as noted above, is influenced by the Kleinian notions of the early mother–infant relationship.

But it is by no means only Foulkes and Bion who espouse the view of the group as mother. There is a strong tradition emphasising the metaphor of the group as embodying the nurturing, containing functions of the mother. Pines (1978) offers a sensitive picture:

> At a very deep unconscious level this group, an entity greater than any one member, on which all are dependent, which all need to be valued and accepted by, which nourishes them with its warmth, which accepts all parts of them, that understands pain and suffering, that is patient yet uncompromising, that is destroyed neither by greedy possessive primitive love, nor by destructive anger, that has permanence and continuity in time and space, this entity is basically a mother.
>
> (Pines 1978, p. 122)

Much of the related literature, however, emphasises the 'bad' characteristics of the group as mother. Schindler (1966), Durkin (1964), Glatzer (1987), and Green (1983) all suggest that harsh, punitive, depriving, or abandoning fantasies of a mother experienced either intra-psychically or in external relationships are projected onto the group. Gibbard and Hartman (1973), in the area of small group research, suggest that the longing in the group for an idealised mother to fulfil Utopian fantasies may conceal awareness of the destructive aspects of the 'mother' group. The same authors, though, also point out the healthy aspect of idealisation: some degree of idealisation is needed to offset mistrust of the group and to encourage cohesion and collaboration.

Prodgers (1990) strongly advocates the notion of the dual nature of the group as mother. He presents a picture of the paradoxical qualities of mothering itself: life-giving and nurturing, yet also withholding and depriving, devouring and ensnaring (Raphael-Leff 1984). This form of duality, Prodgers argues, is inherent in the psychotherapy group. He contrasts the views of Foulkes and Bion on this issue. Whereas they agree on the mother symbolism of the group, they differ radically in their interpretation of its meaning. Foulkes idealises the group and avoids the negative implications of the group as mother; Bion emphasises its negative, regressive aspects to the exclusion of nurturing and development. The dual nature of the group as mother embraces both aspects.

Prodgers' emphasis on the dialectical nature of the group process and his analysis of Bion's and Foulkes' opposing interpretations resonate strongly with my own views. What is interesting is that this balanced perspective, unusual within the classical group therapy literature, emerges from a symbolic consideration of the group as mother. This includes a full awareness of the destructive potential of the group which parallels the concept of the anti-group and does so in a framework of transformation and change. The symbolic maternal link is not surprising: the powerful conscious and unconscious resonances of the mother–infant relationship inevitably occur in group psychotherapy and the metaphor provides a rich associative context for interpretation of group phenomena. At the same time, it is significant that a possible point of reconciliation can be reached only within a symbolic framework, as if more direct consideration of group behaviour precludes this degree of integration. Again, I would ask whether there is something about the group itself that engenders this obfuscation and polarisation, a form of splitting that is reflected in both the experiential and the conceptual domains.

THE ANTI-GROUP AS A CRITICAL PRINCIPLE

The notion of the dual nature of the group as mother highlights the possibility of holding together the opposites of creation and destruction within a single conception of the group. The strength of the maternal symbol, which is universally recognised in the psychoanalytic and psychotherapeutic literature as having conflicting aspects, seems to make it possible to bind these opposites together in the group context. One of the aims of this book is to develop the notion of a dialectical relationship between constructive and destructive processes in the group. Here the anti-group takes its place not so much as a descriptive principle concerning the phenomenology of group life but as an abstract, critical principle that seeks to restore dialogic balance to our understanding of the group.

A feature of postmodernist philosophy and criticism is an emphasis on the 'structure of opposition'. This is a term used by Dews (1987) to denote a situation within which opposite pairs of concepts are organised hierarchically, with one part of the pair dominating and suppressing the other in a tradition of thought. Dews describes how 'Western metaphysics relies on a series of opposites – between mind and body, the intelligible and the sensible, culture and nature, male and female – in which one part is elevated above the other, but can only be so prioritised through denigration of its dependence on its contrary' (p. 10). The elevation or idealisation of one pole (e.g. optimism) depends on the suppression of the other (i.e. pessimism). Elevating the suppressed pole creates tension and upsets the uncritical and idealised acceptance of the other. Going back to Freud, as highlighted in Chapter 2, Thompson (1991) points out that in 'Analysis terminable and interminable', he espoused a view that is in line with the deconstructionist position. He opposed pessimism to optimism, regression to progression, disintegration and fragmentation to integration and unity, death to life, Thanatos to Eros, and incompleteness to completeness. In each instance, Freud emphasised the pessimistic side and de-emphasised the side that embodies synthesis and coherence. In so doing, he challenged our sometimes uncritical acceptance of developmental progress.

Deconstruction of the group therapy literature reveals a similar structure of opposition, exemplified in the work of Foulkes and Bion. Each elevated one side of the pair of opposites of optimism–pessimism to the exclusion of the other. The concept of the anti-group aligns itself to a large extent with the pessimistic view. The fragility of the group as an entity, its vulnerability to loss, change, and disintegration, and its susceptibility to destructive projections arising from intra-psychic and interpersonal tensions make it important to reinforce and uphold this aspect of the structure of opposites.

Disintegration itself constitutes a theme in postmodernist thought. Dews (1987) postulated the 'logics of disintegration' as a position which challenges the notion of progress in knowledge, philosophy, and society. He links his views to those of Adorno (1966), who, like Foulkes, was a member of the Frankfurt School. Unlike Foulkes, however, Adorno's concept of the 'negative dialectic' challenges interpretations of reality as a temporal movement toward ever more coherent and differentiated forms of integration: historical progress can be understood, in some instances, as advancing towards less and less unity and towards increasing antagonism and incoherence.

In the psychoanalytic realm, Freud questioned the assumption of progress in psychoanalytic treatment. His reasons for this were, firstly, his view that there were limits to ego integrity: he suggested that psychopathological factors may ultimately disorganise the ego so that its integratory power is weakened. Secondly, he argued against the unity of the analytic process, especially with respect to the role played by transference: he believed that there were latent conflicts in the psyche that were separate from the transference and that these (and the transference itself) might not be fully dealt with in treatment. Thirdly, he questioned the notion of unqualified progress in development, emphasising that developmental forces could lead to disintegration rather than integration and that these could run counter to the aim of the analysis. Overall, Freud believed that the harmonious state of ego mastery aspired to is more apparent than real. Progress in psychoanalysis is likely to be partial, incomplete, and open to reversal through disintegratory forces both during and after treatment.

These issues are of the utmost importance to the concept of the anti-group. The general points Freud highlighted about the obstacles to development and the limitations of the analytic process apply similarly to group analysis, compounded by the particular characteristics of the group which intensify some of these problems and add a few of their own, e.g. the greater complexity and unpredictability of the group process and the diminished opportunity for individual work, resulting, at least potentially, in a greater sense of incompleteness. The counter-argument to this is that, in providing a very different therapeutic context, the group offsets some of the limitations of individual analysis. The provision of a therapeutic milieu with several people in a facilitating capacity, linked to the generativity of the group matrix, may provide a wider range of therapeutic and restorative possibilities than does one-to-one analysis. These possibilities notwithstanding, the overall complexity and variability of the group process, and its particular susceptibility to aggressive and destructive forces, indicate the need to take a serious view of this perspective. This 'corrective pessimism', however, is not an end in itself: it seeks to bring into relief the potentially destructive aspect of group life in order to strengthen its dialectical relation to creative group processes. Freud adopted a similar view:

> Only by the concurrent or mutually opposing action of the two primal instincts – Eros and the death-instinct – never by one or the other alone, can we explain the rich multiplicity of the phenomena of life.
>
> (Freud 1937, p. 243)

CRITICISMS OF THE CONCEPT

I am aware of using the term 'the anti-group' to cover a variety of perspectives of the psychotherapy group: as a descriptive metaphor, as an explanatory paradigm, and as a critical principle. The concept has widened since I originally introduced it and to the reader it may appear to be over-inclusive. I take responsibility for this, but suggest that, at this stage of the development of the concept, it is useful to allow a measure of elasticity rather than confining the concept too tightly.

There are other actual or potential criticisms of the concept that I wish to address. In England, the concept has been received with positive interest by the group-analytic community. Some relief has been expressed that the unmentionable could actually be mentioned, that a difficult aspect of group life could be named, and that an important gap in the Foulkesian model could be addressed. However, there have also been some critical voices. Some of the issues raised and my response to them are as follows:

1 *The term is too concrete. It suggests a static phenomenon, a thing, that occurs in the group in a largely invariable way.*

   I am mindful here of the view of Ashbach and Schermer (1987), who argue against the introduction of concrete structures in conceptualising group behaviour. I agree with them and do not intend the anti-group to take this form. I see the anti-group more in the nature of a construct, an abstract, metaphorical proposition that seeks to describe a highly variable process in different groups and even in the same group, rather than as a concrete, static entity. Examples in the following chapter will make this clear.

2 *The term is uncomfortably similar to the 'Anti-Christ' and carries religious overtones with a strong implication of primary evil.*

   This meaning was not intended. The concept has a psychological and not a religious basis and supports a notion of healthy ambivalence rather than a moralistic conception of good and evil.

3 *The term implies an anti-group position on the part of the user, as if the concept itself were synonymous with hostility towards groups and group therapy.*

The concept does not imply an anti-group position in the sense of devaluing or seeking to undermine the group in general and the therapy group in particular. Rather, it aims to illuminate the paradoxical nature of groups and their destructive potential, essentially in order to maximise the creative power of the group. In this sense, the concept is essentially and deeply *for* the group.

Chapter 4
Clinical illustrations of the anti-group

This chapter paints a broad canvas of the anti-group in its differing forms. Previous chapters have dealt mainly with conceptual and theoretical aspects of the anti-group, but here the balance shifts towards the description of actual groups that illustrate the defensive, disruptive, and disintegratory forces that characterise the anti-group. Most of the examples are taken from the clinical setting of group psychotherapy, but consideration is also given to 1) staff support or 'sensitivity' groups, which differ from psychotherapy groups in having the work task as their main focus, and 2) experiential training groups, which generally aim to promote awareness of interpersonal and group processes.

The expression of the anti-group, and the particular form it takes, depends on a host of factors, particularly the nature of the group, the composition of its membership, the developmental stage of the group, and the relationship between the group and the therapist. These factors are reflected in the following examples which, for convenience, are grouped under three main headings:

Psychotherapy groups
- the start of a new group
- different level of the anti-group – individual, sub-group, and group-as-a-whole
- group breakdown
- flawed development of a group
- manifest and latent anti-group
- alternation between pro-group and anti-group

Staff support groups

- a psychiatric ward team
- a general hospital staff team

Experiential training groups

- a group in a psychotherapy training course

These examples broaden our perspective on the anti-group, so that the influence of context on destructive group developments starts to become apparent. It will be seen that the intensity of the anti-group varies considerably and that it is necessary to distinguish levels of severity so that a differentiated, as opposed to a global, undifferentiated, picture can evolve. This has a direct bearing not only on the nature of the group but on the management of the anti-group, which will be taken up more fully in Chapters 7 and 8.

Before proceeding, it is important to make a statement about the value of group psychotherapy. I operate on the assumption that many, if not most, psychotherapy groups work well, that it is possible in groups to achieve depths of psychological awareness and emotional growth that are unique to this psychotherapeutic setting. Also, in later chapters, particularly Chapter 9, I provide an example of group transformation that, I believe, more than illustrates the value of group psychotherapy. But in order to develop my argument about the anti-group, I have of necessity predominantly selected examples of failure and distortion in the development of the group. The difficulty is to maintain a balanced perspective on the rewards and risks of group psychotherapy, and if this chapter temporarily unbalances this position, it is with the aim of ultimately achieving a balance.

PSYCHOTHERAPY GROUPS

Group A: the start of a new group

It has been noted (see Chapter 3) that the anti-group is likely to find dominant expression at the beginning of the group. Anxiety, doubt, and ambivalence about attending the group are bound to be uppermost at the start: this, coupled with the unformed character of the group and its susceptibility to projection at various levels, creates fertile ground for the early manifestation of the anti-group. The nature and intensity of anti-group projections at the start may also be an indication of what lies ahead for the group. Early expectations and conflicts may be predictive of the future development of the group.

The following example is of the first six months of a group-analytic psychotherapy group that took place in the out-patient department of a psychiatric hospital. It was a mixed-sex group of patients with serious emotional problems. Two members had been psychiatric in-patients and at least two others had suffered major disorganisation in their lives and relationships.

This group, which I have also referred to in a previous publication (Nitsun 1994), serves as a central reference point in this book, as it vividly illustrates some salient and developing themes. I also describe it in greater detail than other groups and more closely analyse the imagery and symbolism as a way into the psychopathology of the anti-group.

The first session was to a large extent dominated by Georgina, a 40-year-old woman who announced to the group that she had decided to reveal at the outset a problem which she believed she would otherwise conceal for the rest of the therapy. Ten years earlier she had had an operation to enlarge her breasts. This involved putting a prosthesis in her breasts, which had resulted in their becoming hard and lumpy. She believed this made her breasts unsightly and unpleasant to touch. Because of this, she had withdrawn from physical relationships with men and her diminished self-confidence had resulted in her generally becoming more and more socially isolated. She felt there was something false, artificial, damaged, and disfigured about her and that any intimacy would reveal this to others. She went on to tell the group that about a year earlier she had suffered a serious emotional breakdown and had been admitted to the psychiatric hospital. She described schizophrenic-like symptoms: going utterly to pieces, losing the sense of connection between mind and body, incoherent thinking, and strange fantasies about the contents of her body.

Georgina's story was in many ways symbolic, even prophetic, of what was to follow in the group. For some weeks, the anxiety level in the group was extremely high and members seemed under pressure to generate an excited atmosphere of chatter. Commonly, at the start of a group, there are tense, prolonged silences, but in this group silence was pre-empted by intense verbal activity. Yet, there was something hollow about the communications, as if the group was developing a false self (Fried 1979) in order to hide the underlying anxiety about emptiness and aggression. When the defence failed, the group slumped into a long period in which inertia alternated with resentment about being put into the group. The anger was voiced very strongly by two members who had been in individual therapy with the conductor before being transferred to the group. One of these, Barry, compared the group very unfavourably and unflatteringly with individual treatment. His idealised account of his individual psychotherapy aroused considerable interest and envy in the other participants. For a time, individual therapy became the symbol of everything good and everything that was missing in the group: privacy, safety, trust, intimacy, love. This was the longed-for state of oneness, of total containment, that was opposed by the reality of being in this new group with its frustrations and difficulties.

There developed a pattern of criticism of the group. The voice of the anti-group frequently came from Nigel, a markedly counter-dependent man who made scathing attacks on the group and the conductor, claiming that this was a meaningless and purposeless exercise. Although this member aroused hostility in other members of the group, no one challenged his derogatory view of the group – if anything, he seemed to be the elected spokesperson of the group (Horwitz 1983). The same member began to engage the others in complicated and frustrating verbal battles, which led to highly confused states in the group where the point at issue was drowned in a sea of babbling and angry tongues, rather like the Tower of Babel analogy mentioned in Chapter 3. In this atmosphere, the group had its first drop-out, a young woman called Arlene. Soon after this, another patient dropped out and morale in the group sank. When a new member, Norman, joined the group, he went round the group asking participants whether they felt they were benefiting from the group. With the exception of Georgina and Tim, a low-profile member who said he thought the group helped 'a bit', the others asserted that the group had no value to them. When the conductor commented that this was early days yet, the point was disregarded. The consensus was that the group was unhelpful, probably a futile exercise altogether. This attitude may have been an indirect reaction to Norman joining the group, expressing disguised hostility towards him and the conductor for bringing a newcomer into the group, but the survey did seem to sum up the group's opinion at the time.

There followed a period of progress in the group. In spite of the resentment caused, the introduction of two well-chosen new members appeared to have a beneficial effect. Combined with a greater capacity for reflectiveness in the group, communication became more coherent and resonant across the group. In spite of all the misgivings, the group was beginning to help (see Chapter 10 for further details). Then came the first break in the group and, with it, a recrudescence of anti-group material. A sense of impending disaster pervaded the group in the sessions leading up to the break. Maureen described how the council house she was living in was in danger of collapsing; it was one of a group of houses that had been built in a faulty way in the 1930s, with inadequate foundations. The analogy of the group collapsing during the break was all too obvious. The symbol of the house suggested that the group in fact may have acquired properties of safety and containment, but the fear was that its underpinnings were too weak and that it would disintegrate during the break.

If the group had acquired an, as yet unrecognised, value to the participants, this was counteracted by the force of the anti-group. As if to deny any attachment to the group, a wave of anti-group reactions immediately preceded the break. Nigel launched a stinging attack on all of psychiatry, psychology, and group therapy in particular. It was all a load of rubbish, he said. But Nigel also mentioned his continuing depression and how he had recently felt suicidal. There was a moment of anxious concern in the group. Perhaps at that moment, the group contemplated not only Nigel's possible suicide, but a group suicide occasioned by the anti-group and its concomitant wish *and* fear that the group would be destroyed.

In fact, the group survived the break and gradually strengthened and transformed, becoming a genuinely therapeutic group (this process is described in detail in Chapter 10).

Although the group was later to undergo a significant transformation, the threat from within itself in the early stages was very real. Returning to the first session, it is instructive to consider the symbolic meaning of Georgina's revelation of her anxiety about her breasts. I believe Georgina was voicing anxiety not only about herself, but about the group, perhaps on behalf of the group. The predominant theme in her story was one of damage. Paradoxically, the operation that was meant to produce fullness and beauty had led to disfigurement and humiliation. This, in my view, symbolised the very early anxieties in the group about a damaging intrusion resulting in fragmentation. Anzieu (1984) suggests that the deepest unconscious anxiety at the start of the group is about bodily dismemberment. This ties in with the objective state of the group at its inception – it is a dismembered entity: there is no cohesion, and its state of fragmentation both mirrors and provokes fears of fragmentation (Nitsun 1989). Underlying the intense communication at the start of the group may have been one of the deepest fears – madness, echoed in Georgina's vivid description of her schizophrenic-like symptoms in the first session.

The breasts Georgina described in the group could also be seen a symbol of the early feeding relation of mother to child. In this light, the disfigured breast may represent a fantasy of the nature of the group. Through projective identification, the group is perceived as a damaged breast, unable to nourish, provoking attacks which further destroy it. No amount of positive suggestions and reassurances from the group to Georgina could change her despair about herself. There was a profound challenge in this to the group. She had been damaged once by treatment: could the group rectify this or would it repeat the trauma in some other form? A similar question, I believe, lurked in the mind of the group membership as a whole – could this group, in the disturbing setting of the psychiatric hospital, actually help or would it repeat a frightening, damaging early experience?

The unconscious aspects of the imagery of the group are highlighted here so as to locate the origins of the anti-group in early developmental experience. The essence of the anti-group, in intrapsychic terms, is the bad mothering experience, which evokes a sense of frustration leading to fantasies of attack, which further weaken or damage it, marring the relationship of the container–contained.

This was a group of very disturbed patients, more so than is common in group psychotherapy, but their disturbance heightens and illuminates the psychopathology of the anti-group. Interestingly, as will be seen in Chapter 10, this degree of disturbance did not prevent the group from becoming a powerful context for therapy: the group continued to run for six productive years.

Group A: different levels of the anti-group

The group described above illustrates points made in Chapter 3 about the anti-group as manifested at different levels of the group system: individual, sub-group, and group-as-a-whole. These occurrences are usually parallel or interactive, since the group functions as an overall system, but they can also be separated for purposes of explication.

The individual level

Nigel, described above as the 'voice of the anti-group', illustrates the anti-group occurring strongly at the individual level. From the beginning, he was fiercely and unrelentingly critical of the group. He claimed that he came only because he was told to do so by the conductor ('who presumably knows what he's doing') and that he stayed because no one had told him to go: nevertheless, he considered it a complete waste of time. The rest of the group held similar, if not as extreme, views in the early stages of the group. There was a gradual shift in overall attitude and group atmosphere towards the more appreciative and optimistic, except for Nigel. Paradoxically, he involved himself more and more in the group, becoming more open and interactive. But this, seemingly, made no impact on his negative view of the group. He carried on a lone vendetta against the group even when its therapeutic momentum developed and the grounds for criticism were much lessened.

A brief look at Nigel's life helps to explain his anti-group position. He was a 45-year-old man whose marriage of twenty-two years had ended in a traumatic break when his wife left him for another man. It gradually emerged both that his marriage had been a bitter experience and that the bonding of his family group as a whole was very weak. He had practically no contact with his two children, which gave the impression of a fragmented family unit. He was also socially very isolated. The overall impression was of a person whose relationships with his family and social milieu were marked by an anti-group position. It was this bitter, lonely experience of social groups that he brought into the psychotherapy group and projected onto the group.

There is a question about why he was so unremitting in his view of the group when he attended regularly and involved himself and why the rest of the group tolerated it. In part, he served as a container for the anti-group so that the rest of the group could get on with the therapeutic task. Also, Nigel might have been able to involve himself only on condition that he could denigrate the group. This would allow his participation while avoiding the shame of admitting his interest and dependence on the group. By allowing him to do this and not unduly challenging his position, the other participants enabled Nigel to stay in the group and make use of it as best he could.

The sub-group level

Barry and Maureen, the two participants who had been in individual therapy with the conductor, identified with each other in their resentment at being moved to a group rather than continuing individual therapy. Their position in the group became a focus of attention, with considerable interest in how they would resolve their ambivalence about being there. Barry dealt with his by idealising individual therapy, Maureen by emphasising how she felt betrayed by the conductor: both maintained that they did not want to be in the group. Together, they represented a curious form of Bion's pairing basic assumption. It was not so much that their partnership would create the Messiah, as in Bion's formulation, but rather that they had seen the Messiah and lost him. This pairing functioned as an anti-group sub-group which attracted others, like Nigel, to join its ranks.

The group-as-a-whole level

Manifestations of the anti-group at a group level have previously emerged in the description of the early stages of development of Group A. 'The Tower of Babel' symbolised the failure of communication in the group and the way this led to unproductive confusion and conflict. The negative reactions to Norman's 'group survey' when he joined the group further reflected anti-group attitudes in the group as a whole. But it is also useful to see how the group as an entity gradually acquired a therapeutic function.

The dilemma posed by Barry and Maureen, the pair described above, gradually became owned by the group-as-a-whole. The difficulty of losing a valued, exclusive relationship and the resistance this created towards group membership was a theme that other participants could identify with. Initially, this identification fuelled the anti-group in the group-as-a-whole, but later it became a focus for understanding and therapeutic sensitivity. On one occasion, Maureen brought to the group a dream she had had which dealt with the early loss of her father and, by association, the conductor. The dream symbolised her desperate efforts to reconcile the hurts of the past with the present opportunities of the group, and was understood as such by the group. The dream made an important impact on the group, heightening participants' awareness of the disappointment and resentment that lay behind their own anti-group positions. In this way, an anti-group residing in an individual or sub-group can be useful to the group by highlighting the paradoxical demands of the group in a part of the group and then helping the individual(s) – and hence the group – to confront and accept the paradox.

Here, the anti-group manifested in individual and sub-group levels acquired a therapeutic value to the group-as-a-whole. In a group that had developed less constructively, the sub-group might have been disowned by the overall group or had a malignant effect on group development.

Group B: the breakdown of the group

The previous illustration was of a group that ultimately had a favourable outcome, whereas the following example is of a group that was destroyed by the anti-group. There was a gradual escalation of anti-group attitudes in the course of the group, focused on a particularly antagonistic individual member, whose actions finally led to the group's disintegration.

This started as a mixed-sex group in a day-hospital setting. With five men and two women, the group was strongly weighted towards men. This produced from the start an uneasy relationship between the sexes. The men alternated between a show of indifference to the women and a taunting, mocking stance, which barely concealed their longing for closeness with the women. This put the two women in a difficult position; they expressed considerable feelings of discomfort, towards each other, the men, and the group-as-a-whole. The conductor, a male, was aware of these dynamics but had difficulty elucidating them in the group: communication in the group had a concreteness that prevented reflection and exploration. The tension between the sexes became too difficult to handle: first, one woman dropped out, then the other. The conductor's intention was to replace the women and to rectify the balance of sexes in the group, but the group had become more difficult to handle and the conductor decided to try to deal with existing tensions in the group before bringing in new members.

The loss of the female members appeared to have a demoralising and regressive effect on the group. The five men became very self-absorbed and unable to interact with each other. One of them, Leslie, was very depressed and accident-prone. A series of accidents he sustained outside the group, including a fairly serious car-crash, aroused considerable anxiety and despondency in the group, as if fearing that a self-destructive process was at work. Another patient, Alan, was extremely critical and in the group his criticism became increasingly directed at the conductor, the other members, and the group-as-a-whole: his message was that they were all to blame for the mess that the group was in.

There was a sense that it was extremely difficult for anyone in the group to progress. An underlying demand to conform to a disempowered patient role pervaded, as if development and change in one member could arouse intense resentment and envy in the others. One patient, Hugh, unexpectedly began to use the group more productively than the rest, challenging the inertia of the others, and showing evidence of gains he was beginning to make in the group. This attracted much attention of an ambivalent sort, the group-as-a-whole at times appearing to be on the verge of a breakthrough. In this atmosphere, Alan, the very critical member, became increasingly tense and demanding. He resented not being the centre of attention and would succeed in drawing attention to himself by explosive outbursts of anger and blame. The group became extremely tense again, practically paralysed by the fear and resentment instilled by Alan. Finally, in a fit of rage, Alan got up from his chair clutching a heavy glass ashtray and hurled it at the conductor, barely missing him. Alan then rushed out of the room, never to return again.

The group – and the conductor – were traumatised by the event and a few sessions later the group ended in a fragmented, unresolved way. Attendance had faltered badly in the last few sessions. The conductor's attempts to hold the group together, to examine what happened, and to deal with the aftermath, all failed. The members gradually disappeared. In the last session, the only one present was the conductor.

The destructive impact of the anti-group in this example appears to have originated in the sexual tensions at the start of the group. Unexpressed longings and competition among the men for the women, and possibly vice versa, created an impasse which led to the women withdrawing from the group. No doubt the loss of the women repeated an earlier sense of abandonment, and the group itself became identified with a frustrating, abandoning object, tantalising and unsafe. This intensified anxiety about participating in the group, throwing the individuals back onto their isolated selves. The usual cut and thrust of a group could not be tolerated: competition and progress assumed threatening proportions. Alan was clearly the member who could least tolerate development in the group and represented a violent part of the group that chose literally to attack and undermine the group. He was clearly unsuitable for conventional group psychotherapy, and the example highlights the vital importance of selection and group composition, which will be returned to more fully in Chapter 7 on technical considerations. But it is equally clear that Alan acted as a siphon for the severe anti-group that evolved in this group.

Group C: the flawed development of a group

The dramatic and unequivocally destructive outcome of the above group is relatively unusual in group psychotherapeutic practice. More usual are the subtler manifestations of the anti-group, weaving in and out of the developmental fabric of the group. These manifestations are unlikely to destroy the group, but may impede its progress and limit therapeutic gains. In the following example of a group that ran for three years, there were periods of relative trust and co-operation and some members acknowledged the benefit they gained from the group, but the constructive side of the group was frequently sabotaged by the contrary, negativistic, and oppositional voice of the anti-group.

The group was an out-patient psychotherapy group of mixed-sex membership in an NHS setting. This group was from the beginning markedly ambivalent about dependence. Whereas most groups at the start display at least a measure of dependence on the conductor, seeking his or her approval and guidance, in this group there was repudiation of the conductor's authority. Dependence was rejected in favour of precocious leadership battles and escape from the group, particularly in the form of erratic attendance and drop-outs. In various ways, this was a classic flight–fight group, in Bion's basic assumption terms.

The histories of individual members revealed sharp breaks in the continuity of parental care, with death, divorce, and adoption all featuring strongly in their early family lives and leading to fragmented childhood development. Adult relationships were mostly disturbed and highly unsatisfactory. Marked interpersonal defensiveness was reflected in excessive hyper-sensitivity and prickliness, hiding strong expectations of disappointment and potential for rage. This mistrust extended to interactions within the group. Communication was jagged and fraught. There were frequent misunderstandings and unproductive conflicts, leaving a sense of frustration that was often blamed on the group. 'It's impossible to sort these things out in a group,' one member said. 'No one is really interested in anyone else's problems.'

Attempts at sharing were often counter-productive and confirmatory of participants' negative expectations. One dominant member, Tony, managed to set up a vicious circle in which he took up considerable time in the group, was attacked for his self-centredness, withdrew into a sullen silence, and then sought to dominate the group all over again. Another member, Alison, locked the group into double-binding interchanges. She would tantalise the group by saying that she needed to share important information about an extra-marital affair she was having, but feared exposing and humiliating herself. The group was drawn into a game in which they were required to persuade her to share her secrets. She would then open up, only to return the following week and say that she had felt considerably worse after her revelations. She had felt misunderstood and criticised by the group, confirming her belief that she should not trust anyone with her confidences. The group felt perversely used on these occasions, only to rise to the bait the next time the opportunity arose.

Alison's reaction is an example of what could be described as *contaminating communication*, a process whereby communication in a group ends in a member feeling shamed and sullied.

Responses of this sort are often symptomatic of an underlying anti-group at work, the perverse communication both feeding and reflecting a destructive group process. The concept of contaminating communication is explored more fully in Chapter 5.

In this example, the difficulties were aggravated by the group's resistance to group process exploration. The conductor's attempts to address the tensions and conflicts in the group were frequently met with denial and hostility. The suggestion of an unconscious aspect to group behaviour was viewed with suspicion and interpreted back to the conductor as an invention of his mind. Attempts at abstraction and linking were ridiculed.

The conductor found this a highly frustrating and undermining group and experienced many sessions as an ordeal. A termination date was set for the group well in advance, but, not surprisingly, it proved difficult for the group to work constructively towards an ending. Two people left prematurely during the termination phase and the others attended erratically, as if to pre-empt the ending. This made it practically impossible to deal with issues of separation and loss, and the group ended on an unsatisfactory note.

Group D: the manifest and latent anti-group

In Chapter 3, a distinction was drawn between the latent anti-group, which may remain dormant in the psychotherapy group, and the manifest anti-group, which expresses itself more directly. A circular relationship between the two was suggested: the latent, underlying fear and suspicion of the group predisposes participants towards negative experiences and judgements of the group; actual frustrating and painful experiences in the group confirm underlying anti-group attitudes; this elicits manifest hostility towards the group, and so on, establishing an anti-group constellation.

The actual interplay of latent and manifest anti-group tendencies in a group may be difficult to disentangle. However, there are times when the process is more obvious than others. In this example, an analytic psychotherapy group in a private practice setting had been running for some months. Membership of the group was middle-class, professional, and there was a tendency to treat the group as a pleasant chat over a cup of tea. The usual anxiety about unfamiliarity and self-exposure was evident at the start of the group, but the group fairly soon settled into a co-operative mode of functioning. If anything, the atmosphere was too co-operative, as if the group was succeeding in being a 'good', compliant group. Much of this obscured considerable emotional disturbance and distress. Several members suffered serious interpersonal alienation and had family backgrounds in which there were chronic and crippling tensions. Some members had become estranged from their families of origin and harboured deep resentment towards them.

In the group, conflict and personal exposure were carefully measured: there was enough to keep the group ticking over but *just* enough to avoid rocking the boat. The conductor sometimes felt the group lacked genuine aliveness. His comments on members' considered and considerate tones were usually met with wry smiles and nods of agreement. If the group developed at all, it was towards an intellectual earnestness in which strong feelings were recognised but held at bay.

Some of the fragile composure of the group was challenged by a sudden drop-out. A male member unexpectedly left the group without warning: his only communication was an answering machine message that he was not returning. The event triggered marked unease in the group. There was a sense that all was not well in the group, but because negative reactions in the group had been so restrained, it was difficult to comprehend the action of the drop-out. Vague feelings of guilt in relation to siblings and questions about the group's responsibility for individual members constituted themes in the subsequent sessions.

The atmosphere was complicated by the introduction of a new member into the group. This was a man, Paul, who differed from the others in certain respects: although professionally qualified, he was unemployed and tended to identify with the counterculture. He described himself as a 'lapsed Buddhist', and presented a challenging attitude towards authority and traditional structures. He introduced an irreverent note into the group, which at first was found refreshing and stimulating. But his challenge to participants' assumptions and his playing on their sensitivities became increasingly uncomfortable, eliciting suspicion and hostility towards him, and a particularly strong adversarial response from another male member, Brian. In one session, gathering hostility between the two men came to a head, erupting into open, acrimonious conflict. There was talk of physical violence, with one challenging the other, 'I dare you to say that to me outside this group'. Paul proceeded to denigrate the group, saying that the whole thing was 'a con' and that he 'must have been mad to join the group in the first place'.

The conductor had difficulty intervening, but eventually was able to confront Paul, suggesting that he was bidding for the leadership of the group and that this was what had provoked Brian's anger. By this time the atmosphere in the group was so charged that the interpretation aggravated the conflict, probably because it exposed leadership issues that had not previously been dealt with in the group.

There followed a turbulent, unstable period in the group with erratic attendance and 'bad' behaviour like members not informing the group of absences. When the members were together, the previous co-operative sense yielded to bickering and complaints about the group. Participants felt in a double-bind: intellectually they knew the conflict was a natural part of the group process but emotionally they feared that this could be destructive to themselves and the group. Their fears were to a large extent realised when Paul dropped out of the group, followed by a female member who had been hovering on the edge of the group for some time. A sense of despair and disintegration set in. It took the group and the conductor almost a year to reconstitute the group and the turbulent period remained etched on the group memory for some time. There was a sense that the events of this period were not properly understood or assimilated into the development of the group and a fear that a similar explosion could happen again.

The dynamics of this group can be seen in the light of a strong latent repressed anti-group in the 'foundation matrix', Foulkes' term for the underlying potential of the group that is there at the start. Evidence supporting this hypothesis is the social alienation and underlying rage at the family unit that was present in several participants, suggesting a shared internalized anti-group constellation. In the group this was hidden by a compliant mode, not unlike the group 'false self' described in the first example in this chapter and explored more fully by Fried (1979). The presence of Paul, an anti-authority and anti-structure figure in the group, unearthed the latent anti-group attitudes of the other members. An attempt was made to project these entirely onto Paul, but, when this did not succeed, the group plunged into a manifest anti-group with all the attendant symptoms of a group in entropy: spiralling conflict, impasse, drop-outs, erratic attendance, and threatened group disintegration.

The challenge to this group might in other circumstances have been a watershed, providing the group with the opportunity to strengthen and deepen by facing and surviving conflict, rivalry, and profound doubt. But the latent anti-group was probably so strong and resistant to genuine disclosure and working-through that its manifest expression in the group produced a vicious circle leading to destructive group behaviour.

This is an example of the insidious effect of a latent anti-group insufficiently recognised and challenged in the early stages of the group. It suggests that *early* cohesiveness and co-operation in a group is not necessarily a favourable sign, and points to the difficult but important task of reading the 'sub-text' of a group that may contain clues to an anti-group constellation.

Group A: the alternation of 'pro-group' and anti-group

Therapy groups are prone to sudden, sharp and seemingly inexplicable fluctuations. These can go both ways: towards the constructive and towards the destructive. In the absence of any other term, I am using the term 'pro-group' to describe the positive, constructive aspect of groups that facilitates development. This can be seen as thesis to the anti-group as anti-thesis. Groups need and benefit from their pro-group component, but this is not uncommonly subverted by the anti-group, and sometimes in surprising ways.

The present illustration comes from group A, which was described at the start of this chapter. As noted, this was a group with a strong anti-group that gradually developed into a cohesive and therapeutic group in which the pro-group became increasingly consolidated. Well into its constructive phase, where pro-group attitudes predominated, one session was marked by the sharing of very positive life-changes that some members were experiencing. There was full attendance at the group and a sense of pleasure in these achievements, confirming the positive change that had occurred in the group and promoting an attitude of optimism. The next session was a complete contrast. Of the eight members, three were present. Reasons given for non-attendance were on the surface valid and linked to complications in members' daily lives. But there was a sense that something was amiss. The conductor was so surprised by the reversal of group cohesion that he could not see the likely connection with the previous meeting. In retrospect, this became clearer: the marked progress of some members had stirred up envy and feelings of inadequacy in other members but this could not be expressed in the 'good' group, with its display of affiliation and admiration. Instead, it was enacted the following week by members' avoidance of the group. This group instability, in fact, continued for several weeks.

Envy remained very difficult for this group to express and deal with, resulting in avoidance and rationalisation in the group. In Chapter 5 on the determinants of the anti-group, it is suggested that envy is a powerful factor in creating negative reactions to the group. Particularly where envy remains unexpressed and unassimilated in the group, it can have an insidious effect. The group itself becomes identified with the creation of envy and humiliation, and, through a process of projective identification, it becomes both enviable and contemptible. Dynamics of this sort may explain the unpredictable nature of psychotherapy groups, in which good sessions with full attendance and positive group spirit are followed by fragmented groups with poor attendance and weak group spirit. In most groups, this is part of the dialectical interplay of constructive and destructive, leading eventually to a strengthening and integration of the group, but, in some groups, envy and other determinants of the anti-group may seriously undermine development.

Oscillations of this sort are of course common in most forms of psychotherapy. Much of psychoanalytic theory and technique is addressed to the recognition and understanding of negative therapeutic reactions. My own experience, however, is that these oscillations occur with greater speed and intensity in group than in individual psychotherapy. Very probably, feeling states are accelerated and magnified in groups because of the greater number of participants. As part of this, anti-group reactions can occur with great suddenness and strength.

STAFF SUPPORT GROUPS

The focus of this book has so far been almost entirely on the psychotherapy group. But this is only one form of group in the complex matrix of groups in the mental health setting.

Another common form of group is the staff support group. There are various definitions of staff support groups (Bramley 1990), but I am referring here to a regular, usually weekly or fortnightly, meeting of the staff group as a whole to explore the dynamics of the group in relation to the work and task context, with the help of a facilitator. The purpose of the group is to enable and improve work performance by clarifying and dealing with tensions that obstruct the fulfilment of the task.

My use of the term 'support group' is tempered by an awareness that in reality these groups are by no means universally experienced as supportive. Quite often, the reverse applies: they can be perceived as highly threatening, even destructive. The one example of such a group so far given (Chapter 3, pp. 56–7) indicated the anti-group reaction that was sparked off by the mere proposal to run such a group. Recently, a well-known organisation in the UK specialising in the residential treatment of disturbed individuals and families, in which regular staff 'dynamics' groups had been run, took a position on these groups. They noted the dissatisfaction many staff members experienced with support groups, the perception of the groups as destructive, and the ambiguous or unsuccessful outcomes of the groups. In order to remedy the situation, they drew up a document trying to clarify the purpose of these groups, to provide guidelines for their implementation, and to set criteria for the selection of facilitators. The doubts and uncertainties about staff support groups expressed here reflect some of the problems inhering in these groups.

Staff support groups can be seen as similar to psychotherapy groups in that they aim at self-understanding and group development through the group process. However, they differ from therapy groups in important respects. They are groups not of strangers but of people who may spend a good deal of time together and whose purpose in doing so is primarily work-related and not therapeutic. Participants are not generally referred for support groups, nor do they necessarily seek out the group: quite often, the decision to hold the group is made by a senior member or members of the team and the rest of the group is expected to attend, sometimes voluntarily, sometimes compulsorily. Staff arrive at the group with an established set of concerns and often powerful existing interpersonal relationships, positive and negative, since work groups tend to arouse considerable feelings of affiliation as well as rivalry and competition. There are generally also pervasive issues about hierarchical position, belonging and exclusion, power and control. These issues are usually not overtly recognised or openly discussed at work, and staff support groups may challenge members to bring them out into the open. Not surprisingly, this creates a feeling of threat in the group.

Also, unlike a psychotherapy group, members of a staff support group have to face each other and work together after the group. This raises anxious concerns about boundary issues, about confidentiality, and about the degree of disclosure that can be risked in the group.

These sensitivities are compounded by the emotional impact of working with psychologically disturbed or disabled clients, as in the mental health setting. One immediate difficulty for staff is the demand placed on their personal resources: they work in emotionally charged settings in which intense feelings may be aroused in them but they are expected to exercise considerable understanding, patience, compassion, and restraint. They have to deal with their own identifications and counter-identifications with patients. These identifications stir up deep-rooted, primitive intra- and interpersonal dynamics in staff, all of which are likely to influence the process and outcome of the staff support group.

This combination of elements makes the staff support group a potentially strengthening experience in which tensions and hidden dynamics can be clarified and defused. Equally, however, there is the risk of activating unwelcome conflict and exposure, and the possibility that this could create additional problems rather than solving existing ones.

The staff support group in some ways illustrates and exaggerates some of the problematic aspects of psychotherapy groups, previously noted. Complexity of task and purpose are marked and the paradoxical demands placed on members are, if anything, greater in staff support groups than in psychotherapy groups. These phenomena render those groups particularly prone to anti-group developments. Here, two contrasting examples are presented, one in which the anti-group became embedded in a disintegratory process, the other in which group difficulties were satisfactorily and constructively resolved.

Group E: a staff support group on a psychiatric ward

The following vivid, complex example illustrates not only the powerful infiltration of the anti-group in a vulnerable setting but the way in which this both reflected and generated technical problems in managing the group. The staff group took place on an acute admission ward in a psychiatric hospital. The motivation for setting up the group came from the two most senior members of the team, the consultant psychiatrist and ward nurse manager, who felt that the team could benefit from group facilitation. The team consisted mainly of doctors and psychiatric nurses, with the occasional presence of paramedical staff. The problem, as presented by the consultant and the ward manager, was that the team lacked cohesion. There was an uneasy distance between the nurses and the doctors, the junior nurses, in particular, perceiving the doctors as superior and aloof. This was felt especially in relation to the consultation psychiatrist, who was seen as a sometimes benevolent, sometimes despotic leader of the team.

Two important aspects of the setting up of the group stand out. One is that the majority of the staff team was not consulted on the question of whether to hold the group or not. The second was that the purpose of the group was not entirely clear from the beginning, other than a rather vague idea that enhanced cohesion would improve teamwork.

A further problem concerned the choice of group facilitator. The consultant psychiatrist took the lead in inviting the facilitator, an individual psychotherapist and one-time colleague of his of whom he had a highly favourable opinion. The facilitator had had little contact with psychiatric hospitals and had misgivings about undertaking the task. She was also aware that her previous contact with the consultant would be a complicating factor. However, much encouraged by the consultant, she agreed to run the group.

The group got off to a difficult start. Erratic attendance and a rotating set of absences resulted in a group that was never the same from week to week, creating fundamental discontinuities that made it impossible to establish a sense of the group as a whole.

Negative views of the support group were openly expressed. Several members said they had previously been in similar groups and found them to be destructive. Others expressed hostility and reluctance at having to attend. The direct expression of such feelings may have opened the way for understanding and compromise, but there was a rigidity about these views that made them very difficult to penetrate. Boundary issues were prevalent from early on. One member expressed considerable concern that negative comments were being made after the group about individuals who had in some way revealed themselves in the group. Discussions were held about procedures to protect personal boundaries and confidentiality, but agreements reached seemed fragile. There was a pervasive lack of trust in the group.

Interaction in the group tended to be stiff and hierarchical. Most of the talk came from the senior members, while the juniors, particularly the nurses, sat in tense silence. If difficult or controversial issues emerged, these either led to strongly polarised views or were quickly aborted, with sharp expressions of feeling that led nowhere. When problematic interpersonal encounters took place, potentially with useful outcomes, these were usually followed by flight reactions, changes of subject and implicated members staying away from subsequent groups. Painful experiences in the group could not be tolerated, as if resolutions had to be found immediately, or else the group was confirmed in its uselessness. There were repeated discussions about the pointlessness of the group, with demands on the facilitator to provide guidelines and structures.

The facilitator was aware of various sources of tension in the team that were hinted at in the group but seldom explored in any depth. These included considerable problems in handling very difficult patients on the ward and feelings of antagonism towards the management structure of the hospital, which was perceived as critical and unsupportive of the work of the team. Where these issues were discussed, there were strong projections onto the non-staff groups, the crazy patients, and the uncaring management. There was little willingness to look inward, to reflect on how these problems might be generated within individuals or the staff team as a whole. The facilitator had the impression that awareness was not lacking but that the fear of exposure was so great that shared awareness could not be risked. This added to a feeling of helplessness in the team and disempowered the support group, so that it functioned as a detached entity, cut off from a fuller sense of internal and external reality.

Not surprisingly, the conductor found her task an extremely

difficult one. Her usual analytic approach, involving a fair measure of therapeutic distance and an interpretative stance, was not welcomed by the group. The threats and ambiguities created by her approach triggered a wave of hostile projections onto her and the group. Her attempts to encourage the group to reflect on its own process were criticised, even ridiculed. One nurse complained that all the group ever did was to talk about what was going on in the group. When it was suggested that this might be of benefit to the team, helping them to understand and improve their functioning, the response was one of amazed disbelief.

The consultant psychiatrist, perceiving the therapist's difficulties in the group, developed a pattern of coming to her aid. He would argue on her behalf, explain her interventions, and sometimes express exasperation at the group's resistance to the analytic approach. This perpetuated in the mind of the team the pairing relationship between the consultant and the facilitator, with barely concealed suspicion that they were in some form of collusion. This widened the gulf between the consultant and the team, and that between the facilitator and the team, and it also seemed to alienate the ward manager, who had initially supported the undertaking.

An incident that took place outside the group, fairly late in its development, suggested that some of the hierarchical and professional differences were as prevalent as ever. A drug company, via the consultant psychiatrist, invited the staff team to a promotional dinner at an expensive restaurant. This could have been an opportunity for shared enjoyment, but the traditional divisions manifested themselves at the party. The consultant and the other doctors sat at the most prominent table in the restaurant, while the nursing staff as a group were placed at a remote table on the periphery of the restaurant. There was practically no contact all night between the two groups, with the nurses feeling rejected and humiliated. One of the junior nurses reported this event in the support group. By that stage it seemed more a statement of despair about things ever changing than an expression of hope that they could or would change.

Finally, a disruptive incident on the ward led to an intense confrontation in the support group that heralded the ending of the group. A male nurse had been accused of verbally abusing and threatening a female patient. In the group, he did not altogether deny this, but blamed the doctors for leaving the nurses to handle the most difficult patients without support or supervision. This provoked an angry backlash from the consultant psychiatrist about the standard of nursing care, which in turn triggered a powerful outburst from the ward manager towards the consultant. Among the consultant's counter-criticisms was the observation that the nurse in question had very rarely attended the support group and that, had he done so more regularly, the problem might have been prevented. This unleashed the full fury of the critics of the group, who suggested that the group had done little other than stir up destructive feelings and so make matters worse. Emotions in the group were running high when the time came for ending and, given the importance of the issues, the facilitator allowed the group to over-run for 15 minutes.

The following week, another nurse attacked the facilitator for allowing the group to over-run, pointing out that there had been an obsessional emphasis on time boundaries, and that she, the nurse, had once been criticised for coming late to the group. The facilitator encouraged the group to understand this attack in the context of the previous group and events on the ward, but the angry splits in the group made it impossible to reflect on these dynamics and the group ended in disarray.

At this point, the facilitator, who had felt increasingly exasperated with the group, decided that she had had enough. She announced to the group that she was leaving in two sessions' time, giving the group practically no time to address the recent escalation of problems and the prospect of the group terminating. The group ended on a highly unsatisfactory note, with a realisation of the worst fears and fantasies of the group – that it would lead to destructive conflict and disintegrate in the process. Several members of the team decided to continue meeting themselves, but the venture soon petered out.

This group had all the hallmarks of an anti-group. There were fundamental problems in the way it was set up, including the lack of consultation with staff and the choice of a facilitator who was ambivalent about the task and probably ill-equipped in terms of training and previous experience. These factors suggested a failure 'script' in the primary construction of the group, as if the group was set up to fail. Splitting mechanisms that were already present in the multi-disciplinary team and probably rife in the psychopathology of patients treated by the team – yet seldom recognised or explored in the support group – were enacted in the dynamics of the group to unfortunate ends. The split between the consultant–facilitator pair and the rest of the group was symptomatic of this process.

The group revealed pervasive difficulties about boundaries. This included a diffusion and confusion of boundaries, as in the question of what belonged inside and what belonged outside the group, as well as a rigidification of boundaries in other contexts, such as the hierarchical differences between staff and the bitter inter-professional rivalry. These difficulties should be seen not only as a reflection of the internal problems of the group but as expressions of the tensions created within staff groups by the constraints and demands of the organisation at large – a point which will be explored more fully in Chapter 11.

In the support group itself, the problem about boundaries reached its highest peak in the angry criticisms of the nurse who complained about the ambiguities and double standards surrounding the time boundaries of the group. Her attack on the group and the facilitator was a powerful condenser of the many confusions and conflicts that had made this an untenable group.

Group F: a staff group in a general hospital

A staff group that grappled with the anti-group and had a favourable outcome is described here by way of contrast. The group was a team of nurses working on a specialist medical ward for the treatment of anorexia. The request for the staff group came from the team as a whole, although members varied in their motivation and willingness to attend. The facilitator was a psychologist based in the same hospital who otherwise had no contact with the unit or its staff. The group started meeting on a fortnightly basis, later asking the facilitator to increase this to weekly meetings.

The staff team regarded their work as difficult and highly frustrating, with rewards that were few and far between. The patients in their charge were mainly adolescent females suffering from severe anorexia. They spent weeks or months on the ward receiving intensive physical and psychological care. Their illness was sometimes life-threatening and their extreme thinness was epitomised in a popular image of them as ghosts who could be seen wafting through the corridors of the hospital. There was a marked degree of anxiety in this work: the spectre of deterioration and death was never far away and staff felt a considerable burden of responsibility.

The anxiety about these patients' physical survival was paralleled by concern about the primitive psychological states to which they had regressed. Their level of psychopathology was very pronounced but staff often found them impenetrable as human beings. They communicated very little about themselves in personal terms, their affect was flat, and they tended to resist any inquiry into feeling states or emotional problems. This was what staff found so frustrating: the apparent depths of distress and disturbance, masked by the symptoms, that could not be reached. Staff reported an atmosphere of deadness, decay, and overwhelming boredom on the ward. The only emotional life was between staff themselves, and it became clear that this was highly pitched, with frequent and intense conflict, to the extent of generating a fear that the staff team could implode.

These dynamics entered fully into the staff support group, all the more so when the frequency of the meetings increased. There was an intense level of communication with a high degree of expressed emotion. Much of this focused on a male nurse who adopted a highly aggressive attitude towards the female nurses, who in turn reacted with helpless rage. Personal revelations of childhood sexual abuse flooded into the group, as did themes of rape and sexual violence in general. Intense confrontations also occurred between some of the female nurses, with themes of rivalry and envy predominating. For some weeks, there was a sense that the emotions in the group could get out of control, that the group could not withstand the degree of conflict and disturbance. Members of the group acted this out in various ways. The aggressive male nurse powerfully challenged the purpose and value of the group. He absented himself from the group on several occasions, sending contemptuous messages about the group to the facilitator. Towards the end of one meeting, another nurse got up prematurely and accidentally switched off the lights in the room. There was a gasp of surprise in the room, as if the other members resonated with an action that symbolised the wish to shut down the group or to remove the focus on all the painful, threatening subjects that had been unearthed in the group.

Several factors staved off the encroachment of the anti-group. One was the facilitator's own support system. He was a member of a supervision group of psychologists to which he could bring the full weight of the group's concerns, enabling him to share his sense of being overwhelmed and perplexed by the intensity of the group's reaction. The supervision group also helped to clarify the dynamics of the staff support group. Increasingly, it became apparent that the staff were enacting the emotional disturbance that could not be expressed by their anorectic patients. They were playing out the adolescent problems of development that were repressed by the patients – conflicts over sexuality, aggression, and rivalry, with underlying anxiety about the primal elements of male and female genitality and intercourse. For these patients, conscious contact with these fantasies and impulses was frightening and their unconscious choice was to stifle their instinctual development. Staff were receiving the projections of the patients, no doubt stirring up unresolved areas of conflict and anxiety in themselves, but then enacted to an excessive and potentially dangerous degree as compensation for the lack of inner emotional reality in the patients and the atmosphere of non-communication on the ward. Insight into this dynamic relationship, combined with the determined efforts of the facilitator and the support of his supervision group, helped to make this a useful and valued group.

The seriousness of the underlying dynamics in this staff–patient–support group constellation should not be underestimated. At the core of the problem was a fantasy of death, arising in the patient group as an anti-libidinal reaction to the threat of adolescent sexuality. The staff's dramatic enactment of some of these themes could be seen as a way of keeping alive psychic development in their patients, of preserving the life force. They did this in the face of considerable threat to themselves as a work group, so that the danger of a symbolic death was ever present. In the support group, this was reflected in the encroachment of the anti-group, itself an expression of anti-libidinal forces (see Chapter 6, pp. 142–3).

In various ways, this is an example of a successful staff support group, since the group provided a place where staff could bring destructive projections, identifications, and counter-identifications, with the opportunity to contain and transform them in the interests of caring for patients. The success of this staff support group in its containing function can be contrasted with the failure of the group in the previous example. There, the safety of the group, the clarity of boundaries, and the support for the facilitator herself were all missing, so that the group became host to multiple destructive projections. Both examples, though, illustrate the potential of staff support groups to become anti-groups, and the considerable demands on the facilitator to understand and deal with powerful and primitive group processes.

EXPERIENTIAL TRAINING GROUPS

Another common form of group is the so-called experiential group in the context of individual or group psychotherapy training. The main purpose of such groups is to give participants an insight into interpersonal processes in the group setting, although the exact aim may vary from course to course, and there is not unusually an ambiguous sense of the group's purpose. These are not meant to be psychotherapy groups, although at least a measure of therapeutic work may be achieved. The groups benefit from their highly resourced membership: the trainees are pre-selected, and are usually intelligent, sensitive, and aware, often having had previous experience of psychotherapy. However, these groups have some of the inherent problems of staff support groups, particularly those of boundaries and confidentiality, and they may also run into difficulties which can be serious and disturbing.

Group G: an experiential group in a psychotherapy training course

The present example is illustrative of severe difficulties in the development of an experiential group, closely linked to instability in the organisational context. This was a group of first-year trainees undertaking a three-year psychotherapy course in a training institute. The experiential group was a mandatory requirement of the course. The facilitator was an experienced female group psychotherapist.

The host training institute was going through a period of tumultuous change. A crisis of leadership had led to serious organisational difficulties and financial problems, resulting in the dismantling of existing structures and plans for radical restructuring. The group of trainees in question started their course in the throes of this organisational change. Their particular course, one of several in the institution, was beset by staffing problems, a conflict of value systems, and confusion of direction. The students not only picked up these tensions but perceived the staff as highly critical of them. They felt that unreasonable demands were made on them, with little support, and that their difficulties were interpreted as psychopathology. From early on, an atmosphere of mistrust and hostility pervaded the course.

Parallel difficulties occurred in the experiential group. In the first session the facilitator found it necessary to alter the physical arrangement of the room. She had arrived to find the chairs arranged in a circle, as expected, but with no table in the centre of the circle. As a group therapist used to working in a particular way, she commented on this and decided to move a table from the side of the room into the centre. This triggered a wave of criticism from the trainees, who expressed the view that the facilitator was imposing a rigid group-analytic structure on the group and that this probably betokened further arrogance and rigidity on her part.

The group got off to a tense, uncomfortable start. The next few sessions reinforced the unease. In this atmosphere, a male trainee displayed marked persecutory feelings and soon afterwards dropped out of the group and the course. The other trainees blamed the course, but also the unsupportive nature of the experiential group and the facilitator's interventions. Like the staff on the psychotherapy course, she was perceived as harsh, judgemental, and prone to making penetrating, persecutory interpretations. The more she tried to understand this from the trainees' point of view and to address their difficulties, the more impotent and ineffective she was made to feel. She periodically highlighted the connection between the students' anger with her and their anger about the course, suggesting that they were transferring their rage onto her. There was some agreement with this interpretation, but, ironically, it reinforced the trainees' feelings.

The facilitator was aware from early on that the trainees had their own informal group that met at the pub after the experiential sessions. If anything, this was flaunted before her, as if to make her aware of her exclusion and to vaunt the 'pub group' as a close, cohesive group in contrast to the tense, fragmented experiential group. There was clearly a split operating between the two groups: the good pub group, unhampered by authority, group analysis, and the facilitator, and the bad experiential group, which was rapidly degenerating into an anti-group.

In the second of three terms, the facilitator felt that the group's struggle and her efforts had begun to pay off, and a more benign, constructive, atmosphere entered the group. Her relationship with the trainees seemed to improve and they appeared somewhat more settled in their psychotherapy course. However, after the next break, at the start of the third and final term, there was a resurgence of hostility in the group. This was paralleled by the increasingly intense problems of a female trainee related to both the psychotherapy course and her personal life. In a state of near emotional breakdown, the trainee decided to withdraw from the course, and, hence, the experiential group. A sense of ultimate failure and blame spread through the group. Yet, again, the facilitator was accused of contributing to, if not causing, the trainee's problems. The profoundly negative associations the group had acquired now made it impossible to deal constructively with issues of separation and loss as the group drew to an end. How could there be any regret, disappointment, even ambivalence about ending, when the group had been so bad?

Throughout the running of the group, the facilitator had been in a state of distress. She had no external support in relation to the group, realising afterwards that she could have lightened her burden by obtaining supervision. On reflection, she felt that she had been caught in a trap of her own independence and fantasised omnipotence: the belief that, alone, she could make this group better. She remembered how she felt leaving the group after the last session to go to the underground station and take the train home. Standing on the platform waiting for the train, she felt overcome by emotion. The tears welled up inside her and she stood on the the platform sobbing uncontrollably for some time, letting go of her profound sense of hurt, exhaustion – and relief.

This painful account of a highly destructive group merits comment on several levels. One concerns the theme of context, which has been referred to in relation to several previous examples. In this case, the chaos and conflict in the training institute had a devastating effect on the experiential group. The external context of a group can be seen as a form of environmental mother which is required to hold and support the group as it undergoes its complex development, a view which is explored in Chapters 7 and 11. From this, it follows that an organisation in crisis will have a detrimental effect on the group. In this illustration, the organisational disturbance was intensely mirrored in the experiential group, as if the group was compelled to play out projections of a destructive mothering (or parenting) experience. Not only did the organisational matrix and the experiential group matrix closely mirror each other, but the facilitator was the recipient of marked projective identifications which were extremely difficult to disentangle in the group. A form of 'malignant mirroring' (Zinkin 1983) was at work. The facilitator was clearly identified with the staff of the institution, arousing considerable envy and resentment, and the group's repudiation of her ability represented an omnipotent triumph over the hated authority.

A linked theme is brought to light with devastating clarity in this group: the impact of the anti-group on the conductor. The facilitator was an experienced and competent group psychotherapist, her difficulties suggesting that competence is not necessarily a protection against the infiltration of the anti-group. The experiential group was as much anti-facilitator as it was anti-group. This is a common connection: an alternating focus of blame on group and conductor. Significantly, what the facilitator lacked for herself was a supportive 'mothering' context, such as supervision or consultation with a colleague, in which she could have shared the burden of running the group. The fact that she chose not to do this may be an indication not so much of professional misjudgement on her part as of the strength of unconscious pressure on her to absorb and enact the projection of a failed capacity to conduct the group and so to become a devalued object.

CONCLUSIONS

A range of groups in clinical and linked settings has been presented – psychotherapy groups, staff support groups, and experiential training groups – all illustrating the marked susceptibility of the group to anti-group developments. Some examples indicate the strength of the group matrix to withstand and reverse the infiltration of the anti-group, creating a transforming group experience – a theme that will be explored in later sections of the book. But mostly the examples illustrate points made earlier about group characteristics and tensions that predispose the group to anti-group manifestations. The illustrations, I believe, confirm the relevance of the concept of the anti-group, as a descriptive construct and a critical principle that challenges the conventional optimism in the field of group psychotherapy. In the area of staff support groups and experiential training groups, there is a particular dearth of literature; the present examples, although clearly selective, indicate the marked potential for difficulties in these settings and the toll that is taken on conductor and partipants alike.

Themes which emerge with some consistency in these examples form the basis for more detailed exposition in later chapters – the composition of the group, technical issues in handling the anti-group, the individualisation of the 'anti-group voice' in a particular member or members, the conductor's role, and the influence of context on the formation of the anti-group. The examples illustrate the primitive origins of the anti-group in deep-rooted, developmentally early fantasies and conflicts about relationships, including the clash between self or individual and group needs, the link between intra-psychic and interpersonal dynamics, the complex interplay of transference and counter-transference phenomena in the group, and the powerful influence of primitive perceptual and defence mechanisms, especially denial, idealisation, projection, and projective identification. Finally, the illustrations in this chapter suggest the importance of going beyond clinical groups to understand the well-spring of the anti-group in the wider social arena – in family groups, organisations, and the culture at large, all of which are explored in later chapters.

Chapter 5

Determinants of the anti-group I
Regression, survival anxiety, failures of communication, projective identification, envy

One of the underlying theses of this book is that the demands of group existence themselves arouse considerable anxiety and potential for regression. Psychotherapy groups, while offering opportunities for resolution and development, nevertheless in some respects heighten anxiety and regressive potential. Previous chapters outlining the concept of the anti-group and providing clinical illustrations have suggested some underlying determinants of this difficult phenomenon in groups: the paradoxical characteristics of the therapy group; the projection of severe psychopathology into and onto the group; the failure of the holding environment; the disruptive influence of wider contextual factors; the distortion of the mirroring function of the group; and the breakdown of the conductor's containing function. But this picture is incomplete without a corresponding understanding of the psychopathological processes that are brought to the group by the individual members and that are expressed in their interaction with one another. *The interlocking of group-specific factors with the psychological characteristics of the membership generates the distinctive nature of the group, including its position on the anti-group continuum.*

The following two chapters explore the psychopathological phenomena in the group membership that contribute to anti-group developments. This is an ambitious task, since it embraces the full sweep of individual and group psychopathology. My vantage point is largely that of object relations theory, which, like James (1994), I see as complementary to group analysis. The link between internal representations and external relationships – the bedrock of all object relations theory – together with the emphasis on projective and introjective processes, I consider to be essential for the understanding of the psychopathology of the antigroup. Additionally, an understanding of the impact of early developmental trauma on later psychosocial adjustment – which is integral to object relations theory – is crucial. I consider as particularly relevant Klein's description of the paranoid-schizoid and depressive dimensions of experience; Bion's theories of linking and containing; Fairbairn's analysis of the early splitting of the ego; Balint's theory of the basic fault; and Winnicott's notion of environmental support or failure and its impact on the experienced self. The work of these 'classical' object relations theorists is extended by that of contemporary writers, such as Bollas (1987) and Kernberg (1965, 1980, 1991). These understandings are supplemented by the insights of self-psychology, which has been shown to have important implications for group relationships (Bacal 1985; Harwood 1992) and which, I will suggest, can help to clarify aspects of anti-group formation.

As a guiding principle, I start from the conception of the *group as object*. This formulation is implicit or explicit in the views of numerous writers. In Bion's work (1961), for example, the notion of a *group entity*, established through the operation of the basic assumptions, in essence describes a group object. Anzieu (1984) more explicitly describes a group object created through the fantasies and projections of the group membership. Jacobson (1989) describes how the group becomes 'an object in the cultural field'. In the group as object, properties of the group stimulate the perceptions and projections of the membership, combining to establish the group as a form of container in which both recognised and disowned psychic phenomena are vested and in which shared object relationship systems reside. Once established, the group as object, an entity in its own right, invites its own form of object relationships with the group membership, in a way which powerfully influences further development. In the case of the anti-group, the group as object becomes a fragile, dangerous, or aversive container, and it is the evolution of this process which forms the subject of this and the subsequent chapters.

The question of causality arises in any discussion of determinants. As Maratos (1994) argues, we are less inclined in contemporary psychological thinking to accept fixed notions of causality, and more inclined to consider the coexistence of phenomena without necessarily assuming a causal relationship. It is important to clarify that I am not attempting to propose that one or even several factors determine the anti-group in any absolute way. The factors I suggest vary considerably from group to group. In so far as I subscribe to the notion of causality, this is a model of circular rather than linear causality, taking account of the systemic view of groups described previously (see Chapter 3, pp. 61–2).

The determinants I propose also vary in their degree of speculativeness. Some, like the notion of failed communication in groups, are discernible phenomena; others, like the primal scene, reach into the unconscious regions of the group and are in the nature of hypothetical constructs.

There is a large degree of overlap between the determinants, but, because of the wide span covered, I have divided this section into two chapters. This chapter deals with regression, survival anxiety, failures of communication, projective identification, and envy. Chapter 6 deals with interpersonal disturbances, the primal scene, aggression, and the death instinct.

REGRESSION

The regressive tendency of people in groups is one of the most perplexing aspects of group life in general, in social, cultural, and political spheres. Even in more sophisticated societies, people in groups resort to regressive beliefs and actions with sudden and violent intensity, reminding us of the primitive forces lurking behind the veneer of civilisation. Destructive aggression itself has regressive components: the lack, or loss, of conscience and concern that accompanies destructive acts towards others is a dehumanising form of regression.

In Chapter 3 it was suggested that the paradoxical aspects of therapy groups themselves create contradictory, antagonistic, and regressive pulls in the membership. In groups, there is a dual process of regression, emanating on one hand from the pressures of group life and on the other from the psychic structures of individual members.

Freud's original work *Group Psychology and the Analysis of the Ego* (1921) concentrated on regressive forces in large groups. Freud emphasised the primitive, impulsive, unreflective behaviour of hordes or mobs, attributing the sense of immediate closeness between individuals in these groups to the projection of their ego ideal onto the leader. This stimulated group members' strong identification with the leader as well as with each other. These mutual identifications create a sense of unity and belonging but at the expense of ego functioning in the group: perceptual and cognitive balance is weakened. As a result, powerful, normally unconscious needs and impulses erupt, often under the sway and direction of the leader.

Bion's observations on small group dynamics (1961) have previously been described, with an emphasis on the deeply regressive processes creating the basic assumptions. In Bion's conceptualisation, the *absence* rather than the presence of directive leadership awakens regressive forces in the group. The frustration of the members' wish for explicit leadership unleashes powerful, archaic fantasies concerning the leader and the nature of the group. In attempting to give the group structure and direction, the members resort to the primitive organisation of the basic assumptions. In some respects, these satisfy deeper longings but they erode the capacity of the group to think and to work. In Chapter 3, I suggested that for all their apparent 'groupiness', basic assumption groups are anti-groups: their regressive formations undermine group functioning in the sense of coherent interrelatedness.

Undoubtedly, Bion's technique of group leadership – a highly distancing one – contributed to the regression he noticed in these groups. This leadership style is generally considered to be disadvantageous as a mode of facilitating therapy groups, but it nevertheless highlights an inherent dilemma in analytic group psychotherapy: the primitive processes generated can precipitate an excessive degree of regression. The group-analytic model is a more benign one than the Bionian, the therapist more actively attuned to the needs of the group. However, the task of the group remains open-ended and the leadership essentially non-directive. The rationale is that this stimulates a deeper level of communication and relating in the group, including the evocation and projection of unconscious material. Additionally, as Foulkes (1964a) emphasised, this encourages the assumption of authority by the group itself, in this way strengthening the group. However, the situation is sufficiently unstructured and ambiguous to trigger regressive processes and these can be counter-productive, even detrimental, to the group.

These considerations highlight the issue of task definition. Miller and Rice (1967) emphasise the defining role of the primary task for the existence of the group: without a clear task, the group flounders. In therapy groups, where the level of anxiety is in any case likely to be high, the ambiguity of the task exacerbates anxiety. Such ambiguity may arouse other disturbing emotions, such as feelings of inadequacy and shame (Amati Sas 1992). The defence mechanisms elicited in states of regressive anxiety are usually of the most extreme sort: projection, projective identification, and splitting. The therapeutic purpose of mobilising these defence structures is their loosening and eventual replacement by more benign defences or adaptive measures, but the arousal of these defence systems in the group may create a regressive process which forecloses rather than facilitates group development.

The regressive impact of the group has been considered from different vantage points. One perspective concerns confusions of identity. Brigham (1992) focuses on the intra-psychic aspects of individuals' responses to the group, in which there is an activation of part-object relationships as members attempt to relate to the aggregate that is the group. The multiplicity of members and potential relationships requires a continuous sorting out of self-images from object-images, a constant necessity to distinguish 'I' from 'you' and 'we'. In this context, self-representations that form the basis of self-identity are threatened by the infiltration of aspects of the part-objects: projective and introjective identification are mobilised and destabilise the sense of inner identity.

> Potential for loss of identity in the group is an important part of the regression and contributes in large part to the anxiety evoked in group situations.
>
> (Brigham 1992, p. 251)

These conditions not only result in a fragmented sense of self and other, but predispose members to perceive the group as split, most often in a good/bad dichotomy. The bad object may be located outside the group in the creation of an external enemy but equally may invade the group itself, resulting in attacks that disempower the group. Although such schisms in turn exacerbate anxiety and discomfort, since they heighten the perception of danger from within or without the group, they may have the paradoxical effect of uniting the group in the face of threatened fragmentation. Bion (1961) gives the example of a markedly uncooperative group that was at the same time a very united group, the point being that its very negativity gave the group cohesion. This is an important aspect of the anti-group: the creation of a negative, sometimes destructive, counter-group unity that works against the therapeutic purpose.

The alternative to this defensive unity is a prevailing sense of fragmentation, which in a different way feeds into anti-group formation. Since individuals in psychotherapy groups often have an underlying sense of fragmentation, the mirroring of their fragmentation in the destructuring process of the group – particularly in an unstable group with drop-outs and erratic attendance – may create a destructive sequence. As described in Chapter 3, the group mirrors and heightens the fragmentation most feared by patients: this leads to their repudiation of and withdrawal from the group; this further weakens and fragments the group; and so on, in a vicious cycle. In this way, projective identification and the failure of containment are linked to the regressive group process.

Kernberg (1980) emphasises the problem of aggression in the context of group regression. He suggests that the primitive object relations and defence mechanisms evoked in a regressive group atmosphere are conducive to particularly intense forms of aggression. Again, the issue of structure is important. In groups which are more highly structured, aggression can be channelled towards the decision-making process and can be displaced onto perceived leadership characteristics of those in positions of authority. But in groups which are relatively unstructured, aggression emerges more directly and intensely. In the small group, the defensive value of erecting an external enemy is not as available as it is in the large group, where outer-directed hostility contributes to intra-group cohesion. In the small group, there is an uncomfortable sense that 'the enemy is in the midst of the group itself'. In my view, this is likely to result in distorted ways of dealing with aggression internally, one of which is to locate it in the group as object or container, thereby extruding aggression from self – and other – representations, and from the interactional domain, onto the group itself. The group is experienced as if it creates aggression and hostility. The anti-group is a fantasy of the group as filled with the negative accretions of hostile part-objects. This has the defensive value of protecting members from a full recognition of their own aggressive and destructive tendencies, but at the same time undermines and potentially destroys the group.

Various writers, particularly Pines (1978, 1994b), point out the parallels between this order of group functioning and the psychopathology of borderline patients, in which the sense of inner continuity and intact ego boundaries is severely disrupted. For much of the time, the group may function in a borderline state, hovering on psychotic formations. Where the membership of the group is predominantly composed of borderline patients, the parallel becomes stronger and the challenge to the group more profound.

Kernberg (1980) also describes the activation of infantile sexual features in group regression. Normally disassociated or repressed aspects of sexuality are elicited, often with intense fantasies and longings. At the same time, anxiety and prohibitions about sexual expression are evoked, with harsh super-ego type attributions projected onto aspects of the group and the group leader. In itself, this can further group regression. In a later section (Chapter 6, pp. 138–43) I explore the reawakening of the primal scene in the group, linking this to the regressive–aggressive constellation described above.

The regressive impact of groups, in my view, has a curiously ambiguous status in the field of group work. In Bion-inspired group relations events, such as the Leicester Conference, considerable value is placed on the mobilisation of regressive dynamics in groups as a learning experience. In parallel, writers such as Kernberg (1980) and Kibel (1992) describe clinical situations in which regression is almost if not actually fostered so as to heighten the primitive elements of the group process. As Kernberg points out, the group then becomes an outstanding forum for the study of both group and individual psychopathology. But this attitude can seem strangely dissociated from the deeply problematic reality of group life in many contexts. The group becomes venerated as an object of study, regressive processes adding to its fascination. The opposite tendency in group work is the idealised notion of the constructive potential of groups, in which the notion of group regression is virtually absent. It appears to be difficult to establish a serious but balanced basis for group work that elevates neither the regressive nor the constructive to the exclusion of the other. This dichotomy also influences the metapsychology of groups and creates rigid ideologies of group life that reflect rather than transmute the regressive processes we normally seek to understand and harness.

SURVIVAL ANXIETY

The previous section highlighted the intense regressive anxiety that the group is capable of generating. Here, I propose that at root this anxiety is concerned with survival, both physical and psychological. Uncontained, this intense anxiety feeds directly into the anti-group.

I start with an example taken from personal experience:

> In the early 1970s, when the encounter group movement was at its height, I attended a two-day regression workshop. The function of regression in this situation was to take participants back to earlier periods in their lives, for the purpose of uncovering and reworking painful early experiences.
>
> At the beginning of the workshop, the leader went round the group, asking people to say who they were and why they had come. One participant stood out from the rest. A middle-aged man in a group of younger people, he said he had family problems that had driven him to seek help. He had not known where to get help but his impression of the group was that he had made the wrong choice. There was a quality of enormous unease about the man – his very presence radiated fear and hostility.
>
> After the introductions, the leader asked people to think of childhood scenes that they might enact in the group. When it came to the man in question, he became particularly anxious and hostile and refused to participate. He got up to leave. There was a wave of protest from the rest of the group, demanding that he stay. But he shot out of the room. In an instant, the entire group got up to try to stop him. The man began to run, followed by the group. The chase continued for several blocks. There was a sense of brutal intent in the pursuit as if the man would be seized and forcibly brought back to the group. But he escaped from view.

This incident could be understood from several perspectives: the impact of the theme of regression on the group; the question of what this man represented to the group; the speed and intensity with which the projections occurred; and the potentially violent response of the group. What is evident above all is the terror that I believe struck deep into the heart of this man. He sensed that the group was not right for him, that it was potentially dangerous. When he fled, it was as if he was fleeing for his life.

I have used this example to highlight the degree of anxiety that may be evoked in the group. Writers in the Kleinian mould generally refer to this as a paranoid-schizoid level of anxiety, in which the threat of annihilation constitutes the dominant mode of experience (Segal 1979; Steiner 1993). Bion (1961) regarded psychotic anxiety as at the core of group experience, necessitating the basic assumptions as defensive formations. Ganzarain (1992) based his object relations group therapy largely on the evocation and alleviation of psychotic anxiety in the group. Some writers, for example Ashbach and Schermer (1987), question the use of psychopathological terms to describe anxiety in the group. It is undeniable, however, that extreme anxiety can be triggered in the group and I suggest that this can be understood as survival anxiety in two domains:

- the fear of physical attack with a corresponding anxiety about injury and death;
- the fear of assault on the psychological self with a corresponding fear of psychic annihilation.

The fear of physical attack can be seen in actual and symbolic terms. Anzieu (1984) suggested that there is an underlying fear in the group of bodily dismemberment. He also describes a fantasy of the group as a mouth that can devour the group members. If these images at first glance seem far-fetched, this is lessened if they are seen as illuminating primitive bodily experiences and sensations in the group, particularly in states of severe and overwhelming anxiety.

Bick (1968) described a state in infancy in which there is an absence of a 'psychic skin'. Here, the entire self is felt to be extremely vulnerable: in physical terms, it is as if the body had no protective membrane and all the body contents could spill out. Even once established, there is a sense that the psychic skin could be ruptured and the psychosomatic self endangered. I believe that in certain states in groups, adults experience a comparable anxiety. In some poorly organised individuals, with a sense of inner fragmentation, the threat of *exposure* in the group may be associated with this severe degree of anxiety: unwanted or forced exposure might evoke a fear of the psychic and bodily contents spilling out uncontrollably.

More generally, human beings are afraid to face their vulnerable animal selves, their physicality, their mortality. Becker (1975) has described the 'denial of death' as a denial of actual death and of our underlying physical vulnerability. Considerable effort goes into the attempt to block awareness of these frailties. The group is capable of piercing the protective membrane, of cutting through the defences to expose basic human fear in all its forms, corporeal and existential. Yalom (1975) suggests that shared awareness of these vulnerabilities is part of the curative function of the group. The realisation that we are not alone in facing these fears – indeed, that they are universal – is strengthening. However, I believe there are instances when these fears remain silent and cannot be shared: they may be too raw, too sensitive. In other cases, they may be heightened rather than assuaged by communication. Here, experience in the group may be felt to be a painful, aversive reminder of deep vulnerability.

The fear of annihilation of the psychological self – the 'I' or 'me' at its deepest and most private – is best explained in terms of self-psychology. Kohut (1971) suggests that if the early self fails to receive adequate mirroring it becomes depleted and fragmented, reacting with great anxiety to the absence of empathy and validation. As various writers have proposed (Bacal 1985; Harwood 1992; Stone 1992), groups often have great potential for providing the mirroring and idealising self-objects that enhance the self. But, equally, overwhelming feelings of shame and humiliation may be aroused in interaction with others (Pines 1987), reinforcing rather than assuaging states of narcissistic injury and severely challenging the fragile self (Mollon 1993). In the states of regressive anxiety described above, the self may feel not just deprived, but intolerably threatened, inducing a retreat from the group.

Anxieties concerning the survival of both the physical and the psychological self are pronounced at the start of the group. The initial example in Chapter 4 is a vivid illustration. I have not yet run a group in any setting in which there was an absence of anxiety at the beginning, and often this is intense. In an earlier paper (Nitsun 1989), I interpreted this heightened anxiety at the start in developmental terms that link the individual and group. Like the infant–child, the group in the first few weeks, even months, is in a state of unintegration. The group does not have a boundary: the 'group skin' that Anzieu (1990) described is absent. There may be questions about whether the group will survive. This is analogous to the rudimentary organisation of the infant in this first period of life. Winnicott (1960) emphasises the importance of the maternal holding environment at this stage. Without this, the infant is exposed to what he calls 'unthinkable anxiety', anxiety about falling apart and totally losing touch – a condition very similar to that described by Bick as preceding the acquisition of the 'psychic skin'.

Most groups survive these initial difficulties to become more or less cohesive units in which the group acquires a boundary and an identity. The achievement of the 'group skin' in Anzieu's terms parallels the formation of the 'psychic skin' in Bick's view of infancy, both achievements facilitating psychic integration. Where the group fails to achieve this elementary cohesion, however, the level of survival anxiety in the group may remain very high. Even in groups that become more cohesive, it is likely that early survival anxieties will be reawakened at different points, plunging the group into new periods of sudden, intense anxiety. This may happen when changes impinge on the group, e.g. breaks, the absence of the conductor, sudden drop-outs, explosive outbursts – events that threaten the fragile boundaries of the group.

The group at different times arouses and re-arouses a sense of trauma. The analogy of the birth process is a useful one. Eigen (1985) has suggested that Bion's conceptualisation of early development has at its core a sense of catastrophe, an early psychic disaster – like the experience of birth – that led to a painful sense of differentiation and separation. I would speculate that the catastrophe lurking in the group in some respects has to do with death, as suggested above, but in other respects it may concern birth. The quality of heightened anxiety at the start of the group is redolent of very early separation anxiety, as if the familiar must be left behind to countenance the new and the uncertain, symbolised by the passage of the foetus from the womb. Later on in the group, familiar elements of the self are surrendered to the group and a new self is born through identification with the group: another form of birth. For all its potential for psychological growth, this experience may engender a new sense of potential catastrophe – of total loss of self, protection, containment. Curiously, in this sense, the symbolisms of birth and death in the group are closely linked. (For an interpretation of the group as womb see Elliott, 1994.)

The paradoxical nature of the group is again reflected here – the group creates the very anxieties it seeks to allay. At the deepest level, these are anxieties about survival. Their containment can profoundly strengthen the individual and the group. But the failure of containment may impregnate the group with the dread of a catastrophic beginning or ending. A group created in these circumstances is itself born in fire, strongly predisposed to the ravages of the anti-group.

FAILURES OF COMMUNICATION

Group psychotherapy, including group analysis, is essentially a method of communication. Foulkes asserted, 'psychotherapy is identical to the ever-increasing process of communication itself'. Within this, verbal communication is of overriding importance. Foulkes talks about 'translating' the autistic language of the disturbed individual into words that have a shared and 'ever-articulate' meaning. Schlapobersky (1994) refers to 'the language of the group', in which words are the paramount medium of expression, facilitating the movement from monologue to dialogue to discourse. Rogers (1987) emphasises the importance of 'putting it into words' in the group, offsetting the insidious non-verbal communication of projective identification.

What happens in the group when words fail? When words cannot be found? When heightened feeling states of anxiety and anger cannot be conveyed in words? Or when words ignite powerful emotions that cannot be communicated? In the previous example of the man who fled the regression workshop, there was very meagre communication. He mentioned that he had sought help because of a breakdown in family relationships but did not explain this. There was no discussion about his discomfort in the present group. A powerful atmosphere of mistrust suddenly enveloped his relationship with the group, precluding communication and leading to potentially violent acting out.

Failures and distortions of communication are an integral part of the anti-group process. I believe the problems of communication in groups to be more widespread than is generally recognised. There is a sense in Foulkes' writing that the sheer fact of being in a group, with support from the conductor and the other members, creates a transformative context in which gaps in communication are naturally remedied: in time, communication will flow. I believe this is part of Foulkes' over-optimism about groups in general and verbal communication in particular – an idealised view he shares with many other individual and group psychotherapists. What I see is enormous variation in the capacity for verbal expression in individual participants and in the ability of groups to help overcome the impasse and alienation that arise from failed communication.

It is important to recognise that verbal communication may be inherently both limiting and threatening. Lacan's view (1977, 1982) is that the Self can never be entirely understood by the Other, creating an inevitable gap in communication. Bollas (1987) observes that whole areas of self-experience are incommunicable – 'the unthought known'. Ogden (1988) notes that discourse between subjects is frequently blocked by unconscious thoughts and feelings that are too frightening or unacceptable to put into words. He also refers to

> other sorts of fears such as the unconscious anxiety that aspects of oneself are so private, so central to an endangered sense of being alive that the very act of communication will endanger the integration of the self. Still another form of anxiety that disrupts the intersubjective discourse is the fear that one's life-sustaining ties to one's internal objects may be jeopardised through any sort of discourse in which one relinquishes control over one's internal object world by sharing knowledge of it with another.
>
> (Ogden 1988, pp. 21–2)

Several of my previous examples illustrated failures of communication in the group. The following is a particularly dramatic example.

A group in a psychiatric hospital setting consisted of both in-patients and out-patients. One of the in-patients, Neil, was a successful salesman who had been admitted to the hospital in a state of agitated depression. Throughout the group, he had difficulty conveying the depth of his distress. He appeared on the surface to have everything he could wish for: a personable man, he had a good job, home, wife, and children. But, as his stay in hospital and attendance at the group continued, he appeared to deteriorate even further. An important change in the group seemed to affect him: a male co-therapist, towards whom he had positive feelings, left and was replaced by a female Neil did not seem to like. This was apparent in his manner but he was unable to express or explore his feelings in words. However, this was just the tip of the iceberg. Neil seemed very disturbed and conflicted about events at home that he could not communicate in any detail. The group tried in many ways to draw him out but to no avail. He became more and more introverted, more distant, more inaccessible.

The shock came one Monday morning. During the weekend, Neil had driven his car to a lonely spot, poured petrol over himself and set himself alight. All that was found was the charred wreck of a car and a man. The event had a deeply disturbing effect on the group. Although in time it returned to its normal working mode, the group remained haunted for years by the spectre of Neil's end. A sense of powerlessness about Neil's inability to share his inner self was mingled with feelings of guilt that the group had failed him.

This is an illustration of a profound gap in communication. This gap is not unique to group therapy: it could as easily have happened in the context of individual therapy. But its occurrence is a demonstration of the limits of communication in the group setting: the group was unable to facilitate communication in any way that could help this troubled man. Judging from the way he killed himself, Neil probably had deep underlying problems about aggression, his inability to externalise his rage resulting in his violent attack on himself. In the face of overwhelming sadness, anger, despair, confusion, words often fail. The more complex the disturbance and the more fragmented the sense of self, the harder it is to put thoughts and feelings into words.

People not uncommonly say that they find it harder to communicate in groups than in dyadic situations. The presence of others watching and listening, the fear of criticism and humiliation, the anxiety aroused by inter-member comparisons are among the reasons given for this difficulty, as suggested in the section on the 'paradoxical characteristics' of therapy groups (Chapter 3).

In another group, Cynthia regarded her main problem as her inability to express herself in the group. A relatively confident talker in the one-to-one situation, she found herself tongue-tied in the group. She described her difficulty in finding a space for herself and how, when she wanted to say something, she was eclipsed by other members. When she did speak, she fumbled for words. In an individual meeting with the conductor, she decided to aim at improving her participation and expressiveness in the group. But she ran into the same difficulties again and became progressively demoralised. In despair, she left the group.

I see communication difficulties of this sort as a powerful source of anti-group attitudes. The problem can manifest itself at an individual member level, as in Cynthia's case, within several members, or in the group-as-a-whole, resulting in states of intense communicative impasse.

Stern (1985), from the perspective of infant developmental research, describes words as 'double-edged swords'. On the one hand, they are a wonderful way of opening up new channels of communication and relating; on the other hand, they are symbols or abstractions rather than direct expressions of states of mind, and they can leave vast tracts of inner experience incommunicable. Stern also suggests that words encourage the development of a false self. By providing a social channel of expression, with external referents, communication may be split off from inner truth or meaning. Fried (1979) describes the development of a group false self which lacks genuine interchange. This, I believe, may be a product of the over-valuation of verbal communication in groups and a relative neglect of the incommunicable self that yet needs recognition and understanding. Equally, I believe that little attention is paid to non-verbal communication, which is often an authentic and powerful route to awareness. 'Words lie, the body does not' (Perls 1972).

The development of a group false self was illustrated in Group D (see pp. 87–90), in which an apparent 'groupiness' formed around highly verbal, articulate discussions in which participants hid rather than revealed their true selves. When the illusion of the 'good group' was exploded by the challenges of a new member, this triggered a strong anti-group.

Interpersonal communication in groups cannot be considered

without reference to the concept of attunement. This concept, which is at the centre of contemporary developmental psychology (Stern 1985; Emde 1991), has also begun to inform understanding of the communication process in groups (Brown 1994; Pines 1990). In essence, it describes the sensitive receptiveness and responsiveness of one individual to another. Stern describes it as the single most important process in the early mother–child relationship, strongly influencing the individual's developing sense of self. He also describes the failures of attunement in relationships and what he refers to as 'misattunement'.

In the psychotherapy group, attunement is a vital process. Most participants have suffered from a lack of adequate attunement in their early lives and their current relationships may be marked by failures of attunement. In theory, the therapy group provides an excellent setting for the development of attunement. The opportunities for inter-subjective relationships are considerable, amounting to what Foulkes called 'ego training in action', and, in many groups, this process is at the core of creative individual-group development. But in some groups the propensity for attunement is so diminished that the group is experienced as a repetition of earlier failures of attunement rather than a context for new learning.

In the previous example of 'flawed group development', Group C (pp. 86–7), there was a description of Alison's problematic relationship with the group. She had great difficulty communicating her distress, particularly that concerning a painful triangular relationship. When she did communicate, she experienced her sharing in highly negative terms. She felt misunderstood and criticised by the group, the other members in turn feeling misinterpreted and frustrated by her. This led to a state of chronic tension surrounding her interactions with the group, which seemed to become more and more toxic.

The above is an example of misattunement. This general process of failed communication can have specific adverse consequences. I use the term *contaminating communication* to describe a phenomenon I have observed in a variety of groups in which a participant reports feeling worse after communicating a part of the self. This seems to take two forms. The first is where the very act of revealing oneself to the group is experienced as noxious. This often occurs in people who are highly guarded in the group, so that the communicative act is regarded as a considerable risk and its consequences as potentially damaging (as described by Ogden). This is not necessarily related to the quality of feedback the person receives: it is the act of revelation itself which is believed to be destructive.

The second form of contaminating communication is where, following the communication, the person attributes feeling worse to negative feedback in the group. As in Alison's case, this is usually linked to a sense of being misunderstood, criticised, and attacked. This perception is often a misinterpretation of the intentions of other group members, so that a mutual process of misattunement is instigated: the main communicator feels misunderstood and criticised, which leads her to blame the group (or members), who in turn feel misunderstood and unfairly criticised. In both forms of contaminating communication, the individual may also have strong underlying anti-group attitudes which are confirmed by the failed attempts at communicating, and this may then be invoked as a reason to reject or withdraw from the group.

I have used the term contaminating communication because of the strong sense of contamination attributed to the communication. The individual reacts as if contaminated through the medium of sharing and the sense of contamination not uncommonly spreads to the group through a process of mutual identification. This phenomenon could be regarded as the group equivalent of 'malignant mirroring' as described by Zinkin (1983). It also represents a corruption of 'exchange', a term Foulkes (1964a) used to denote the interactive communication process in groups.

The emphasis has so far been on interpersonal communication, on the language that unites or divides people. Another perspective on communication relates to the domain of thinking as a basis for the communication process. Here, I refer to the constellation that includes thinking, the attribution of meaning, and the linking process. These internal processes subserve the communication process, in so far as words are expressed thoughts, and disturbances at the level of thought impede and distort verbal communication. The group presents an enormous challenge to this internal processing function: it is a highly complex situation generating myriad internal impressions and feelings that require practically continuous monitoring and connecting in order to make sense of the experience.

The place of thinking in psychopathology has become an important area of study in psychoanalysis. Here, Bion's work (1962, 1967) is seminal. He hypothesised that the capacity to think is established in the context of early object relationships. To begin with, sensations, perceptions, and feelings are 'things in themselves', unmetabolised entities seeking 'a container to transform them into thought'. The original container is the breast, which, in conjunction with the infant's preconceptions, forms a 'thinking couple'. In turn, this is internalised as 'an apparatus for thinking thoughts', becoming the foundation for all subsequent thinking and the interpretation of meaning. Various writers (e.g. James 1994; Gordon 1994) have identified this as an important process in the group, postulating that the group is analogous to the container that helps to transform incoherent and unconscious perceptions into coherent thought.

Yet again, the group offers a double-edged sword. Most writers emphasise the positive opportunities in the group for the translation and transformation of the inchoate. But, as I suggested in Chapter 3, the complexity and unpredictability of the group also make considerable demands on the thinking apparatus, in some respects mirroring the confused and chaotic states of mind that are in search of transformation. This disorganising process takes a dangerous turn if a group-destructive process is at work. If factors such as envy, rage, and hatred of dependency are prevalent in the group, there is a tendency not just passively to register regressive thought processes but actively to seek to undermine cognitive and emotional connections. Bion (1959) described this as 'attacks on linking', in which the capacity to generate connectedness is violated. Ogden (1980) similarly described a disruption of the ability to create and interpret meaning. Gordon (1994) draws attention to the emotional and interpersonal connectedness that subserves thinking (captured in Bion's notion of $-k$) and illustrating the failed communication in a group arising from $-k$. Thinking internally and communicating outwardly are intricately linked in the creation and negation of meaning in the group, with a strong susceptibility to distortion and derailment.

PROJECTIVE IDENTIFICATION

The failures and distortions of communication described in the previous section lead naturally to a consideration of projective identification, a primitive mode of communication that is a pervasive aspect of group process. Kibel (1992) described 'projective identification as the driving force in groups'.

Since Melanie Klein originally formulated the concept of projective identification there has been considerable elaboration of the process. More recently, it has also been recognised as of crucial significance in group relationships (Horwitz 1983; Rogers 1987; Roitman 1989; Zender 1991). There are many perspectives and definitions of projective identification. Zender (1991), in the context of group psychotherapy, gives a useful definition of projective identification as 'a dynamic, interactive process by which an individual (the projector) has the fantasy of evacuating unacceptable or endangered mental contents by behaving in such a way as to evoke similar contents or characteristics in another person. The projector then identifies with the content in the recipient, and to some degree reinternalises the outcome, if the recipient has managed the contents in an integrative way' (Zender 1991, p. 118). This process of the *management* of the received contents of the projective identification and its consequent re-internalisation are a central part of the psychotherapeutic process, intimately linked to the quality of the container–contained relationship. But the process is a delicate one, easily derailed, since the force of projective identification can have a disorganising and destructive effect on both projector (the contained) and recipient (the container). This is particularly relevant to the group situation, in which the plural membership is conducive to frequent and intense projective identification between members. Furthermore, the group as object itself can play host to malignant projective identifications, becoming a mirror of the hostile projections of the membership. In many ways projective identification lays the foundation of the anti-group.

> The preceding example of Alison's contaminating communication with the group can be interpreted as a particular instance of projective identification. Attempting to convey some painful aspects of herself, Alison expected these to be immediately contained and absorbed by the other group members. However, their comments indicated that they were separate people with independent minds who were unwilling to assimilate unquestioningly her communications.

Alison perceived their response as an attack, attributing to them the malice that she feared in herself but could not acknowledge as possibly spoiling her relationships outside – and inside – the group.

Projective identification takes various forms. It most commonly occurs in dyadic situations but it rapidly filters into interactions in the group and affects perception of the group as a whole. In its positive form, it approximates the process of mirroring that Foulkes emphasised in groups. Foulkes described the group as a hall of mirrors, suggesting that participants discovered themselves in others in a way that enhances self-awareness and self-understanding. Zinkin (1983) challenged this, pointing out that the mirroring could produce an aversive reaction, leading to a hostile, persecutory relationship between the two people involved – 'malignant mirroring'. The limitation of Zinkin's analysis is that, while identifying malignant mirroring as occurring with particular intensity in groups, he did not take account of the group context as influencing the pair caught up in the psychic battle. This point was highlighted by Gordon (1991), who suggested that what appears to be projective identification emerging from one individual or between two individuals may be a product of unconscious *group* dynamics of splitting and projective identification.

It is an important thesis of this book that projective identification is a crucial medium in the formation of the anti-group. It acts as a force determining the potentially destructive character of the group by an evacuation of dangerous internal contents onto the group as object and container. This can happen through direct attacks and demands on the group. Zender describes how 'the group becomes contaminated with negative affects and impulses, as the members in the throes of projective identification psychologically vomit on the group, making intense and unrealistic demands for nurturance'. Alternatively, the process of massive projective identification onto the group happens in more insidious ways. Instead of overt demands on the group, the membership, in the grip of a narcissistic defence system, attempts to eradicate the recognition of dependency needs by spoiling the therapeutic function of the group.

Rosenfeld (1971) formulated the concept of *the gang* to describe an internal process that seeks to obliterate need, dependency, and, in particular, envy, by denying external reality and so protecting an omnipotent internal object. The gang is conceived as a mafia-like internal constellation which, through perversely sadistic self-protective devices, guards the inner self against the threat of emotional vulnerability. The outcome is the severance of all nurturing ties, a rupture which in fantasy feeds the omnipotent object but in reality destroys the capacity for emotional growth.

The gang is a useful metaphor for the anti-group, suggesting a particular form of projective identification in which an internalised destructive group is externalised and projected onto the real group. Even in normal group development, the group is not uncommonly described by the membership as a form of gang, although usually with playful associations: the 'A Team', the 'class of 89', the 'famous five', 'a bunch of hoodlums', and so on. In the anti-group scenario, these benign versions of the gang are replaced by a sinister version, in which the group is projectively identified as a destructive mafia-like organisation.

In Group A, described in Chapter 4 and explored more fully in Chapter 10, there was at one point unexpected progress in some members' lives. Since this progress was not uniform across the group, it appeared to evoke considerable envy in the less successful members. The envy was not expressed directly: instead, it became deflected into attacks on the group. There was still a body of opinion that the group was valueless. This was expressed even by patients who were themselves improving. The devaluation intensified when two members communicated their plans to leave the group, saying that it was harmful rather than helpful to them. Everyone agreed and the session ended on a note of unanimity about the group's failure.

During the session, Georgina, who described herself as having once been a 'gangster's moll', initiated a discussion about London's criminal underworld. This was like a journey into a sinister underworld, with its distorted morality, reaching a frightening destination when Georgina mentioned that she knew the Kray brothers (East End criminals notorious for their brutal crimes). Malcolm then mentioned, rather cheerfully, that he had once played in a band at a party given by the Kray brothers. The theme then disappeared as suddenly as it had appeared.

I was puzzled by the group material at the time but on reflection could see it as evidence of 'the gang' – a symbolic glimpse into the perverse side of the group that would demand conformity to its rules, the denial of emotional growth and progress, and an attack on its own source of growth – the group itself. The devaluation of the group that unexpectedly followed evidence of progress in participants' lives could be interpreted in these terms. It is as if a destructive, gang-like organisation was precipitated by the envy that enveloped the group. This served temporarily to obliterate the real value of the group.

In more extreme versions of the projective process, the group verges on psychotic formations. The content and intensity of the projective identifications become increasingly violent. Bion noted how attacks on linking, in their extreme form, result in a splitting of the perceived object into minute, often bizarre fragments. Since the multiple nature of the group, in adverse circumstances, invites fragmentation of perception and thought, these elements may play host to psychotic-like perceptual splitting and projective identification. The following is an example of this process as represented by an individual group member.

Sally, a patient in a psychiatric out-patient group, had a long history of psychological breakdown, with several admissions to the hospital. She was diagnosed 'schizo-affective'. In the group, she was a quiet, withdrawn member, seemingly detached for most of the time, but with occasional flashes of intense involvement. A period during which she participated increasingly in the group culminated in a sudden resurgence of psychiatric symptoms, as if her increased involvement was too threatening to her fragile equilibrium. A dramatic deterioration followed and she was admitted for some weeks to an acute psychiatric ward. While there, in a state of paranoid anxiety, she told the ward staff that the group had been a very frightening experience with some sinister, inexplicable goings-on. She described how the conductor had writhed on the floor like a snake. He had also insisted on her involvement in the group and shouted at her across the room. The other group members indulged in strange acts. One man wore a succession of female wigs and experimented with facial make-up that kept altering his appearance. Another masturbated in a bath and lay there watching the water run out, as his sperm bobbed to the surface of the water. Sometimes, the whole group got up and engaged in weird contortions.

This is a vivid illustration of the degeneration of thoughts into bizarre splits, as if reversing the usual transformation of unmetabolised experience into structured thought. Sally's perceptions have become 'things in themselves', objects infused with a bizarre life of their own. Primitive sexual symbols are intertwined in the imagery, as if unconscious or dream material has lost its censorship. This degree of conceptual regression is unusual in groups and is likely to be evinced only by particularly disturbed individuals like Sally, but the illustration opens a door onto the unconscious life of a group in which the threat of intimacy precipitated severe perceptual regression.

The story about Sally has an interesting outcome. With the encouragement of the conductor, she returned to spend several years in the group. During this time she was gradually able to involve herself in the group without undue regression. She developed an idealised transference towards the conductor that had a highly erotic charge, suggesting that her previous 'bizarre' sexual projections onto the group reflected her as yet disowned desires and were predictive of her later intense involvement. The other members had considerable difficulty in accepting Sally's relationship to the group, particularly her bizarre associations that raised fears that this was a mad group. However, there was enough support to contain her in the group and to help her gradually understand and manage her tendency to erupt in primitive, regressive ways.

Sally's case is an illustration of how powerfully de-repressed, psychotically charged material can be reintegrated in the self and the group as part of the containing function. But this was achieved with great difficulty, highlighting the delicate balance in the container–contained relationship. Within this, the intensity and quality of projective identification will strongly influence whether the outcome is creative or destructive.

ENVY

Envy is readily evoked in groups and is crucially linked to the anti-group. This has already emerged in previous sections, particularly in relation to projective identification (see above). As Melanie Klein pointed out in her original formulation (1957), envy has considerable destructive potential, since it harbours deep-rooted antagonistic impulses towards the good object, aiming at its annihilation or the spoiling of its enviable properties. Klein gave envy primacy in her view of emotional development, seeing it as instinctually based, with oral-sadistic and anal-sadistic tendencies. Self-psychology gives an important alternative explanation. Rather than arising from instinctual drives, envy is seen as a consequence of narcissistic injury. In the language of self psychology, frustration of self needs leads to rage, fragmentation, and depletion. Envy represents a variation of narcissistic rage (Stone 1992). The impulse to destructiveness is the self's attempt to get rid of the threatening envied object in order to quell the painful feelings of self-injury and worthlessness.

Envy is nowhere more apparent than in the therapy group. Being in a group often confronts the individual with a painful sense of difference. Members of a group, particularly heterogeneous groups, usually vary considerably in physical and psychological attributes, and this readily evokes unfavourable self-comparisons. Members also vary in their progress in the group, some developing rapidly, others slowly, if at all. Comparisons with other members and the conductor are an inevitable consequence. The group is ripe with potential for envy.

Envy is usually defined as operating within a dyadic, two-person relationship, but in the group it is manifested in a variety of ways. Several of the examples in Chapter 4 highlighted such instances. In Group B (pp. 83–5), Alan's envy was whipped up by virtually any success in the group, leaving him feeling deprived and enraged to the point where he was driven to attempt a physical attack on the conductor, heralding the disintegration of the group. Here, envy could not be tolerated or spoken of: it triggered a form of primitive acting out in which the impulse to destroy the object(s) of envy succeeded in destroying the whole group. In Group G (pp. 101–4), envy on the part of the student group members towards the facilitator appeared to be the mainspring of attacks on her that contributed to the toxic atmosphere of the group, leaving the facilitator and the group feeling wasted by the experience. In Group A (pp. 90–1), envy of progress in the group stimulated attempts to undermine the group in the form of a destructive gang that strove to deny need and dependency.

Dealing with envy in groups is particularly difficult. The acknowledgement of envy usually leads to a sense of humiliation and shame, making it one of the most difficult feelings to admit to oneself and others. As such, it is rendered particularly prone to deflection by projection and projective identification. This illustrates what Kreeger (1992) described as 'envy pre-emption', a term that highlights defensive strategies aimed at reducing or negating both the experience of envy in the self and the danger of envious attacks on the self. Klein herself described several defences against envy, including devaluation of the object and devaluation of the self. But these attempts at envy pre-emption usually fail. They may lead to collusive agreements between members of the group to deny or deflect envy, while the underlying force of envy remains intact. It can then express itself in insidious ways. Group D failed to confront envy for some time, only to find it erupting in an explosion of rivalry and hatred that constituted a powerful anti-group (see Chapter 4, pp. 87–90).

The destructive potential of envy can, of course, be reversed in a reparative or therapeutic experience. When a group works well, it can be particularly helpful at recognising members' assets and strengths and so counteracting feelings of envy and concomitant shame and humiliation. Here, the group provides what in self-psychology are described as mirroring and idealising self-objects (Wolff 1988). But a group in which destructive envy predominates will have great difficulty facilitating such restitution.

An anti-group constellation is particularly likely to arise when the envy is directed at the group itself. There may be powerful underlying envy of the group, not towards the conscious representation of the group but towards the group as a symbolic container, unconsciously representing the mother, the breast, or the womb – the original sources of envy. This process is intensified by the need to maintain the splitting between good and bad objects. Examples of such splitting are groups in which the conductor is idealised and the group devalued or in which another form of therapy, particularly individual therapy, is idealised and the group devalued. The process of maintaining the bad-group projection is reinforced by the phenomenon of retaliatory anxiety that results from the projection of bad feelings onto an object: retaliation is feared, as if the projected bad feelings will return to attack the self. Envy harbours a wish to attack and a fear of attack. The group is felt to be dangerous when it stimulates envy.

Envy can be seen as an important component of the *negative therapeutic reaction*. This refers to the worsening of the patient's condition in the face of apparent therapeutic gain. In classical psychoanalytic theory, this is related to a punishing super-ego which requires the continued suffering of the patient (Sandler *et al.* 1973). Object relations theory, however, tends to consider envy as the mainspring of the negative therapeutic reaction. Segal (1993) points out there is usually an element of triumph over the defeated analyst – this assuaging the patient's envy of the power and capability of the analyst. The phenomenon of negative therapeutic reaction is more commonly described in relation to individuals in the psychoanalytic setting, but it has equal relevance to the group, at both the individual level and the group-as-a-whole level. The destructive response of Group A to progress in the group, symbolised in the operation of an intra-psychic gang, could be viewed as a negative therapeutic reaction. More generally, the anti-group can be seen as the group expression of a negative therapeutic reaction, obstructing and undermining therapeutic gain.

Envy is usually distinguished from jealousy (Klein 1957, Kreeger 1992). While envy is traditionally regarded as occurring in a two-person relationship, jealousy is viewed in triangular terms: jealous feelings in an individual arise in response to the perceived relationship between two others. But, as Stone (1992) points out, there is usually an element of envy in jealousy, as the jealous person may envy the attributes of the rival (this will be explored more fully in the section on the primal scene). Similarly, there is usually a strong measure of envy in rivalry. Rivalry, which is usually a more openly manifested response than either envy or jealousy, is a pervasive feature of group life and often finds intense expression in psychotherapy groups. Rivalry for achievement, for dominance in the group, for the admiration of the other members, for the special attention of the conductor – even for who has the worst problem, as Kreeger (1992) ironically notes – are all familiar themes in groups. But the element of envy may give rivalry a particularly deadly sting. In some groups, rivalry may be played out to extreme degrees, with one member usually the bitter loser. In this situation, the cohesion of the entire group may be threatened, as in Group D, where the rivalry between two men instigated a continuing anti-group reaction in the group-as-a-whole.

Greed is also associated with envy. In Klein's formulation (1952, 1957), greed arises in response to an insatiable appetite, linked to envy of those who are seen to have more or to be satisfied with what they have. Like envy, greed is potentially destructive since it depletes and exhausts the object. In groups, the common problem of 'sharing space' is compounded by greed and its reaction formation, i.e. those who use all the space and those who use none, often building up to a crescendo of criticism and anger, in which the issue of sharing space becomes a destructively competitive focus.

The above considerations suggest that envy should be seen not so much as a unitary phenomenon occurring within a two-person relationship, but as a complex response that can infiltrate the group in various ways: silent, unspoken envy which none the less may be devastating in its effect; envy that is disguised or displaced; destructive playing out of envy between members; profound envy of the conductor; and finally envy of the group itself in its symbolic significance as the generator and container of experience. Since envy is generally so difficult to acknowledge and accept, it is particularly prone to expression through projection and projective identification, in this way increasing its insidious and potentially corrosive effect on the group.

Chapter 6

Determinants of the anti-group II
Interpersonal disturbance, the primal scene, aggression and hatred, the death instinct

Group experience is made up of a complex interaction of intrapsychic, interpersonal, and group-as-a-whole responsiveness. Frequently, participants have difficulty managing the shift from their individual position to a group-member position, the challenge unleashing powerful and potentially regressive emotions. This chapter initially focuses on the disturbances triggered by a shift from the position of 'singleton', a term used by Turquet (1975), to multiple relationships, and the way in which the anti-group can arise as a response to the anxiety and frustration experienced as part of these changes. This includes the impact of 'the primal scene'. Further, the chapter traces the sources of aggression and hatred in both individuals and groups and ends with consideration of the controversial psychoanalytic notion of the death instinct and its putative role in the genesis of the anti-group.

INTERPERSONAL DISTURBANCE

The group processes explored so far have emphasised the regressive impact of early object relationships. These do not involve interpersonal relationships as such, other than as primitive expressions of part-object identifications and frustrations that tend to perpetuate a fragmented sense of self and other. Yet, one of the major aims of group psychotherapy is to facilitate relationships and to strengthen interpersonal capacity in individuals' personal lives.

A paramount wish of most human beings is a relationship with another person, the forming and maintaining of an interpersonal bond that satisfies the basic need for love, intimacy, and emotional support. But the group offers something different: the relationship to a group of several people. There is an immediate tension here between what may be desired and what is available. The conflict is manifested at the outset in the preference many people show for individual over group therapy. This was mentioned earlier in Chapter 3, where I reported my experience of selecting patients for group-analytic psychotherapy in the context of an NHS clinical psychology service: most people's first choice is individual therapy. This is vital information and the reasons for it are not difficult to come by: in general, people want individual rather than group therapy because they believe it will be safer, more containing, more personally focused, and more rewarding. Part of this is understandable since there is a great emotional investment in the early dyad of mother and child, and since states of severe psychological disturbance in later life often generate a wish to restore the primacy of the early one-to-one relationship. Numerous writers have referred to the longing for such a relationship that can vary from a striving for intimacy with a separate person to fantasies of total merging with another (e.g. Glasser 1985). In Balint's terms (1968) this is based on an idealised fantasy of total togetherness, of a perfectly containing relationship. This is often needed to compensate for the 'basic fault' – profound early disappointment in emotional development, with consequent rage and emptiness. The disturbing experience of early catastrophic loss or trauma and its destructive – and self-destructive – consequences is strongly described by Balint:

> If any hitch or disharmony between subject and object occurs, the reaction to it will consist of loud and vehement symptoms suggesting processes either of a highly aggressive and destructive, or profoundly disintegrated nature, i.e. either as if the whole world, including the self, would have been smashed up, or as if the subject would have been flooded with pure and unmitigated aggressive–destructive impulses.... This primary relationship is so important to the subject that he cannot tolerate any interference with it from outside, and if anything contrary to his needs or wishes happens, he simply must resort to desperate methods.
>
> (Balint 1968, p. 71)

This quote crystallises two themes of great relevance in the present context: the overriding importance of the 'primary' relationship and the destructive effects of its loss or unavailability.

The preference for individual therapy can be seen as an expression of the more or less universal longing for an idealised one-to-one relationship. The prospect of group therapy in various ways runs counter to these expectations. The individual has to deal with the very sense of interpersonal difference and complexity that created problems in the first place. Participation in a group may accentuate the longing for a one-to-one relationship. The dominance of part-object relationships, the confusing crisscross of communication, the problems about sharing and competing may all intensify the desire for a relationship with one other person. Of course, this is to some degree possible in the group: the other participants are people who, in principle, are available for whole-object relationships. But, as Brigham (1992) points out, establishing a dyadic relationship in the group context is complicated by the impingement of other members. Whether through others' feelings of envy or jealousy of the relationship, or simply through the presence of others in the group, there is always a demand to attend to the rest of the group. 'In the end,' says Brigham, 'the whole-object relationships, which are counter-regressive when taken singly, combine to have a schismatic effect, returning one to the problem of the relationship to the group as a whole' (p. 255).

Similar issues pertain to the relationship with the conductor. The leader is likely to be the person in the group towards whom the wish for a dyadic relationship is most keenly felt. The conductor's role generally confers on him or her immediate attributes of power and attractiveness that make him/her the object of desire in the group. This is intensified by members' transference reactions, unresolved longings and attachments from the past. Further, the conductor may be perceived as embodying all the part-objects in the group, so that the relationship with this one person comes to contain or represent all relationships within the group. The conductor in this sense pulls the group together, in almost a literal way, for the individual member, so offsetting fears of fragmentation and alienation.

Needs felt in relation to the conductor are potentially manifold: for the symbolic integration of the various personae in the group, for dependence, for the elevated pleasure of 'special child' status, and for the fantasised fulfilment of romantic and erotic longings. But these desires entail a large measure of frustration: the conductor is there to understand dependency, transference, and other longings towards him, not to gratify them. In most groups, this area of frustration is an inevitable and necessary one in the maturing of group members and is generally resolved to a relatively satisfactory degree. But in other groups, frustration of these desires, particularly within the context of dissatisfaction with the group-as-a-whole, can create deep disappointment and bitterness. The anti-group may emerge in parallel to the loss of belief in the capacity for an idealised, primary relationship: the group is invested with the properties of the uncaring, abandoning object; it may be treated with the hatred and disdain deemed fitting for such an object. The group may then be abandoned as a mirror expression of the individual's own sense of abandonment.

The theme of the frustrated longing for a relationship is illustrated in the same group in which Sally's psychotic breakdown occurred (see pp. 127–8).

> The group was nearing its end. In the years that it had been running as a slow-open group, several members had come and gone, with varying degrees of resolution of their problems. Now, just three members were left in the group – Claire, Harry, and Sally. Very different as individuals in most respects, but one point united them: their disappointment in the search for a close, enduring relationship. Claire was married but experienced this as a lonely, loveless relationship. Harry was a homosexual whose lover had suddenly left for a far-off country. He had an acute sense of loss and feared that he might never see his friend again. Sally had a strongly romanticised transference towards the conductor. She had struggled to accept the reality that her wishes could not be fulfilled but in the last stage of the group again became deeply preoccupied with the relationship. All three individuals had shown more than the usual difficulty in using the group. In tandem with their preoccupation with the single relationship they sought, they had been limited in their capacity for group relatedness.
>
> The last session of the group was hardly a group at all. The three patients sat in near silence, each enveloped in his or her own individual sense of loss and desperation. Drawing their attention to their common plight did little to galvanise responsiveness or interaction. The suggestion that this might be a strong defence against the loss of the group,

and, for all three, the loss of the conductor, was acknowledged but not taken up. Their individual absorption in their disappointed longings made it virtually impossible to explore any of these issues and the group ended on a note of loneliness and emotional isolation.

In terms of relationships, group psychotherapy makes complex demands on participants, in so far as it invites, or requires, relationships at several concurrent levels: to other individuals in the group, to the conductor, and to the group as an entity in its own right. Given that transference and counter-transference enter at all these levels, complicating the conscious here-and-now aspects of relationships, the task for the individual of dealing with this dense interpersonal matrix is a formidable one. In its positive form, this is in essence the socialising function of the group and for many participants it has a strengthening effect. But where the capacity for interpersonal relating is particularly limited, and especially where there is a traumatic link to a damaged primary relationship, the group may present a challenge of overwhelming difficulty.

This is one reason why people are often reluctant to join groups: the dual sense of an interpersonal demand they believe they cannot sustain and an interpersonal wish that cannot be met. In ongoing groups, participants not uncommonly revert to their wish for individual therapy. Usually, this is at a time of considerable frustration of their personal needs in the group and this may require sensitive understanding if an escalation of anti-group attitudes is to be prevented.

These considerations highlight the universal dilemma of individual existence vs. group belonging. Foulkes saw group-analytic therapy as providing a new opportunity for social connectedness. De Maré (1991) used the term 'koinonia' to describe the spirit of community engendered by the large group. These aims are of profound relevance in an alienated world. But the conflict between individual and group interests is compounded by people's wish for a more or less exclusive dyadic relationship, and the depth of this longing may counter the promise and benefits of wider social relating.

THE PRIMAL SCENE

Early sexual theories and fantasies have a particular relevance to the group in that they reflect notions of the connection between the sexual and the social. Psychosexual development is not only about sex in its purely instinctual form: it embraces perceptions of the self in relation to others, in two-person, three-person, and group relationships. My particular interest in this area led me to explore the notion of the primal scene as an explanatory paradigm for group development (Nitsun 1994). Rather like the concept of the anti-group, this is presented not as an absolute schema for all groups, but as a theme that varies in its expression in groups, drawing on actual and symbolic experiences.

The concept of the primal scene has a universal significance in psychoanalytic discourse. Differing theoretical emphases concern the constructive and destructive aspects of the fantasised scene and the significance this has in the child's mind. Freud (1908) drew attention to the view of parental intercourse as a sadistic act, essentially an attack by the father on the mother. Melanie Klein (1928) elaborated further on this, seeing the primal scene generally as impregnated with powerful aggressive fantasies. In part, this reflects the child's envy and hatred of the parental union, which through projective identification contaminates the parental representations and makes them dangerous to each other and the child. Bion (1961) extrapolated this to the group. He suggested that the basic assumptions are 'secondary to an extremely early primal scene perceived in part-object terms and associated with psychotic anxiety and mechanisms of splitting and projective identification' (p. 164). In this interpretation, as Brown (1985) highlighted, the basic assumptions serve as a defence against the deep ambivalence and anxiety experienced when confronted by the relationship of the parental couple.

Bion believed that the fantasy of the primal scene could be traced in the material of the group. He argued that the group evokes very primitive fantasies about the content of the mother's body, linked to the early primal scene, in so far as 'it seems to assume that part of one parent, the breast or the mother's body, contains amongst other objects a part of the father'. This interpretation, which initially strikes one as an over-elaboration of primitive fantasy, has nevertheless been borne out in my own experience of running groups. The example of Group A in Chapter 4 provides a striking example. Here, in the very first session, a female patient described a breast operation she had had in which the prosthesis left inside her had resulted in damage to her body and self-perception. I suggest that this image might be a condenser for fantasies of the primal scene linked to an unconscious construction of what might happen in the group (see p. 80).

The primal scene normally serves as a precursor of the Oedipus complex. In the latter, the child becomes more actively involved as a rival for one or other of the parents. The nature of the primal scene as envisaged by the child has a strong influence on the later oedipal constellation, in which the emerging degree of aggression and retaliatory anxiety are crucial components. Klein sees the resolution of these conflicts occurring through the depressive position, in which the child recognises its separation from the parental couple and, through a process of mourning, reaches the capacity for concern and reparation. This helps to imbue the parental couple with constructive qualities and to internalise a more harmonious union between them.

In a previous paper (Nitsun 1994), I argued that the concept of the primal scene has considerable relevance to group development, in the following ways:

- as a symbol of the origin, unity, or disunity of the family, the primal scene fantasy influences the conception of the group, its origin and destiny;
- the perception of gender characteristics and the understanding of sexual relationships as originally constructed in the primal scene are projected onto the group membership;
- curiosity, as well as inhibition about sexual matters, in response to anxieties generated by the primal scene, is located in the group;
- creative or destructive qualities deriving from the primal scene are transferred to the group.

On the latter point, the group requires a spirit of healthy as opposed to defensive idealisation in order to develop (Gibbard and Hartman 1973). The shared group fantasies of the primal scene may determine the extent of idealisation vs. devaluation of the group. In the previous section, I explored the important part played by envy in the genesis of destructive group developments. There, envy of the breast was presented as the underlying paradigm. Here, the focus shifts to envy of the parental couple and their creative capacities. Meltzer (1973) suggests that in addition to the usual protagonists of the primal scene, there enters another member: the outsider, the stranger to the family, the enemy of parental creativity, of love. This figure, usually represented as part of the self, is malicious in its intent towards the idealised family and sets out to destroy it. I believe that a similar process occurs in the group as a dawning entity and that a part of the group represents this kind of malevolence, often unconsciously or barely expressed, but aimed at undermining the group.

The fantasy of the primal scene is usually symbolically rather than actually expressed in the group: it is often communicated in condensed form, as in the example of the breast operation that had a damaging outcome. In some groups, however, there is explicit material concerning the scene, and this not uncommonly reveals the deep ambivalence and hostility towards the parental couple. Detailed material about this can be found in my previous paper on the primal scene (Nitsun 1994) but the following is a further vivid illustration:

> An image from an analytic group stands out as a symbol of the hostile repudiation of parental sexuality. Sandra, who was having an extra-marital affair with a married man, Bob, had taken a cleaning job in the family home that Bob shared with his wife and children. Sandra's access to the house gave her various opportunities to observe the life of the family, which filled her with a mixed sense of envy and triumph. She described how on one occasion she was in the marital bedroom when through the window she saw Bob with his wife and children in the garden. She was filled with furious envy and resentment, hating her exclusion from Bob and the family unit. The wife was ill and in a wheelchair at the time and had her back to the house. Bob, though, seemed to be aware of Sandra's hovering presence inside the house. In a fit of pique, Sandra stripped off all her clothing and stood naked at the window. The moment he noticed this, Bob rushed back to the house to attend to her. Sandra had succeeded in her aim of tearing him away from his family.
>
> Sandra's affair, and her intense reaction to it, could be seen as a re-enactment of her relationship with her parents. She loathed her parents' closeness which she felt excluded

her. She desperately wanted to be close to her father and could not tolerate being anything less than his first choice.

In the above group, Sandra was one of several voices of the anti-group, since the group was suffused with anti-group reactions. In other groups, there tends to be a particular person who becomes the voice of the anti-group: for example, Nigel in Group A and Paul in Group D (see Chapter 4). In all these instances, the antagonists had backgrounds of considerable friction with their own families and had become estranged from them. In various ways, they exemplified what Meltzer described as 'the outsider, the stranger to the family'. In all these cases, their role as the voice of the anti-group was probably heavily invested by the rest of the group, so that they carried their groups' projections of hatred towards the family.

The dark underpinnings of the primal scene may account for the anxiety and shame that often surround the exploration of sexuality in the group. Members' current sexual preoccupations are likely to derive, in part, from their earlier sexual theories and fantasies. Revealing sexual wishes and concerns means revealing the deeper recesses of the primal scene. My impression is that, of all subjects dealt with in groups, sexuality is perhaps the most highly charged. Given the difficulty of talking openly about sex in groups and exploring its ramifications, there is a danger that the more primitive, destructive aspects of the primal scene will be acted out in the group, in either disguised or overt fashion.

In Group A, long-standing tension between Nigel and Maureen culminated in Maureen's misunderstanding of a point Nigel was making about his failed marriage. This triggered a strong confrontation between the two. Nigel humiliated Maureen by saying that she was a 'stupid female who never listens and always gets things wrong', and she flew into a rage with him. There had previously been discussions in the group about who and what Nigel and Maureen represented to each other, given their continuing mutual hostility. Following the present confrontation, another member asked Nigel whether he might be displacing onto Maureen the great anger he harboured towards his wife. Nigel retorted, 'If she were my wife, I would have her on the floor!' Maureen reacted with disgust and rage. Nigel's remark had conveyed both sex and violence, suggesting a re-enactment of a much earlier scene, perhaps a sadistic primal scene between the parents.

In this group, there was a useful processing of the event by the group as a whole, followed by an improvement in Nigel and Maureen's relationship. But in other groups this sort of dramatic enactment, imbued with the force of earlier fantasy, could seriously disrupt relationships and damage the safety of the group.

In some groups, the predominant ethos is one of inhibition of sexuality, the group as object representing a punishing, repressive force. In Group C (described in Chapter 4) there was a flamboyant display of sexuality coupled with contempt towards the primal couple. But in reality there was a repression of actual sexuality, with guilt and shame about sexual desires and relationships.

Groups in which there is a large degree of sexual repression, possibly cloaked by an outward show of sexuality, as in the above, illustrate a process which is captured in Fairbairn's (1952) notion of the *anti-libidinal* ego. This is one of three main ego-states described by Fairbairn – the central ego, the libidinal ego, and the anti-libidinal ego. The latter describes an internal process (also referred to as 'the internal saboteur') that punishes and controls libidinal desire (the libidinal ego). The impulse to repress and destroy represents 'the angry despair of the original unitary infantile ego over the non-satisfaction of its libidinal needs and its consequent turning in part against these needs themselves' (Guntrip 1961, p. 365).

The anti-group can be seen in some cases as a strong embodiment of the anti-libidinal ego. In several previous examples, it became apparent that, when the group awakened emotional and sexual needs, an oppositional, counter-attacking process was instigated, which led to a deadening or fragmentation of the group.

In healthy development, the central ego in Fairbairn's theory strengthens its grasp on emotional reality and a mature conscience is established. In groups, this can be seen to occur as part of the group gaining its own authority. Here, a benign authority encourages the enjoyment of life in its various forms, while accepting the necessity of some repression and some frustration. But in defensive development, a harsh, aggressivised morality predominates, attacking the imperfect object and its frustrations as well as the creation of libidinal need.

A group that is distorted by the anti-libidinal ego is itself deprived of the libidinal charge necessary for growth.

AGGRESSION AND HATRED

The phenomenon of aggression has penetrated most of the perspectives on the anti-group so far considered. But the terms 'aggression' and 'destruction' have been used fairly loosely and interchangeably and it is necessary to differentiate the varying forms and degrees of these phenomena. The subject is taken up again in Chapters 7 and 8 in terms of its technical implications for conducting groups, but here some theoretical underpinnings are considered.

It is important to recognise the ordinary, healthy, constructive forms of aggression that commonly occur in the group and are an intrinsic part of individual and group development. Foulkes (1964a) believed that most aggression could be canalised into constructive channels in the group and saw communication as the vital process whereby this is achieved. Rothenberg (1971) described anger in similar terms: anger resulting from frustration is a common experience, easily aroused in groups, and has a positive communicative function. It acts as a signal to others that there is a source of frustration or distress. Openly communicated and received, anger may lead to some form of resolution or reconciliation. This is very different from the pathological forms of aggression in which direct communication is likely to be absent, distorted or exaggerated, in which the intent is largely destructive, and in which the conflictual issue tends to remain unresolved. These forms of aggression have deeper intra-psychic roots and are related to severe disturbances in object relations. They tie up closely with processes of splitting, projective identification and regression, and they form an important substratum of the anti-group.

Kernberg (1991) described the continuum of aggression in terms of severity of response – irritation (mild), anger (moderate) and rage (maximal). To this, he adds hatred as a concentrated and organised expression of rage. In the context of the anti-group, the most relevant forms of aggression are rage and hatred.

Rage can be seen as the core affect in severe aggression. It seeks to eliminate or destroy a source of profound pain or frustration. Additionally, unconscious fantasies that develop around rage activate both an all-bad object relationship, and the wish to eliminate it, and an all-good object that must be restored. Rage tends to operate in a sporadic way, expressing itself in acute attacks of intense feeling. Beyond rage is what Kernberg regards as the most severe and dominant of all the affects – the complex and elaborated affect of hatred. Here, rage is organised into a stable pattern of intense and enduring affect.

Kernberg sees hatred as anchored in character, in a way that includes powerful rationalisations and distortions that subserve its primary aim: to destroy the object. Hatred is further differentiated in terms of degrees of intensity from mild to extreme. In *mild* hatred, the objective is to dominate and control the object. The search for power over the object potentially invokes sadistic elements but in a limited way. In *moderate* hatred, the individual's wish, conscious or unconscious, is to make the object suffer. The aim is not to eliminate the hated object but to maintain a close link with it in the enactment of a relationship between persecutor and victim. The *extreme* form of hatred demands the annihilation of the object. It may be expressed literally in murder or in a massive, destructive devaluation of the object. This devaluation may generalise to other objects in the form of a symbolic destruction of all objects: this is observable in severe antisocial personality structure. This extreme form of hatred may also be directed against oneself, as in suicide, in identification with the hated object: self-attack might seem to be the only way of destroying the object. Sadistic elements in varying degrees pervade all these forms of hatred, as does masochism to some degree, since in hatred directed against the self there is a large masochistic component.

Before examining the anti-group in terms of these conceptions of hatred, it is necessary to provide a dynamic formulation of the link between destructive aggression and the anti-group. The phenomenology of the anti-group is synonymous with aggression against the group. How does this come about? As suggested in previous illustrations and theoretical considerations, it happens when the strength of pathological aggression is either very difficult or impossible to assimilate in the interactional sphere of the group. This will occur when rage and hatred are so overwhelming that they cannot be communicated, contained, or understood, or when the threat of their enactment in the group is felt to be too dangerous. Since the group as object is identified with the containing, nurturing function, but is frequently experienced as intensely frustrating and painful, it invites a massive projection of the overall constellation of aggressive feelings. This can be seen to have a defensive function: by providing a receptacle for these affects, the group agglomerates into a single whole the separate sources and foci of aggression that may exist within and between individuals in the group. Of course, as has been shown in several examples, extreme aggression directly expressed between members – and towards the conductor – can also have a destructive effect on the group. This is likely to occur when there is a collusion on the part of the rest of the group, usually through projective identification onto the warring parties, or through the lack of a sufficiently strong good object to contain the rage and hatred and facilitate resolution.

Hence, the anti-group can be seen to arise in two contrasting situations: where the expression of aggression is inhibited and displaced onto the group and where it is expressed uncontrollably in a way that makes the group seem dangerous and inflammatory.

Kernberg's formulation of the different types of hatred is categorical in emphasis but provides a potentially useful framework for considering differing degrees of intensity of the anti-group. Group C, described both in terms of the intermittent impact of the anti-group (pp. 85–7) and the hostility towards the primal scene (p. 142), could be seen as of *mild* anti-group intensity. Its overriding concern was with control and domination, expressed in a strong desire to gain power over the conductor, the parents, and the overall group process. Elements of sadism crept into this, as in the pejorative view of the primal scene, but this did not get out of hand: the group continued to function in an ambivalent way. Group G, the student psychotherapy training group (described on pp. 101–4), could be seen as of *moderate* anti-group intensity. The group was filled with rage, but it was kept alive, seemingly almost to torment the conductor and to maintain a persecutor–victim relationship with her. Group B, the group that broke down under the impact of the anti-group, could be described as of *extreme* anti-group intensity. The main antagonist's hatred was itself of an extreme kind. The overwhelming frustration, rage, and envy he experienced in the group activated a powerfully bad object that had to be destroyed. This was enacted in the group in a physical attack that probably harboured murderous feelings, and led to the annihilation of the group. The rest of the group may have colluded with this, reflecting a strong underlying anti-group constellation in the group as a whole.

Kernberg's theoretical analysis of the origin of extreme aggression is also relevant to the anti-group. He regards this as a 'fixation to the trauma'. This is a condition in which the individual – under the domination of hatred – remains intensely linked to the frustrating, depriving, or attacking object. This object is experienced as needed but all-bad and as having destroyed or 'swallowed up' the ideal, all-good object. 'The revengeful destruction of this bad object is intended magically to restore the all good one, but in the process it leads to the destruction of the very capacity to relate to the object' (1991, p. 229).

Translated into group terms, this formulation helps to make sense of the sometimes obdurate and intransigent quality of the anti-group. Behind the aggressive demands and attacks of the anti-group lies the longing to restore the good object. But this is precluded by the destructive behaviour of the group. The resultant frustration and despair feed the cycle of hatred that in turn maintains the anti-group.

THE DEATH INSTINCT

The death instinct occupies a controversial place in psychoanalysis, its original home. Relating it to groups and group analysis, in particular, is even more problematic. This is in spite of the fact that Foulkes himself embraced instinct theory and, as is probably *not* widely recognised, expressed considerable belief in the existence of a death instinct. Describing it as a 'universal biological phenomenon', Foulkes (1971, p. 246) claimed that it was indispensable in understanding destructive and self-destructive forces and that, in line with Freud's view, it was 'the best simplification'.

I first introduced the concept of the death instinct in Chapter 2, supporting the view expressed by Thompson (1991) that its value might lie not in the adumbration of a concrete, causal phenomenon but in the formulation of a critical principle that challenges our assumptions about psychoanalysis and human development. I compared the concept of the anti-group with this perspective of the death instinct in so far as the anti-group is a similarly abstract principle, although not without implications for actual group behaviour. I also drew attention to the fact that, although Foulkes gave considerable credence, at a philosophical level, to the concept of a self-destructive force, he stopped short of investigating its impact on the psychotherapy group and instead evolved a largely idealised picture of the group.

It remains to consider more fully the relevance of the concept of the death instinct to the anti-group, not only as a parallel principle, but as connected experientially, and possibly aetiologically, to the origin of the anti-group. I have deliberately left this to the end of the chapter in order to link any evaluation of the concept to the preceding illustrative and theoretical material.

But, first, an overview of the concept and its current status. Freud (1920, 1923) originally described the death instinct as a biological drive to return to the inorganic. Life brings with it strife, conflict and upheaval: in the death instinct, there is a longing for the cessation of life. Linked to this is the Nirvana principle, the fantasy of peace attained through an inanimate state. The death instinct, of course, is part of a dual instinct theory, in which Thanatos (the death instinct) exists alongside Eros (the life instinct). This needs emphasising as critics of the death instinct tend to judge it as a unitary, all-pervasive state, which was not Freud's intention. It is the flux and the conflict between the life and the death instincts which is seen as core in human existence.

The death instinct is closely related to aggression, which was dealt with in the preceding section. Aggression is the death instinct turned outwards. Melanie Klein (1946, 1952) elaborated this point. Part of the death instinct is projected onto an external object which thereby becomes a persecutor; the other part, which is retained in the ego, turns its aggression against the persecutor. In this way, the death instinct accounts, varyingly, for the wish for annihilation, the fear of annihilation, and, paradoxically, the force to withstand and combat the threat of annihilation. The latter is another point worth highlighting: that aggression arising from the death instinct may be seen not only as destructive but also as serving to protect the life instinct.

I introduce here a statement by the physicist Hutten (1983) which expresses views that are strongly consistent with the arguments presented in this book: 1) that creativity is close to death or destruction; 2) that integration is linked to differentiation; 3) that the presence of a disintegratory force in human experience can be seen in common-sensical rather than theoretical terms.

Creation cannot be achieved without death: integration is not possible without some fragmentation of the previous, incomplete, or incorrect, integration of a level, or set of informational levels. Only in this manner, too, can differentiation – the more varied and flexible use of information on a given level – go together with increasing integration. I know that many people do not wish to accept the 'death instinct': but all the cells of our bodies are mortal, they die and are shed all the time, and how can this natural process not be represented in our unconscious fantasies? *To accept the biological reality of death and its emotional consequences is an indispensable requirement, in my view, when processes, both in the individual and within the group, are discussed.*

(Hutten 1983, p. 158, italics mine)

The present theoretical status of the concept is reflected in two contrasting recent papers on the death instinct. One is by Segal (1993), who writes in the Freudian–Kleinian tradition which generally accepts the validity of the concept. The other is by Maratos (1994), who examines the concept critically within a largely group-analytic framework. A viewpoint similar to the latter is presented in comments by another group analyst, Zulueta (1993).

Segal (1993) argues unequivocally for the clinical usefulness of the concept of the death instinct. She demonstrates the infiltration of the death instinct into individual psychopathology as well as the material of the psychoanalytic encounter. She describes how recognition of the death instinct significantly changes her understanding of the patient and how, in some cases, the insight is used to constructive ends. She concludes that in favourable circumstances a confrontation with the death instinct can mobilise the life instinct.

On the conceptual side, Segal suggests that the concept of the death instinct need not necessarily invoke biological explanations and that it can be explained on purely psychological grounds. On the side of life, the individual's awareness of profound need leads to object seeking, psychological growth, and love. On the side of death, there is a striving to annihilate need with all its pressures, frustrations, and pain. This leads to a withdrawal from objects, the cancellation of psychological growth, and the longing for non-existence. This formulation implies a revision of the notion of a death instinct and its replacement by a formulation that roots the death motive in the psychological domain.

Maratos' (1994) article is, equally unequivocally, an attack on the theory of the death instinct. It is an impassioned attack, which includes some important points about the over-valuation of causal explanations, which he sees as one of the main flaws of the concept. However, his remaining argument seems biased on several counts. First, Maratos claims that the concept of Thanatos was predominantly a product of Freud's painful life experiences, with little relevance to clinical or universal issues. Although the concept was no doubt partially an expression of Freud's personal difficulties — no theory, especially of this magnitude, can be stripped from the person of its originator — it was essentially concerned with clinical problems in the application and outcome of psychoanalytic treatment (as highlighted in the 1937 paper, 'Analysis terminable and interminable'). On the wider front, Freud was also intensely aware of the destructive forces surrounding him. It is no accident that the death instinct was first proposed at the end of World War I and elaborated on the eve of World War II. In fact, Freud's concept of the death instinct has been recognised as prophetic in its dark vision (Gay 1989).

Second, Maratos regards the concept as uncritically and slavishly accepted by psychoanalysts. The reverse applies. Many psychoanalysts have sought to refute the concept (Ricoeur 1970; Brenner 1971; Hamilton 1976; Berenstein 1987). It has not gained widespread acceptance in the psychoanalytic realm. Third, Maratos describes the concept as being removed from 'reality' and proposes other beliefs and understandings that are closer to 'reality'. But what is reality? The notion of a single, unitary reality is outmoded: in the late twentieth century we mostly subscribe to the notion of a complex set of 'realities', with writers such as Maturana and Varela (1980) arguing persuasively that 'reality' is subjectively and plurally constructed rather than a unitary, objective fact.

Finally, Maratos opposes group-analytic psychotherapy to the concept of the death instinct: 'Group therapy can provide the new experience on which a new understanding of "self and other can emerge"' (1994). This statement is similar to a comment by Foulkes quoted earlier (pp. 27–8), in which group analysis is presented as a revolutionary new approach that transcends the limitations of other approaches. This vein of somewhat crusading optimism tends to deny the existence of aggression and self-destruction and, in so doing, perpetuates the split between an optimistic 'good' and a pessimistic 'bad'. As previously noted, this split is largely characteristic of the group psychotherapy literature and group analysis is no exception.

Maratos' repudiation of the death instinct is echoed in a book on the roots of destructiveness by another group analyst, Zulueta (1993). The main argument here sets relational approaches to understanding destructive behaviour against what are presented as orthodox Christian and psychoanalytic viewpoints concerning 'original sin'. While the interpersonal aspects of destructive behaviour, particularly those rooted in emotional frustration and rejection, are crucially important, the book tends to polarise the nature–nurture controversy in a way that heavily concretises the death instinct and invests it with archaic beliefs, such as 'inherent evil'. This renders the concept unworkable and also deprives it of its suggested value as a critical or metaphorical principle.

Returning to the anti-group, what further light can be thrown on any possible connection with the death instinct? It seems to me that an important distinction needs to be made between phenomenology and causality: the one does not necessarily imply the other. Hence, much of the illustrative data presented on the anti-group can be seen as descriptively and phenomenologically consistent with an interpretation linked to the death instinct. This applies particularly to cases where there was a complete breakdown of the group, leading to total disintegration, suggesting that a powerful self-destructive tendency may have been present in the group. In other cases, the group might not have disintegrated but progress was stifled by intensely destructive group relationships, including those towards the conductor. In some groups, this degree of overt destructiveness was missing but the group barely came alive: any hint of spontaneity or progress was stifled by a subterranean process of repression and distortion. These groups are reminiscent of what Joseph (1982) describes as 'addiction to near-death', a malignant form of self-destructiveness that she relates to the death instinct and that is seen as maintaining a state of suspended psychic animation.

Additionally, some of the processes accompanying the anti-group, such as the insidious operation of envy and projective identification, the omnipotent denial of emotional need and dependency (as in 'the gang'), and the perverse collusions to maintain states of impasse and suffering, are in line with elaborations of the concept of the death instinct described by writers such as Rosenfeld (1971) and Steiner (1993).

An important question concerns whether the hypothetical death instinct is mediated via the individual or the group process. As I see it, both may apply. Undoubtedly, the presence of particularly disturbed and destructive individuals generates attitudes and behaviour that can profoundly and adversely influence the group: numerous examples of this were given in previous illustrations. Anzieu (1984) suggests that, in spite of the power of group-as-a-whole phenomena, the group process may be unconsciously organised by the fantasies and attitudes of a particularly dominating member. The alternative situation is one in which the group itself, through pervasive projections, embodies a process akin to the death instinct. Here, the group as a whole becomes a poisonous container, acting as a siphon for the self-destructive process.

It is impossible on the basis of these illustrations, however, to say that the death instinct, as an *instinct*, is concretely and causally related to the anti-group. It is more possible to align these observations with Segal's (1993) reinterpretation of the death instinct in psychological terms, seen as a wish for self-annihilation in the face of unendurable frustration and suffering. But, ultimately, the importance of the concept of the death instinct, as I see it, remains as a critical principle that reminds us of the regressive and disintegratory aspects of human behaviour and guards against therapeutic over-optimism and idealisation. That this is as true for the group as for the individual should, by now, be abundantly clear.

It is important to clarify the relationship between the anti-group and the death instinct. The anti-group should not be seen simply and uncritically as the group equivalent of the death instinct. I have suggested a possible link between the two, particularly when the death instinct is reinterpreted in psychological terms, as above, or in the much more broadly biological terms suggested by Hutten (1983), as described on pp. 147–8. The aetiology and phenomenology of the anti-group are more complex and multi-faceted than that implied in the classical version which roots the death instinct in a biological drive.

The last two chapters have considered the determinants of the anti-group under several headings. These headings, though, are more convenient than they are clinically and experientially real, since the primitive processes they describe are fundamentally linked. Overall, they attempt to explain the failure of the group process to contain the destructive developments arising from intolerable intra-psychic, interpersonal, and more broadly social pressures that are elicited in the group. The group as object then itself becomes a receptacle for the hostile and malignant part-object projections that impugn and fragment the therapeutic frame. That this process is not an all-or-nothing affair and that an anti-group component is a natural part of the development of most groups is emphasised. Also, that, even in its more pathological manifestations, the process can be understood and managed or transformed is already suggested in a number of the previous examples. The potential for clinical management and therapeutic intervention forms the subject of the succeeding chapters.

Chapter 7
Technical considerations in dealing with the anti-group

To what extent is the anti-group preventable? How might it be prevented? And if it is not prevented, how is it best managed to the therapeutic benefit of the group? This chapter addresses these questions but with an important caveat in mind. This is that the anti-group usually has a developmental function in the life of the group, that it represents a challenge to the strength and survival of the group, and that it may contain the seeds of transformation. At the same time, the creative potential of the anti-group exists in a delicate balance with its destructive potential. A constructive outcome, as we have seen in many examples, can by no means be assumed in psychotherapy and related groups. It is wise therefore to consider how to maximise the group's creative potential and to minimise its destructive tendencies.

This requires a reassessment of some of the fundamental aspects of running an analytic group. Here, I aim not so much to provide an exhaustive review of these factors as to evaluate these issues from the perspective of the anti-group. I suggest that 1) there is an absence of robust guidelines on some crucial technical concerns, 2) this reflects the confusion in the overall field, the plethora of overlapping and sometimes conflicting theories, and the scarcity of information about basic group processes, particularly the negative aspects of the therapy group, and 3) most importantly, the confusion about technical issues creates ambiguities and anxieties in the running of the groups, which, if unprocessed, may unwittingly set up an anti-group constellation.

Given the range of factors to be considered, I have separated general technical considerations from detailed aspects of the role of the conductor, which are dealt with in Chapter 8. In the present chapter, I focus on the following aspects of group psychotherapy:

the setting (physical and organisational); selection (criteria and procedure); drop-outs; and preparation for the group.

There are important contributions in the literature to these areas, and these will be highlighted, but I will also point out the deficiencies and ambiguities I consider to be most apparent. Selection is the area I see as most problematic, no doubt because it is such an important but complex aspect of the psychotherapy group. In order to extend our perception of this area, I will highlight three interrelated concepts – bonding capacity, the 'passion for proximity', and the group-object relation. These indicate a move away from individually based selection criteria to group-related considerations.

It is useful to start with a conception of the overall context of group psychotherapy. This I derive from Winnicott's theory of the 'holding environment'. In this concept, Winnicott (1963a, 1963b) considers the need of the infant for an environment which provides the safety of physical as well as emotional holding. This context enables the infant to depend on a reliable, consistent, and emphatic presence that minimises the overwhelming anxiety resulting from excessive environmental impingements. It facilitates the infant's capacity to develop object relatedness, including the ability to make reparation for destructive actions or impulses.

The concept of the holding environment has been widely adopted in the understanding of the analytic treatment frame. Modell (1976, 1988a, 1988b) has elaborated the concept to suggest that the holding environment operates as a silent but necessary backdrop to all analytic work. Slochower (1991) has extended the concept to focus on the holding needed by borderline patients, whose range of disturbance and unpredictable behaviour requires a particularly firm but unretaliatory frame. The concept clearly has relevance to the group-analytic therapy group, as James (1994) and Tuttman (1994) have described. The presence of a group of approximately eight people, each with distressing and often complex problems, which are usually quickly transferred and enacted in the therapy group, if anything accentuates the need for a holding frame. Hawkins (1986), relating the concept to the group, highlights Winnicott's distinction between the environmental mother and the object mother. The environmental mother provides a predictable setting and 'actively provides care in handling and in general management'. The object mother, on the other hand, is the mother who excites or frustrates, arousing and satisfying – or not – the child's urgent needs. Hawkins suggests that in terms of vision, the object mother can be thought of as in central vision, encountered 'head-on', whereas the environmental mother is related to peripheral vision, safely present in the background. Overall, the group can be viewed as an environmental mother supporting the patient as he/she struggles with the object mother.

Much of this and the following chapter underscore the importance of the holding environment for the safe development of the group. Failures and distortions of the holding environment are seen as exacerbating the likelihood of pathological manifestations of the anti-group as opposed to its developmentally appropriate expression in the group. In this chapter, emphasis is placed on the 'general management' functions required to establish and strengthen the group and thereby secure the holding environment. This view is fully congruent with Foulkes' notion of 'dynamic administration', which describes the conductor's core function as creating and maintaining the group setting.

THE SETTING

The setting can be divided into the physical setting, including the group room and the immediate physical environment, and the organisational setting, which refers to the nature of the organisation in which the group is conducted.

The setting of the group is fundamental in providing a containing framework. Group analysts usually attribute considerable importance to the setting (Van der Kleij 1983), reflecting Foulkes' emphasis on the influence of the social domain and Norbert Elias' concept of 'figuration' which highlights the network of social inter-dependencies. Simpson (1995) gives a sensitive account of the severe disruptions of a setting in the National Health Service and the impact this had on the running of psychotherapy groups. He notes the close correspondence between the vicissitudes of the setting, the therapist's state of mind, and the dynamics of the groups.

Group analysts, however, may be distinguished from other group psychotherapists in their strong emphasis on the setting. Yalom (1975), for instance, in his otherwise comprehensive treatment of technical factors in group therapy, devotes just a few lines to it. Overall, I believe, the significance of problems in the setting has been largely underestimated as a factor contributing to faulty group development.

The physical setting

The physical setting defines the spatial context and boundaries of the group. It need hardly be said that a controlled, consistent setting including a comfortable, neutrally furnished room, with uniformity of seating, is a basic requirement of the group. Although most group therapists would see the necessity for this, it is surprising how frequently complications arise in the arrangement of chairs, heating, ventilation, and so on. It is also striking how this impacts on the group. Groups can spend whole sessions complaining about the physical setting, seemingly holding up the work of the group, while members unite in their condemnation of the setting. In itself, this may be useful material, there to be understood as part of the group's development, but it can assume a dominating influence. Particularly in the early stages of the group, when there is heightened concern about the nature of the holding environment, the physical setting – as for the infant in relationship to the mother – is vital. It is the equivalent of the 'psychic skin' (Bick 1968), previously mentioned in Chapter 5, which in early development helps to contain internal chaos. 'Like the infant's skin, the group circle embodies both the concrete external and the abstract internal or psychological functions of containing' (Foguel 1994).

The surrounding building has a linked significance. Deficiencies or oddities in the environment are quickly spotted by group members and rapidly enter the material of the group. Again, this material adds grist to the mill, but an understanding of what it means in terms of the structuring of the holding environment helps to make sense of the group's sometimes obsessive concern with the physical surroundings.

> In an experiential training group, the material of the first few weeks was dominated by complaints about the small, cramped, overheated room, in which members felt they had no physical or emotional space of their own. The chairs lacked uniformity and several were uncomfortable, adding to a sense of unwelcome difference. The surrounding building was dilapidated, with a maze of corridors, and access to

the toilets was difficult. Members were highly critical of these features, and the only cohesion they showed in the early period was in their shared indignation about the setting. One member described how he had looked for the toilet and ended up in a broom cupboard that was stuffed with an old mattress. If the group symbolically was trying to establish the environmental mother, it was meeting with frustration and confusion. This was a sticky, resistant group that remained tense and uncomfortable for most of its duration, with occasional flare-ups of intense hostility between members that precipitated great anxiety in the group. It was as if in the absence of a safe comfortable environmental mother, the 'object mother' was too dangerous to confront.

Of course, it is well-nigh impossible to provide a perfect setting for therapy groups in which there are no impingements from without, but the impact of perceived or actual flaws in the setting may be expected to infiltrate the consciousness of the group and potentially to undermine a sense of trust in the holding environment.

The organisational setting

The wider organisational setting of the group has both powerful and subtle effects on the group. Again, group analysts are closely attuned to these effects. Sharpe (1995), in the context of group-analytic supervision, refers to the therapist's 'responsibility to the external context' and provides a guide to organisational issues that need consideration:

- The part the therapy groups are perceived to play within the organisation;
- The 'climate' around the group – positive and negative aspects. Who, if anyone, is the conductor answerable to?
- Who control(s) the immediate setting of the group and availability of its members?
- Identifying allies and opponents. Who feels threatened by the group's existence?
- Mustering support/fostering alliances: 'playing politics';
- Planning actions to solve problems and minimise trouble;
- Negotiating through conflicts;

- Maintaining a good climate around the group and keeping the 'outside' in the picture.

(Sharpe 1994, p. 158)

Here, I explore some salient features of the organisational context and show how failures to deal with the setting can lead to anti-group developments. To start with there is the social significance of the organisational setting. Context informs the social meaning of the group (Hopper 1985). A group run in a psychiatric hospital is contextualised very differently from a group in a private practice. The organisation constantly influences the group's perception of itself, as it struggles to find its own identity. A therapy group has no intrinsic social identity, other than as a collection of strangers who come together for the purpose of having a therapeutic group. As the group develops a sense of itself, it becomes a group in a network of groups, taking its identity, in part, from the ambient social milieu. In a hospital or clinic situation, there are obvious associations with pathology and the patient role, and these associations will be internalised in a group's developing identity, often in unfavourable ways. My years of working in a psychiatric hospital have convinced me of the power of this process of internalising the external milieu. However, the process works both ways: projection onto the environment and the other patients of feared inner fragmentation and madness and a re-introjection of these perceived characteristics.

A further aspect of the social setting concerns the organisational dynamics that define the environment as a living system. Particularly in times of organisational conflict and change, these dynamics are highly active and tend to leak out to all aspects of the system. Therapy groups are often acutely aware of the vicissitudes of the organisation and any hint of disequilibrium can affect the group's own sense of safety, paralleling and mirroring internal threats within the group, and vice versa.

The anti-group may then reflect destructive processes in the organisation at large, partly through a process of projective identification with the organisation and partly because organisational stress may impact on the group in very real ways. Group G, the student psychotherapy group, is a vivid example (Chapter 4). The chaos in the host organisation had a noxious effect on the experiential group and in turn a great deal of the group's chaos was projected onto the organisation. This could be seen as a form of malignant mirroring within the organisational system.

Adding to the complex matrix of organisational group dynamics is the conductor's role in the organisation. How the conductor fits into the system and how he or she is affected by the organisational dynamics is an intrinsic part of the leadership brought to the group. The members are likely to pick up conscious and unconscious cues from the conductor, particularly those revealing information that in some way affects the status and meaning of the group, as well as its safety and continuity. Since these dynamics are unlikely to be spelt out openly, they are further distorted by members' fantasies.

The following example illustrates the interacting effects of several dimensions of the organisational setting:

> Group A had been meeting for about 6 months. The setting was a group room in the psychiatric hospital. Participants had to walk through the corridors of the hospital on the way to the group and sometimes encountered long-stay patients who looked and behaved in bizarre ways. Participants reacted with considerable anxiety and some aversion, as if there was a fear of contamination. In this phase, there was also great anxiety about exposure, as if the act of self-revelation was dangerous. There were fears of being discovered to be mad and of being compulsorily admitted to the hospital. The conductor's role as head of a department was equated with sweeping powers to diagnose insanity and force detention on patients.
>
> The group room had observational facilities, including a one-way screen and microphones. On one occasion, the group arrived to find the mirror exposed. This aroused enormous suspicion and anger. In spite of strong assurances, members were convinced that the eyes and the ears of the authorities were upon them. This reaction was symptomatic of pronounced paranoid anxiety in the early stages of the group, reflecting the fragile trust in the group context. The sense of threat emanating from the organisation remained an issue for some time.
>
> A few months later, the sudden unavailability of this room resulted in the conductor having to find an alternative venue. He managed to book a large, pleasant room in the

education centre of the hospital, a building removed from the main hospital and treatment centres. There was an enormous sense of relief and appreciation in the group. Whether it was the changed setting or the fact that the group had begun to mature, or both, the group became more relaxed, self-exposure became less threatening, and members began to work more actively at the therapeutic task.

At a later period in the group, rumours started circulating about hospital closure and staff redundancies. The membership picked this up and became anxious about the threat to the continuity of the group. For some months, members remained acutely sensitive to any hint of organisational change, including the possible loss of the conductor. These perceptions were not out of line with the difficult organisational reality at the time and the conductor found it a difficult challenge to help to contain the patients' anxiety when he was himself caught up in the spiralling organisation change.

This example illustrates the penetrating effects of the setting at several levels on the group – the physical environment; the social significance of the psychiatric hospital; the setting as a container of madness; the meaning of an altered setting, when the room was changed; the threat of wider organisational change; and the conductor as a mirror of the setting. This particular group both survived and became a strongly viable therapeutic unit. But in more fragile groups, the impact of a troubled setting may be more destructive and add powerfully to the anti-group.

This analysis is consistent with a fundamental group-analytic principle: that individual, group, and social contexts are strongly interdependent. One of the greatest influences on Foulkes was Norbert Elias, whose theory of 'figuration' emphasises the inseparability of the individual and society. Within this, institutions have a major influence on groups and individuals (Gfäller 1993). Here, the emphasis is apparently very different from the intra-psychic and interpersonal focus in the previous chapter on determinants of the anti-group, but not if the group is seen as occurring at the interface of internal and external worlds. The anti-group, too, I suggest, occurs at this point of intersection, condensing into a destructive mirror the mutually reflecting processes of psychic and organisational threat.

SELECTION

Selection may appropriately be described as 'the obscure object of desire' of group psychotherapy: so little is known about such a vital part of the process. Without question, the composition of the group profoundly influences its therapeutic outcome. As Yalom (1975) says, 'the fate of a group therapy patient and a therapy group may, in large measure, be determined before the first group therapy session' (p. 219). Selection and group composition undoubtedly influence the extent of anti-group developments, making it necessary to have clear parameters about this basic technical consideration, but the situation we find is a complex and ambiguous one.

It is important to clarify that I am focusing here on selection for group-analytic 'slow-open' groups with a mixed or heterogeneous membership. These are to be distinguished from homogeneous groups, which, although less part of the group-analytic tradition, are increasingly described by group analysts. Here, selection criteria are to some extent circumscribed by the specificity of the population for whom the group is targeted. Some examples of homogeneous groups that have been reported in the group-analytic literature are: groups for adult survivors of child sexual abuse (in Nitsun 1995a); forensic psychotherapy groups (Welldon 1993; Schlapobersky 1995); and groups for alcoholics (Stevenson and Ruscombe-King 1993).

The situation is very different in groups where wider diversity is the aim. On the one hand, diversity is one of the essential strengths of heterogeneous psychotherapy groups (Thyssen 1992); on the other, it creates problems about balance, proportion, and the degree of difference the group can tolerate and benefit from (see Chapter 3, p. 50).

Brown (1991) gives a useful account of the assessment and selection procedures for long-term, heterogeneous groups at the London-based Group Analytic Practice. He is realistic about the limits and problems of analytic group therapy. Questioning Foulkes' (1975a) assertion that group psychotherapy is indicated whenever psychotherapy is appropriate and that its range is broader than that of individual psychotherapy, he points out that the demands of long-term group analysis are considerable and very different from those of other group approaches. He emphasises the need to consider for each patient their motivation, the practicality of long-term group psychotherapy, and their capacity to respond positively to the analytic, exploratory approach in a group. He also highlights the importance of criteria such as psychological mindedness and ego strength.

Sensible and sensitive as these criteria are, they tend to be rather general and difficult to assess, and several apply equally to individual psychotherapy, blurring the necessary distinction between the two modes. More generally, use of group selection criteria is also complicated by the fact that we are never selecting an individual in isolation but in relation to a group context – a point I will develop below. Finally, even where criteria are regarded as essential for group selection, it may be difficult implementing them in the less than ideal circumstances in which many group practitioners work. The frequent time pressure to get groups going and to maintain them in the face of difficulties, as well as the common problems of recruiting a critical mass of suitable patients, are aspects of the group mode of therapy that easily lead to unfavourable compromises in selection.

Yalom (1975) provides a range of criteria for selection for mixed psychotherapy groups, paralleling those suggested by Brown above. He also highlights criteria for exclusion from groups, i.e. factors which contra-indicate group membership. He mentions 1) reality factors, such as difficulties about time commitment, 2) external stressors, such as impending divorce, which are too preoccupying at the time, 3) group deviancy, by which process people become isolates in groups, usually through personality features which prevent them from fitting in, 4) severe problems of intimacy, and 5) fear of emotional contagion. Yalom bases these observations on studies of group drop-outs. Interestingly, he points out that these factors could have been checked out prior to the patient entering the group, indicating exclusion rather than inclusion, but in many cases this did not happen.

These descriptions are relevant in the present context, in so far as they portray individuals who are likely to contribute to anti-group developments. While I hesitate to enlarge the focus on individual characteristics, for reasons outlined further below, my own observations in clinical practice lead me to mention the following as presenting particular problems.

Highly aggressive individuals, particularly within a borderline personality constellation. It stands to reason that highly aggressive people, who are easily frustrated and provoked and quick to attack, are likely to have a disruptive effect on the group. Variations in aggressiveness are to be expected in any group, and can be seen as part of a natural continuum, but the sort of individual who stands out is subject to powerful and unpredictable outbursts of rage, often fuelled by envy, with little or no sense of responsibility for these sudden, intense, and demanding responses. These patients tend to be impervious to the group and conductor's attempts to help them understand the source of their reactions and they can end up destroying the group in the process. Alan in Group B (Chapter 4) was a typical example. Tuttman (1994) has given a compelling description of difficulties encountered with aggressive, acting-out participants.

Isolated, schizoid individuals. It has been noted quite frequently (e.g. Grotjahn 1972) that these individuals are difficult as group members and that they have a high drop-out rate. These patients epitomise Foulkes' description of the 'sick' individual who is isolated in the social group. In many ways they are precisely the sort of individuals we wish to be able to help in group therapy, so that they might strengthen their ties with their own communities, but this is achieved with great difficulty. They are not openly group disruptive in the way the aggressive individuals described are, but their suspiciousness, reserve, and isolation in the group contribute in a different way to anti-group tendencies. My impression is that they often have enormous pools of repressed rage and envy that are blocked off in the group and that they also block the capacity of the rest of the group to express these feelings. There also seem to be vast areas of interpersonal vulnerability in these patients that dare not be touched in the group. Rather than exposing and expressing the anti-group, they help to inhibit it, and this insidiously reinforces destructiveness towards the group.

Patients with severe early trauma. It goes without saying that many patients who enter group therapy have experienced serious early loss and deprivation. Although there are reports of very successful homogeneous groups with people of this kind, notably Liesel Hearst's example of deprived mothers (1981), my own experience is that, if a mixed group is composed largely of such patients, the combined and cumulative traumata may have a negative effect on the group. Severe anxiety about abandonment, unless very carefully dealt with, can become a self-fulfilling prophecy which has a disintegrating effect on the group and repeats the traumatic event.

The suggestion is by no means that all patients with these characteristics are automatically excluded. Much depends on the individual, since there may well be compensating factors. Also, the balance of personalities in the group needs to be given precedence. A participant who may be very problematic and uncontainable in one group may participate usefully in another, depending on the rest of the membership.

Although Yalom's researches and my own impressions may be of use in establishing criteria for inclusion and exclusion, I believe the difficulty in developing a coherent set of selection criteria for group therapy may reflect, again, the absence of coherent models of group treatment. Hence, the factors described above remain somewhat *ad hoc*. Although the concept of the anti-group does not in itself provide a complete theory of group therapy, it does offer a particular perspective which may be of value in thinking about selection. The main implication of the anti-group for group composition is that the group requires members' contributions to the survival and strengthening of the group and can be damaged by the presence of participants who are excessively prone to attacking or undermining the group, in either overt or covert ways, and those who are unable to integrate with the group in an ongoing way. This perspective has led me to consider additional participant variables that relate less to conventional diagnostic and personality categories and more to considerations about group membership and commitment. I tentatively suggest the following:

Bonding capacity. For a group to become a group and not just an aggregate of individuals, it is necessary for participants to be able to bond with each other and the group. We know from the work of Bowlby (1977, 1988) that early patterns of interpersonal attachment have a crucial effect on individuals' later capacity to bond, and that difficulties in bonding are associated with considerable anxiety, frustration, depression, and aggression. Although the group is meant to provide a corrective experience for people with problems of attachment, it also paradoxically depends for its own development on the bonding propensities of its members. The group provides a context for bonding but also depends on the component bonds established. This is not meant to imply that we should select only patients who are already capable of effective relationships – if so, they would not need therapy in the first place – but we may need to consider carefully again the *balance* of participants in terms of their bonding experience and capacity. Weak bonding potential may contribute to anti-group development, whereas stronger bonding capacity will help to build the group and offset destructive group developments. The identification of differences in bonding capacity may be aided by current research and assessment instruments, such as the Adult Attachment Interview developed by Mary Main (George *et al.* 1985).

The passion for proximity. An interesting and potentially useful concept of interpersonal relatedness appears in a paper by Mendez *et al.* (1988). They refer to a 'passion for proximity'. This describes an interpersonal situation in which people seek and enjoy relationships. The inference is that both social situations and individual people vary on this criterion. The concept suggests a continuum, at one end of which is the passion for proximity, and at the other end what could be called an 'aversion to proximity'. This may provide a novel perspective on criteria for selection and composition in group therapy.

Mendez *et al.* relate this concept very interestingly to family systems and come up with a view of the family that is relevant to the therapy group.

> The constitution of a family is a non-rational phenomenon that takes place when there is a passion for living together in physical or emotional proximity. Therefore, a family disintegrates when this passion is lost, or when this passion cannot be maintained through separation.
>
> (Mendez *et al.* 1988, p. 22)

This observation applies similarly to individuals in a therapy group. It suggests a view of the anti-group as a constellation in which it is not only aggression that is a key factor but also the absence or diminution of interpersonal relatedness due to a lack or loss of the passion for proximity. This construct is similar to the concept of *valency*, as originally proposed by Bion (1961) and elaborated by Scharff and Scharff (1991). Mendez *et al.* continue:

> As a consequence, since a family is defined as a particular kind by a particular configuration of conversations, when such a configuration of conversations disappears, the family disintegrates as a family of that kind, but a new family may appear

in its place if the persons that compose it do not lose their passion for living together.

(Mendez *et al.* 1988, p. 22)

Departing for a moment from selection, this statement has important implications for continuity and change in group analysis. Since any longer-term group will evolve and change over time, there is a question about the extent to which the members, consciously and unconsciously, will seek to stay together under the changed conditions, e.g. when the 'configuration of conversations' alters, and, hence, whether the group continues or not.

The implications for group selection here are not yet clear, but the link between characteristics that define the passion or aversion to proximity and the continuity of the group is a promising line of inquiry, connecting selection more clearly to a dynamic view of the continuing group process.

The group-object relation. I introduce here a term to describe the way individuals characteristically perceive and relate to groups – the group-object relation. I derive the term from object relations theory and suggest that in addition to the commonly recognised set of object relationships, i.e. one-person, two-person, and three-person relationships, there is an internal representation, unique to each individual, of the group as object. This is thought to originate in the primary family group, as suggested in the section on the primal scene (Chapter 6, pp. 138–43), and to generalise to other groups, such as peer groups, school groups, work groups, and social groups. These influences may generate a characteristic, relatively consistent view of groups which ranges from highly positive to highly negative, and in which characterologically based anti-group attitudes may first take root. Such forms of the group-object relation will then influence the individual's characteristic group behaviour, in terms of criteria such as the seeking out vs. withdrawal from groups, excitement vs. anxiety about groups, and pleasure vs. displeasure in the experience of groups. The group-object relation includes the person's idiosyncratic expression of aggressive and destructive tendencies in groups, in the way Foulkes originally described the 'neurotic' or 'psychotic' position as disrupting the social network and as has been illustrated in the foregoing clinical examples.

My impression is that selection for groups takes insufficient account of this group-object relation. Interviews are likely to be focused on the more commonly recognised object relationships – to self, to other, and to two others – with little recognition of the supra-ordinate relationship to groups as social entities. Yet, exploration of this particular pattern may yield valuable and more precisely relevant information about prospective participation in a therapy group than the traditional areas stressed in the selection process. Brown (1991) adopts a similar perspective in his suggestion that when assessing for groups we consider the 'social birth of the person'. He refers here mainly to the family context in which the individual is born and the way this affects later group relationships.

A brief survey of individuals who were highlighted in previous examples as having a group-destructive orientation, and contributing to, if not leading, the anti-group, indicates powerful underlying disturbance in the group-object relation. For example, Alan, whose attack on Group B led to its demise, was isolated and virtually an outcast in his primary family group. He was a misfit in school and peer groups, and had a record of destructive behaviour in work groups. Alison, who in Group C evolved a pattern of contaminating communication, had intensely jealous relationships within her original family group, was deeply resentful of her marriage and embarked on an extra-marital affair which nearly destroyed another family. These are extreme examples but less extreme variations may also have important implications for group membership.

The emphasis here is on the individual's own group-object relation, but with an understanding that this is, in part, a product of the role he or she was required to take in groups, particularly the primary family group. Similarly, in therapy groups, such difficulties do not operate in a vacuum, but in interaction with others. In fact, the speed and intensity with which such destructive and self-destructive roles are established, in collusion with the group, make it all the more important to recognise the dangers in advance. Knowledge of individuals' group-object relation, including the past occurrence of specific processes such as bullying, victimisation, or scapegoating, may help to prevent casualties in the group and the group itself becoming a casualty.

The above proposals for selection criteria for groups – bonding capacity, the passion for proximity, and the group-object relation – encourage a move away from selection based on individually based variables, such as intelligence, psychiatric diagnosis, and simplistic personality classifications, to a systemic perspective of the group-defining characteristics that link a particular individual to the particular group in question.

There is an irony in the degree of emphasis that needs to be placed on the importance of group-related as opposed to individual-centred criteria when selecting for groups. This should be axiomatic but is not. A sub-theme in this book concerns the inconsistencies that have filtered into the professional practice of group psychotherapy, inconsistencies that suggest subtle but powerful forms of resistance and prejudice towards the group as a viable unit. The paradoxes surrounding selection may be another example of this.

Another inconsistency in the selection process is related to the context of selection. Selection for groups is typically made by the conductor in individual interviews with the client. But my experience is that people are often very different in the one-to-one context than they are in the group context. I have known individuals who are highly communicative in a dyadic situation to freeze up in groups and others who are reticent in the one-to-one to open up easily in groups. The transfer of impressions from one situation to the other is questionable. Further, even if an individual is judged as suitable for group therapy in general, there is no guarantee that he/she is suited to the particular group in question. The task of matching individual to group is an important one that lacks operational guidelines and relies largely on the personal intuition of the conductor. All sorts of subjective factors may enter into these decisions. The conductor carries the group transference and his own counter-transference and these phenomena may infiltrate the selection process. Where there is a strong anti-group dynamic present in the group, and possibly where the conductor himself has negative feelings towards the group, unconscious factors may adversely influence selection. In this case, the 'wrong' choice of an individual member may be unconsciously determined, adding to the potential for group-destructive processes.

The absence of more clear-cut selection criteria than currently exist, compounded by the relative neglect of group-related criteria that link the prospective member to the group in specific ways, renders the group selection process vulnerable to a variety of distortions and errors of judgement. The selection process may itself then become embedded in an anti-group matrix. The complexity of variables affecting the success of group membership ultimately makes it difficult to be prescriptive about selection criteria, but careful attention to the process and not only the content of selection may help to limit errors of judgement and, hence, the potential for pathological group development.

DROP-OUTS

Few events in the group are as symptomatic of an anti-group as drop-outs. Dropping out, particularly in the absence of forewarning or explanation, is an anti-group act in itself. It is indicative of dissatisfaction with the group, arising from excessive anxiety, frustration, or anger. It is usually experienced by the remaining members as an attack on the group, leaving them feeling rejected and abandoned. It tends to arouse doubts about the value of the group, as well as guilt about imagined responsibility for the loss. As noted in Chapter 3, dropping out can be contagious. The sudden departure of one member may be followed by another, producing a chain reaction which can rapidly deplete the group – 'like rats leaving a sinking ship' – and creating a real threat to the survival of the group. This also has a demoralising effect on the conductor, who is faced with the task of holding the group together and finding replacement members. Some degree of drop-outism is to be expected in a therapy group (Yalom 1975), but excessive drop-outism is usually a sign of a serious anti-group at work, and, in turn, contributes to an intensification of the anti-group.

Selection has been emphasised precisely for the above reasons. Flawed selection will increase the chances of dropping out: greater control of the selection process, particularly if carefully attuned to the needs of the specific group, is likely to minimise the rate of drop-outs.

Drop-outs must also be seen in terms of the group-as-a-whole. The drop-out, who is likely to embody a negative group-object relation, may be collusively chosen to enact an anti-group position, so that the remaining members can either confirm their commitment to the group by denying their ambivalence, or use the dropping-out to justify an escalating anti-group.

These observations have implications for the handling of drop-outs. Most therapists would probably agree with a relatively active approach to the drop-out, encouraging the participant to remain in the group wherever possible. The effort to retrieve the drop-out may be successful, helping to re-integrate the individual in the group. However, there are obviously limits to how far this can go: no amount of exhortation can bring back a member who is determined to leave. When the drop-out does leave, there is the question of how to handle the event in the group. My impression is that, after the initial surprise, disappointment, and anger, most groups quite quickly rally and proceed with the business of the group. This may be a healthy reaction, getting on with the repair of the group rather than dwelling on past disappointments, but there may also be a defensive aspect to it. Loss and feelings of abandonment may be denied, adding to the unspoken store of frustration and regret, later to emerge in a gathering anti-group. The opposite situation is where a drop-out or loss leads to a form of pathological mourning. This may happen when the circumstances surrounding the loss are unknown or mysterious or when an idealised member is experienced as taking something so important from the group that it can never be replaced. The event of a drop-out is therefore of considerable significance in the development of the group and careful attention should be paid to the group dynamics preceding and following the member's departure.

But there is a different and balancing perspective. The above discussion assumes that drop-outs are inimical to the progress of the group. If this is true in many cases, in others the reverse may apply. The group may strengthen in response to the leaving of a member who did not fit in with group norms and who, through a negative group-object relation, instigated anti-group developments. Such individuals often hold the group to ransom, drawing considerable attention to themselves and disturbing the progress of the group. Notwithstanding the strong possibility of projection onto this member by the rest of the group, and the need to illuminate this process, it may be in the group's interests – and those of the individual – to let this person go. Holding on may simply reinforce destructive group patterns.

> In the first few months of an out-patient group, Catherine's overwhelming anxiety about participation was apparent to all. She was terrified of having to speak and of being put on the spot. Her problem impeded the movement of the group since members frequently stopped to show Catherine

concern and support. Discussion about what the group was defensively doing in relation to Catherine was unproductive. It also led to Catherine blaming herself, only compounding her anxiety. When she first broached the subject of leaving the group, this was met by a wave of protest from group and conductor alike, who seemed to feel it was their responsibility to rescue Catherine and keep her in the group. However, when she finally did leave, after several more sessions, the group's disappointment was tinged with relief. The others could now get on with the work of the group. Furthermore, Catherine's departure made space for a new member of the group who turned out to be an excellent addition and helped to transform the atmosphere of the group.

In spite of the assertion that groups collude to create deviant members, a balancing principle emerges from the above – it is an illusion to believe that groups can cater for all members. Recognition of this limitation, with consequent exclusion of some members or acceptance of the loss of others, may be instrumental in the sifting process required to establish a cohesive, operative group. In this view, drop-outs may be seen as part of a natural process of group self-selection, offsetting errors that may have been made in the selection process. Spero (1986) concludes that drop-outs are a natural part of the group psychotherapy process and that their management by the conductor and remaining patients has therapeutic value. However, careful judgement is required to distinguish this from a destructive cycle of dropping out or from denial of the negative impact of an untoward loss. The group itself will usually help with this distinction, indicating through its progress or regression what the meaning of the loss might be.

PREPARATION FOR THE GROUP

It is generally accepted that a period of preparation, usually in a series of meetings with the conductor, is a useful preliminary to entry into the therapy group. Yalom (1975) suggests that this is an important way of correcting misconceptions about group therapy, including the notion that group therapy is second best to individual. He also recommends this as a way of establishing congruence between group goals and individual goals, helping the patient to see that commitment on his part enhances group cohesiveness and that this in turn will benefit him as an individual.

This is a sensible approach, but with one qualification. This concerns the patient's potential bonding within the dyadic format. Yalom sees this as helpful: in the group, the patients' identification with the conductor will encourage the acceptance of group goals and provide a stimulus for group participation. However, I have known cases in which the opposite occurred: the primary bonding with the conductor and the satisfaction with the individual sessions competed with group membership. In one case, a female patient who had had four preliminary meetings with the conductor lamented the loss of this exclusive contact and for months resisted involvement in the group. This situation is akin to patients who progress from individual to group therapy but experience this as a loss rather than a gain. An example was seen in Group A (see Chapter 4, p. 82), in which two participants who had previously been in individual therapy with the conductor formed a hostile pairing group of their own. Individual preparation with the therapist may reinforce the idealisation of the one-to-one therapeutic relationship and the denigration of the group – a factor worth taking into consideration in the preliminary phase, even though preparation, in overall terms, is an important pre-therapy requirement.

Other forms of preparation for group therapy are less generally recognised and potentially more difficult to implement in the clinical setting. In particular, I am thinking of ways of dealing with commonly experienced communication difficulties in analytic psychotherapy groups. Many patients do not have, or feel they do not have, the verbal or expressive abilities to facilitate group participation. Although group-analytic therapy aims to promote communication across the group, this may run adrift where there are serious communication difficulties within the group, creating an unwelcome sense of exposure and invasion rather than support, as suggested in Chapter 3. Such difficulties may be offset by participation in a pre-therapy group, aimed at strengthening communication potential, possibly in a more structured, supportive way. In the psychology service I run, this happens informally when a patient attends a brief, focused group such as anxiety management or assertiveness and progresses on to a longer-term psychotherapy group. Quite often, these patients themselves ask for an extended and more exploratory group setting and my experience is that they enter the group better equipped than those who have no previous group experience. The positive experience in a preliminary or pre-therapy group can increase motivation and confidence about participation in a long-term analytic group.

A review of some basic technical considerations in running analytic psychotherapy groups raises many questions about the assumptions underlying group psychotherapy practice. There are indications that confusion and lack of clarity about procedures for setting up and maintaining the group may generate anti-group processes. It is also suggested that this confusion is, in part, symptomatic of the lack of an adequate conceptual and empirical model of group psychotherapy and that the gaps in theory and practice may unwittingly – or unconsciously – allow the infiltration of anti-group attitudes. At the same time, it is likely that due attention to these processes will help to limit the undue development of the anti-group. There is a considerable need for further conceptualisation and research and some pointers in this direction are suggested, particularly in the area of selection. The present state of confusion places considerable demands on the group conductor, whose role in handling the anti-group is crucial, and it is to this area that we next turn.

Chapter 8

The role of the conductor

The anti-group presents a formidable challenge to the group conductor. Whereas in the course of most long-term analytic groups, the therapist can take a reflective observer's position, or one in which he merges imperceptibly with the group, more active intervention is generally necessary when anti-group states predominate. As the conductor has chief responsibility for the maintenance, facilitation, and containment of the group, the nature of his interventions strongly influences the outcome of the anti-group. However, his interventions cannot be separated from his attitude to the group, including counter-transference responses evoked by the anti-group which can be intense, perplexing, and very difficult to manage. This chapter approaches the role of the conductor via two linked areas of consideration – the technical interventions available in dealing with the anti-group and the counter-transference issues that influence interventional style.

Foulkes (1964a) introduced the term 'conductor' in order to emphasise the facilitating as opposed to the directive role of the group therapist: he likened it to the function of an orchestral conductor. Linked to this, Foulkes encouraged a shift away from the authority of the conductor to that of the group, a process he described as a 'crescendo' in the authority of the group and a 'decrescendo' in the authority of the conductor (1964a). Although some group analysts, for example Behr (1995b), question the utility of the term, it is mostly regarded as a cornerstone of the group-analytic approach. The term 'conductor' distinguishes group analysis from other forms of group psychotherapy, but the content of this chapter is relevant to group psychotherapists in general, particularly where an analytic approach is practised.

THE CONDUCTOR'S INTERVENTIONS

Attitude to the anti-group

Without at this point delving too deeply into subjective factors in the conductor – as these are fully explored in the second section of this chapter – it is necessary to say something about attitude towards the anti-group. A fundamental consideration is whether the conductor agrees that a phenomenon akin to the anti-group exists. In my view, the therapist who expects unhampered progress in the group, combined with more or less unequivocal acceptance of the group setting on the part of the membership, is bound to be disappointed, frustrated, and potentially at a loss in leading the group. The conductor who is attuned to negative therapeutic processes, and the unique forms these can assume in the group, is more likely to regard the anti-group as a natural part of the group process and to be ready to meet it when it appears or to be aware of its potentially more insidious and pathological manifestations. Importantly, the membership will also take its cue from the conductor, repressing or expressing anti-group attitudes in line with what the conductor appears to accept.

Closely linked to this is the conductor's bias towards aggression as constructive or destructive. Of course, there are both constructive and destructive forms of aggression, as outlined in Chapter 6, but beyond this is the conductor's own tolerance of aggression in the group. Gans (1989) states that the positive value of hostility is often unappreciated and underestimated. He draws attention to the view of Slavson (1964), a pioneer in group therapy, that the expression of hostility is *the* most important therapeutic vehicle. Gans argues that expression of hostility is a sign of hope: anger can initiate change and lead to forgiveness, reparation, and a deepening of bonds. But a therapist who is anxious about aggression and fears it as destructive will inhibit its expression. There is also a difference between theoretical belief and personal tolerance. A group conductor may in theory accept the importance of aggression in the group, but balk at its expression, particularly if directed at himself, and this will override conceptual belief. The anti-group, like other forms of aggression, may arise suddenly and very powerfully in the group, and this can be very testing of the conductor's resilience.

The value of periods of conflict or instability in the group is supported by Hawkins (1986). Although periods of group instability, including erratic attendance and drop-outs, have a disorganising and demoralising effect on members, they also offer members the opportunity to explore the meaning of this in the context of discontinuities in their lives. Very often, the unstable group consciously or unconsciously evokes memories and feelings about early periods of instability in the holding environment. If this is understood and integrated, it can have a healing rather than disruptive effect on the members and the group. But this will, to a significant extent, depend on the conductor's reading of such events and what attitudes to group disruption and dissension he displays to the membership.

Recognising the paradoxical demands of the group

Acknowledging that there are some inherent contradictions and limitations in the group, as seen from the perspective of the participants, may help to address the deep frustration and disappointment that can lead to anti-group formations. Although much of the anti-group is fuelled by the constellation of psychopathology in the membership, it is, in part, a natural reaction to the problems created by the group. A conductor who fails to recognise this may react defensively to members' criticisms of the group and this may produce an unhelpful polarisation of views, the conductor seemingly very pro-group and the membership determinedly anti-group. Sharing an awareness of the group's limitations and contradictions with the membership may avoid the tendency to blame patients for their resistance and hostility and provide a means of encouraging them to examine what it is in *them* that responds so strongly to the complex requirements of group participation.

Maintaining the group position

One effect of the anti-group is to sabotage the group as a unit, so that attention is forced back onto individuals, pairs, and subgroups. The conductor may unwittingly be drawn into this, colluding with the rejection of the group frame. This may happen imperceptibly, since a shift in focus from group to individual and sub-group is part of the natural oscillation of the group process, with ongoing reversals of the figure–ground constellation. But this is different from an attack on the group position generated by the anti-group, and some effort is required on the part of the conductor to distinguish these processes and to maintain and restore the group position, where necessary.

In an NHS out-patient group, several members complained about the severe set-backs they had recently suffered. This was linked to the perceived inadequacy of the group as a treatment modality. There was general agreement that the help the group offered was very limited and superficial: some members believed that it actually made them worse through a process of contagion. One man described how he had felt much worse the previous week after hearing another's catalogue of fears and complaints.

As the group continued, members turned more and more to the conductor to engage him in one-to-one discussions. The conductor, himself worried by the degree of apparent regression in members of the group, became aware of being drawn into a series of dyadic interchanges, as if each patient was taking it in turn to have individual therapy with him. This recognition helped him to reverse the process by simultaneously engaging other members of the group and promoting group discussion. This created a horizontal spread of communication that re-invested the group with energy and interaction.

In this example, the threat to the group frame was enacted in the form of a dependency basic assumption: an idealised view of the conductor as the source of all help. As described in Chapter 3, the basic assumptions represent attempts at subverting the group task, so constituting an anti-group. The conductor needs to be watchful of the group's propensity to do this and his own susceptibility to collusion with anti-group processes. Maintaining the group position is a core component of this task.

The connecting function

The connecting function dovetails with the previous point about the group position. The effect of the anti-group is often a fragmenting one, splintering the connections between individual and group, feeling, thought and meaning, in a way that is captured in

Bion's concept of 'attacks on linking'. Given the complexity of the group process, and its many strands of conscious and unconscious mentation, this aspect of the anti-group can be particularly group destructive in its effect. Making connections, which includes synthesising and integrating, is a basic psychotherapeutic function, but it becomes especially important in the face of the disintegratory impact of the anti-group. The linking function needs to be strongly represented by the conductor, a point illustrated by Gordon (1994) and Hinshelwood (1994) and generally endorsed in the therapists' interventions described by Kennard *et al.* (1993).

> In the previous example, there appeared to be no connection between the different individuals who complained about their deterioration and perceived the group as failing to help them. They became more and more separate and isolated from each other, reflected in their striving to engage the conductor in one-to-one discussions.
>
> Recognising the compartmentalising effect this was having on the group, the conductor was also able to perceive a common thread that linked the individual stories. This concerned a sense of failure in the face of imminent and potentially valuable personal change, e.g. one patient was about to risk starting his own business, another was approaching the anniversary of his stopping alcohol abuse, and a third had recently entered a serious emotional relationship. The conductor pointed out the link between the participants' reactions, suggesting at the same time that breakthroughs in development are very challenging and may precipitate a temporary regression. The connecting comment produced a reaction of surprise and relief in several members, also evoking interest in each other through mutual identification. The theme was actively taken up by the group, as part of the renewed flow of the group.

The linking function is particularly relevant during times of group instability. Conditions and symptoms of group instability, such as breaks, erratic attendance, and drop-outs, tend to have a disruptive effect and, in an anti-group context, can lead to a severing of connections and an attack on the sense of group. When the group is unable to maintain connections, it is vital that the conductor continues to do so.

Positive connotation

In the example described above, the connections made by the conductor not only linked the separate members of the group but gave their negatively valenced experience a positive connotation. This helped participants to gain a more constructive perspective on their difficulties. The conductor's intervention also challenged their assumptions that the group had not helped them. Although not explicitly stated, the refocusing on their progress pointed to the help that the group had in fact given them. The act of recognising this connection, and the shared understanding generated by it, was itself a demonstration of the positive value of the group.

The technique of positive connotation or *reframing* is by no means unique to group therapy: in fact, it is more commonly practised in family therapy and other systemic therapies (Coyne 1985). But it may be particularly useful in dealing with the negativism of the anti-group. This could apply at the various systemic levels of the group. For example, at the individual-member level, a particular participant may be taking a distinctly strong anti-group position. Instead of this being interpreted in negative terms, the participant could be complimented on his courage to speak for the sceptical side of the group or even freeing the other members to relate constructively to the group by his holding the anti-group position.

Yalom (1975) advises the group therapist to draw attention, wherever possible, to the beneficial effects of the group, using individual members' gains as illustrations. He suggests doing this deliberately as a way of offsetting negativism and demoralisation in the group. This approach is more active and directly encouraging than is characteristic of a group-analytic approach, but the idea of highlighting the positive, even *in* the negative, may be of value in dealing with the anti-group.

Interpretation

There is less emphasis on the interpretative mode in group analysis than there is in individual psychoanalysis. Pines (1993) describes interpretation as 'a last resort' in group-analytic work. This is linked to an overriding belief in the integrative power of the group itself, the conductor's responsibility being to facilitate and empower the group rather than to make sweeping or penetrating interpretations – what Foulkes called 'plunging interpretations'. Horne (1992) describes the process whereby the group comes to make its own conscious, preconscious, and unconscious interpretations, providing an overall therapeutic function which includes but does not depend on the therapist. However, these considerations do not preclude the judicious use of interpretation by the conductor.

It seems to me useful to distinguish two main types of interpretation in group analysis – what I would call the broadly interpretative function and the focused interpretation. The broadly interpretative function I see as consisting of all the aforementioned interventions – connecting, reframing, integrating – that serve to make coherent sense of otherwise disconnected and inchoate material. There is little doubt about the value of these forms of interpretation in therapy groups in general and in relation to the anti-group in particular. The focused interpretation I see as more in the realm of analytic interpretation relating to unconscious phenomena and deeply rooted anxiety–defence constellations. Such an interpretation may be focused on the primitive aspects of the fantasy of the group as object, epitomised in the sorts of constructs described by Anzieu (1984), explored in a general way in Chapters 5 and 6 on the determinants of the anti-group and illustrated more fully in Chapter 9 on the transformational process.

However, there are dilemmas involved in adopting the interpretative mode in groups. The anti-group is a sign that the therapeutic alliance in the group, often in relation to the conductor, has broken down, and, with it, the capacity for reflection and insight. Making an interpretation in this context, particularly about deep-rooted disturbances, may therefore be counterproductive, fuelling rather than assuaging some of the primitive forces that generate the anti-group. This includes feelings about the act of interpretation itself, including envy of the conductor and hatred of the content of the interpretation, particularly if it touches on vulnerabilities that the anti-group seeks to conceal. On the other hand, interpretation that is sensitively judged in terms of acceptability and meaningfulness to the group, particularly if addressed to the collaborative capacity of the membership (in so far as an element of this is likely to exist even in the face of the anti-group), may go some way towards putting the anti-group into perspective. Congruence, timing, and the manner of the interpretation are as important, at least, as the act of interpretation itself.

Similar considerations apply to the question of group interpretations, i.e. interpretations which are addressed to the group-as-a-whole. Group interpretations of this sort are less a part of the group-analytic model than they are of the Bion–Tavistock tradition. Yalom (1975) calls these 'mass group process commentary' and argues against their value. Pines (1993) similarly regards them as non-therapeutic. Those who are against group-as-a-whole interpretations tend to see them as having an alienating effect on the group. On the other hand, Anthony (1983), one of the founders of group analysis, points out that group interpretations can have a 'groupifying' effect, bringing the group together in a spirit of mutual identification and shared understanding. In the anti-group situation, this may be a useful way of counteracting the splintering effect on the group and encouraging a group identification other than through the shared negative identification predicated on an anti-group.

Further questions concern the directness with which the anti-group is addressed. Is the term 'anti-group' used by the conductor? Are the characteristics of the anti-group spelt out to the group? Is negative group behaviour directly interpreted in anti-group terms? My own practice is not to refer to it directly, or to use the term as such, since this may encourage a concretisation and simplification around the concept in the group, when what is required is a greater understanding and control of the processes that the anti-group sets in motion. This is similar to the approach Brown (1985) suggested in relation to dealing with the basic assumptions in groups: highlighting process rather than encapsulating a set view of the group. Of course, intervention styles and contexts vary. A group facilitator reported that it was very useful to introduce the concept of the anti-group, in so many words, into a difficult staff support group she was running. But context may be the issue here: what is relevant and useful in a staff group may not be so in a therapy group.

Where the anti-group construct is incorporated in an interpretation to the therapy group, it is probably most usefully linked to an overall understanding of the process which interconnects symbolic and transference elements in the individuals and the group as a whole. The following is an example of a focused interpretation which aimed at identifying and analysing an anti-group process, but on the basis of broader interpretative interventions that preceded the deeper interpretation.

In this once-weekly NHS out-patient group, there had been several weeks of particularly erratic attendance. This was marked by an attitude of indifference on the part of absentee members. They did not generally notify the group about their absences and, when they returned to the group, they offered little if any explanation for being away. The group felt distinctly unstable and there was a barely concealed view that it was all a waste of time.

One ongoing theme in the group concerned the absence of adequate emotional care in participants' early lives. Most members felt neglected or cruelly dominated as children. This was exemplified by Brendan, who had remained preoccupied with the way his mother had fostered him and his siblings out when they were small children.

In this session, the focus shifted from children being cared for by parents to children caring *for* parents. This was particularly the case with elderly parents. Helen described her great resentment at having to look after her elderly father who was ill and very demanding. Helen's mother had died when she was young and Helen had felt that she was deprived of maternal care. This link was revived and clarified in the group, the conductor suggesting that Helen's resentment at caring for her father was compounded by her sense of never having been adequately cared for herself, particularly by her mother.

Brendan then described a return of his 'phobias' about drinking and eating food that had been prepared by other people. He believed that the drinks were laced and the food poisoned. The group discussed this for a while, and the conductor suggested that Brendan's 'phobias' about food and drink might represent an underlying feeling that, emotionally, his rejecting mother had poisoned rather than nurtured him and his siblings.

Towards the end of the group, two members announced that they would be absent the following week, one of them for several weeks in a row. Some other members complained about the poor attendance at the group and there was a lurking feeling that the group might disintegrate.

The conductor drew several themes together into a focused interpretation concerning the anti-group that was made in two or three stages. This was that the members were behaving in an uncaring way towards the group, like neglectful, even cruel, parents to a child or child to parents. In fact, they were treating the group as badly as they had felt treated as small children. The problem was that by not looking after the group, they were in a sense poisoning it: the group could not survive without their attention and attendance. Instead, it might weaken and die. The difficulty was that, faced with a poisoned group, they might well not want to return – to see it might be to face the parts of themselves they felt had almost died from emotional neglect and this was very painful. The interpretation resonated deeply within the group.

The core of this interpretation concerned a developing anti-group, seen here in the light of a process of projective identification that imbued the group with the destructive properties of a depriving and neglectful parent–child relationship. The anti-group represented the failure – the 'poisoning' – of the container–contained relationship. The interpretation aimed at understanding the members' projections onto the group and giving these back in a modified and acceptable form. Overall, this was a complex interpretation with a group-as-a-whole emphasis but this was made on the basis of preceding interpretations concerning individual members, so that it did not appear suddenly as a 'plunging' interpretation. It also incorporated the imagery and symbolism in the group material, making the interpretation congruent with the language, themes, and metaphors of the group. Further, it was integrative, in that it linked several dimensions – individual to group, past to present, and symbolism to reality. It is presented as an illustration of how the interpretative mode, in both its broad and its focused forms, can be employed in dealing with the anti-group.

Dealing with aggression

Problems of aggression and hatred are an inherent part of the anti-group, as discussed in a previous section on the determinants of the anti-group (Chapter 6, pp. 143–6). It follows that dealing with the various manifestations of aggression in the group is crucial. The subject of aggression *in* groups has been considered more fully in the literature than aggression *towards* groups, and what follows is a combination of impressions gleaned from other writers and my own further reflections on the subject.

An initial requirement is the location of aggression in the group. The concept of location, as formulated by Foulkes (1968), is in my view a very useful but under-used one. It is also very relevant in dealing with group aggression. As previously mentioned, the anti-group can be seen as an accumulation of aggressive responses springing from a variety of different sources in the group and condensed into the anti-group. I use the term 'defensive agglomeration' to describe this process. Handling the anti-group in the first place then requires a deconstruction of this process and a disentangling of the various sources of aggression in order to locate the main focus or focuses of aggression. A number of previous examples described the expression of aggression at the individual, pair, sub-group, and group-as-a-whole levels, illustrating how insufficient recognition of these particular conflicts resulted in a displacement of aggression onto the group. These examples demonstrated how the anti-group concealed aggression occurring at alternative levels within the group. The more these can be identified and tackled independently, the less likelihood there is of a mass attack on the group itself. Unchallenged and unresolved aggression in all these spheres confirms fears and fantasies of the group's destructive power and can end up projected irrevocably onto the group.

A second requirement concerns the differentiation of various kinds of aggression. In the section on pathological aggression (Chapter 6, pp. 143–6), differing degrees of aggression, such as anger, rage and hatred, were linked to differences in their dynamic origins and intentions. Recognising these differences may be helpful in adopting a method of dealing with the aggression in the group. For example, anger is more readily communicable and understandable than other forms of aggression and, with minimal intervention on the part of the conductor, may be resolved through group interaction. Rage and hatred are more deep-rooted and the aggression contained in them more destructive in intent. These characterologically based reactions represent a greater therapeutic challenge and require a deeper understanding on the part of the conductor. The judicious use of interpretation may be important here.

Not only is it useful to differentiate different forms of aggression, but there is also the notion of *differentiated aggression*. This is Fairbairn's term (1952) to describe aggression, or libido in general, that is directed towards the object in a clear, decisive form. Psychoanalytically, it is analogous to biting in the later oral stage of development as contrasted with sucking in the early oral stage. In the group, as Rogers (1987) points out, biting is saying what you think. It is the direct expression of feeling as opposed to the concealment and displacing of feeling that occurs in undifferentiated and displaced aggression. It is important for the conductor to encourage the expression of differentiated aggression in the group, so as to offset the tendency for aggression to be diffused and redirected into the anti-group.

Some useful aspects of handling aggression noted by other writers include:

- *Understanding hostility and aggression in terms of the developmental stage of the group* (Gans 1989)

The various stages of the group are characterised by different tensions and frustrations, in turn creating differing forms of aggression. For example, the 'stranger anxiety' and sensitivity at the start of the group elicits a different form of hostility from the struggle for control and power in the subsequent stage. The first may generate hostility born out of fear, the second aggression arising from rivalry for dominance.

- *Recognition of the defensive function of hostility and aggression* (Rosenthal 1987)

Aggression can be utilised as a resistance to work in the group at an individual, sub-group, or group-as-a-whole level. Aggression may hide considerable anxiety about exposure and intimacy. It can also be seen as an indirect or disguised communication of unexpressed, even opposite, feelings. For example, hostility may emanate from feelings of being frustrated by important others who are loved and admired. Here, aggression may be seen as arising from the frustration of relationship needs, as described in Chapter 6, and serving a defensive or self-protective function.

- *The conductor drawing the aggression onto himself* (Ormont 1984)

    Members' aggression in and towards the group may be displaced from the conductor, who is the original source of frustration. Where the aggression becomes particularly stuck, as in the scapegoating of a member, it may have an unblocking effect if the conductor redirects the aggression back onto himself. Expressing direct anger towards the conductor is one of the most difficult things to do in a group and the conductor's ability to handle this openly and constructively is an important containing and modelling experience for the group (Tuttman 1994).

None of these approaches in themselves provides the whole answer to dealing with destructive aggression in the group, but they do offer the conductor a measure of control in understanding and tackling the ramifications of aggression. This is an important counterbalancing force to the disorganising impact of the anti-group, where this is linked to excessive problems of aggression. Particularly if these methods serve to empower the group-as-a-whole, they are worth building into the conductor's repertoire of interventions.

THE CONDUCTOR'S COUNTER-TRANSFERENCE

Conducting an analytic group generally requires close monitoring by the conductor of his personal reactions, and this requirement is heightened by the anti-group. Ashbach and Schermer (1987) have commented, 'The group leader ... is subjected to particular counter-transferential pressures centred around group issues as well as individual transferences. In particular, massive projective identification onto the leader and the struggle for separation from him present particular problems which test the limits of his *neutrality, empathy, and forbearance*' (pp. 6–7, italics mine). Hence, although the previous section suggested ways of approaching and intervening in relation to the anti-group, the use of these approaches will in large measure depend on the conductor himself, what personal responses are evoked in him, and how these are translated into interaction with the group.

In overall terms, we return to the issue of containment. As therapist, the conductor fundamentally represents the containing function of the group. In the course of ordinary group development, this function is to a large extent assumed by the group, as it grows stronger and more autonomous. But in the anti-group condition, the containing function of the group breaks down and there is added pressure on the conductor to supply this. The conductor may find himself very challenged. The anti-group is likely to evoke powerful feelings in him too, stirring up a host of conscious and unconscious attitudes that threaten his capacity to 'hold' the group, in particular testing his 'neutrality, empathy and forbearance'.

These considerations bring us directly into the area of the conductor's counter-transference. There are differing views of counter-transference. Kernberg (1965) drew a distinction between the 'classical' approach, in which the therapist's counter-transference is seen as an unconscious resistance to the patient's transference, and the 'totalistic' approach, which views counter-transference as the therapist's more general response – thoughts and feelings, conscious and unconscious – to the therapeutic encounter. The classical approach sees counter-transference as an impediment to the analysis: the totalistic approach regards counter-transference as a valuable adjunct. Both psychoanalysis and group analysis have moved closer to the second perspective. Linking this to the group and the varying expressions of counter-transference, Prodgers offers a wide definition:

> Counter-transference may be seen as the conductor's emotional response to the group and particular individuals in the group, within the context of the conductor's own personality and training analysis.
>
> (Prodgers 1991, p. 398)

Various aspects of this definition will be highlighted in the discussion below.

The conductor's identification with the group

Is the anti-group also anti-conductor? Various alternatives are possible. In some cases, there is an apparent split between group and conductor: the group is bad, the conductor is good. In other cases, there is a close symmetry between the two: group and conductor are both bad. The conductor is often blamed for creating the anti-group.

The conductor is very likely to identify with the group – it is his idea, indeed his creation – and there is naturally an investment in the development and success of the group. In part, this reflects altruistic wishes towards the group, but, in part, it reflects a narcissistic identification with the group, in which the success or failure of the group is seen by the conductor as a reflection of his own competence as a group therapist. The conductor's self-esteem is at stake, and, particularly if there are deeper than usual narcissistic needs in the conductor, the effect on him of the anti-group may be devastating. The therapist's narcissistic vulnerability may be one of the most decisive factors in group psychotherapy. The conductor's loss of confidence in himself and the group may weaken considerably his containing function, even his will to continue. This is aggravated by projective identification and counter-identification (Grinberg 1973), in which messages from group to conductor and vice versa are transmitted in a noxious mirroring process.

Problems arising from the conductor's over-identification with the group are just one indication of the need for therapist differentiation in this complex setting. This will be determined by the conductor's own degree of ego identity and self-awareness and points to the importance of the training analysis in shaping the link between self and therapist identity. As in any analytic work, problems unresolved by the training analysis are likely to find their way into the implementation of the therapeutic role.

The conductor's group-object relation

In Chapter 6, I suggested that it would be useful to develop the concept of an individual's group-object relation as distinct from more usually recognised one-, two-, and three-person relationships. The group-object relation describes the internal representation of groups that is the product of the individual's group history and the way his attitudes towards groups have been externalised and enacted in the social milieu. This will determine responses to present group situations, usually in a way that confirms the internal representation. Like everyone else, the conductor has his group-object relation and the fact that he is a group therapist does not mean that his internal representation of groups is uncomplicated or resolved. If anything, he may have chosen this field as a way of working out problems in his own relationship to groups.

The anti-group can be seen as rooted in the negative internalised representations of the group. For all his training and personal group analysis, the conductor may be struggling with his own anti-group. If this is the case, the emergence of the anti-group in the therapy group may be very difficult to cope with, mirroring his own ambivalence and hostility towards the group. This may be compounded by the sense of narcissistic injury described above. Difficulties of this sort may be encountered by therapists who undertake a group training after having practised a different form of therapy, particularly individual. For some, the transition may be a smooth one, but for others there may be a conflict of therapeutic values. Mayer Williams (1966) described the struggle trainees had in adopting a *group* therapeutic frame and the way this was exacerbated in those with an individual therapy background.

Part of the group-object relation is the capacity to keep the group in mind. This notion highlights the individual's capacity to construe groups as entities and to maintain a group construct. In both cognitive and emotional terms, this is a complex achievement. In Piagetian terminology (Inhelder and Piaget 1958), it requires the development of 'formal operations', which are the basis of abstract thinking, since the group itself is an abstract concept. Emotionally, the complex demands associated with a group may make it difficult to hold in mind.

The following example from my own experience illustrates the ongoing struggle to maintain the group as object and to keep it in mind.

> An experiential training group I was running was due to resume after an unusually long end-of-year break. I had found this an excellent group and one I had greatly enjoyed conducting. To my surprise, I found that, as the time to resume drew nearer, I was reluctant to return. I felt a strong burden of responsibility towards the group. I also had difficulty imagining it as a group and could call forth only fragmented impressions of the group.

On reflection, I realised that I was feeling overwhelmed by groups in general. During the break, I had had experiences in my family group, work group, and social group that had all been demanding and difficult, that had left me with a sense of the fragility of groups and the problems of taking a leadership role in groups. I feared having to concentrate and get involved in the training group all over again. I feared being invaded and swallowed up.

Back in the group, it was striking that a large part of the membership felt the same way. They found it difficult to disentangle themselves from the rest of their lives and re-involve themselves in the group. At first, there was silence and resistance, but gradually, as these feelings came to light and were explored, the group re-established itself. I wondered if the impasse had signified a deeper anti-group that was concealed by the collaborative and cohesive nature of the group. Perhaps the real violence in the group had not yet surfaced. In the next term, this became a conscious issue in the group. Holding the group in mind may be complicated by a conscious or unconscious sense of the aggression lurking in the group.

The leadership role

The above example points to another crucial dimension of the conductor's group counter-transference – the way he experiences and implements the leadership role, at both conscious and unconscious levels. Training influences this, but more unique personal features undoubtedly determine the perception and enactment of this role. The leadership function emanates from the deeper recesses of internalised models of authority. These may contain powerful and primitive elements that conflict with the civilised function of being a group analyst. They are all the more likely to be stirred up by the anti-group with its demands and attacks. The regressive impact is unlikely not to touch the conductor. In order to maintain the therapeutic stance, he has to balance his own regressive tendencies with the leadership function required of him. His own anger, rage, fear, cruel-authority parts and anxious-dependent parts all threaten to derail his leadership.

The challenge to leadership is underlined by the complexity of the group process and its tendency towards fragmentation. As

Brigham (1992) points out, the multiple membership of the group results in a regression to part-object relationships which can have a schismatic effect on the group. The leader has a crucial integrating function in these circumstances: his leadership is required as a way of pulling the group together. But how this is done, and the extent to which it is achieved, depends on qualities in the conductor. He needs to maintain a position of neutrality, to keep the whole group in mind, and to avoid splitting in his response to the group members. When groups function well, they usually provide this integrating function themselves, but, at times of stress and fragmentation, there are particular pressures on the conductor to fulfil this role. This may challenge deeply his own degree of ego integration as well as his capacity to maintain an integrated group-object relation.

Group analysts prefer the notion of conducting the group to that of leading it (Foulkes 1964a). While this has valuable implications for the facilitation of the group, it can obscure the fact that crucial elements of leadership are subsumed within the conductor's role. Unrecognised, the leadership function may generate significant difficulties, particularly in the face of the anti-group with its implicit challenge to authority and its intense projections onto the leader. These issues are further explored in Chapter 9 on the group transformational process.

The conductor and projective identification

The central significance of projective identification in the group process closely links group and conductor in an ongoing system of psychic attributions. It is important that this is seen as a two-way process, since it is not only the group that projects onto the conductor but the conductor who projects onto the group, a point that emerges in several papers on projective identification in group therapy, e.g. Roitman (1989) and Zender (1991). We have already explored the former situation: the significance of the conductor's containing function in relation to the membership's projective identifications and the problems arising if this breaks down, particularly if the group is left to carry intolerable affects and conflicts: a blueprint for the development of the anti-group. But what of the reverse situation, when the group is the recipient of the conductor's projective identification?

In a general way, Foulkes (1964a) was impressed by 'the

overwhelming influence' of the conductor on the group. More particularly, he was concerned about the effect of the beginner on his group, seeing the novice conductor as especially prone to making the group reflect his own inner conflicts. Foulkes (1964a, p. 162) described a situation in which the individuals in the group all became 'personifications of part aspects of the conductor', e.g. 'the shadow', 'the scapegoat', 'the conductor's favourite', and 'the conductor's assistant'. Foulkes referred to these as forms of counter-transference, but Prodgers (1991) correctly points out that this is more in the nature of projective identification on the part of the conductor than counter-transference.

Foulkes believed that, with experience and further analysis, the therapist will be able to avoid grossly projecting onto the group membership. That personal and/or group analysis helps in this process is undoubtedly true, but the resolution is never complete and freedom from projective identification, both as receiver and giver, is an illusion. Even experienced therapists run into difficulties of this sort, if only because each group is unique and evokes particular responses from the conductor. It is important to recognise that projective identification between group and conductor can work both ways. Given the conductor's paramount responsibility for shaping the group, through selection, composition, administration, setting group norms, and interpretation, there is enormous scope for the conductor's projections onto the group. The conductor may be the unconscious instigator of an antigroup, through projective identification of complex, disavowed parts of himself, probably within the domain of the group-object relation. But equally in groups with a given membership where the conductor was not responsible for setting up the group, such as in training contexts, the outcome of anti-group developments will be strongly influenced by the conductor's projective counteridentification.

The conductor and aggression

Technical aspects of dealing with aggression have been considered in the section on the conductor's interventions. However, this is incomplete without taking full account of the countertransference phenomena evoked by group aggression.

When assessing the conductor's response to aggression, a distinction must be made between a theoretical belief system and the experiential impact of dealing with aggression. Most therapists of a psychodynamic persuasion would probably endorse the value of recognising and expressing aggression in psychotherapy. However, this is different from engaging fully with aggression in the therapeutic encounter. In groups, the suddenness, intensity, and amplification of aggression can be disturbing and threatening to all concerned, including the conductor.

The way the conductor deals with his own aggression is probably a strong determinant of his response to aggression in the group. The extent to which he externalises or internalises anger and aggression, his sensitivity to perceived aggression, his quickness to aggressive response, his anxiety about aggression, his sado-masochistic tendencies are all potent factors in influencing his interactions with the group and the culture established around aggression.

Tuttman (1994), in a commendably open way, explores the impact of the conductor directly expressing his aggression in the group. Particular difficulties arise if the communication of inappropriate aggression on the conductor's part leads to a derailment of his therapeutic stance. Gans (1989) describes several such situations: the leader may collude with the group in scapegoating a hated member; he may respond with retaliation to a group attack; angry challenges to his authority may provoke the leader to control or criticise a rebellious member; unable to distinguish destructive from healthy expressions of hostility, the leader may fail to set limits, thereby permitting abusive interactions to take place. Limit setting can be a vital intervention in dealing with the anti-group. There may be times when the conductor needs to intervene actively in order to stop destructive acting out and his judgement about such events will be influenced by his personal response to group aggression.

A parallel tendency exists in the leader's inhibition of aggression for defensive reasons. He may demonstrate his preference for a 'good group' rather than a hostile group by encouraging norms which emphasise caring and discourage real anger. Through reaction formation, he may turn retaliatory impulses into apparent love, relinquishing the opportunity to work through aggression. Sceptical of the benefits of aggression, in spite of theoretical beliefs to the contrary, he may encourage premature closure. Out of a need to be liked, he may fail to recognise hostility disguised as idealisation. Anxious to be a 'good conductor', he may discourage appropriate expressions of hostility such as dissatisfaction with anti-therapeutic norms, anger over real violations of self by others, and critical responses to therapist mistakes (Gans 1989).

To sum up, the conductor's difficulties with aggression may result either in his encouraging inappropriate, destructive expressions of aggression in the group, including his own, or in his inhibiting appropriate and useful aggressive responses. Either way, the group will be felt to be unsafe and either way may be a route to the anti-group. According to Winnicott (1949), 'hate in the counter-transference' is a natural response to the demands made of the analyst and owning such hatred is an essential part of the analytic process. This is at least as relevant in group analysis as in individual analysis. In the group, the intensity of hate in the counter-transference, in proportion to group processes of amplification and intensification, can be especially powerful and the need for self-monitoring correspondingly important.

Professional and training issues

Prodgers (1991) refers to an aspect of the conductor which he calls the 'professional counter-transference'. This represents the particular biases and blind spots of the school of psychotherapy to which the conductor belongs. As Kennard *et al.* (1993) have shown, training influences the nature of the conductor's interventional style in conscious and acknowledged ways. But it may also influence the conductor at a deeper level, equivalent to what Bollas (1987) called the 'professional *unconscious* counter-transference'. This describes those aspects of psychoanalytic training and practice that become internalised without conscious awareness.

I have previously suggested (Chapter 2, pp. 27–30) that, if there is a single, dominating blind-spot in group analysis, this is the idealisation of the group, coupled with a denial or neglect of its destructive aspects. Prodgers (1990) sees this as an overemphasis on the positive aspects of mothering. Karterud (1992) suggests that the idealisation of groups in group analysis is linked to the idealisation of the founder, Foulkes. Either way, there is an institutionalised professional counter-transference that may get in the way of perceiving the destructive potential of the group and of equipping the conductor adequately to deal with it.

Another aspect of the training context is the conductor's transference to his own training analyst. Prodgers suggests that this is seldom resolved. Since all therapists internalise their training and, at some level, their own therapist, unresolved (positive) transference may result in split-off hostile intra-psychic processes based on identification with the aggressor. These processes may engage the conductor in unconscious retaliatory action if material sensitive to his unresolved transference emerges in the group. I would suggest that the aggressive aspects of transference and counter-transference may be especially problematic in group-analytic training, especially in relation to the institutionalised, idealised group-object relation that tends to influence the culture of group analysis, potentially making it difficult at a fundamental level to get to grips with the anti-group.

The need for support

Groups in which there is a dominating anti-group take a considerable toll on the conductor. The confusion of self and group, the ravaged self-esteem, the sense of powerlessness, and the struggle to contain one's own hatred and aggression, all within the complex system of personal and professional issues described above, can be deeply perplexing. This points to the essential need for supervision and support. Supervision, which may be on a formal or an informal peer basis, should help to clarify the group process, the source of the anti-group, and the conductor's role in exacerbating or assuaging it. It should lend support when the anti-group seems overwhelming and unmanageable.

The need for support in this situation is closely linked to the concept of the group as a holding environment. The conductor needs holding if he is to facilitate the holding capacity of the group. This is akin to Winnicott's (1960) description of the mothering task, in which the mother needs to be supported by the father (or substitute), the wider family, and the community in general, if she is to give of her best to the infant.

Considering supervision beyond the training context, Behr (1995a) asks whether this should be regarded as an essential part of professional practice or a luxury which few can afford. On the basis of all that has been said, I would argue the former.

The consequences of a lack of support and supervision in the face of a strong anti-group may be highly unfavourable. The conductor is likely to become increasingly drawn into a destructive enmeshment with the group, in which objectivity and the capacity for repair are gradually destroyed. There was a vivid illustration of this in Group G, the student psychotherapy group, in which the conductor experienced a rising sense of helplessness and despair in response to the relentless attacks on her and the group. She recognised her need for support and supervision only when the group was practically over and it was too late. By then, she had suffered a severe blow to her confidence and an erosion of her belief in the salvageability of the group.

It seems fitting to end this chapter on a note emphasising the importance of the holding environment. In one way or another, most of, if not all, the aspects of dealing with the anti-group covered in the last two chapters are related to this – the physical environment of the group, the maintenance of group boundaries, the impact of the host organisation, the interventions aimed at containing through clarification, linking, and interpreting, and, finally, the role of the conductor as a person who needs to be securely held in his own personal and professional matrix. Of course, this process is seldom perfect or complete, in the same way that the group itself cannot provide perfect holding. In fact, this itself is a vital part of psychotherapy, since it is in the spaces between, the inevitable areas of frustration and disillusionment, that much of the therapy actually takes place – a theme that will be developed in the next chapter on group transformation. At best we can aim, like Winnicott's universal mother, to be 'good enough', recognising that at least a degree of failure is inevitable and that this can be helpful, if openly admitted to ourselves and shared in a supportive environment.

Chapter 9

The transformational potential of the anti-group

Previous chapters have emphasised the destructive power of the anti-group and have suggested ways of minimising or harnessing it. But a qualification has constantly been brought forward: that the anti-group has a crucial place in the creative transformation of the group. This chapter explores this thesis more fully. It is suggested that the anti-group forms an essential part of the dialectic of creative and destructive forces in group psychotherapy, that it is in the movement between the two poles that the group develops, and that it is in the opposition of thesis and antithesis that a new synthesis, a transformation, may take place. In the complex system that is the developing group, the antagonistic force of the anti-group helps to shape the identity of the group, to define it as an autonomous and self-regulating system, and to evolve its therapeutic value system. It helps to strengthen and deepen the crucible of change that is the therapy group.

There is a growing interest in the psychotherapy group as a transformational experience, in terms of both the group as an entity (Zinkin 1989; Rance 1992; Powell 1994) and personal transformations within the group (Boyd 1991; Lear 1991). This is a natural corollary of the therapeutic task, since transformation is closely linked to therapeutic progress, but it could be argued that the group has particular transformational properties given its depth and width: it reaches deeply into the intra-psychic *and* social origins of self, while enhancing intersubjective relationships and becoming, as Jacobson (1989) puts it, 'an object in the cultural field'.

The view of the analytic group as a transformational process is in line with a tradition of philosophical thought on the 'logics of change' (Morgan 1986). Much of this theoretical background emanates from the work of scientists and philosophers who have explored the processes of change at a universal level. Bohm (1980), for example, presents a model of reality as constantly changing, with flux and transformation at the heart of change.

In group analysis, the transformational perspective is rooted in Foulkes' vision of the group matrix. The transpersonal qualities of the matrix, in which elements of culture, history, mythology, and the personal and collective unconscious all coalesce, interconnecting the lives of eight or more people, and traversing the domains of past, present and future, provide the basis for transformation. The unfolding of the group matrix is in essence a process of transformation. Exploring the different meanings of the word 'matrix', Roberts (1993) emphasises its definition as a 'place where something with structure, often alive and perhaps extremely valuable, is held during its formation or transformation' (p. 93). Roberts goes on to suggest that 'the group matrix can be viewed as a context in which a safe and remarkably deep regression may be obtained, with a potential for enabling a significant new formation or transformation of major personality elements' (p. 93).

To what extent, and how, do aggression and destructiveness figure in the transformation? De Maré *et al.* (1991), outlining their vision of koinonia in the large group, describe the transformation of hate as essential to this process. They make the point that hate constitutes valuable psychic energy which seeks and is capable of transformation. In contrast to Bion (1961), who suggests that frustration – and hate – essentially have to be tolerated, de Maré *et al.* believe that such passive acceptance could result in chaos and meaninglessness. Therefore, the therapeutic system must be structured in a way which can contain and transform hatred. They see the structuring of the large group as facilitating dialogue, which in turn transforms hatred. While I agree with these views about the transformational potential of hatred, and their general points about structuring and containment, I see the process of transformation in different, perhaps more complex, terms. Verbalisation and dialogue are important aspects of the process of transformation, but they are aspects rather than the whole picture. The transformational process in groups has important developmental and systemic aspects which go beyond the verbal realm and it is these that I now consider.

THE ELEMENTS OF TRANSFORMATION

The preceding observations illuminate the transformational potential inherent in the group matrix. However, Foulkes' broad conception of the matrix, tending towards the universal and the idealised, makes it difficult to distinguish the elements of transformation and to determine how the processes of change actually occur. In order to get a clearer picture of the process, it is necessary temporarily to step outside the group psychotherapeutic frame and to call on models of change and transformation that have alternative roots.

The following section is devoted to some key perspectives on transformation and change. Three main approaches are examined: the cybernetic model of mutual causality; the concept of autopoesis; and the dialectical perspective of change. These are complemented by more psychoanalytically based notions of development: the concept of reparation in the context of aggression and survival; the transformational object; and the transitional object/space. The place of the anti-group in each of these perspectives is examined, leading to an overall view of its paradoxical relationship with creative forces in the group.

The cybernetic model

This model emphasises mutual rather than mechanical causality: instead of A causing B, the relationship between A and B may be understood as a consequence of belonging to the same system of circular relations. The model has become incorporated in systems theory in general, but its relevance to the group process requires explication.

Maruyama (1963) focuses on the notion of positive and negative feedback in determining system dynamics. Negative feedback occurs when a change in the system initiates changes in the opposite direction, so balancing the initial change. This process is fundamental in maintaining stability in systems. Positive feedback, by contrast, occurs when a change triggers a spiralling escalation of change. Here, more leads to more and less to less. Together, these feedback loops explain why systems gain or maintain a given form and how this form will be transformed over time. The initial stimulus that sets the change in motion, in either a balancing or an unbalancing way, is described as a 'kick'. But such kicks are not in themselves the cause of the actual outcome. They trigger transformations already contained in the logic of the system.

This model offers a useful framework for understanding the anti-group in systemic terms. The anti-group can be seen as contributing a 'kick' to the evolving group system that triggers either negative or positive feedback, resulting in different outcomes, but determined by potential transformations that already exist in the group. Take, for example, the event of a drop-out, previously described as symptomatic of an anti-group process. Where this elicits 'negative' feedback, the rest of the group will rally and strengthen, counterbalancing the impact of the change occasioned by the member dropping out. However, it can also elicit 'positive' feedback: the drop-out instigates a chain of drop-outs and the group may be denuded of members in a short space of time. In either case, the outcome is influenced by the inherent potential of the group either to cohere and hold or to split and fragment.

This process can be linked to the notion of a latent and a manifest anti-group, more fully described in Chapter 3. The nature of the manifest anti-group (the conscious behavioural expression of anti-group forces) is determined by the strength of the latent anti-group (the reverse also applying in a system of circular causality). In itself, the relationship between the manifest and latent anti-group can be viewed as a transformational element, since this relationship is in flux and contributes to the development of the group. In turn, this highlights the fact that group transformation can be either constructive or destructive. Prodgers (1990) points out the threatening, destabilising aspects of transformation: this helps to guard against too narrow and idealised a view of transformation.

The relevance of the cybernetic model in this context is that it places the anti-group in a circular transformative relationship to the group rather than seeing it as a static entity that influences the group in a one-dimensional way.

The concept of autopoesis

Working within the constructivist tradition, Maturana and Varela (1980) coined the term 'autopoesis' to describe the ability of living systems to create and perpetuate themselves. The term is made up of the words 'auto' (self) and 'poesis' (creation, production). Autopoetic or living systems are defined by three principal features – autonomy, circularity, and self-reference. The aim of such systems is ultimately to produce and reproduce themselves: their own organisation and identity is the outcome. Their underlying quest is fundamental: to survive. This process is echoed in Cox and Theilgard's (1987) concept of 'poesis' – the creation of that which was not there before.

Maturana believes that because a living system is an autopoetic system it is also structurally determined. The overall organisation of a living system is maintained by the circular process of continuing self-referral, so that the changes it undergoes are determined by its own organisation and structure. This implies a phenomenon Maturana calls structural coupling: the relationship between a structurally determined system and the medium in which it exists. If an organism is able to continue functioning as a living autopoetic unity, it must be coupled to its medium: structural coupling is the basis of all human and animal interactional systems. The more complex the organism, the more 'structurally plastic' it can be, i.e. plastic in the sense of being able to make constant changes as a result of interacting within itself, its environment and other structurally plastic systems. A structurally plastic system will readily become richly coupled to its environment. Within this environment, other systems, through interaction, become increasingly coupled to each other. Among humans, many such systems are formed, in which the establishment of a consensual domain, generally based on language, leads to its identity as a 'family', 'club', 'school', and so on. Language can be regarded as a fundamental part of the structural coupling of human systems.

The concept of autopoesis is very relevant to understanding the analytic psychotherapy group. While the conductor initially conceives of and sets up the group, the aim of the group is to gain a large measure of autonomy, and to achieve structure, unity, and continuity as a group. Increasingly, its structure determines its development and character. The individual members of the group can be seen as structurally coupled to each other and the group, and the group itself becomes coupled to its environment. Language, of course, is the fundamental mode of communication in the psychotherapy group, establishing its consensual domain. In the same way that a family and a club are established and maintained through their own consensual language, as noted above, so a therapy group is born and bred through communication and, for as long as it remains structurally coupled, survives.

The anti-group can be seen as that part of the group which challenges its increasing self-referencing mode and structural coupling. Since the anti-group may be regarded as antagonistic to the evolving group culture, this can result in the destruction of the group, but, assuming it continues, there are two alternative outcomes: 1) there is a rejection of anti-group elements that conflict strongly with the group – they are not structurally coupled; 2) the challenge to the group results in an accommodation on the part of the group so that structures and processes in the group are changed accordingly. In both cases, the anti-group contributes to the evolution of the group, either as a negative force that paradoxically serves to define the group's existing structure and identity or as a contradictory force that is assimilated into the group, forming a new structure and identity. This is akin to what Maturana calls 'a new configuration of relationships'. In constructivist terms, the anti-group represents a 'perturbation' that causes a temporary deregulation of the group, with one of the two outcomes noted above or a combination of the two – some consolidation of existing structures and some accommodation in other structures. This view of the group as a living, sentient system parallels the cognitive structures described by Piaget (1952), in which maturation proceeds on the basis of assimilation and accommodation.

The concept of autopoesis contributes to the recognition of the anti-group as an essential parameter in the creation and continuity of the group.

The dialectics of change

Of the various theories presented here, the dialectical model is the most widely represented in group analysis (Cortesao 1991; Blackwell 1994; Brown and Zinkin 1994; Schlapobersky 1994). At the same time, the notion of the dialectic is very loosely applied in group analysis, serving as a broad principle to describe the link between complementary states. In this section, the dialectical perspective of the group is given a closer, more specific focus: that of the interplay or struggle between creative and destructive forces, seen as the ground upon which processes of integration and transformation can occur.

In order to establish a conceptual framework within which to explore this process, it is worth digressing briefly to examine the dialectical tradition of thought. An excellent summary is provided by Morgan (1986). He notes that any phenomenon implies and generates its opposite – good and evil, life and death, day and night, hot and cold are all pairs of mutually defining opposites. In each case, one side depends for its existence on the other: we cannot know cold without hot, day without night, and so on. Opposites interrelate in a state of tension that also defines a state of harmony and wholeness – the dialectical interplay paradoxically unites the opposites. Morgan suggests that this tension might be at the basis of all change, that flux and transformation could be an expression of contradictory tendencies through which phenomena change themselves.

The history of the dialectic can be traced back to ancient Taoist philosophy, which describes the way of nature (the Tao) as influenced by a continuous interplay of two opposites, *Yin* and *Yang*. These notions entered Western thought to become a recognised dialectical view of reality strongly associated with theorists such as Hegel and Marx. Reviewing the overall contribution of the dialectical standpoint, Morgan writes:

> A dialectical imagination invites us to embrace contradiction and flux as defining features of reality... encouraging us to recognise that the parameters of organisation define the rallying points for disorganisation, that control always generates forces of countercontrol, and that every success is the basis for a potential downfall.
>
> (Morgan 1986, p. 265)

The dialectical framework also ties in with a rich vein of thought in the development of psychoanalysis. Recently, a number of writers, including Thompson (1991), Ogden (1989, 1992a, 1992b) and Webb *et al.* (1993), have drawn attention to the dialectical perspective as central to the psychoanalytic discourse. Thompson's (1991) particular concern, as described in Chapter 6, is to reinforce Freud's theory of the death instinct in its dialectical relationship with the life instinct, thereby also clarifying its significance as a critical principle that counters the uncritical strand of conventional optimism in psychoanalysis. Webb *et al.* (1993) focus on the contribution of Lacan, who stated that 'psychoanalysis is a dialectical experience'. Lacan was especially concerned with the search for truth in the discourse between two (or more) subjects. Here, truth is seen as emerging not in any absolute sense but as a relative phenomenon in the movement between the speaking subjects.

But, within the psychoanalytic domain, it is Ogden (1992a, 1992b) who has elaborated most strongly and most clearly the dialectical perspective, proposing it as *the* frame of reference for the development of psychoanalytic theory. He traces the dialectical strand of thought as beginning with Freud and continuing through post-Freudians such as Klein and Winnicott. He then draws these themes together into a coherent statement of the dialectical process, which includes a notion of the decentring of self. Ogden sees the dialectic as a process in which opposing elements each create, preserve, and negate the other: each exists in a dynamic, constantly changing relationship with the other. Neither has any conceptual or phenomenological meaning except in relation to the other. Each interrelationship has the potential for integration but each potential integration generates a new form of dialectical tension. 'That which is generated dialectically is perpetually in motion: constantly in the process of being decentred from static self-evidence.' Here is the notion of the decentred subject referred to above, akin to Lacan's view that the phenomena of truth and self are suspended between the elements of a relationship in dialogue.

Within this perspective, Ogden views psychopathology as a collapse of the dialectic in the direction of one or other of the modes of generating experience. The tension of opposites in motion is lost: experience is dominated by a single mode of being. In the Kleinian model, for example, the predominance of either the paranoid-schizoid or the depressive mode is seen not as a developmental arrest but as the collapse of the dialectical movement between elements of experience.

Ogden's vision of the dialectics of experience provides a very apt framework for positioning the group-destructive mode in relation to the group-constructive mode, the relationship between the two seen as both mutually defining and mutually negating. Anti-group and 'pro-group' are the two poles of experience that define the development of the group. Within the interplay of the two, the group itself is decentred as a static object: it is constantly in movement between the opposing modes. The anti-group represents the collapse of the dialectic in the direction of destructive processes, leading to group pathology. The nature of the group pathology will vary in relation to the dominant mode of disturbed experience in the group. In line with the theoretical perspectives presented in Chapters 5 and 6, for example, this could take the form of fragmentation as part of a regressive response, the empathic gulf created by failures of communication, the deadness and despair of the depressive mode, the violence and surrender of the aggressive mode, or the combination of several such modes in the constellation of group-destructive development.

The adverse consequences of a collapse towards group-destructive processes are readily apparent. What are less obvious are the unfavourable outcomes of a collapse in the direction of group-cohesive forces. On the face of it, this would seem to be a contradiction in terms: group cohesion is generally regarded as a *sine qua non* for group development and is positively associated with group identification and commitment. These are ordinarily favourable conditions for the group but in their extreme form they also represent group pathology. Battegay (1976) describes the narcissistic process of self-investment in a therapy group that led to stasis and psychological impoverishment. Wong (1981) similarly describes a pathologically narcissistic group self associated with powerful resistance to change. In non-clinical groups, the dangers of excessive cohesion and commitment become even more apparent. Bohm (1981) has drawn attention to seeming stability and cohesion in social groups as having a deeply self-deceptive component. He sees this as harbouring a belief in the supreme value of perfection, without concessions or compromise. Although this may create strong group identification and cohesiveness in the short term, it renders the group vulnerable to powerful internal or external conflicts with other groups, which can lead to the disintegration of the group. Lifton (1981) suggests that excessive social cohesion in groups may conceal a striving for immortality. Here, a form of 'ideological totalism' is associated with an irrational defiance of death, of the sort enacted to destructive ends in cult groups such as those led by Jim Jones and David Koresh.

These are crucial observations. They highlight the dangers of an *absence* of group oppositional forces. In cases that tend towards the totalistic groups described above, the existence of an anti-group would provide a correcting and balancing force. Doubt and criticism of the group, its ideals and goals, would be a healthy part of the differentiation and survival of the group. This deepens our perspective of the anti-group. While, in some contexts, it may produce group pathology, in others it can provide the opposite, a bulwark against the hidden threats of excessive cohesiveness and over-zealous group commitment, threats that ultimately may trigger the complete disintegration of the group.

The same corrective function of the anti-group can be seen in psychotherapy and training groups. In the following example, a group that idealised itself had to painfully confront its disowned aggression and ambivalence.

> The first six months of this experiential group were marked by considerable progress, with an active and creative group atmosphere. The group itself was also increasingly idealised by its members. But there were hints that something was amiss. Some members felt threatened by the rate of positive change and the expectation of intense group intimacy.
>
> Attendance at the group started faltering. One male member, in particular, stayed away frequently. A scapegoating process set in as the other participants challenged and criticised him. The member in question began to express strong anti-group reactions, blaming the group for its attacks on him. This provoked further hostility from the group and a vicious circle of blame and counter-blame was established. At first, the group was united against the recalcitrant member. But gradually the others, partly in response to the conductor's interventions, began to recognise their own fear and dislike of the group and the times they wished to withdraw from it. This left the group more vulnerable, but it relieved the scapegoat of carrying all the hostility in the group. This resulted in a greater dialectical balance in which ambivalence was more strongly evident. Towards the end of the group, a fuller reconciliation of opposite feelings was achieved with a sense that the group had deepened rather than weakened in the process.

In this group, there was initially a tendency to collapse in the direction of the idealised. This was associated with split-off aggression becoming projected onto a scapegoat. Re-introjection by the group of its aggression was a turning point, producing more balanced development in the group-as-a-whole. As in social groups, the anti-group in the psychotherapy group is a necessary antithesis to the narcissistic over-investment in the group self. It restores the dialectical balance that is necessary, if not essential, for healthy group development.

The survival of the group

The dialectical perspective presupposes the continuous flow of the group, but there is the problematic question of whether, in the face of destructive forces, the group will actually survive. Attacks on the group are fuelled by the wish to destroy the hated and unsatisfying object(s) that the group represents. Underlying this may be a massive fear of catastrophic and annihilating loss. This may have intra-psychic origins, but is reinforced by actual life experiences of loss and abandonment, a constellation which may be enacted within the group. At its worst, the anti-group may succeed in destroying the group, so fulfilling the wish for *and* the dread of annihilation. But the reality is that probably only a limited number of groups actually disintegrate. Even in highly anti-group situations, there is usually enough constructive potential to keep the group alive. From this emerges a hypothesis that the experience of the group surviving in the face of considerable threat may itself be strengthening and contributory to the group's transformation. It confirms the life-giving properties of the group and the individuals in it; it offsets the terror of destructiveness and of being destroyed; and it establishes the group as a viable unit.

> In an NHS psychotherapy group, there was a repetitive cycle of frustration, attack, and hopelessness. Members were uncommitted and attended erratically, and, when present, perpetuated an attitude of distrust and demoralisation in the group. This reached a head when one member made a suicide attempt and another was involved in a motor accident which nearly left him seriously injured. The exact connection between these events and problems in the group was unclear, although the self-destructive element common to both was evident. The group reacted with considerable anxiety to the events and started taking the situation very seriously. The vulnerability of the individuals and the group as a whole struck home, but also a recognition that they had survived. Destructive and self-destructive tendencies

diminished as the group began to consolidate and develop along more reflective and caring lines.

In this example the threatened survival of the group was dramatised in events outside the group – a disturbing way for a group to be faced with responsibility for its self-destructiveness. In less dramatic ways, however, there are usually ongoing challenges to the survival capacity of the therapy group, for example, through drop-outs, irregular attendance, other forms of acting out, breaks that threaten the stability of an already fragile group, critical attacks on the group and conductor, and so on. The fact that the group normally continues and that the conductor and the members are not destroyed is powerful evidence that the life-thrust of the group can withstand these attacks.

This process is quintessentially captured in Winnicott's concept of 'the use of an object'. Linking this to the early mother–child relationship, Winnicott (1968) argues that the mother's capacity to survive the attacks of the infant gives substance to her identity as a separate person. This removes the mother from the sphere of the infant's omnipotent control into an independent existence of her own. 'In this way a world of shared reality is created.'

This concept is particularly relevant to the formation of the therapy group, since the group is initially a diffuse and unintegrated entity, needing time and commitment in order to gain substance and continuity. This is seldom a smooth, linear process, but a gradual oscillation, in which the destructiveness of the membership paradoxically contributes to the strengthening process by confirming the group's capacity to survive. Here, again, the anti-group is seen not as a self-limiting disintegrative force but as an integral part of the transformation of the group. This view also confirms the dialectical perspective of the group, since the threatened destructive 'collapse' may contain the seeds of survival and growth, generating and regenerating the constructive potential of the group.

The creation of the group

Beyond the survival of the group is the notion of the creation of the group. This links with Maturana's notion of autopoesis, described above, but takes account of the threat posed by the anti-group and the way in which this can be transformed into creative group relationships. Understanding of the dynamics of creativity has long recognised the intimate connection between the creative and the destructive (Storr 1972). Stokes (1965) described creation as a form of restitution following aggression. Hanna Segal (1990), who has written extensively about the origins of creativity, says, 'All creation is a recreation of a once loved and once whole, but now lost and ruined object, a ruined world and self.'

These views highlight the process of *reparation* as a core component of the creative act. This is based on the Kleinian concept of reparation as a successful outcome of the depressive position (Klein 1952), a view also taken up by Winnicott (1948). In healthy development, reparative wishes and actions emerge from the constellation of anxiety and guilt in the depressive position. In the case of the group, its survival in the face of disintegratory forces enhances personal responsibility for the group and generates reparative processes that serve the therapeutic development of the group. Symbolically, the group-mother is restored as a source of nourishment and containment and there is a diminution of envious and destructive attacks, with a corresponding increase in the capacity for concern. In the example of Group A, described in Chapter 4 and later in Chapter 10, the group not only survived the impact of destructive forces: it grew closer, more constructive and more concerned. Reparation is closely linked to the therapeutic endeavour, and its emergence from a potentially destructive matrix is a further endorsement of the developmental value of the anti-group.

This leads to a fuller consideration of the creative dimension of the group and the notion of the group itself as an aesthetic object. Several group analysts have written about this recently, all within a transformational perspective of the group. Cortesao (1991) describes the 'aesthetic equilibrium' of the group and links this to the aesthetic qualities of the early mother–child relationship. Rance (1992) proposes an ontological model for the group-analytic process, that of the 'aesthetic transformation'. Here, the individual is seen as becoming him or herself by contributing to the process of the group becoming itself. 'The group provides ... a multidimensional transformational object. This is experienced as the apprehension of the beauty of the unfolding reality of the group and of oneself and others in the group' (1992, p. 171).

These views of group transformation tie in with the tradition of psychoanalytic thought on transformation and aesthetics. An important recent contribution to this tradition is Bollas' concept of the transformational object. Bollas (1987) sees the experience of psychic union in infancy as motivating a search in adult life for an object that provides the transformational function. The search embodies the memory of the early object relation and aims to recapture the original transformation. Various group analysts, such as Rance, have described the group as such a transformational object, although Wojciechowska (1993) has pointed out a difference: rather than stimulating a re-enactment of the original memory of transformation *per se*, the group offers new opportunities for transformation, particularly in members' achievement of a creative and autonomous self. This could be extended to include a process of social transformation, since group-analytic therapy, perhaps more than any other form of psychotherapy, is capable of strengthening the individual's relationship with the wider community, leading to what de Maré (1991) calls 'koinonia', a spirit of oneness with the community.

If there is a problem with the transformational perspective, it perhaps lies in its idealising tendency. The transformational goal itself concerns idealisation, the seeking and experiencing of an ideal state with another or others, but the concept also runs the risk of over-idealising the process. In the context of group therapy, this can create the same unbalanced perspective that has been noted throughout this book. In Rance's formulation, as described above, there is little conception of antagonistic forces in the group. The result is that his notion of the beauty of the group, linked to properties of 'proportion, integrity and clarity', is essentially idealised. This, however, compares with Cortesao's views, where the concept of aesthetic equilibrium includes a dialectical view of both creative and destructive forces. Cortesao speaks of 'negative elaboration', the unfolding of oppositional and negative feelings and forces in the group. 'Group analysis is a way of dealing with Eros and Thanatos in an endless ebb and flow' (1991, p. 271). Also, 'the aesthetic equilibrium cannot (or at least must not) ignore the death instinct' (p. 277). Finally, Cortesao is optimistic about the outcome of such recognition: 'if group analysis, by the transmission of a certain group-analytic *pattern*, induces the analysis and the working through of the death impulses in the matrix, then there will be a great probability of dealing with them in the familiar and socio-communal space' (p. 277).

The latter statement leads to an important realisation: transmutation of the anti-group has a value not only for individual and group, but for the wider sphere of social relationships that links the group to the community.

The transitional object

Winnicott's concept of the transitional object, and the linked notion of potential or intermediate space, has similarly been taken up by group analysts to explain the representation and function of the group. There is some confusion about which is primary – the transformational object or the transitional object. Bollas (1987) sees the transformational object as the original experience and the transitional object as 'heir to the transformational period'. In his view, the transitional object is a displacement of the transformational process from the original environmental mother onto a range of other objects.

Winnicott's formulation of the transitional object is well-known: the 'object' emerges out of the infant's attempts to cope with physical and emotional separation from mother. In the creating of a familiar object as a soothing substitute, the baby also creates its first not-me possession. The transitional space or intermediate area is the space in which this occurs, a psychic space which bridges the gap between infant and mother. This space is neither dream nor reality in its fullest sense, but a link between the two. It ushers in the world of illusion, in which imaginative activity can take place. Winnicott links this development to the capacity to play and to the more adult forms of artistic creation and cultural expression.

Ashbach and Schermer (1987), drawing together the work of group theorists on this issue, particularly that of James (1982), suggest that the therapy group is very much a transitional object in that 1) it gradually replaces the group leader as a source of security and comfort, 2) it is a given reality which also becomes a self-created 'possession' of the membership, and 3) it allows the space for members to develop their cultural expression, in the broadest sense. Schlachet (1986) proposes that the transitional space provides a unity between intra- and interpersonal dynamics in the group: in their work together, the members of a therapy group develop a shared psychic group space deriving from the interaction of the transitional space of each. Jacobson (1989) explores members' notion of the group as an object in the cultural field, 'a small temporary society', which also has its origins in the transitional space of the group.

This all has an important bearing on the group-as-object, the basic paradigm adopted in this book as a framework for considering the anti-group, understandable itself as a particular version of the use of the transitional space. On the surface, the anti-group represents the negative of the transitional process: by deflecting hopeful and constructive regard for the group, it may prevent the group from becoming a transitional object in the first place. However, previous considerations concerning the paradoxical nature of change, including the 'use of the object', suggest that the group as transitional object is achieved in a state of complex emotional development. The anti-group, with its underlying fears of separation and abandonment, makes it all the more necessary to create a group transitional object. This will fill the void threatened by emotional catastrophe; it will provide a breathing space on the tortuous road to maturity; it will offer a context for the dialectical play of experience. The processes involved will be illustrated in the next chapter, which focuses on the transformation of a psychotherapy group.

Play

Winnicott's concept of the transitional space leads naturally on to the phenomenon of play, since play can be seen to originate in the potential space. The relevance of play to the psychotherapeutic process in general and group psychotherapy in particular is captured in Winnicott's original statement, 'it is play that is the universal, and that belongs to health: playing facilitates growth and therefore health; *playing leads into group relationships*; playing can be a form of communication in psychotherapy' (1971, p. 48, italics mine).

Linked to this is Winnicott's famous statement that 'psychotherapy takes place in the overlap of two areas of playing, that of the patient and that of the therapist. . . . The corollary of this is that where playing is not possible then the work done by the therapist is directed towards bringing the patient from a state of not being able to play into a state of being able to play' (1971,

p. 46). In terms of the group, the 'two areas of playing' are of course multiplied several times over, resulting in a particularly powerful frame for the emergence of play – especially important where, as Winnicott indicates, there was a prior absence or inability to play.

The creativity of play not only vitalises the group but stimulates members to use the potential space in an imaginative way, loosening up unconscious processes and creating spontaneous experiments which free the development of the group. Jacobson (1989) notes that play enables members to use the group as a medium in which to experiment with problems before engaging with them in concrete form. I would suggest that this is particularly important in relation to aggressive and destructive processes: these can be symbolised and expressed in the group rather than acted out. This could pre-empt destructive enactment both inside and outside the group. In this way, play can help to modify the intensity of the anti-group.

But a word of caution is needed. While playing can be seen as an antidote to the anti-group, it carries its own risks. Winnicott notes that, although play is usually enjoyable and satisfying, it also leads to high degrees of anxiety, partly through the tension between fantasy and reality, partly through the excitement that is generated by play and that may get out of control. Winnicott describes play as 'inherently exciting and precarious' (1971, p. 61). Where the degree of anxiety is unbearable, this can destroy playing. This could be seen to occur where the aggressive component of play gets out of hand, leading to hurt and blame rather than pleasure. There is a danger that anti-group phenomena may infiltrate the group play space or to be generated by it. In playing itself, therefore, there is a degree of dialectical tension between creativity and destructiveness, a further point which will be elaborated in the next chapter.

The transformation in leadership

Theories of group transformation do not usually address the issue of leadership explicitly: the transformational process is seen as embracing the group-as-a-whole, with the leader included rather than singled out. But the relationship between group and leader is crucial, affecting both deeply, and requires an exploration of its particular meaning within the transformational context.

Small group researchers (e.g. Bennis and Shephard 1956; Slater 1966; Hartman and Gibbard 1974) have observed that a central point in the development of the group is a form of revolt against the leader. The challenge to the leadership is often followed by members' increased collaboration with each other. Bennis and Shephard referred to this as 'the barometric event', postulating that the basis of group evolution is the mobilisation of a rebellious challenge to the leader. Each stage of group development is seen as a step in this direction.

Following the 'overthrow', the combined motives of guilt and reparation lead the membership to internalise the leader's values, to deny the destructive act and to draw closer together. Bennis and Shephard relate this to Freud's *Totem and Taboo* (1913) in which leadership is symbolised by the murder of the father by his sons in the primal horde. This 'oedipal' interpretation is contested by Ashbach and Schermer who interpret the attack on the leader as a pre-oedipal phenomenon in which over-identification and fusion with a maternal identity prompt a move towards autonomy and differentiation.

In Foulkes' group-analytic model, the concept of leadership is modified to represent the group therapist as a conductor rather than a leader (Foulkes 1964a), as set out in Chapter 8. The conductor has a facilitating, catalytic role, avoiding the omnipotent position that participants want to confer on him. Although the conductor clearly holds the authority of the group at the start, Foulkes sees the group as gradually taking over this authority. There is 'a crescendo move in the maturity of the group and a decrescendo move in the authority of the leader' (Foulkes 1964a, p. 63). Foulkes does not link this to the group revolt as such, seeing it more as a purposeful strategy on the part of the conductor to empower the group, coupled with the group's natural tendency to strengthen and gain authority. The apparent absence of a challenge to the leadership in Foulkes' formulation is noteworthy: it reflects the democratic style of leadership and group communication that he was particularly keen to develop. But, in practice, this is seldom a smooth process. The group's assumption of authority can be fraught with ambivalence and conflict, complicated by leadership struggles between members of the group and aggressive challenges to the conductor epitomised in the 'group revolt'. Equally, the conductor's capacity to withstand the projections and aggression generated and to relinquish authority may be severely tested, touching on issues about power and control which I would suggest are more complex than allowed for in Foulkes' formulation. I explore this area more fully in Chapter 8 on the role of the conductor.

It appears that Foulkes' crucial conception of group leadership minimises the aggressive potential in the process, aggression that may be an essential part of the maturing of the group. I suggest that the dual transformation of group and conductor may be subject to the same dialectical interplay described above, with frequent and intense oscillations in the location of power and authority, and with the same risk of unresolved aggression generating destructive solutions and triggering anti-group developments. Of course, the pre-existence of marked anti-group attitudes towards the group will complicate the resolution of the authority issue, potentially adding to the build-up of unproductive aggression and reducing the sense of background safety that makes it possible for group and conductor to deal robustly with the dynamics that propel the shift of authority.

To sum up, the transformational view of the analytic group is a powerful and apposite belief in the potential of the group to change, as an entity in itself, as an object in the cultural field, as a vehicle for democratic leadership, and as a crucible for personal transformations in members' lives. But, rather than this representing a linear process of development, it proceeds along dialectical lines, in which the anti-group and its derivatives play an important part, paradoxically helping to 'construct, deconstruct and reconstruct the group' (Schlapobersky 1995), so defining its therapeutic value. This process is highlighted in the detailed clinical example that follows in the next chapter.

Chapter 10

'Nippets and Imps'
The transformational process in a psychotherapy group[1]

This chapter is devoted entirely to a clinical illustration of the points developed in the previous chapter on the transformational potential of the anti-group. In particular, the group presented illustrates the dialectical movement between creative and destructive forces, the anti-group acting as an essential, recurring polarity in the interplay between opposing tendencies in the group. Within this dialectical matrix, the group gradually gains shape, strength, and identity. It becomes a self-created, 'autopoetic' activity, a transitional space which awakens the zone of play and provides a context for therapeutic transformation for group and conductor alike.

The analysis of the group draws on Foulkes' adumbration of the four levels of the group: the current level, the transference level, the projective level, and the primordial level. Particular attention is paid to the emergence of visual imagery in the group. Arising from the projective and primordial levels of experience, which generate and contain the fantasy life of the group, these images also infuse the transference and counter-transference with the idiosyncratic and vivid life of the group. The transition from primitive, archaic fantasy to images of transformation is the subject of scrutiny in this chapter. This is epitomised in the 'Nippets and Imps' that give the chapter its title. The 'Nippets and Imps' are little sweets that become the focus of free-floating discussion in one of the later sessions described, symbolising and condensing the pathway of transformation chosen by the group. But the symbolism also illustrates the fragility of the process. Within

---

[1] The material in this chapter is based on an unpublished clinical paper presented on the Institute of Group Analysis qualifying course (Nitsun 1989).

the kernel of transformation remains the potential for regression and reversal. The process of resolution is not complete: it ebbs and flows in the paradoxical cycle of change.

The group in question (A) has been referred to several times in previous chapters, notably as an illustration of the anti-group occurring in the initial phase of a therapy group, as well as the manifestation of the anti-group at individual, sub-group, and group-as-a-whole levels (Chapter 4, pp. 76–83). Here we return to the group as it begins to emerge more clearly, though ambivalently, as a therapeutic entity. We follow the group's progress through several further stages which were marked by thematic concerns that touched on issues of loss, abandonment, fragmentation, restoration, and transformation.

THE DREAM OF THE GRAVE

We pick up the group at the end of the first break. Return to the group was marked by a sense of disaffection in the membership. Much of the material in the initial session referred to inconsistent and/or intrusive mothers. The conductor highlighted the theme and suggested that the break might have seemed like an intrusion into the continuity of the group and that it might have been experienced as if an inconsistent and uncaring mother. The interpretation appeared to resonate with the group.

Whereas mothers were very present in the group material, there was an absence of fathers, as if fathers were dead, distant, or ineffectual. This reflected the reality of most participants' lives. In historical terms, the absence or distance of the father had left the child at the mercy of a very powerful mother, without the moderating influence of a third person (see Wooster 1983).

The theme of the lost father then emerged powerfully in the group. This was epitomised by Maureen, who spoke emotionally about her father who had died suddenly when she was 5 years old. One of the most tormenting aspects of his death for her was that he had been buried in a communal grave. She supposed that her mother had not been able to afford a separate burial with a tombstone, so that her father was buried with others in a remote part of the cemetery. The grave had no identity. It was just a mound of earth with several bodies beneath it. The picture of this bleak, communal grave could be seen as a metaphor for the group, in its most depressive mode. Maureen actually referred to the grave as a 'group grave', reinforcing the connection. She was one of the two patients who had had individual therapy with the conductor before joining the group: in her mind, the change had been like being dumped. In the image of the group grave, the other patients were all in the same position, as if the therapy group was, metaphorically, like a heap of abandoned, undifferentiated bodies.

In session 16, Maureen reported a dream about her father's grave. The conductor was present in the dream (representing the link with her father) standing to the side as Maureen went to put flowers on the grave. Instead of placing the flowers on the grave, however, she picked off the flowers one by one and strewed them around the grave. But there were insufficient flowers to go round, even though she tried this in different ways, and in the end she picked them all up again and dumped them in the middle of the grave.

The dream suggested a failed attempt at reparation in relation to Maureen's father's death and the ignominy of his grave. But this was also a signal of the group's early struggle to give up the fantasy of idealised oneness, the clinging to the lost parent, in order to allow the group itself to emerge and to acquire a therapeutic function. This was a recognition of loss that could provide a starting point for growth. Also, although the theme was explicitly related to the father, I believe it contained depressively toned symbolism of the mother. The 'group grave' could be seen to represent the mother's womb and the bodies the dead babies inside the mother (cf. both Bion's and Foulkes' interpretation of the group as representing a womb, also Elliott's (1994) extended treatment of the subject).

This image of the mother, extrapolated from the group material, can be compared to the fantasy of the damaged breast in Georgina's account in the very first group (pp. 77–80). That account illustrated an attempt at a cosmetic solution that did not work, whereas Maureen's dream and the image of the grave seem to go inside the psyche, into the heart of the depression, into the interior of the mother, rather than the disfigured exterior. In this interpretation, Maureen's unresolved mourning in relation to her father can be seen as based on an earlier identification with a damaged mother with a dead inside. For some weeks, the group as a whole seemed in a state of suspended animation, like a state of near-death (Joseph 1982). This was an anti-group of a particular sort – a dead, frozen group, buried in its archaic past.

Gradually, Maureen began to show signs of working through the grief associated with her dead father and of achieving both separation and reparation. For the first time ever, she went to the cemetery where her father was buried. There, she established that the grave contained the bodies of five adults and two children (a further connection with the group: there were seven in the group). She also confirmed her impression of the grave in its barrenness and anonymity. She decided that she would have a wooden cross made for the grave and this she subsequently did. She also spoke about growing a tree at the grave. These were her ways of giving the grave an identity and of saying good-bye to her father.

Parallel to her dealing with her father's death, Maureen gradually came to terms with the loss of individual contact with the conductor. She went through periods of profound ambivalence towards him in the group. For the first time, she was able to express intense anger towards the conductor, while also feeling distressed about her resentment and loss of confidence in him. At these times, the other members were very supportive of her. This had the paradoxical consequence that Maureen came to value the group, which she had initially resented, more and more. For the group, too, this was a crucial development, as it brought to the fore the caring, compassionate side of the members, and enabled them, via Maureen, to deal with the shared problem of disillusionment and loss. There were powerful resonances in the group to Maureen's story about her father, as it awakened memories of the death and dying of loved ones, and the universality of the experience deepened bonds.

Maureen wished to give her father's grave an identity. A parallel theme of identity came up in a multitude of ways in this phase of the group. The individual participants were becoming more clearly identified and personalised. Names and personal characteristics became the currency of the group. Moreover, the group was gaining an identity as a group. It was becoming less fragmented and more cohesive. Its boundary was strengthening. This could only happen when members could begin to mourn the loss of the idealised leader, to accept the existence of the group and to invest it with a therapeutic function.

The relationship of the group as a whole to the conductor –

and his relationship to them – began to show signs of a gradual transformation. Previous associations had suggested that the conductor was perceived either as a distant, idealised figure or as a stern, arbitrary authority who could shift people (like Maureen) around at his will. The conductor's own experience of his relationship to the group in some way mirrored these perceptions. He liked the group but felt distant from it. Part of this was his concern about how best to exercise his role as conductor. How active should he be? How much control did he need to exert over this ambivalent and often fractious group? How interventionist should he be? How open? How closed?

The group seemed to reflect these concerns in a session in which members expressed uncertainty about whether to call the conductor by his first name or surname. The point at issue, I believe, was whether he had to remain the distant authority figure (Dr Nitsun) or become a member of the group (Morris), more like them, human, accessible, vulnerable. During this discussion, Norman said he thought that something had displeased the conductor who had suddenly looked like 'a disapproving rabbi'. In this perception seemed to lie a very real question about how open the conductor was to challenge and change. The conductor was aware of similar questions in himself. To a large extent, this concerned the anti-group process in the group and his own attitude towards it. Could he trust the group sufficiently to let it take its course or did he have to remain vigilant, in control, the 'authority' influencing the direction of the group – still needing to be Dr Nitsun?

These questions continued to have relevance. If the group was beginning to deal with separation and disillusionment, and if the group entity was beginning to consolidate, it still had to contend with the anti-group. Two interlocking forces seemed to evoke an anti-group backlash: 1) the anxiety about positive developments in the group and whether they would last, leading to a form of negative therapeutic reaction, and 2) the envy and envy pre-emption mobilised by successes in the group. One form of anti-group activity in this phase was a pattern of inconsistent attendances. Members seemed to take it in turns to stay away. There were usually rational reasons for their absence, but the effect was to disrupt the group and to make it difficult to maintain continuity. In fact, 'good' sessions, in which there was full attendance and hard work aimed at uncovering and facing painful issues, or open acknowledgement of constructive changes in the group, were usually followed by 'poor' sessions, with low attendance and resistance to the group process – a not uncommon finding in therapy groups. The absences were demoralising to the group and reinforced anxieties about whether the group would survive.

This form of teasing the group was epitomised in the behaviour of Pam, who kept disappearing on holiday to Marbella. She would return looking tanned and glamorous, exciting envy in the others while saying how much she had missed the group. She also seemed the focus for a good deal of tension and rivalry between the men and women in the group. On several occasions, this became viciously confrontative. Although this split probably had a basis in actual male–female differences, I believe it was also fuelled by the anti-group, the male–female dichotomy serving as a vehicle for a potentially destructive group process. For example, the sense of universality that might have been achieved when important aspects of separation and loss were dealt with, as described above, would then disappear, eclipsed by the battle of the sexes. The oscillation between group-cohesive and group-fragmenting processes was a particular feature at this stage of the group.

But improvements in members' lives could not be denied. Norman described how his relationship with his parents had improved, first his mother, then his father. In his mother's case, he felt that he had for the first time begun to appreciate the effect on her of having been a Holocaust survivor, and he linked this recognition to an awareness of the anguish expressed by Maureen in the group. In relation to his father, he revealed an experience that touched the group and also seemed to have symbolic relevance to the question of leadership. Norman was in his parents' bedroom one night and noticed his father's shoes at the foot of the bed. They were old, worn, rather small shoes, and he felt a wave of compassion for his father. Suddenly, this tyrannical man he feared so much seemed ordinary and frail. There seemed to have been a connection here with the conductor as father and the loss of him as the ideal, invincible figure of authority. Perhaps Norman (and, in identification with him, the group) was stepping into the conductor's shoes, thereby assimilating his function into the group. Perhaps their early confrontation of the conductor on the issues of authority, control, and disillusionment – and the conductor's own grappling with these problems – had made it possible for the group to prepare itself to gain a greater authority of its own.

An impending three-week summer break then re-ignited the anti-group. A strong theme concerning pregnancy arose, with disturbing material about abortions and miscarriages. This signified a fear that the group would miscarry during the break. Attendance at the group dropped and in the last session there were just four patients. It was as if the group was enacting an abortion ahead of the break. The morale was very low and the mood depressed. The conductor felt particularly demoralised about the group just before the break, as if he was the recipient of projective identifications he could not comprehend – perhaps connected with the fantasy of an unborn or aborted foetus, echoing the earlier theme of the group grave and its unconscious equivalent of the mother's damaged womb with the dead babies inside. As suggested in Chapter 5, the anti-group may have unconscious roots in deep underlying existential concerns about life and death. Perhaps, in this case, the patients' earlier confrontation of the conductor had also left the group with fears of damaging and destroying him, now exacerbated by the impending break.

For all the progress the group had made in this phase, including the courageous attempt to deal with disillusionment and loss, generating the hope of reparation, it still had a sense of great fragility.

THE GROUP CRISIS

The group got off to a shaky start after the break. There was a good deal of resistance and the conductor's attempts to take up the group's feelings about the break met with denial.

The paradoxical pattern of change continued. Individual progress was now occurring in and outside the group, but the changes were presented very hesitantly, as if too precarious to risk exposure. Attempts at envy pre-emption also continued. In one session, previously described (pp. 126–7), this led to a renewed attack on the group as inadequate and unhelpful, culminating in a wave of threats to leave the group. As previously reported, this generated material about the Kray brothers, the East End criminals who symbolically represented the perverse organisation of 'the gang' as an attack on the need for dependence and emotional growth. In fantasy, the therapeutic group could be replaced by a secret omnipotent gang that despised everything therapy stood for. These counter-developments all represented the voice of the anti-group, continually challenging the progress being made in the group.

But the successes were encouraging. Georgina, the participant with the breast surgery, reported a promising relationship with a man, her first for some years. Nigel, previously described as the 'leader of the anti-group', started opening up and showing his vulnerability to the group. But it was Tim's progress that was particularly striking and that produced a vivid, early image of personal and group transformation. Tim was beginning to succeed in his ambition as a photographer. To his great delight, an article he wrote about 'Urban Weeds' and illustrated with his own photographs was published in a well-known nature magazine. He brought a copy to show the group. The article concerned the wild flower life that grew in the forgotten, neglected parts of the city, such as disused industrial sites and abandoned parking lots. The colourful photographs conveyed the surprising brilliance of these flowers amidst the wreckage of the city. This was like a metaphor for the unexpected growth occurring in the group, for the stirrings of life in the debris of the past. These images produced a striking contrast to the image of the barren, anonymous graveyard that Maureen described in the previous phase, as well as the flowers in the dream that were dumped onto the grave. The urban weeds were the early symbols of transformation, rooted in the soil of change, flowering in the face of neglect and decay.

This phase ushered in what Bennis and Shephard (1956) have called the group revolt. The group started challenging the conductor strongly in various ways, ranging from insistent questions about his technique to criticisms of a no-smoking sign that he was accused of imposing on the group. The challenge was at times very powerful and the conductor had to steel himself in order to avoid being drawn into a defensive battle. This was 'the barometric event', the point at which the group seeks to take over the leadership function, noted in the previous chapter (pp. 214–15) as a crucial moment in the group's development. The occurrence of 'the event' at this particular point may be explained in terms of the fact that 1) the loss of the father, in actual and symbolic terms, had been countenanced earlier in the group, 2) the conductor had already been confronted and had withstood and survived the challenge, 3) the strengthened resources of the group made it possible to attack the leader without fearing that there was nothing to fall back on.

If these developments constituted progress for a number of the participants, however, to others they may have been inimical. Two members dropped out in this phase and this may have been connected with the challenge to authority. Arlene, a very introverted member, sent a letter saying that she no longer needed the group as she realised her salvation lay in religion. She felt very close to God and this was the path she now wanted to follow. In Arlene's case, the challenge to the conductor's authority was probably disturbing: she still needed dependence on an idealised leader. Hence, her return to the highest authority of all – God. Pam, the member who holidayed in Marbella, also wrote a letter to say she was leaving the group. She said she had valued attending the group but had to leave for practical reasons. This felt to the group unconvincing: there was a sense that Pam had not resolved her problematic relationship with the group. At the same time, she had never revealed any overt anti-group reactions in the way other members did. Interestingly, those who were openly critical of the group stayed: those who were uncritical left. This suggests that freely expressed and tolerated anti-group feelings are more conducive to members staying than the anti-group when expressed in indirect and disguised forms.

There was at first a disappointed but low-key reaction to these departures. Then a panicky reaction set in as several other members – Maureen and Barry in particular – announced that they were also intending to leave. A contagion effect had set in, the threatened drop-out chain mentioned in Chapter 3 (pp. 55–6). For a while it seemed as if the entire group was in danger of collapse. The drop-outs had triggered a powerful anti-group reaction and a sense that the group could disintegrate.

Uncannily, this was the week of the devastating hurricane of October 1987. The group had arrived at the hospital to find the awful spectacle of the trees in the grounds uprooted and blown over: a strange mirroring in the natural world of the sense of impending catastrophe in the group. There was an atmosphere of great distress and upheaval in the group, and the threat to its survival produced a clinical regression in several patients. Maureen reported a return of frightening, hallucinatory-type experiences. She had been eating her Rice Krispies for breakfast when she had a disturbing vision of the cereal moving, as if some sinister force was activating it from underneath. Georgina reported seeing a bath flannel repeatedly changing colour in front of her eyes – she felt her mind was playing tricks on her. These experiences reflected the sense of a loss of control, of a deep upheaval in the natural world and in the group, reviving patients' innermost fears of fragmentation and loss.

This was a great test of the group's resources but it mobilised the healthy part of the group that could respond in a reparative way. Several members urged Maureen not to leave, saying that she was in no state emotionally to go and that she still had important work to do in the group. Nigel, with whom she usually had an abrasive relationship, told her that he would personally be very sorry if she left and that she was the person in the group he valued most. All this had a containing effect on Maureen and she settled back into the group, becoming one of its most committed members. In Barry's case, he decided to stay until the following year, when he left in a planned, constructive way.

THE 'NIPPETS AND IMPS'

Following the crisis, the group not only survived – it strengthened. This was a period of intense transformation. As described in the previous chapter in relation to Winnicott's concept of 'the use of an object', the capacity of the group to survive destructive threats and attacks resulted in a regeneration and the group became stronger, freer, more expressive. There was increasing use of the transitional space in the group, the zone of play. In session 37, there was a group event – the 'Nippets and Imps' – that crystallised the transformation of the group.

The session started with a discussion about how parents, often criticised and reviled, had their own problems and difficult childhoods. Georgina communicated a story from her mother's childhood. Her mother had greatly admired a female teacher who had a very elegant way of eating little sweets that she pressed out of a container into the palm of her hand. Georgina demonstrated this action to the group. Georgina's mother had longed to emulate the teacher's refined style, but she had no money to buy the sweets, so she stole a shilling from the mantelpiece and went out to purchase a box of the sweets. She came home, sat down in front of the mirror and proceeded to imitate the teacher's movements, dispensing the little tablets from the box into her hand and with her fingers daintily bringing them to her mouth. She was fairly pleased with this but felt that she did not quite match her teacher's delicacy of movement.

This prompted members of the group to say they thought the sweets must have been Nippets. They remembered these from their childhoods, tiny, black, sharp-flavoured sweets that indeed came in a little box with a dispenser. Other participants remembered them as Imps and there followed a lively debate about whether they were Nippets or Imps and whether in fact Nippets and Imps were the same or different. There was a great absorption in the topic and an unusual closeness in the group. The humour in the interchange grew as members discussed whether they liked the sweets, the general consensus being that the box and the dispenser were more desirable than the sweets themselves. The humour turned into hilarity when Maureen described how, as a child, her husband, Charles, loved the sweets and looked forward to visits from his grandfather, who gave him two Nippets each time and four on his birthday. Norman asked if the tablets were for enjoyment or constipation, and the hilarity grew.

This was one of the most playful episodes in the group's development, certainly the first that involved the group so fully and so vividly. In the rest of the session, which returned to more overtly serious matters, there was a warmth and closeness that was striking.

It was as if from this moment the group was a different group, even though the potential for transformation had been there earlier on and was probably gradually coming to fruition. The conductor, too, felt differently about the group. He relaxed much more into the group, losing his tense self-consciousness about his role as conductor and his nagging doubts and fears about the group's development. How did this happen?

The name 'Nippets' is an invented word that evokes various associations. One obvious association to 'Nippets' is 'nipples'. The association suggests that the symbolism in the material was related to the early mother–infant feeding relationship. The various details of the story are open to differing interpretations, but, overall, can be seen as images of the infant in a playful feeding relationship with the breast. In this interpretation, the little box and the dispenser represent the breast and the nipple respectively, and the detailed hand and mouth movements described relate to images and experiences of holding and fondling the breast, while sucking at the nipple and tasting, chewing, swallowing, and spitting out the milk. The group's delight in the discussion was a re-evocation of the warmth and play of the infant at the breast. It appeared to be essentially a good experience – even though the Nippets were not to everyone's taste, there was a sense of being able to tolerate the element of distaste. In this way, a potentially 'bad breast' experience can be transformed into a 'good breast' experience, or at the least, ambivalence can be tolerated.

Further associations to 'Nippets', aided by the *Oxford English Dictionary*, suggested the following: A 'nipper' means a child, usually a boy, and is often used colloquially in a playful way. 'Snippets', which is nippets prefaced with an S, refers to a 'small piece' or 'snipping' and in the plural refers to 'detailed fragments of knowledge or information' or 'odds and ends'. The verb 'nip' means 'to go nimbly' but also has the negative association of pinching and squeezing sharply; also to 'pinch off ... check the growth of (espec. in the bud)'. Interestingly, 'Imp' has a similar meaning to some of the above: it refers to a 'mischievous child', also with connotations of play.

The emphasis on play in these associations is mirrored in the way play, as a theme and a process, was repeated at several levels of the material – Georgina's act of story-telling, her mother's engagement with the sweets in a form of imitative play, and the group's playful response. The focus on sweets clearly evoked childhood associations and feelings – children love sweets – and this stimulated imaginative activity and humour in the group. An important part of this was the play on 'Nippets' and 'Imps', as if the little sweets were imbued with a fresh, almost magical significance, investing the whole with the quality of dream meaning and feeling. It is as if the group members all became nippers and imps themselves, mischievously creating a charmed circle around the story of the little girl and her sweets. Winnicott's statement (1971) that play facilitates growth, that it leads into group relationships, and that it can be a form of communication in psychotherapy strongly comes to mind, as does Anthony's (1983) description of the therapy group as 'a magic circle'.

The importance of play in this group is heightened when we consider that it started as a group of very disturbed, depressed, and anxious individuals, whose capacity for play in their own lives, in the sense of spontaneous and shared enjoyment, had been damaged. To have reached a point in the group where play entered so freely suggests that there was growing trust in the group (Winnicott points out that trust is a necessary precondition for play). In turn, the satisfaction gained from the play reinforced trust in the imaginative function of the group.

In line with the emphasis on play, the 'Nippets and Imps' episode seemed also to be about the creation of a transitional space in the group. Here, following the views of James (1982) and Schlachet (1986), the group is seen as a transitional area in which the members of the therapy group develop a shared psychic space, derived from the interaction of the transitional space of one another, in which interpersonal transactions and transformations can take place. No doubt the group had slowly been in the process of establishing the transitional space, but it emerged with particular clarity in this episode. The little box of sweets in the story had the symbolic properties of a transitional object, an object that links past to present and future, and this paralleled the creation of the group itself as a form of transitional object.

An important aspect of play is the role of imitation. We know that the transitional object is usually established in response to separation from the mother, that it serves to some extent as a substitute for the mother and also represents qualities of the mother. In Georgina's story, the fact that the girl does not entirely succeed at emulating her teacher seems less important than her attempt to do so: the transitional object is created not as an exact replica of the mother but as an entity that combines aspects of the self, the mother, and the external world. The parallel in the group was the way the membership needed to create the group in recognition of its separation from the conductor. This involved incorporating aspects of the conductor in the group, indeed the conductor as a physical presence, and also qualities associated with him, such as therapeutic values and skills, even if these could not be perfectly represented.

Linked to this is a further association to 'Nippets': its similarity to the conductor's name, 'Nitsun'. Speculative though this may seem, it is relevant to the process of the group becoming a transitional or transformational object. Like the sweets that are tasted and incorporated in the child's inner world as a symbolic link with the teacher/mother, so the conductor and his qualities are assimilated and internalised in the group. Freud, in his 1921 paper on group psychology, described the ritual eating of the father as a symbolic incorporation of his power; this is the dynamic suggested in connecting 'Nippets' with 'Nitsun'. It may also be a consequence of the 'barometric event', in so far as the challenge to the conductor's authority and the mourning of his loss enabled the membership to assimilate his function in the group.

It is important that in this session the conductor perceived a dramatic change not only in the group but in his own role. He became totally absorbed in the spirit of the group – the playful regression to childhood, the intricacies of the word play, and the sheer release of humour in the group. It is as if the assimilation of his therapeutic function by the group was mirrored in his own transformed experience in the group. He acquired a greater confidence in the group itself and a diminished sense of pressure to *lead* the group. In this sense, the transformational process in the group was paralleled by a transformation in the leadership function.

It is interesting to consider the 'Nippets and Imps' session from the perspective of the group's evolution over the previous year, specifically in relation to unconscious images of the group. The symbolism followed a line of development from the initial image of the group as a damaged breast (the failed cosmetic surgery), via the group as womblike depressive container (the group grave), to the Nippets and Imps, representing a return to the breast but in joyfully reparative form. These could all be seen as fantasies of the formation of the group, viewed in unconscious terms as the mother and parts of the mother's body (Bion 1961; Foulkes 1964a). Hence, the 'Nippets and Imps' episode appears as the culmination and transformation of several fantasies about the early development of the group, particularly in its maternal, containing function (and paralleled by the absorption of the paternal function into the group).

A last point concerns the creation of an aesthetic moment in the group. The concern with form in the story – the child's preoccupation with the *way* her teacher dispensed and ate the sweets, mirrored in the group's experimentation with new forms in the group space – links up with the notion of the aesthetic properties of a transformational experience (Bollas 1987). This is 'aesthetic' in the sense of the felt experience of a 'processing form' that integrates previously fragmented experiences of self. Here, the significance of 'snippets' as a variation of 'Nippets' comes to the fore: the snippets are the fragments of self-experience and knowledge that are assimilated and integrated in the transformational process of the group. The group debate about whether the sweets were Nippets or Imps, what they tasted like, and whether they were liked or disliked was all part of this processing, through identification, differentiation, and integration.

DISCUSSION

The development of this group illustrates the major points concerning group transformation outlined in Chapter 9.

The anti-group is seen as representing pervasive themes about anxiety and distrust of the group process, as a defensive container of the regressive and aggressive tendencies of the membership, and as a continuing challenge to the evolution of the therapeutic function of the group. There are several instances of how the latent anti-group became manifest in a continuing cycle. But the anti-group also emerges as the counterpoint to the development of the group as an object. It is the group's capacity to withstand the destructive threat that strengthens its identity and function as a therapeutic group. By turns, it becomes the self-created autopoetic activity described by Maturana and Varela (1980), a transitional object, and a play space for experimentation and transformation. The containment of the destructive process also facilitates the reparative function of the group, deepening its healing potential. This is paralleled by the 'aesthetic elaboration' of the group (Cortesao 1991; Rance 1992), in which the formal qualities of the group acquire definition and proportion, providing a satisfying and coherent frame for the therapeutic experience. The transformation of the group is also linked to transformation of the leadership function, as the group relinquishes its dependence on the idealised conductor, assimilates his therapeutic role, and allows him to become both conductor and member of the group. But this is achieved only gradually and with a struggle. Reaching what Foulkes (1964a) described as a 'crescendo in the maturity of the group and a decrescendo in the authority of the conductor' was more difficult, ambivalent, and conflict-ridden for all concerned than might have been expected on the basis of Foulkes' original description of the process.

It is in the dialectic of creative and destructive *per se*, however, that this example is most powerfully illustrative. This is reflected not only in the movement between constructive and destructive forces, but also in the mutually generative relationship they have to each other, so that creative and destructive can be seen to contain each other. As noted in a previous section on the 'logics of change' (pp. 197–207), the stimulus for change triggers transformations already contained in the logic of the system. This reaches its quintessence in the Nippets and Imps episode. The little sweets are a source of great delight but they have a sharp edge – they are sweets with a bite, bitter little sweets that are not entirely to the liking of the group. Yet, they can be enjoyed and entertained as a symbol of play and growth. Equally, the delight in the stories about the sweets is edged with a manic excitement, as if hiding some underlying anxiety. Perhaps the clue lies in the association of 'nipped in the bud', representing the threat of development being destroyed at its inception. In this sense, the anti-group is not far in the background of transformation. If anything, it exists in the very process itself, negating but also evolving and creating the group's constructive potential.

In clinical terms, this group went on to become a strongly therapeutic group lasting for six years with some outstanding individual outcomes. But the anti-group was there to be dealt with at different stages, each time serving to re-evoke and reconstitute the therapeutic potential of the group – and to challenge and redefine the relationship between group and conductor.

Chapter 11

The anti-group in the wider social sphere

This chapter deviates from the essentially clinical focus of this book by turning its attention to the social reality outside the consulting room. It proposes that anti-group forces may be intrinsic to the socio-cultural domain: that there exists a phenomenon that could broadly be described as *the culture of the anti-group*. This sets the concept in a wider context which includes political, cultural, social, and historical dimensions, although the same influences are ultimately reflected in the themes and images of the psychotherapy group (Hearst 1993). Viewed in these terms, the anti-group is subject to the same forces of 'figuration' described by Norbert Elias as influencing the full continuum of psychological experience.

Three main settings – the family, organisations, and the wider culture – are examined separately, but with the understanding that they represent a single universe. Within this universe there is a pervasive cycle of creation and destruction, progression and regression, with periods in which there is a collapse in the direction of decline and disintegration, a view which coincides with Toynbee's (1972) analysis of cultural change. This is similar to the dialectic that fuels the psychotherapy group and its potential for growth or reversion to a static and extreme position (see Chapters 5, 9, 10 and 12). The psychotherapy group can be seen as a form of social organisation itself, created within the framework of a wider organisation (the hospital, clinic, private practice, NHS, etc.). Schermer and Pines (1994) note that the therapy group cannot be separated from its context and that there may be an insidious influence from context to group in the existing social order: 'Primitive regression is an increasingly impinging and insistent aspect of the ongoing context within which all group psychotherapy is conducted' (p. 3).

At the same time as linking the psychotherapy group to the wider culture, it is important to differentiate it. Psychotherapeutic provision is created not simply to mirror outside reality but to understand it, grapple with it, and transmute the destructive influences that may penetrate individual lives. This is achieved, particularly in group therapy, through the co-operative, creative, and reparative propensities that are inherent to human beings and that offset the impact of destructive processes. That the group can offer new cultural opportunities that have a transcendent value for individuals caught up in the spiral of social rupture is demonstrated in two examples in this chapter: one in the familiar setting of group psychotherapy (p. 246), another in a staff development group in a work setting (pp. 255–8).

The latter reference to the work organisation highlights a further aim of this chapter: to contribute to the framework of a group-analytic model of organisational intervention. In parallel to my argument about group psychotherapy, this requires greater attention to group-destructive processes than has hitherto been part of the group-analytic tradition. In organisations, destructive intra- and inter-group relationships are often the nub of the problem.

DIFFICULTIES OF THIS APPROACH

There are very real difficulties about extending a clinically based concept, such as the anti-group, to the world of phenomena outside the consulting room. One such difficulty is the risk of reductionism. This would be true of any attempt to formulate universal principles about complex social phenomena. Hoggett (1992), commenting on the application of individual psychoanalysis to social issues, questions the degree of conviction with which we can move from the highly personal, internal world of the patient to the sphere of collective pathology. He asks:

> How can we generalise from our analysis of the world of the autistic child or the successful but 'borderline' adult personality to what often seems like the madness of normal life, whether we consider this in terms of our complacency in face of the prospect of mass extinction, the development of intimate

attachments to commodity objects or the collusion of otherwise intelligent and sensitive workers in the maintenance of depersonalised human interactions?

(Hoggett 1992, pp. 71–2)

In support of my own approach, I would argue that the clinical insights applied here are *group* and not individually based. The group perspective is much closer to the collective. It is rooted in an appreciation of the social context. Le Roy (1994) describes the group as being an intermediate position between the individual intra-psychic dimension and the social dimension. But this still equips us with limited means to grasp the full force of flux and change in the cultural domain. Part of the difficulty is the broad generalisations that already exist in popular commentary on the cultural order. We are confronted with repetitive images not only of commodities but of the cultural fabric itself: 'the information superhighway'... 'cyberspace'... 'global decay'... 'the new communitarianism'. As we move towards the twenty-first century, visions of the future assume an apocalyptic scale, predictions of a transformed universe alternating with those of total destruction. It is difficult to enter this field of discourse without using the same language, making the same generalisations, while knowing that they reflect profound and often more complex issues than are immediately apparent. This is also true of using the concept of the anti-group in this context: it might over-simplify very diverse and complex phenomena. With these considerations in mind, however, I suggest a tentative hypothesis:

The threat of destruction in the wider culture both generates and reflects a form of anti-group at the core of our civilisation and this sets the context for fragmentation or defensive survival of institutions and groups at successive levels of the cultural ethos.

Here an attempt is made to clarify these patterns and to discover whether any common dynamics traverse the various cultural domains that harbour anti-group forces. The small analytic group serves as an interweaving point of reference, a prism which reflects these processes and at the same time contributes particular ways of understanding them.

THE PRESENT CONTEXT

It is both a commonplace and a disturbing reality that our present social order is in the process of turbulent change. Hoggett (1992) describes our age as 'the culture of uncertainty'. He suggests that late-twentieth-century politics is 'all about dancing on the edge', that if the odds are not quite against us surviving, then we cannot be sure about our children and our children's children.

On the more immediately social front, Skynner (1989), in an address at the Fortieth Anniversary of the Institute of Marital Studies, London, observed:

> There is increasing concern at the effect on marriage and the family of what has appeared, at least on the surface, to be a progressive breakdown in the structure of society. In the western world over the past forty years our values have become increasingly individual, rather than group-centred, swinging the balance away from social cohesion towards personal freedom, often regardless of its social consequences. We have been losing the concept of duty, role, place in society, and of authority and order, including the former influential role of the father, the extended family and the community. There has been a decline in the influence of religion, in the force of social expectations, and in respect for law.
>
> (Skynner 1989, p. 188)

Many would argue that these are not 'degenerative changes', as Skynner refers to them, but his description conveys the essence of social instability in the past few decades and the rejection of group or collective values in favour of the individual. Skynner goes on to point out that these changes have been paralleled by the emergence of new forms of relationships and new possibilities for integration. He refers, in particular, to a more organic and holistic order, in which the resources of both women and men are recognised, an increasing concern for the environment coupled with an awareness of ecological consequences, and an increasing sense of responsibility for world conditions.

Skynner made these pronouncements in 1988. Some years later, it is evident that much of what he said remains true, but that the growth he describes is constantly challenged by the forces of regression, irresponsible waste, and disintegratory change. Our civilisation often seems poised on a knife edge, 'dancing on the edge', as Hoggett says.

How are these processes reflected in three major social institutions – the family, the work organisation, and the wider culture – and what light do they throw on the anti-group in the world outside the consulting room?

THE FAMILY

The family is a relatively enduring social institution as opposed to the 'small temporary society' of the therapy group (Jacobson 1989). But it is also presently an institution in crisis, with increasing questions about its viability (Frude 1991) and speculation on the precise reasons for its embattled position, a debate described as the 'war over the family' by Berger and Berger (1984).

In recent decades, there has been trenchant criticism of the family from different quarters: from feminists, who have seen it as an instrument of oppression of women and of rigidification of male–female roles generally; from left-wing critics, who have seen it as a vehicle for capitalist ideology, with an emphasis on competition and consumerism, resulting in alienation between people; and from social critics, such as Laing (1976), who has seen it as a defensive organisation that reacts to dangers in the community and interiorises and enacts psychological violence as a way of dealing with external threat. These criticisms all imply some form of anti-group process, in which existence in a family is perceived as inimical to both individual and group.

Criticisms of the family as an institution have been paralleled by a progressive breakdown in conventional family structures. These include the erosion of the extended family network in Western society, a reduction in the number and size of family households, a rise in the rate of separation and divorce, an increase in the number of single-parent families, and the emergence of non-traditional families, such as homosexual couplings and parenting through new forms of fertilisation.

There is increasing evidence of domestic violence associated with the family: child, marital, and elder abuse are now so frequently reported that our perspective on family norms has changed radically. Other forms of social pathology, such as crime, violence on the streets, vandalism, drug abuse, suicide, and child prostitution, have all been attributed to family breakdown and the weakening of parental authority and guidance.

The family is indeed embattled. Not only has it been the subject of savage criticism in past decades, but it has undergone massive structural transformations, and it continues to be a vulnerable point in an ever-changing society. The call to 'family values' of the Bush administration in the USA and the Conservative government in the UK in the late 1980s and early 1990s expressed a recognition of this crisis and an attempt, albeit rather hollow, to restore the conventional value system enshrined in the family.

The healthy family

Understanding of the family cannot be separated from its social context, since external factors are bound to impact on family dynamics. It also raises the question of what constitutes a healthy family and whether this can withstand the vicissitudes of external change.

Scharff (1982) describes the family as 'an institution which has a course of development of its own. Its basic task is to provide stable attachment figures for each of its members while simultaneously promoting their individualised development' (p. 221). Attachment theorists emphasise the family as 'a secure base' from which further social development can take place, an empathic springboard that equips the individual with the capacity to form relationships with individuals and groups outside (Bowlby 1988; Glenn 1987).

Skynner (1989) suggests that the ability to cope with change and loss is a key requirement of the family. This is strengthened by the positive resources within families as enhanced by three factors: 1) a strong parental coalition and a clear parent–child hierarchy; 2) a good support system which includes the marital relationship, the family itself, the extended family, and the wider community; 3) a sense of connection and meaning provided by a value system that transcends the present family.

Le Roy (1994) emphasises the need for a form of psychic envelope in the family. This concerns the creation of safe boundaries for the self and is achieved when the individual has a 'sense of being held' (Winnicott 1960) in an envelope (Bick 1968) or a skin (Anzieu 1989). He also cites Bion's (1962) concept of the container–contained to describe a parenting function that requires the support of the wider family network in order to become a safe envelope with a coherent sense of meaning.

The family as group and anti-group

Although the family as a social unit has been the subject of much study, there is relatively little focus on it as a functional or dysfunctional *group*. Most of what the above writers have said about the family could be translated into small group terms, with the wider family network representing an ambient large group, but this needs to be made explicit. In this section, the group aspects of the family unit are explored, providing a framework within which to consider the expression of the anti-group as an antithetical force in family life.

The family is a highly concentrated form of group, since the ties are blood ties, the level of interpersonal contact probably greater than in most other groups, and its history stretching much further back in time. In this context, the usual group-related issues of boundaries, status, leadership, authority, closeness and distance regulation, autonomy, and role differentiation all take on a heightened significance. Seen from a group perspective, Frude (1991) has pointed out that the family has 'emergent properties': it is more than the sum of its parts. Synergies occur within families, leading to the family's own 'construction of reality' in which a principal component is the representation of the family itself. This is the precursor of the group-object relation, a concept I introduced in Chapter 7 and explore more fully below.

The family has in common with the psychotherapy group an evolutionary thrust. Both the individual family member and the group as a whole go through stages of development and periods of transition, which mark the evolving character of the group: transformations, progressions, and regressions occur in a dialectical interplay. The developmental stages not unusually trigger crises in the family. Hoffman (1981) notes that within the family life cycle, crises centre around members entering and leaving the system. She describes these as crises of accession (e.g. a new baby) and crises of dismemberment (e.g. divorce, death). As Skynner suggests, the ability to cope with change and loss across a wide range is a key requirement of the family.

As in psychotherapy groups, a family in conflict does not necessarily portend disaster but expresses the mounting pressure to deal with change and achieve a more complex integration. However, where the underlying emotional constellation in the family is weak or seriously in conflict with itself, the change cannot be absorbed and the family breaks down: symptomatically, as in the psychological collapse of one or more members; or in the fragmentation of the family, as in separation and divorce.

Weinhold (1991) listed the following characteristics of a dysfunctional family: rigid and compulsive rules; rigid and compulsive roles; family secrets; a very serious and burdened atmosphere; no personal privacy and unclear personal boundaries; a false sense of loyalty to the family; resistance to outsiders; embargo on strong feelings; conflict between family members denied and ignored; resistance to change; fragmentation and isolation; and triangulation to create alliances against others.

Frude (1991) highlights the main characteristics of disturbed families as: enmeshment or symbiotic closeness; its opposite in disengagement and interpersonal distance; poor communication with a high degree of ambiguity; lack of sharing and support, making problem solving difficult; intolerance of differences; lack of conflict resolution, with residues of hostility and damaged relationships; destructive rage; and avoidance of painful family matters, including deviant behaviour such as sexual abuse or physical violence.

There is a large degree of overlap between these two descriptions. They are also highly congruent with descriptions I have given of the anti-group in the psychotherapeutic setting. In a general way, they are the family equivalents of the anti-group. They also raise specific questions about the survival and continuity of the family in the face of such conflict and disunity.

The issue of continuity ties in with the concept of family history. The present-day family is crucially affected by the preceding generations. Williams (1989) refers to families as 'transmission belts of pathology'. Typically, difficult and dysfunctional patterns are repetitions of problems in earlier generations, often transmitted unconsciously but with powerful effects on present-day behaviours. Abuse of various sorts often follows this pattern. Masterson (1981) refers to the compulsion to repeat acts of cruelty as the *talionic impulse*: one of the deepest and most ancient of human impulses. Families repeat and reinforce such destructive and self-destructive patterns over several generations.

The genesis of the family as anti-group

Whereas the study of individual psychological development usually starts with the mother–infant relationship, study of the family begins with the parental couple. Even Winnicott, whose overriding concern is the early mother–child relationship, emphasises the importance of the parents in determining integrative and disruptive factors in family life (Winnicott 1965b). The emotional maturity of the couple, the nature of their relationships, their vision of the family, their relationship with their own primary families, and their integration within the wider community are all critical factors in influencing the kind of family they create.

Each parent brings to the new family the biological and psychological legacy of his or her own family history, and this is passed on to the children. Moreover, the way the two family lines come together in marriage or some other form of partnership is crucial in determining the positive or negative valence given the emerging group. Marriage can be seen not only as a ritual joining two people in partnership, but as an agreement, conscious and unconscious, to extend the family line – or not, as the case may be. These decisions are not purely biologically driven: they reflect deep-rooted beliefs about the value of the family and its future. Whether children are conceived, how many, and what sexes they might be are important aspects of the agreement, even though they are not always within conscious control.

The family is a highly complex network, a dense tapestry with many interweaving threads, past, present and future, conscious and unconscious. But, as Frude suggests, it has emergent properties, synergies which create a whole that is greater than the sum of its parts. A central aspect is the family's own representation of itself; and here, I suggest, lies its investment as group or anti-group, a group that will develop and thrive, in spite of obstacles, or a group that will turn in on itself, in a destructive enmeshment that will undermine the freedom and independence of individual members, or in splitting and fragmentation, which lead to the disintegration of the family group. Most families struggle with the opposing forces of integration and disintegration, and, in spite of the high rate of separation and divorce, the majority of families stay together. Here, the anti-group constitutes a point of tension without leading to disintegration.

The emphasis has so far been on social and interpersonal processes that determine a family's conception of itself, but the intrapsychic dimension is also important. In Chapter 6, I drew attention to the primal scene as a symbolic component of family and group development. Taking a broader definition than usual, I described the primal scene as a condenser of conscious and unconscious factors influencing the phantasy of the parental relationship. It has constructive or destructive elements, which may affect the direction and form of family relationships as a whole. In developmental sequence, it is followed by the Oedipus complex. Here, the child grapples more actively with its own intense longings and rivalries in relation to the parental couple. Where the Oedipus complex is mainly unresolved, this is a blueprint for a form of anti-group: the deeply frustrated rivalry and the failure to establish a positive identification with one or both parents weaken and potentially enmesh the child in a destructive triangular relationship which can have detrimental effects on the family as a whole.

A positive attitude towards the family entails a measure of healthy idealisation. This is complicated if the parental couple generate excessive envy of their relationships and their creative capacities. Meltzer (1973) refers to 'the enemy of the family' as an internal representation that is hostile towards the idealised family and seeks to destroy it. This tendency may be present in an individual member or may infiltrate the family as a whole.

It is important to recognise that it is not only parents who bring integrative or disruptive factors to the family group: children have an essential role in this, too. Winnicott states:

> It cannot be too strongly emphasised that the integration of the family derives from the integrative tendency of *each individual child*.... The parents, in their efforts to build a family, benefit from the sum of the integrative tendencies of the individual children ... each infant and child *creates* the family.
> (Winnicott 1965b, pp. 46–9)

Winnicott goes on to consider the disintegration of the family brought about by a lack of development in the individual child or by a child's illness. He observes disturbed tendencies in children which show themselves as an active need on the part of the child to break up anything that is good, stable, and reliable in family life. An example is the antisocial tendencies of the deprived child, who can be very destructive of family life. This is the active expression of Meltzer's 'enemy of the family', the hostile enactment of an anti-group attitude towards the family.

Ultimately, of course, it is neither parents nor children in isolation who determine the integration or disintegration of the family. This depends on the interactions of the generations in the synergy of the family.

This highlights the primary family experience as the template for what I have termed the group-object relation (see Chapters 7 and 8). Positive or negative group experiences in the family form the basis for constructs of groups in general. The psychotherapy group often reveals the connection between these domains of experience as transferred to the interactional sphere of the group. Although, as in therapy groups, there are opportunities in groups more generally for corrective experiences, these may fail when the individual or group is under the sway of a dominant anti-group mode deriving from pathological family group experiences.

Cross-sectional and longitudinal family approaches

The anti-group perspective on the family can be developed in two complementary ways: as an approach to understanding the current difficulties of the family (the cross-sectional approach) and as a perspective on the inter-generational history of the family (the longitudinal approach). In the following example, the cross-sectional and longitudinal views of the family as an anti-group are presented in parallel, but it becomes apparent that they are closely intertwined.

> The cross-sectional view is like a snapshot of the family in its current circumstances. The family in question is a unit of five: father (48), mother (43), James (21), Arthur (17), and Maddy (11). Father is an engineering repairman on the railways, working shifts. Mother has a part-time clerical job. James (21) is unemployed and has bouts of serious depression, withdrawing for long periods into his room. He is socially isolated. He has received psychiatric help and a diagnosis of schizophrenia has been mooted. Arthur (17) is meant to be studying for the GCSE certificate but has more or less dropped out of school. He has been on probation for minor offences and spends most of his time with his

friends, roaming the streets, glue-sniffing, and sporadically taking other drugs. Mother is a chronic worrier who has a poor relationship with father and has become close to Maddy (11), the youngest child, who is pubertal and a sensitive, confused girl. This is practically the only perceptible alliance in the family, and mother tends to triangulate with Maddy against father.

There is little interpersonal contact between most members of the family. For years, they have had no activity as a family group. There is practically no sharing of problems: for example, there has been no open discussion about James' problems, there is no constructive interaction, and no expression of conflict that leads to resolution or reconciliation. Occasionally, there are bursts of vicious anger between father and sons, which seem only to deepen the tensions in the family. Father has on occasions physically abused his two sons. They regard him with a mixture of fear and loathing.

The absence of family life is most apparent at evening mealtime, which could be an opportunity for the group to come together. But father almost invariably eats on his own, either before or after a shift. Mother tries to bring the children together at mealtime but rarely succeeds. James prefers to eat in his room, if at all. Arthur is seldom home and, when he is, hurriedly consumes snacks in the kitchen. Maddy usually sits down briefly with mother at the dinner table but she eats very little and usually leaves the table after a short while. She shows signs of anorexia. Mother sometimes complains openly about feeling isolated and unappreciated, but she gets little response. Beneath the tension and lack of communication in the family, there is an absence of trust, suppressed rage, and a lurking sense of despair.

These are all the hallmarks of the family as anti-group. Family members do not enjoy or want to be in the group. They pull apart rather than together. Their distress is expressed in acting out and psychiatric symptoms rather than communication.

The *longitudinal* view of the family reveals a deeply troubled history, going back several generations. The following is a brief summary:

Both parents are Irish, having emigrated to England, met there, and married. Their relationship was from the beginning problematic in that father is Catholic and mother Protestant. Both families, particularly father's, rejected the partnership at the outset. Father's family disowned him and his new family. Mother's family continued contact with their daughter but not their son-in-law and made only distant contact with the children.

Father's father (PGF) had been a heavy drinker and petty criminal who had become estranged from his wife and children. There had been several early deaths in the family (three children had died in infancy or early childhood), with a pervasive sense of mutual blame among the remaining members. PGF had actually been accused by some family members of killing his children through neglect. Father had an intensely hostile, confrontative relationship with PGF and his proposed marriage to a Protestant was a defiant gesture that succeeded in breaking all links with his family.

Mother's family had been marked by the early death of her father (MGF). Her mother (MGM) had brought up three daughters on her own. She had dealt with the death of her husband by becoming both mother and father and telling her daughters that men were unreliable and dispensable.

The 'new' marriage became burdened by feelings of guilt and resentment, both at the partners' primary families and, increasingly, at each other. There was a deep sense of a mistake having been made, irrevocably. The survival of the partnership was based more on routine and dogged defiance than any positive affiliation and there was no parental pride in the family they had created. The family was poorly integrated in its local community. In part, this was through shame about the children's problems, particularly James' psychiatric illness. An attitude of mistrust towards outsiders was one of the few subjects that momentarily united the family.

The longitudinal view of the group indicates that the family was created in an oppositional context which from early on undermined the value and integrity of the family group. The marital union, far from being supported by the respective families, met with profound disapproval, and the children grew up in an atmosphere of almost total estrangement from the wider family network. At the deepest level, there may have been a sense that the family should never have existed. The continuity of the family beyond their immediate nucleus, in fact, seemed to be in question. The children showed no interest in developing relationships that would ultimately perpetuate the family line. James' withdrawal and social isolation almost guaranteed this; Arthur was more interested in substitute outlets, such as drugs and anti-social acts; Maddy's incipient anorexia suggested possible problems of later sexual identification that would complicate her proclivity for a partnership and a family of her own. If indeed the children failed to form partnerships and procreate, this would lead to the fulfilment of the most destructive anti-group fantasy: the dissolution of the family.

Although the plight of this family seems particularly severe, my clinical experience suggests that it is not that unusual. Behind the surface of marital and family conformity, the semblance of conjugal happiness, often lie inherent contradictions in the very formation of the family that predispose it towards dysfunctional development and a threatened outcome. Current difficulties in the family are then understandable not so much as the problems of individual members, or even their existing relationships, but as the culmination of an inter-generational history which has built-in destructive and self-destructive elements.

The place of psychotherapy

To imagine taking any members of the above family into psychotherapy, either individual or group, is to countenance the profound struggle that would be required to overcome the despairing messages of the past. In a group, one could imagine the membership as a whole sinking under the weight of this particular family history. Destructive patterns of family life, such as described above, can become replicated in the group, contributing strongly to its anti-group potential.

Yet, it is important to recognise the enormously positive value a group can have for an individual who has known only fragmentation and isolation in the family context. Not all unfavourable histories constitute insurmountable problems for the group. As we know, an individual's own potential can transcend the constraints of past and present. In a favourable context, this can be brought to the fore in a healing way.

> Nina (aged 25) joined an ongoing psychotherapy group in an NHS setting. A shy, awkward young woman, severely lacking in self-esteem, she had considerable difficulty becoming part of the group. Her position here mirrored her life situation. As an infant, she had been fostered out to a succession of homes, ending up in a family with ten other children. She had been made to feel a total outsider there, unwelcome and inferior, particularly by a controlling and denigrating foster-mother. Nina was gradually able to talk about these events in the group and also her recent experience of seeking out her natural parents. She discovered that her father had disappeared soon after her birth and that her mother had become a long-stay patient in a psychiatric hospital. Her search had confirmed her deepest fears about her origins.
>
> The unfolding of this story in the group aroused great sympathy for Nina. This came particularly from two women, themselves mothers, who provided the group with two different sorts of mothering: Lela, a doting, sentimental Jewish mother, and Kay, a spunky cockney mother. These two women took a special interest in Nina, providing something of the maternal care that Nina lacked in her own life. To some extent, this was matched by the paternal interest shown in her by two men in the group, who tended to give her practical advice and support.
>
> Nina made considerable progress in the group. For the first time in her life, she started going out with men. Her self-esteem strengthened. Towards the end of her stay in the group, her success was symbolised in an event outside the group: she ran the London Marathon. She raised over one thousand pounds in sponsorship for a charity and became a local celebrity. The group delighted and shared fully in her success: it was as if she had run for them as well as herself.

The restorative potential of the psychotherapy group is nowhere more evident than in this example. An individual who had never found a family or a home found it in this group. The legacy of an anti-group history does not have to be destructive and the therapy group can help to transform it.

ORGANISATIONS

My knowledge of organisational behaviour stems from various roles, as a head of department in the National Health Service, as a staff consultant in mental health settings, and as a member of learned institutes. In each of these settings, I see the organisation from a different perspective, some as an insider, some as an outsider, but what is common to most, I believe, is the troubled heart at the centre of the organisation. In some cases, my sense of these difficulties is a background factor as I carry out my usual tasks, in others the organisational stress intrudes sharply on the conduct of my role. I am often reminded of the discrepancy between the organisational ideal, the aims and objectives of the organisation, its mission statements and logical strategies, and the reality of its functioning, in which conflict, confusion, and irrational behaviour abound.

A similar view is propounded by Schwartz (1990). Coming from the organisational consultancy field, he describes the evolution in his mind of the concept of two types of organisation, the 'clockwork organisation' and the 'snakepit organisation'.

> One type was a textbook organisation. In it, the organisation is all about and is concerned solely with carrying out its mission; people are basically happy at their work; the level of anxiety is low; people interact with each other in frictionless, mutually supportive co-operation; and if there are any managerial problems at all, these are basically technical problems, easily solved by someone who has the proper skills and knows the correct technique of management.
>
> The other type of organisation, the 'snakepit' organisation, is just the opposite of the textbook projection. Here, everything is always falling apart and people's main activity is to see that it doesn't fall on them; nobody really knows what is going on, though everyone cares about what is going on because there is danger in not knowing; anxiety and stress are constant companions; and people take little pleasure in dealing with each other; doing so primarily for their own

purposes or because they cannot avoid being so used themselves. Management problems here are experienced as intractable and managers feel that they have done well if they are able to make it through the day.

(Schwartz 1990, p. 78)

Schwartz believes that the snakepit is a far more accurate description of most organisations than the clockwork analogy. However, he identifies a common tendency in organisations to perpetuate an illusion of superiority and perfect control. This illusion he attributes to a narcissistic process in which the organisation invests itself with grandiose aims and qualities that remove it from realistic contact with its task and from a balanced appreciation of how it is, or is not, achieving its task. This Schwartz sees as potentially leading to a state of organisational decay. The consequence may be serious technical or financial failure and eventual organisational collapse.

Hirschorn (1988) similarly describes the deployment of 'social defences' in which people retreat from role, task, and organisational boundaries into fantasied solutions and self-created boundaries. These defences distort and depersonalise interpersonal relationships within the organisation through primitive processes of isolation, splitting, scapegoating, and projection. They undermine work relationships and impair the group's capacity to accomplish its task. Hirschorn regards anxiety as the basis of these processes: anxiety about the nature of the task, performance of the task, and perceived role in the organisation. This anxiety mobilises defensive strategies which lead to destructive actions between individuals and groups and this exacerbates rather than reduces the anxiety.

Schwartz's and Hirschorn's views are both strongly influenced by the Tavistock approach, which is largely derived from Bion's writings, particularly the theory of basic assumption groups. The model was developed by Elliott Jaques (1955) and is epitomised in the seminal paper by Isobel Menzies-Lyth (1959) on social systems as a defence against anxiety. This study revealed the way in which nursing staff's anxieties on a hospital ward led to the splitting of the task in defensive and bureaucratic ways.

A clearly distinctive approach to organisational problems has not yet emerged from group analysis, though there is reason to believe that the model has considerable applicability in the organisational field. One reason for this is that the study of organisations is in essence the study of group behaviour. Organisations are large groups which usually comprise a system of hierarchically organised smaller groups. The culture of the organisation can be understood in large part in terms of the nature of interactions within and between groups, as well as the interaction between the organisation as a whole and its environment. Within this context, as Hirschorn and other writers suggest, boundaries of groups are particularly important points of perception and activity: much of the dysfunction in organisations occurs at the boundaries.

It is within this framework that the concept of the anti-group can be introduced as a means of describing the pathological group processes that occur in organisations. The same key questions about group integrity, survival, and development as previously noted apply strongly in organisations, and the same polarities of integration–disintegration, progression–regression, and creativity–destructiveness define the working group as it organises itself in relation to its task. But, of course, the context is different from either psychotherapy groups or family groups, and it is necessary to consider the particular demands of organisational life to which people at work are subject. These could be described as follows: the pressures of employment and conformity to a work routine; the pressures of job performance; the anxiety about job security; the pressures of authority and hierarchical relationships; the stratification and overlap of work roles; the pressures of group vs. individual identity in a corporate environment; and the interpersonal tensions generated by a competitive work environment.

These 'pressures' are not unique to organisations but they are heightened in the organisational frame and create tensions and disruptions in group relationships. Schwartz's notion of the 'snakepit' is in many ways the organisational equivalent of the anti-group. The lack of trust, survival anxiety, distorted communication, false sense of group identification, and interpersonal alienation he describes are similar to the anti-group as described in psychotherapy groups and in families. The parallel between a dysfunctional organisation and a dysfunctional family has also been highlighted by Skynner:

Occasionally an isolated hospital or clinic will achieve public notoriety because it is exposed as functioning like a really sick family, isolated and at loggerheads with most colleagues and the local community because of its deviant values, and showing such pathological features as splitting, blaming, scapegoating, evasion of responsibility and failure to fulfil its assigned task on many levels.

(Skynner 1989, p. xli)

In organisations, the quality of group relationships has an important bearing on the level of productivity. Excessive group tension and conflict is likely to lead to lowered productivity, undermining the chief purpose of the organisation. The common symptoms of organisational fall-out are:

- High sickness and absence rate
- Poor recruitment and retention
- High accident rate
- Ineffectual and conflictual leadership
- Low morale
- Poor productivity

In all these instances, the hidden factor may be an absence of group cohesion and commitment and the presence of unbearable tensions which create particular stresses for the individual. In these circumstances, the workplace is experienced as unsupportive, threatening to the emotional and physical well-being of the employee. At its worst, the workplace becomes a paranoid-schizoid environment, a nightmare existence.

Morgan (1986) draws attention to the unconscious aspects of corporate life, in which powerful sexual and aggressive wishes complicate the relationships required to perform the organisational tasks, often leading to destructive acting out. He introduces the metaphor of the organisation as a psychic prison in which individuals are trapped in seemingly irrational, disturbing relationships that are only tangentially related to the task at hand. White (1988) similarly describes 'incest in the organisational family' as distorting work relationships and potentially destroying individual lives.

These are bleak visions of organisation life. The image of the snakepit, the narcissistic illusion, and the psychic prison highlight organisational pathology at its extremes, with little place for the creativity of individuals and groups. The difficulty, as in other forms of group, is the thin line that exists between creative and destructive, a phenomenon that is especially relevant to the fulfilment of work tasks.

Creative and destructive forces in work groups

It is necessary to keep the overall organisation in mind when attempting to understand the behaviour of specific work groups, since groups in organisations are so interdependent and linked to the wider system. However, this perspective can be complemented by more detailed examination of the dynamics of work groups observed as units in their own right. Here the dialectic of creative and destructive emerges with particular clarity and relevance.

Leaving the world of organisations for the moment, a vivid illustration of a creative group in conflict with itself is found in the novel *The Commitments* by the writer Roddy Doyle (1987), set in Dublin in the 1980s. The novel was also successfully filmed under the same name (director, Alan Parker, 1991). 'The Commitments' is the name of a self-styled pop or 'soul' group, as they prefer to be known. The story traces the evolution of the band from a ragbag of musicians and singers to a strong, dynamic group. In the first part of the story, there is an explosion of creativity as the band comes together, the problems of forming a group superseded by the energy, drive, and enthusiasm of the members. Then, just at the point where the group has finally made it, and in fact stands poised for greater things, there is an eruption of destructive behaviour and the group falls apart. Almost overnight, a group that lived and breathed the excitement of creativity is no more.

The story is told in recall by the leader of the band, Jimmy, who himself is an important instrument in the creative–destructive interplay of the group. Analysis of the developing narrative reveals that all along there have been underlying tensions that can no longer be contained as the group reaches its zenith. Identifying these features is instructive in understanding the way in which an anti-group can develop in work groups. In each feature, there is a creative element which shades into a disruptive or destructive one. The features are:

1 *The leadership*. Jimmy is something of a visionary leader. 'The

Commitments' are his inspiration and he has great ambitions for them. But once the group is established, Jimmy is uninterested in its day-to-day management, in helping the group to consolidate and survive. He prefers his fantasies of fame and glory. On the night the group breaks down, Jimmy is nowhere to be seen.

2 *Rivalry.* There is intense rivalry between the lead singer, a talented but obstreperous young man, and the female backing singers. In the early stages, this seems healthy for the group: it has an energising effect. But the rivalry deepens and becomes a source of tension, keeping the group on edge.

3 *Envy.* The same male lead singer's talent excites considerable envy in others, fuelled by his taunting, provocative behaviour. On the night of the group's great triumph, his boasting is more than others can bear and he is viciously beaten up by a follower of the band. Although the singer's gifts have contributed greatly to the success of the group, the destructive aspect of envy is greater than recognition of his value.

4 *Sexuality.* The three female backing singers all fall for the same, rather unlikely man in the band. Their separate affairs are hidden from each other until the night of the big explosion, when knowledge of these goings-on erupts and sparks off a frenzied back-stage fight. Earlier on, these clandestine affairs added a secret intimacy to the group, but the jealously unleashed has a destructive effect.

5 *Individual vs. group orientation.* As the band develops, the members are for the most part committed to the project. But by the time the group finally comes together, individual directions have started leading members away from the group. One wants to become a jazz musician, another is more attracted to matrimony than the music business. The name of the group, 'The Commitments', is ironical, since in the end it is the loss of commitment that leads to the disintegration of the group.

The dynamics described above are common to work groups, although they are played out with particular ferocity by the The Commitments. They vividly illustrate the tension between creative and destructive forces and the way this can get out of control. Such challenging processes may ordinarily be contained by strong leadership, but flaws in the leadership style, which in Jimmy's case become apparent only when the maintenance and survival of the group is at stake, create a gap in the holding function and the group falls apart.

Although the description here concerns the dynamics of a small working group, the overall theme echoes the processes described in relation to larger organisational dysfunction: the impact of destructive group tensions that are not primarily linked to the task and that are exacerbated by the retreat from reality into fantasy, as epitomised in Jimmy's flawed leadership.

Although The Commitments have been looked at as an independent group, not embedded in an organisation, the question of context is a vital one. The context of The Commitments is an economically ravaged Ireland with dwindling prospects for young people. Ironically, The Commitments' success, had it lasted, would have protected them from these privations. But there is a sense in the story that the deprivations of the external world may be so strongly internalised that, in the end, The Commitments may themselves be seen as a victim of environment blight, a failure of the holding environment to support initiative and creativity. This theme is explored more fully below in the section on 'The Culture'.

Organisational change

The significance of the external environment is compounded by the accelerating rate of organisational change that has been a feature of our times and that has resulted in massive degrees of instability in organisations. The combination of economic scarcity, the recession of the late 1980s and early 1990s, the widening gap between demand and resources in public services such as health and education, and the rampant influence of technological change has produced a deeply uncertain organisational world which affects not just organisations in their entirety but groups and individuals at all levels of the organisational matrix.

This uncertainty has a corrosive effect on the integrity of the workforce. In order to survive, group is set against group, individual against individual. A typical example in the UK was the decision by the Arts Council in 1994 to fund only one of three national orchestras, with an implied threat to the survival of the other two. The orchestras were invited to submit a business case for funding and a series of fraught negotiations ensued. Newspaper reports described the internecine strife that developed between the competing orchestras which previously enjoyed a friendly rivalry but were now pitted against each other in an intense struggle to survive.

Ruthless competition, disengagement, interpersonal alienation, hostile withdrawal, and downright betrayal are the products of a dog-eats-dog environment. Group cohesion survives mainly in the face of suspicion of other groups, a fragile cohesion born of fear and self-protectiveness that can easily splinter if competition for survival takes root *within* the group.

The impact of organisational change and uncertainty highlights the normally containing function of the organisational matrix. Le Roy (1994) has pointed to the necessity of a stable external frame in order to ensure continuity of self and relationships between selves. The organisation ordinarily has a function akin to the environmental mother and, when this breaks down, its containing function is destroyed. The safety provided by the external frame is replaced by a sense of danger, and primitive anxieties and defence mechanisms abound. One of these is projective identification: here, as described in the anti-group formation of the psychotherapy group, the unbearable mental contents are evacuated onto the organisation as a whole, making the organisation in fantasy a monster. An example of this is the present conception of the UK National Health Service. Once revered as an exemplary organisation with a strongly containing frame for patients and staff, it has become, through a series of policy and funding changes, a fragile structure that provokes powerful projections of a depriving and uncaring organisation, a starving monster that feeds off itself.

Reparation and staff development

Although the contemporary organisational world is a perplexing one that can produce serious individual and group dysfunction, it is counterbalanced by the capacity of human beings not only to survive adverse circumstances but to restore order and to maximise the opportunities for creative adaptation. This may be especially true in organisations which, for all their problems, usually provide opportunities for constructive action. Added to this is the natural desire people have to restore wholeness in the face of projection and fragmentation. Hirschorn (1988) suggests that reparation is a cardinal motive in the work environment. It can be achieved in various ways – through objects successfully made, services rendered, or healing the splits in interpersonal relationships. Hirschorn comments:

> Although people rely on social defences to contain their anxiety and consequently scapegoat clients, customers, or co-workers, they also desire to restore their experience of wholeness and repair the real or imagined psychological damage they have done in devaluing others. This desire for reparation helps to limit the level of social irrationality in any group setting and provides a strong basis for moments of group development.
>
> (Hirschorn 1988, p. 10)

Schwartz (1990) links reparation to the depressive position, which entails an acceptance of reality, a sense of limitation, and the capacity for neutrality. 'As part of a process of mutual affirmation with the other, it provides a rich motivational basis for doing good work' (Schwartz 1990, p. 135).

Where organisations have difficulty finding constructive solutions to their problems, they may call in external consultants for advice and support. One way in which group analysts have come to provide a highly relevant input to organisations is in the running of staff development groups, also known as staff support or sensitivity groups (Bramley 1990). These have previously been referred to (see Chapter 4) but merit consideration in the present context.

Groups of this sort are becoming more common in mental health settings, but there is a dearth of conceptual models to describe such activities, possibly because they straddle the complex terrain linking group work and organisational intervention. The group-analytic approach, which has the aim of achieving a democratic form of communication within and between groups, is a useful basis for carrying out such work, although the model, I believe, needs a clearer perspective on organisational pathology, including destructive processes in groups. In what follows, I describe a staff development group I have conducted over several years in which I used a group-analytic approach. The example aims to illustrate the way an anti-group process in the staff group reflected disturbances at the client level as well as changes in the wider organisational context. In order to make sense of this intense mirroring process, I formulated a hypothesis that proposes a core dynamic in the 'inner group' or 'organisational unconscious'.

The staff group in question was a mental health team providing day care for disturbed families. At the time I was invited in as staff facilitator, the group showed all the hallmarks of an anti-group. It was fragmented, lacking in trust, and suffering from a loss of belief in its value as a team. In the previous twelve months, several members had left the team in rapid succession and those remaining felt abandoned, demoralised, and anxious about the survival of the project.

I contracted to meet with the group for fortnightly meetings of 1½ hours each. In the first six months of these meetings, a traumatic past event, that had led to the weakening of the group, was revealed. A husband and wife couple attending the day centre as clients had come to dominate the community in a frightening way. Presenting as a powerfully united couple, they claimed a section of physical space in the day centre as entirely their own. The husband, in particular, behaved in a taunting, provocative way. Several patients stopped attending the day centre out of fear and the staff team felt highly threatened and unable to intervene. The male staff felt particularly anxious and impotent in the face of the husband's aggressive threats. Finally, a violent incident in the residents' community sparked off by the husband resulted in the police coming in and the couple was removed. But the incident left the community shaken and the staff group fragmented.

In the course of the staff development group, it became apparent that there were weak relationships between male and female staff, with a fear of coupling in case this aroused suspicion and envy in the rest of the team. Male–female rivalry was much more readily expressed than male–female bonding. A connection could be made with the disruptive client couple who expressed the reverse tendency by demonstrating an aggressive and exclusive heterosexual coupling. One interpretation was that the staff team could not deal effectively with the couple because of their unresolved anxiety about male–female relationships; another was that the client couple was destructively enacting something for the staff team. Either way, there was a serious problem about boundary regulation, with projections between staff and clients occurring in an uncontrolled and damaging way.

In addition to the dynamics of staff–client group relationship, the wider organisation, a social services unit, was going through a crisis. Much of this concerned the planned merger of two separate services, each of which had to make sacrifices in order to merge, and this was proving highly problematic. At a metaphorical level, this could be interpreted as a form of organisational coupling that was threatening to all those involved. It could be seen to have set the problem of coupling at the widest organisational level.

Finally, hypothesising a core dynamic in the organisation, it is suggested that within the inner group of the organisation – the organisational unconscious – was a disturbing fantasy of a violent, devouring couple that cowed those around them into defensive submission. (See Chapter 6, section on the primal scene.) In this process, the urge to couple on the part of the others was denied and powerful sexual impulses were projected onto a couple that had both heroic and scapegoat functions.

Interpretation of these dynamics was not directly made to the staff group: rather the connections were intuitively established in the staff's own exploration of their difficulties. The awareness gained made staff much more conscious of the need for boundary regulation. There was also increasingly free discussion about relationships in the team, including the tensions surrounding cross-gender communication. The following year, a similar incident threatened to implode in the community, but this time staff were able to see the warning signs and to deal with the problem in advance. The overall experience had a strengthening effect on the team: their number increased and their confidence returned. Male–female relationships improved and difficulties in this area were more openly confronted. This example demonstrates how an anti-group arose in the staff group, then how the process of disintegration in the team could be reversed by appropriate intervention in which the group-analytic approach with its understanding of boundary dynamics helped to mobilise the reparative tendencies of the group. In this case, the intervention was assisted by the psychological-mindedness of the team and their anxiety to avert a similar trauma.

The group-analytic method has considerable potential with relatively small staff groups of the sort described but it is not clear whether it can make a similarly positive impact on wider organisational pathology. Here, median-group or large-group approaches may be more relevant. Large-group dynamics are often akin to organisational processes, including the intensification of primitive emotions and the threats to individual identity (Turquet 1975). However, as various writers, including Skynner (1989), have pointed out, there may also be states of creative depression in large groups, which, if maintained, can deepen relationships, promoting a sense of wholeness in the individual, the group, and the wider context – koinonia, as described by de Maré *et al.* (1991).

The difficulty is that the tide of organisational change has currently gained a frightening momentum of its own, potentially dwarfing the efforts of supportive intervention. Here, we enter the wider arena of culture and politics: organisational life is determined by powerful forces outside itself, and it is to this dimension that we now turn.

THE CULTURE

The previous sections on psychotherapy, family, and organisational groups have all suggested that destructive forces in these contexts are related to vicissitudes in the cultural domain. This is consistent with a group-analytic perspective, which regards the essence of the person as being social not individual and the dynamics of the social in turn being related to the broader cultural frame. It also fits with mainstream social theory which seeks to dissolve the dualism between individual and society, while recognising the crucial contribution of both to the social order (Layder 1994).

In spite of this emphasis, the primary focus in group analysis since its inception has been the small analytic psychotherapy group. Awareness of cultural forces is mediated through the therapy group and seen in terms of the individual and interpersonal rather than culture being viewed as a subject for study in itself. Thus, Hearst states:

> It is my contention that the small analytic group contains

and discloses the historic, social and cultural dimensions in its individual members and that these must be taken into the field of vision, if one is to do justice to its full potential.

(Hearst 1993, p. 393)

In recent years, however, there has been a growing interest among group analysts in exploring the reverse relationships – how culture and its changes impact on individuals and groups, including the psychotherapy group. Le Roy (1994) describes 'the double dimension of culture which *defines* and *contains* a person as transmitted in groups, the family group and socially organised groups or institutions' (p. 182). Traumatic sources in the cultural container continually threaten to disrupt these groups. For example, primary groups, such as the family, are adversely affected by parental and transgenerational family pathology and weakened cultural codes (see the example in the previous section on the family for an illustration of this process, pp. 242–5). Secondary groups or social institutions are also disrupted by current or past traumata, including wars, political violence, migration, and rapid cultural change.

This leads naturally to an exploration of the cultural origins of the anti-group. I suggest that we can see culture itself as generating and struggling to contain anti-group forces that seep through all our institutions. At times of rapid cultural change or transformation, the threat to group integrity is all the more pronounced. I suggest that this is particularly the case at present, that we are undergoing a process of massive cultural transition and that this highlights the crucial significance of both group and anti-group identifications in influencing the quality of social life. This covers a huge area of concerns, most of which are beyond the scope of this chapter, but some of the main parameters are outlined below.

Politics and the group

Politics largely concerns the relationships between groups and within groups. The nature of an individual citizen's tie to his or her community is moulded by the dominant political perspective of the day. In the UK, for example, if we take the two main political parties, Labour and Conservative, we see immediate differences in their notion of community and how the individual relates to that community. Labour emphasises the collective spirit that underlies community, seeking to strengthen mutual collaboration and support as a way of facilitating the individual, whereas Conservative emphasises the individual's autonomy in a competitive environment driven by market forces.

It is clear that in the last sixteen years or so, the Conservative government has created a society in which the value placed upon individual freedom has superseded the notion of group or community. When Margaret Thatcher became prime minister in 1979, she encouraged popular resentment at what was seen as too much taxation, too much bureaucracy, and, in particular, too much collectivism. In Mrs Thatcher's own words, there was no such thing as society.

The impact of this ideology on Britain is currently undergoing intense review. There have arguably been some benefits, which include: the 'modernisation' of Britain; increased opportunity for segments of the population; and perhaps a greater capacity for self-reliance. But there is also a common view that the sharp rise in social unrest and disintegration may be at least partly related to Thatcherite philosophy. An ideology of individualism creates a society of winners and losers, but neither of them is ultimately satisfied. The losers end up marginalised and disaffected, while the winners are driven more and more by the need to acquire. This undermines values which may be of more fundamental importance in their lives, such as relationships, altruism, and a sense of social responsibility.

These social consequences translate into the psychological symptoms that we see in our consulting rooms. The desolation and damaged self-esteem of the unemployed is matched by the desperation of the workaholic and the accompanying loss of intimacy and relatedness. Lasch (1979) describes ours as a narcissistic culture in which people are preoccupied with their image while finding themselves unable to relate to others. Clinically, narcissism has become the focal problem of our age, the psychotherapeutic literature reflecting an urgency to understand and treat problems in which an excessive preoccupation with the self hides an underlying sense of estrangement and despair (Kohut 1971; Johnson 1987).

My purpose in outlining the link between politics and social reality is not so much to condemn a particular belief system, i.e. Conservatism, as to make the point that the phenomena of the group, whether pro-group or anti-group, are generated and reflected in the cultural container. In what direction the causal relationship flows is a further consideration. I have suggested above that the sense of community is established largely through the political reality of the time. But the reverse could also apply: that ambivalence about group membership, in this case, is so widespread that it is picked up, expressed, indeed exploited, by the prevailing ideology of the day.

The breakdown of established structures

The twentieth century has increasingly seen a breakdown of traditional structures covering a wide area from territorial and ecological structures to structures of thought and belief. To continue the point about community above, it is true that the investment in community as a valued entity is influenced by the politics of the day, but it is also the case that for some decades territorial communities and therefore local identities have been breaking down under the pressure of geographical and social mobility. In this situation, social attachments become shifting and tenuous, since each move means starting again, and there is a withdrawal from the effort required to build up and maintain groups. The group as the focus of social life disintegrates and a sense of anxiety and strangeness about groups sets in: anti-group attitudes that are similar to those described in relation to the psychotherapy group. As Schwartz (1990) suggests, the motive for group membership may become one of use and exploitation rather than affiliation.

The spread of technology and the volcanic growth of information brings with it widespread obsolescence and information redundancy. Jobs, roles, skills that are needed one day are irrelevant the next. Institutions that served a purpose are no longer required. This is paralleled by crises in personal identity and a loss of faith in the spiritual domain. Although in themselves these phenomena do not necessarily have a direct bearing on group life, they weaken and destroy the ties that bind people together in groups and communities.

In an anti-group culture, the phenomenon of group affiliation can become polarised between a loss of affiliation at one extreme and total, all-consuming affiliation at the other. I refer here to the extremist religious or political groups in which there is an overwhelming identification with an ideology, a leader, and the group as an absolute community. Here, individuality has no place. Instead of the division between self and other, there is a complete merging of self and other. These groups were referred to earlier in terms of the dangers of extreme cohesiveness (Chapter 9). Ultimately, as has been documented on many occasions, these groups end up destroying themselves. We may conclude that they harbour split-off anti-group attitudes that are all the more vicious for never being allowed to surface or be seen. But there appears to be a powerful attraction to fundamentalism in both the Western and Eastern worlds: the surrender of individual identity to omnipotent leadership and an idealised, totalistic community. On a lesser scale, the temptation – and the danger – in our psychotherapeutic institutions of enacting an ideological totalism has previously been noted, as has the function this might provide in preventing internal splits (see Chapter 2).

Technological change

As the twenty-first century approaches, the speed of technological change is at once exciting and frightening. More and more it becomes apparent that what is at stake is not only the future of technology but the very nature of the society we live in.

Critics vary in their interpretation of whether this change will benefit or damage our culture. *Visions of Heaven and Hell* was the title of a Channel Four television series (February 1995) that set out to debate this question. Looming large was the subject of the Internet, a vast computer network linking some 30,000,000 people in a system of immediate communications. Here, the vision of community takes a radically new form. Instead of a geographically based community with known boundaries and stable referents, we enter the world of the virtual community. Communication no longer occurs within the confines of a familiar group but within 'cyberspace', a potential space that dramatically transforms the nature of communicative relationships.

The optimistic view is that technology can bring us together and can give us a greater sense of community in a divided world:

> This is a new definition of community for the twenty-first century. It does not merely yearn for how things used to be. It confronts the reality of modern life – that we are more

mobile, that change is a constant condition, that we live in a global economy.

(Harrison 1995, p. 11)

The sceptical view, however, is that technology fuels the very problem it claims to be solving: that, instead of helping people to re-connect, it will help to drive them further and further apart. A large part of this is the substitution of ordinary face-to-face encounters between people, and the potential for closer, more intimate relationships, with communication through a symbolic order mediated and dominated by computers.

> A vision of a person in the early twenty-first century presents itself. He has lost his position in the workplace and has set himself up in an office at home, surrounded by a fortress of computers and linked systems. He has practically no contact with anyone all day but traverses the myriad pathways of the Internet, making fleeting contact with people in distant parts of the world. He lives in a social bubble, a computer cocoon. He is sheltered not only from the immediate pressures of his personal life but from the aggression and violence that continue unabated on the national and international scenes. He has no part to play in this, no particular convictions about it.

The loss of personal contact and the implications this has for the social domain are summed up by Charles Handy:

> As somebody once said, if I is to be fully I, we have to belong to We. And the big question is 'who is We?'. To a lot of people in the past it was the organisation; and a hundred years before that it was the village, which incorporated the work organisation. But now for many people we've taken away the village and we've taken away the work organisation, and so it's not at all clear who 'We' is.
>
> Now through my computer I belong to what's called a virtual community – a lot of people I can contact just by pressing buttons. But to me a virtual community that I can only talk to by typing is not the same as people I can actually touch and feel.
>
> (Handy 1995, p. 15)

When previously considering political systems, there was a

question about the extent to which politics influences the degree of value placed on community vs. the extent to which it picks up and exploits what is already there, in terms of social anxiety and ambivalence. So with technology. Are people rearranging their lives at a greater distance from each other because computer technology requires adaptation to a differently structured existence? Or are they embracing technology because it offers a refuge, a seemingly safer and more satisfying means of communication than person-to-person relationships?

A further concern is the developing cleavage between the computer 'haves' and 'have nots'. It is increasingly apparent that computers are accessible to only portions of the population – the informed, the rich, the technologically skilled, mainly inhabitants of the developed world. People outside these spheres are likely to become increasingly excluded. Even in the 'affluent' cities, it is likely that there will be technological advancement within the computer nerve centre of the city, with oceans of poverty and ignorance on the outskirts. This developing condition has been referred to as 'techno apartheid' and is described by Petrella:

> Because technology is creating more and more poverty while creating more goods and more services, the consequence will be the emergence of a cleavage between the world of the integrated and those armies of excluded people in Africa, in Asia, in Latin-America, in Europe, in North-America and Japan. And they are going to witness a kind of new global apartheid based primarily on scientific and technological factors.
>
> (Petrella 1995, p. 16)

We see the symptoms of anti-group everywhere: groups breaking up, threatened, divided, disenfranchised, not through wars or acts of violence (as will be discussed in the next section) but through the paradox of evolutionary progress. Returning to the group-analytic frame, Foulkes' original formulation of the individual as a nodal point in the social network acquires an altered meaning. Although Foulkes (1971) spoke about the transpersonal qualities of the social matrix, reflecting the synergistic potential of the wider group, the individual nodal point was still embodied in a tangible network and the language of communication essentially that of the spoken word. In the virtual community, the nodal point becomes a tiny speck floating in a vast, mysterious cyberspace periodically illuminated by the word of the computer.

Destructive forces in the cultural container

In the previous sections, anti-group tendencies contained in cultural changes such as increasing social mobility and technological advancement were considered, as opposed to the erosion of the group through overt attack. In this section, more direct aggression between and within groups is examined. The problem of human destructiveness is universally recognised, although Zulueta (1993), in a recent examination of the phenomenon, commented that we still do not understand why, as Storr (1968) put it: 'we are the cruellest and most ruthless species that has ever walked the earth' (p. 9). In the twentieth century alone, there have been two world wars which between them led to the death of some 100,000,000 people. As the century moves to a close, the killing continues, in the former state of Yugoslavia, the dismantled Soviet Union, and the battlefields of Africa and Asia. At a domestic level, this is matched by rising violence of every conceivable form.

Although these are acts committed by one group against another, reflecting *inter-group* hostilities, the long view, when seen in terms of the overall human predicament, is that these are self-destructive acts. Ultimately, they threaten our existence as a species. In parallel to Storr's quote above, Dixon (1988) has questioned why we have become not just the most destructive species ever but 'the most *self-destructive* animals ever to stalk the earth' (p. 8, italics mine). Dixon cites Higgins (1978) who, in his book *The Seventh Enemy*, refers to human beings as their own worst enemy. Higgins suggests that there are six interrelated threats to the survival of the human race – over-population, increasing scarcity of resources, degradation of the environment, nuclear abuse, the food crisis, and galloping technology. Together, these threats combine at an accelerating rate to lead us towards the ultimate catastrophe – extinction. Higgins suggests that only one thing could save us – ourselves. But far from doing so, we seem to be caught in an uncontrollable spiral, moving relentlessly towards the brink. Hence the title of Higgins' book – the seventh enemy is ourselves.

Higgins' predictions were made almost twenty years ago but they ring true today. Our self-destructive potential continues to be widely quoted. Morgan (1986) cites evidence that we are slowly eating ourselves to death. Our food is adulterated by myriad additives that could have toxic effects, particularly in the long term. Similar threats stem from environmental pollution. In spite of continued warnings from scientists and others, the pollution continues, with mounting evidence of the destruction of the global environment. The most worrying aspect is that this is our host environment, the earth we depend on for sustenance and survival. This is another version of the culture of the anti-group, where the group represents the human species imperilled by itself in its biological and social continuity.

Returning to the political domain, we see the great difficulty of achieving and maintaining the integration of larger social and national groups. There appears to be an inevitable hostility between them. Money-Kyrle (1961) saw this splitting as a tendency based on 'propinquity': the natural gravitation towards those who are similar and exclusion of those who are different, particularly when in states of need, with selfish interests in each group leading to competition for resources and inevitable hostility towards the other. Money-Kyrle writes:

> That in a limited world with an expanding population the welfare of one group – whether class, party or nation – can often be secured only at the cost of other groups is a fact we may deny but cannot escape.
>
> (Money-Kyrle 1961, p. 142)

There have been several dramatic examples of this on the recent world scene. In the late 1980s, there was a sense of rising hope as some long-standing barriers between countries were removed. The breaking down of the Berlin Wall, in particular, symbolised the promise of greater harmony between people. A unified world in which difference could be tolerated, even integrated, seemed possible. But in a short space of time, those hopes – at least temporarily – were dashed. A wave of racial prejudice flared up in Germany and suspicion and hostility between East and West resurfaced. The reverse situation occurred in the Soviet Union and Yugoslavia, where previously united countries splintered into violent national groups. The media drew dramatic attention to these events. 'Hate thy neighbour', read a *Newsweek* cover story of late 1992. 'Rape thy neighbour' headed a feature article in the *Independent* newspaper in England, describing the atrocities committed in the former Yugoslavia.

Here, there were group problems of the greatest magnitude. For smaller groups struggling to unite there was intense competition and conflict, making integration impossible: for larger groups, in which there had been a semblance of unity, a process of fragmentation and entropy set in. Groups fell apart: the centre could not hold.

Other examples showed how, in different circumstances, frustration and despair could lead groups to turn in on themselves. In the Los Angeles riots of 1990, members of the black population, frustrated by their lack of prospects, unemployment, and racial discrimination, turned violently against each other. In South Africa, preceding the momentous political change of 1994, the worst violence of a people marked by deprivation and discrimination was turned not outwards but inwards, with ethnic killing on a scale unprecedented in the country's long history of conflict.

Kaplan (1994) has drawn attention to the 'coming anarchy'. He cites examples of how, in parts of Africa, South America, and China, governmental authority has broken down and a rampant, destructive lawlessness has set in. In China, rapid economic growth has resulted in less rather than more order, with vast tracts of the population in chaos. Millions of people are described as wandering across China in search of work, a home, belonging. Social commentators, like Kaplan, regard these as the wars of the future. Increasingly, threats to states will come from inside not outside, with social divisions plunging whole states into anarchy.

If there has been a shift at all in our awareness of our destructiveness, it is towards a clearer recognition that the violence emanates from within us. In this sense, our cultural preoccupations have changed. In the first half of the twentieth century, our thinking about wide-scale aggression was dominated by the impact of the two world wars. Here, for the most part, the enemy was outside us. The threat to our survival came from clearly defined external sources, seemingly beyond our control. But in the second half of the century, our concern about survival reflected the threats from within, generating two major themes concerning our self-destructiveness. The first was – and, to a lesser extent, still is – the danger of a nuclear holocaust. The second, and more recent, is our anxiety about the destruction of the global environment. A third could be seen as the spread of chaos and anarchy in the way described above. These preoccupations reveal a sense of the fragility of our civilisation, but they begin to identify ourselves as the key players in the theatre of destructiveness. This can be seen as a shift from the paranoid-schizoid position to the depressive position in which we begin to take responsibility for our destructiveness. For all the anxiety this arouses, it reflects progress in that the acceptance of responsibility strengthens the possibility of repair.

Whether, though, human beings can deal with the enemy within – minus the rallying point of the enemy without – is an open question. Dixon (1988) points out that much of our irrational, self-destructive behaviour may be the consequence of an absence rather than the presence of an identified enemy. This leaves us facing a dilemma: if aggression, particularly at the wider national levels, can be dealt with only by directing it outwards, by creating and maintaining enemies, and if internal aggression leads to increased irrationality and self-destruction, what choice do we have?

Linking the intra-psychic and the social: a hypothesis

The indivisible link between individual and group, person and culture, has been emphasised throughout this text, but largely in a generalised way. These are such complex domains, occurring at such differing levels of the organisational whole, that to specify exact links is difficult. But consideration of the anti-group in these spheres suggests a point of intersection. We return here to a mirroring analogy: through the prism of the anti-group, we see psyche and social world acting as containers for each other, mutually reflecting each other in an ongoing cycle.

The most relevant intra-psychic paradigm, I suggest, is the failure of the environmental mother to provide a context for the child to acquire the rudiments of a creative relationship to self and other. This includes group relationships, such as the family group, peer group, and social group. Groups become the repository of the hostile part-objects accruing from early maternal failure. This lays the basis for the anti-group, for fear and distrust in groups, and for its corollary in the negative group-object relation (as described in previous chapters, 3, 5, 6, and 7).

Culture, in its widest forms, is reflected in the same mirror: the surrounding ethos, be it earth, world, society, is experienced symbolically as a failing environmental mother. This mother-environment is unable to feed and nurture sufficiently those within it, to provide safety and support. Individuals and groups appear to be picked for special favours (the successful ones, the wealthy, the chosen) while others are left to struggle for mere existence. A wish to repudiate and attack the world, the frustrating environment, mobilises actual or fantasied attacks on it, in the form of depredation of people, property, and the ecosphere. This lays waste to the environment, human and non-human, and the sense of a desolate world, be it in the mind or reality, is confirmed.

The cultural tragedy is reflected in the personal tragedy of the infant with failed maternal support: the tragedy of the infant is reflected in a cultural wasteland of devastation and despair.

Scarcity, I believe, is at the heart of the problem, a deep underlying sense of insufficiency, whether fantasied or real. One of the most haunting images of our time, intermittently flashed across newspapers and television screens, is that of a famished mother in a drought-stricken third world country clutching her starving infant at her breast. This image, I believe, transfixes us because of the shame, horror, and indignation it arouses, but also, at another level, it reminds us of our own most primitive fears of deprivation and decay. These are the mothers of scarcity and it is the psychology of scarcity that is at the root of both personal and cultural disintegration, creating envy of the 'haves' and a rage that seeks to destroy.

The psychology of scarcity, I believe, is universal. In many third world countries, ravaged by war and drought, it is a brutal, incontrovertible fact. But in the developed world, too, in the midst of plenty, there is also a lurking sense of insufficiency. This may also be factual: witness the pockets of deprivation and degradation in inner cities, for example. But even among the well-off, the affluent, the spectre of insufficiency roams, perhaps through some ancestral roots, perhaps through a form of unconscious anxiety, propelling people towards greater and greater gain. Everywhere we see the spectacle of excess, spiralling materialism, galloping profits, as if nothing is ever enough. This is a form of rape and pillage of the environment, making ever-increasing demands on natural resources, depleting the world in order to fill up the unstoppable gap of imagined insufficiency.

We see this theme reverberating through the various groups

we have considered. In group psychotherapy, resistance to the group is often based on a sense of insufficiency – there is too little to go round; one therapist has to be shared; you have to fight for attention. In family groups, a major source of tension is the sense of not being personally valued and loved, as if love is a very scarce commodity that has to be wrenched from other family members. In organisations, the competition is for diminishing resources, jobs, money, recognition, and here the fear of insufficiency is often cruelly confirmed by actual redundancy.

In this way, the deepest internal and the widest external forms of disintegration interpenetrate at the point of environment failure. At the dark heart of the anti-group is the dread of insufficiency, and, beyond that, of extinction.

Group analysis and culture: a critique

The cultural matrix is a field of enormous potential study for group analysis and the underlying group-analytic belief system is highly congruent with such an approach. But is also contains some inherent limitations.

In the same way that Foulkes did little to augment understanding of destructive processes in small groups, so, while recognising the broader significance of culture, he did little to penetrate it in any depth. Society and culture often seem to remain abstract entities in his writing, emphasised in overall terms but lacking the richness of detail. In biographical terms, as suggested in Chapter 2, there is little in his writing that gives the impression of a man who had seen and survived a world war, and, as I suggested earlier, his approach to group therapy seems strangely dissociated from an awareness of the cultural ethos of the time.

These problems are particularly apparent in Foulkes' basic law of group dynamics – a flawed construct, which I believe is predicated on Foulkes' blind spots about both the small group and the social context. This issue was dealt with more fully in Chapter 2, but, in summary, the 'law' flows from the assumption that aggression is primarily located in the individual rather than the group (an assumption which is challenged by the evidence presented in this chapter). Once aggression is dealt with, the theory goes, constructive forces are liberated and lead the group towards the norms of the community of which it is part. My main criticisms of this formulation are 1) the failure to recognise the aggression and destructiveness residing in groups, and 2) the naively optimistic ring of Foulkes' 'sociobiological' view that the therapy group of necessity moves closer to social norms. Given the social distortion and breakdown described throughout this chapter, the desirability of moving closer to such destructive norms is highly questionable.

I believe that group analysis would have more to offer the cultural sphere if

- it were to see the therapy group as continuous with culture rather than as a separate, idealised entity that yet aspires to some of the dubious aspects of society;
- it ceased to shrink from some of the real devastation and destruction enacted within groups;
- it applied its understanding to the forces between and not only within groups, as Brown and Zinkin (1994) have suggested;
- it could view the therapy group as a force for change that challenges rather than conforms to the conventional norms of society.

Ironically, Foulkes underemphasised the power of both psychotherapy groups and the culture at large: therapy groups, since they have a transformational potential that may transcend the constraints of society; cultural forces, because they do not remain static but have their own profound transformational flux, itself precipitating massive change.

Apart from these more conceptual considerations, there is the emotional challenge of the impact of the anti-group which, as suggested in previous chapters, is manifested in destruction and disintegration at varying levels of our socio-cultural life, from intensely personal to the broadly ecological. Here, I refer to the challenge to psychotherapists of whatever persuasion. Hoggett (1992) claimed for psychoanalysis the capacity to repair the social fabric. If this is true for individual analysis, how much more so is it for group analysis which, with its small, median, and large groups, is so close to the social domain? But this depends on a careful understanding of the relationship of therapy groups to the changing cultural context and, in particular, the vicissitudes of integration–disintegration that pervade our social functioning.

Chapter 12

Conclusion
Towards an integrative theory of group analysis

> *'Strangely enough', wrote Foulkes, 'the acknowledgement of the forces of self-destruction and their agencies helps us and makes us therapeutically far more powerful.' (1964b, p. 145)*

The evidence of this book suggests that this is one of Foulkes' most paradoxical statements. Not only does it convey Foulkes' own sense of paradox, but it is paradoxical when viewed in the light of his overall contribution. Foulkes repeatedly affirmed his awareness of the importance of destructive processes, including his strong belief in the death instinct (Foulkes 1964b, pp. 138–9, 145; 1969, p. 24; 1972, pp. 246–7; 1974, p. 275; 1977, pp. 300–5), but stopped short of developing in group analysis a method of understanding and working with these processes that could add to its therapeutic value. His one attempt at doing so (see Chapter 2, pp. 30–1) was limited and formulaic, and did scant justice to the complex relationship between destructive and constructive forces in the group. It is also tied to his questionable 'basic law of group dynamics' which posits that the momentum of the therapy group inevitably, and of necessity, leads towards the norms of the society of which it is part. The result was an optimistic, inspiring view of the group but one that underemphasised the extent to which groups mobilise aggressive and potentially destructive impulses and the threat this may pose to the integrity and continuity of the group itself. As such, it did not address the issue of group as opposed to individual pathology, which also limited the application of group analysis to non-clinical contexts.

The discrepancy between Foulkes' stated belief about the value of understanding destructive processes and the way this is represented in his actual theory and technique to a large extent has formed the substance of this book. Why and how it came about has been considered in historical, biographical, institutional, theoretical, and clinical terms. The concept of the anti-group emerges as a core, critical principle, aiming to restore dialogic balance to the theory while offering a framework for describing and understanding group-antagonistic and disintegrative forces in both clinical and non-clinical settings.

Part of the problem is that Foulkes' writing, and his underlying assumptions, have not yet been subjected in any substantial way to critical analysis. The first fifty years or so of group analysis have seen the proliferation of interest in the approach, the spread of Foulkes' influence to many countries, and a diverse and growing group-analytic literature – all of which attests to the generativity of the approach and its relevance to the contemporary psychotherapeutic endeavour. However, much of the post-Foulkesian literature has taken Foulkes' concepts as givens, seeking to reinforce and illustrate them, rather than to question and debate. It has therefore tended to perpetuate the over-optimistic aspects of the theory, linked to what Karterud (1992) described as 'the cultural idealisation of Foulkes within the group-analytic community'. My brief biographical perspective on Foulkes and the early development of group analysis (see the Prologue and Chapter 2) suggested areas of denial and dissociation which are possibly reflected in the continuing group-analytic tradition. It is as if a process of mourning has failed to take place, perhaps for Foulkes' death, perhaps for the limits and incompleteness of the theory, perhaps for the loss of the ideal in our vision of the therapeutic group.

This said, it is important to recognise the alternative responses that have grown in the group-analytic milieu in recent years. Writers such as Roberts (1993) and Prodgers (1990) have begun to challenge some of Foulkes' more dominant assumptions, to give voice to the side that represents caution and doubt, and to bring into focus the group's potential for destructive and disintegratory processes. This also ties up with a growing view in the USA that 'disorganisation, chaos, death, aggression and unknowing are important and hitherto neglected aspects of groups as of all living systems' (Schermer 1994, p. 31). In this sense, I suggest that the anti-group can be seen as reflecting not only my ideas but a body of thinking that is interested in exploring the reverse side of the group-analytic mirror.

A word about the scope of the anti-group. As the Foulkesian

tradition has largely lacked an adequate balancing force, the concept is applied very widely in this book, covering a complex range of phenomena within psychotherapy groups as well as the universe of groups outside the consulting room. It is recognised that there is a risk of over-generalisation. To use a single term, the anti-group, to describe the multiplicity of phenomena covered may indeed seem reductionist, but it is argued that:

- the anti-group *is* conceived in broad terms to describe a wide range of manifestations that have at their core an ambivalence about group relatedness; and
- the concept is relatively new and this book is exploratory, so that it is appropriate at this stage to follow a discursive path.

The concept makes it more possible to open and extend the debate about creative and destructive forces in groups, to consider them as complementary parts of a pair, to examine the links that join them and the language that separates them. The overall aim is not to destroy what exists but to regenerate and strengthen it. Ultimately, what may be achieved, in line with Foulkes' paradoxical belief, is both a theory and a therapy that are *more* rather than less powerful.

THE CHALLENGE TO GROUP PSYCHOTHERAPY

Many of the difficulties in the group-analytic approach mirror those in group psychotherapy more generally. As this book is concerned with the overall field, I begin with some reflections on the position of group psychotherapy at the present time.

Two linked features mark the current status of psychotherapy: the continuing expansion of psychotherapeutic practice in its diverse forms and the increasing challenges to the ethics and efficacy of psychotherapy. In the last decade or two, this has been witnessed in the unsettling issues raised by critics such as Masson (1990) and Hillman and Ventura (1993), who question the value of all psychotherapy; the critiques by writers representing particular political concerns, such as feminism, lesbianism (O'Connor and Ryan 1993), and class (Richards 1995); the increasing attention to outcome evaluation in health services; and the greater exposure of psychotherapeutic practice in the media.

Interestingly, group psychotherapy has to a large extent eluded the challenges to psychotherapy as a discipline. For example,

Masson particularly lambasts individual psychotherapy but also takes to task a range of other modes of therapy, such as family therapy and Gestalt therapy. Almost the only one missing in his list is group psychotherapy. I would venture that this omission has more to do with the ambiguous status of group psychotherapy than with its being inherently less open to criticism, particularly in the eyes of a critic as determined as Masson. In the introduction to this book, I suggested that anti-group attitudes may influence not only the conduct of psychotherapy groups *per se*, but the surrounding ethos in terms of the status accorded group psychotherapy and the strength of conceptual discourse underpinning theory and practice.

Group psychotherapy needs to stand and be counted with all the other psychotherapies. It has to be judged on similar criteria to the others, to be demystified, to be fully anchored in the critical domain. The more it can confront its own internal contradictions and limitations, the better prepared it will be for these challenges.

This is all the more important given the complex future we are entering. Exploration of the wider social sphere in Chapter 11, in addition to extending our frame of reference, provided a vision of the altered society we encounter as we approach the millennium. There is a challenge to all forms of psychotherapy in the advent of a new century. The twenty-first century looms ahead vast and unknowable in the longer term. But at the point of its interface with the present century, there are particular concerns about the nature of society, the individual, and the quality of interpersonal and group relationships in a highly technological world. Technology offers new modes of communication in transformed communities which are seemingly more integrated than before through information networks but more dispersed and fragmented in terms of direct interpersonal contact.

It could be argued that group is the most socially relevant form of psychotherapy in a world in which local communities are breaking down. It could be seen as a continuing context for group affiliation, a place where the human narrative can continue to be told, and a forum for understanding the complexities of group relationships in a paradoxically shrinking but decentred global network. In order to fulfil this potential, however, group psychotherapy needs the strengthened theory and practice suggested above.

THE PLACE OF GROUP ANALYSIS

The strengths and potentials of group analysis, in terms of its depth, breadth, and its creative possibilities, are implicit in this book. In the same way that it has provided fertile ground for a wide sphere of developments, so it has provided a broad and generous frame for this book. But its limitations and weaknesses have also been highlighted, particularly its dual tendency to over-idealise the therapy group and to underemphasise destructive processes in groups. Foulkes' emphasis on wholes has created an illusion of unity, a problematic situation for a field as complex as group psychotherapy that requires an understanding of the relationship between parts and wholes in the flux and disequilibrium that characterise group development. The Foulkesian concept of the group matrix exemplifies the problem: although a generative concept, it is nevertheless vague and global in a way that obscures the detailed textures of group development.

There is a particular need in the group-analytic approach for a greater emphasis on differentiation. This applies not only to the conception of the group as a generalised whole, as suggested above, but to the notion of *otherness* in relationships between people. In Foulkes' theory, the view of the individual as a nodal point in a social network, reflecting and mirroring other individuals in multiple patterns, although at one level sound in terms of the indivisibility of the social order, at another level underestimates the problems created by difference – the sense of separation, gulf, unknowing, and barrier in relationships. Without accepting this, our best efforts may run adrift.

The evidence culled from a wide range of groups, though admittedly necessarily selective, confirms the view that the constructive potential of the therapy group is easily derailed, leading to severe disruption and threats to the continuity of the group. I suggest that the 'act of faith' that Foulkes ascribed to the practice of group analysis, and that has been adopted by a continuing line of group analysts, is an inappropriate premise for the psychotherapeutic endeavour. Confidence requires, paradoxically, a greater readiness to question and doubt, coupled with a sharper, more reflexive awareness of the assumptions of a given model, its limitations and possible risks.

It becomes increasingly difficult to avoid criticism in a deconstructionist age which challenges the limits of our beliefs and dogmas and explores ways of disentangling and transgressing them. Using this approach, the largely one-sided nature of group-analytic philosophy becomes apparent in its over-optimistic view of the therapy group and of the processes which constitute it, such as communication, resonance, and exchange. In deconstructionist terms, this illustrates the 'logic of identity' (Derrida 1976), in which a stated category of identity excludes a complementary category, or 'the suppression of opposition' (Dews 1987) in which a given tradition of thought emphasises one quality while suppressing its opposite.

In group analysis, the quality that is missing is a realistic form of pessimism. In the wider milieu of group theory, a pessimistic stance is represented, but again to an exaggerated degree, by Bion. Bion emphasised the regressive and destructive aspects of the group to the neglect of its creative potential. His theory of the basic assumptions led him to emphasise pathology and aberration in groups: what he referred to as 'group diseases' (Bion 1961). But much of what he said is pertinent and of undeniable importance in understanding groups.

Bion's theories of the group are in various ways compatible with an anti-group perspective. They help to explicate some of the phenomena observed and in turn, I suggest, are demystified by the application of the anti-group concept. The basic assumptions, in particular, can be understood as differing attempts to find solutions in primitive forms of relationship that are anti-group (see Chapter 3, pp. 66–7) for a more detailed argument).

I have referred to the 'ideological split' between Foulkes and Bion. In its extreme form, it embodies the mutual suppression of opposites which has maintained a polarised view of the therapy group. It represents the dualism between optimism and pessimism that deconstructionists have described as the bedrock of Western language and thought (Hollinger 1994). I am by no means the first to call for an integration between the two, as part of a greater integration in group therapy more generally. But attempts at integration have been piecemeal and faltering, in fact rather more generous on the group-analytic side than on the other (see p. 11), and the sense of underlying opposites in conflict still characterises the field.

Ironically, the need for greater coherence occurs at a time of increasing fragmentation and deconstruction in the social order. This has led some to question the possibility and desirability of greater theoretical integration. Brown and Zinkin (1994), for example, shrink from any consideration of the 'grand theory' in relation to group analysis and fall back on the value of 'partial and provisional insights'.

We are left then with the paradoxical requirement for greater coherence and balance at a time of rapid social transformation and postmodernistic challenges to the whole notion of integration. I believe that, to some extent, the contradiction can be addressed by *incorporating the paradox* in our theory, i.e. a coherent vision of the group would include a sense of its incoherence and disintegratory potential in line with the social processes that have existed in some form all along but that are heightened in post-industrial society. In this way, group-analytic theory would tie in more clearly with the external mould of social and cultural change.

THE CONCEPT OF THE ANTI-GROUP: SUMMARY

The impetus for my formulating the concept of the anti-group arose in the clinical rather than the theoretical domain. But it became apparent that its value might also lie in providing a critical principle that helped to establish, or restore, dialogic balance in group-analytic theory. The concept came with little premeditation: the anti-group represented the negative of the positive processes I had expected to find in the therapy group. This appeared to originate in an underlying fear and distrust of groups in prospective participants and expressed itself in a variety of antagonistic processes in the group. In some cases, this could not be managed clinically in the usual ways and led to an undermining or disintegration of the group. I have given several extended definitions of the concept in previous chapters (see pp. 1, 44–5). I will not repeat these here, except to draw out some salient features:

- the anti-group is a process rather than a fixed entity in groups
- the process varies considerably from group to group
- it has latent and manifest forms
- it occurs at individual, sub-group, and group-as-a-whole levels
- it concerns aggression within but more particularly towards the group
- it derives from both group and individual characteristics, i.e. the paradoxical characteristics of the therapy group (see Chap-

ter 3) generate anti-group attitudes that interlock with projections arising from the underlying disturbances of group members
- it can be seen in dialectical terms, with 'pro-group' constituting the thesis and 'anti-group' the anti-thesis
- it may be seen both as a developmental phenomenon and as pathology (see 'The dialectics of the group' below for clarification)
- it exists in a complementary and potentiating relationship with the creative and transformational properties of the group
- it is mirrored in our wider socio-cultural and political structures.

PHENOMENOLOGY AND THE DETERMINANTS OF THE ANTI-GROUP

The anti-group has functions as both a descriptive construct and an explanatory paradigm. Descriptively, I suggest that the concept is close to the experiential reality of what happens when groups enter a destructive mode. By drawing evidence from a wide range of groups, I have attempted to base the concept in the phenomenology of the group rather than developing a set of purely abstract principles.

The situation is less straightforward when it comes to the determinants of the anti-group. Here, too, I have tried to keep to the facts, but of necessity have ventured into the complex terrain of causality. This generated a number of hypotheses that are explored in detail in Chapters 5 and 6 on the determinants of the anti-group, drawing on object relations theory and self psychology. Some of the hypotheses are easier to verify than others. For example, the proposal that the anti-group is linked to survival anxiety in groups, failures of communication, and interpersonal disturbances is easier to substantiate than hypotheses concerning the primal scene and the death instinct. Ultimately, however, the 'determinants' are meant as process interpretations rather than any form of concrete, causal explanation. As I see it, the processes described have a circular relationship, weaving in and out of a core dynamic process of projective identification in which the group as object becomes a projective screen for the experiential reality of its members. In the anti-group, the group as object is suffused with hostile part-object projections arising from frustrations and conflicts in the current experience of the group and informed by failures in the early holding environment of the participants. By agglomerating the experiences of failure, disappointment, and rage into an attack on the container, the group, the anti-group has the defensive function of allowing participants to disown responsibility for their difficulties and to avoid the pain of learning and psychological growth. This is by no means an all-or-nothing affair and its consequences can vary from disintegration of the group to transformation, in the way described below.

IMPLICATIONS OF THE ANTI-GROUP FOR GROUP-ANALYTIC PRINCIPLES

Does the concept of the anti-group affect our understanding of the group-analytic principles formulated by Foulkes? I refer here to concepts such as the group matrix, communication, resonance, and exchange. I would answer this question in the affirmative on the grounds that the deconstructionist stance of the anti-group alerts us to the 'privileged' position accorded some aspects of group experience by these concepts, while denying or suppressing others.

Perspectives on the group matrix have begun to emphasise greater differentiation in relation to its creative and destructive or malignant potential (Prodgers 1990; Roberts 1993). Similarly, the concept of mirroring has been elaborated to include 'non-dialogic mirroring' (Pines 1982) and 'malignant mirroring' (Zinkin 1983). But some of Foulkes' other concepts remain somewhat mired in their customary usage, to the extent that a degree of atrophy has set in and their more complex and contradictory aspects lost to view. I suggest this is particularly true of the principle of communication. Foulkes stated that 'communication is identical with the process of psychotherapy itself'. This is an over-simplification, and the term is now used in such a general, positivistic way that it has lost its heuristic value. In Chapter 5, I noted failures of communication as a correlate, indeed a possible determinant, of the anti-group. Here, I suggest that the optimistic view of communication itself constitutes an important blind spot in the group-analytic milieu. As Bollas (1987), Lacan (1982), and Stern (1985) have shown, there are categories of identity and non-identity, awareness and non-awareness that elude communication in the usual verbal sense. In some cases, the act of communication, of speaking, is itself traumatic. It confronts the speaker with the experience of gap, disconnection, and schism, rather than releasing him from it. This is compounded in the group situation, where the presence of several others sometimes obscures rather than clarifies communication. In Chapter 5, I introduced the term 'contaminating communication' to describe a process whereby communication is experienced not as enhancing meaning but as fragmenting and spoiling meaning. Recognising this might make it more possible to extend the boundaries of communication, to reclaim for the group and the individual the possible value of dialogue even in these extreme states.

Similar distortions may occur in the other group-specific processes formulated by Foulkes. Exchange, translation, and socialisation – processes that form the conceptual bedrock of group analysis and that provide useful distinguishing points in the theory – are all potentially problematised rather than realised in the actuality of group experience. Ultimately, it would be useful to have a set of redefinitions of the basic group-analytic concepts that could extend their range, giving them greater reversibility and applicability.

MANAGEMENT OF THE ANTI-GROUP

Many of the clinical examples I cited indicated how difficult it can be for the conductor to manage a pathological or insidious anti-group process. But it is crucial that we consider ways of making this possible and in Chapter 7 I suggested a review of some of the fundamental technical considerations in running analytic groups, from the perspective of the potential derailment of the group. Group analysts are generally very careful to protect the setting and the boundaries of the group but there is a lack of information and guidelines on some essential dimensions of conducting groups. I suggest that this allows the infiltration of anti-group processes into the therapeutic setting more readily than might otherwise be the case. Selection for the group is clearly a key consideration, since the constructive or destructive character of the group will undoubtedly be influenced by the nature of its composition. I offered possibly new ways of thinking about selection, including the notions of bonding capacity, the passion for proximity, and the group-object relation. The latter term, which I return to several times in the text, refers to the individual's internal representation of groups and the way this influences actual group relationships.

One of the strongest and most important considerations in the text is the necessity for the conductor to be more active in relation to the anti-group than is usually the case in group-analytic psychotherapy. This begins with the fundamental importance given by group analysts to establishing as firm and holding an environment as possible in which the group can develop. It goes on to take full account of Foulkes' concept of 'dynamic administration'. It then extends our current literature by taking particular account of the pressures on the conductor in dealing with the anti-group, and the technical and transferential concerns affecting him, which are examined in Chapter 8. A variety of interventions were suggested as ways of dealing with the anti-group, such as strengthening the linking function; maintaining a group perspective; and positive connotation, indicating that there are means of taking greater control in potentially disruptive group situations. The conductor's crucial role in influencing the course of the anti-group is evident, but this itself is influenced by the personal and professional matrix in which he is positioned and the counter-transferential responses that are powerfully evoked by the anti-group.

THE TRANSFORMATIONAL POTENTIAL OF THE ANTI-GROUP

I have suggested two alternative approaches to the therapeutic management of the anti-group: one, described above, encourages active leadership in situations where the anti-group threatens to get out of hand; the other proposes a containing, holding function, more passive and receptive, in situations where the anti-group seems to be following a course towards integration and transformation. Ultimately, all effective therapeutic management is holding, but this is achieved more or less actively, depending on the situation. Judging which is which may be difficult and requires an appreciation of the dynamic function of the anti-group at any particular time in the development of the group (see pp. 59–62).

The transformational vision of the anti-group restores a large element of optimism to the debate. Here, rather than being destructive, the anti-group is seen as providing a stimulus for group and personal transformations. How this is achieved was explored in detail in Chapter 9, where I viewed the anti-group in the context of the 'logics of change', noting how, in essence, the anti-group contributes the 'perturbations' that are an intrinsic part of the transformational flux of the group. These perturbations assist the group in becoming a self-regulating autopoetic activity, a transitional space, and a transformational object. The aggressive challenge of the anti-group further contributes to the strength that comes from surviving destructive impulses, in line with Winnicott's notions of 'creative destruction' and 'the use of an object'. From this matrix also emerge the capacity for reparation and the facility to play, which extend and invigorate the group space. Finally, the anti-group is a defining parameter in the dialectical movement of the group, itself a transforming frame for group development. This process is illustrated in detail in Chapter 10 and is referred to again in the section below on integrative perspectives.

While advocating a transformational view of the anti-group, I recognise a danger in this process itself becoming idealised. It is a more complex process, I believe, than is suggested in de Maré et al.'s (1991) concept of the transformation of hate through dialogue. Transformational experience in a group is fulfilling for all concerned, but it is an elusive process, experienced most intensely in moments, to be lost again in the dialectical flux of the group. In some cases, the moment may never occur, allowing for the possibility of less than successful or satisfactory outcomes, and reminding us once again of the limits of psychic development and therapeutic progress.

The transformation of the leadership role I see in similar terms. Foulkes described a relatively smooth transfer of authority from therapist to group, but my own observations and experiences suggest that this can be fraught with anger and ambivalence, to the extent that it kindles the fires of the anti-group in its wake.

THE ANTI-GROUP IN THE WIDER SOCIAL SPHERE

Group analysis regards the essence of the human being as social, not individual. Foulkes was particularly influenced by Norbert Elias' theory of figuration which sees people as existing in continuing developmental lines of interdependency. Within this, social institutions also exist in a line of figurations, moulding and reflecting each other. On this basis, we would expect the anti-group to be expressed at wider social levels than the individual or the small group. Given also what we know about the patterns of social violence and disintegration in contemporary history, it would be surprising not to find phenomena akin to the anti-group in these spheres. Explorations of the family, the organisational workplace, and the culture at large in Chapter 11 all confirmed the above, suggesting that the concept of the anti-group, in its broadest terms, provides a perspective on the complex and contradictory processes in contemporary society.

The overall picture is of a fragile cultural container in which many traditional institutions have either broken down or are breaking down. The pressure of change has generated increased social mobility, the loss of geographical communities, and massive technological advancement which offers new forms of 'virtual' community while fragmenting the social textures that previously bound people together. This situation led me to postulate the culture of the anti-group. On further levels of cultural disintegration, there is the continuing violence within and between nations and the depredation of the environment, to a degree that it is believed could lead to global decay. Here, the anti-group assumes a massive scale as 'civilisation dances on the edge'.

Within this fragile container, the family as an institution has gradually weakened in recent decades. The nuclear family can be seen as a small group struggling to maintain identity, cohesion, and self-esteem in the face of sexual and emotional tensions, as well as the impact of loss and change, all within a cultural framework of rupture and uncertainty. The way the family deals with this, in both current and longitudinal terms, can acquire anti-group characteristics, reflected in fragmentation and disintegration or a symbiotic closeness, which often conceals the threat of internal aggression. Since the family is the first group the individual encounters, these experiences can be seen to contribute crucially to the group-object relation.

The organisational world is similarly subject to disruption and change. This adds to tensions and insecurities about role and intense competition for often diminishing resources. Here, group is often pitted against group and relationships within groups strained to breaking point. The organisational equivalent of the anti-group is embodied in the symptoms of an embattled workforce – rapid turnover; high rates of sickness and absence; high accident rates; low self-esteem; and low productivity. The destructive enmeshment in work groups has led to a variety of images to describe work organisations, e.g. the 'snake pit' (Schwartz 1990) and the 'psychic prison' (Morgan 1986).

The importance of these patterns for the psychotherapy group is two-fold – they generate the problems that impel people to seek help and they define the threatening social context in which psychotherapy groups are conducted. They illustrate what de Maré *et al.* (1991) termed 'transposition' – the way in which a psychotherapeutic group reproduces not only present and past personal relationship but a much broader social context, a point highlighted by Blackwell (1994).

In terms of the application of group analysis to social and organisational intervention, the anti-group perspective also illuminates some possible pathways. I suggest that what previously impeded the organisational application is the absence of a clear group-analytic model and, in particular, a sufficient understanding of group dysfunction and pathology. In Chapter 11, in the section on organisations, I gave an example of a group-analytically orientated staff development group. The staff team involved had been subject to a damaging anti-group process that had begun with a crisis in the client group and that had led to significant staff fall-out. My work was based on a formulation of mirroring occurring at successive levels of the organisation, from the innermost fantasies of the staff team to the outermost organisational concerns. This approach is group analytic in essence, but includes the anti-group as a core concern and aims at the restoration and strengthening of the group.

TOWARDS AN INTEGRATED GROUP-ANALYTIC THEORY

'Group analysts are naturally integrative animals.' This statement by Maratos (1987) is probably true in general terms, given the way group analysis draws on psychoanalysis, systems theory, and social psychology. However, the degree of loose, informal integration that exists is different from a clearly articulated integrative standpoint. The need for a more coherent – and integrative – group-analytic model has been referred to at different points in this book. The concept of the anti-group and its creative potential is presented as a critique of the existing theory but also as a pointer towards a revised theory.

There is the question of how meaningful attempts at integration can be in the face of deconstructionist trends which challenge the notion of the complete or integrated theory, making us aware of the 'illusion of unity' and affirming the value of 'partial and provisional insights', as Brown and Zinkin (1994) suggested. We are left with a dilemma. On the one hand, we require a more integrated theory as a basis for the conceptual, clinical, and applied development of group analysis. On the other, we are wary of the value of any form of 'complete' theory.

A solution to the problem, I suggest, is the formulation of integrative perspectives that utilise the integrative potential of a theory without confining it to a rigid mould. With this in mind, I suggest a series of integrative perspectives that are to some extent implicit in group analysis but that are illuminated and extended by the findings of the preceding chapters and that incorporate the notion of the anti-group. The emerging theory I see as mainly clinical and oriented towards the psychotherapy group, but with applicability to groups in general.

I suggest three main integrative perspectives:

- the dialectics of the group
- the ecology of the group
- the aesthetics of the group.

Each of these is presented separately below, but with the understanding that they represent synchronous rather than discrete aspects of the group, themselves forming a dialectical relationship with each other. Each perspective implies a task or a set of tasks in the conduct of the group and these are also described.

The dialectics of the group

The thrust of this book has increasingly been towards dissolving the dualism present in some analytic approaches to the group psychotherapy. It has also at several points used the dialectical framework to convey the experience of paradox and flux that is a defining characteristic of the therapy group. The anti-group takes its position as a mode of experience that opposes the integrative, constructive 'pro-group' mode, but at the same time generates it in a continuing cycle of mutual creation and negation.

Instead of an either–or culture we have a both–and culture – not Foulkes vs. Bion or constructive vs. destructive but Foulkes *and* Bion, constructive *and* destructive. Within this framework, the group itself is decentred. It is never one thing, a defined, static essence: it becomes what it is in the interplay of different modes of experience.

In this model, the anti-group has both its developmental and its psychopathological counterparts. The anti-group as a developmental phenomenon constitutes the natural resistances and opposition to the group that form one polarity and that mark the group's undulating progress. In 'normal' group development this occurs in a particular phase or as part of the cyclical change in which anti-group alternates with pro-group. In either case, the constructive potential of the group usually prevails. The 'pathological' manifestation of the anti-group occurs when the dialectical movement between modes of experience breaks down and there is a collapse into a single, anti-group mode, resulting in severe impasse, irreconcilable destructive conflict, or disintegration. The dangers of a collapse into the reverse mode, excessive cohesiveness, are equally clear. At best, this can produce symbiosis and stasis; at worst, a delusional investment in the greatness of the group (see Chapter 9, pp. 205–7). Here, the anti-group is crucially needed as a balancing and differentiating mode, a force that counteracts cohesiveness.

Within this frame, the essential task of the group analyst is to facilitate the dialectical flow of the group, to recognise the signs of its collapse, and to help restore its momentum. It involves an appreciation of the value of both creative and destructive moments and a capacity to track the movement between them. In terms of its application to the field of organisational intervention, the same focus needs to be kept in mind – whether and how the work group or the organisation as a whole maintains the momentum of creative reversibility in the face of the interlocking pressures of the work task and the demands of group relatedness.

The dialectical vision is part of a long tradition of philosophical thought, as outlined in more detail in Chapter 9. It is, in fact, implied in much of Foulkes' writing, even in his theory of aggression (p. 32), but is mainly eclipsed by Foulkes' attraction to idealised wholes and his proclivity for mechanical theorising (as in the analysis of group aggression). It is also suggested in some recent contributions to group-analytic theory: for example, in his analysis of communicative pattern in psychotherapy groups, Schlapobersky states:

> It is through this movement – from monologue through dialogue to discourse and back again – that the group-analytic method comes into its own, creating an arena in which the dialectic between the psyche and the social world helps to refashion both.
>
> (Schlapobersky 1994, p. 212)

But I suggest a sharper focusing of the dialectical perspective in group analysis, bringing it out of the theoretical background into the foreground. This perspective would also provide a framework for reconciling some of the other splits that continue in our field and that usually reflect complementary rather than contradictory states. As suggested earlier, the combination of group and therapy to create 'group therapy' produces probably the most complex of all psychotherapeutic approaches. I see the dialectical viewpoint as the one that most meaningfully embraces the full degree of complexity and paradox.

For some, the elevation of the pole of pessimism associated with group-destructive processes may instil a sense of disillusionment and despair. But I suggest this is no more than the giving up of omnipotence and idealisation. Foucault (1984) has addressed a parallel problem in the domain of social theory. His proposed solution is one of letting go, of experimentation, of playfulness (Hollinger 1994).

The ecology of the group

The ecological viewpoint in the human sciences is perhaps most strongly identified with Bateson. In his seminal work *Steps to an Ecology of Mind* (1972), he formulated the principles of how human systems, including groups, are formed and maintained by the communication and interaction of ideas. This perspective has been taken up by a number of group theorists, notably Durkin (1981) and Agazarian (1989). Here, I use the notion of the ecology of the group in a broader sense to describe the evolution of the group as a living system in a particular social landscape. The perspective is close to Jacobson's (1989) view of the therapy group as a 'small, temporary society' and an 'object in the cultural field'. The point at issue is the survival and development of the group as a living social entity. In this perspective, the anti-group is seen not in terms of intra-psychic projection but as an expectable response to a unique set of contexts that facilitate or obstruct the progress of the group. A group may disintegrate if the surrounding context fails to recognise or support its growth.

I consider this an integrative perspective in that it draws together a number of themes and influences that are relevant to the evolution of the group. These may be hierarchically organised in terms of their level of context: the socio-political climate of the day; the organisation in which the group is run; the actual building, the room, the seating arrangements, and so on. Another context is the conductor in his or her professional network; the institutional values and biases that inform his work; his well-being and support; his attitude to the group. The overarching concept is that of context, seen as generating a variety of interacting structures and values that foster or undermine the group.

The ecological view also embraces technical considerations, such as the composition of the membership, that influence the course of the group. Selection is important precisely because it affects the ecology of the group – by recruiting participants who contribute in particular ways to the viability and durability of the group. The way boundary issues are handled, the pattern of drop-outs and how this impacts on the group, the issue of beginnings and endings in a slow-open group – these are all features of the eco-system that is the group.

This perspective is close to Maturana's (1985) notion of autopoesis, the creation of the organism as a self-sustaining entity. Maturana emphasises the importance of structures in this process and, in particular, structural 'coupling', which in groups is reflected in members being coupled to each other and the group and the group being coupled to the environmental medium in which it exists, in order for the group to achieve autopoesis.

The ecological perspective provides a broad framework for the setting up and running of groups, defining a variety of contexts and their interaction as the nexus of integrative and disruptive group processes. In essence, this is the systems theory approach, drawing on the various modes of systemic thought outlined by Blackwell (1994), but I prefer the term 'ecological' as it generates more directly a vision of the group in its multiple contexts as it struggles towards its destiny as a living system.

The main therapeutic task, I suggest, is to develop a reflexive, systemic view of the internal needs of the group in relation to the surrounding organisational environment, its requirements and priorities. The former is assumed in Foulkes' concept of dynamic administration, the latter in Sharpe's (1995) notion of 'responsibility to the external context'. Together, these requirements constitute the ecological perspective of the group.

The aesthetics of the group

Whereas the dialectical perspective can be seen to relate to the experiential flux of the group and the ecological perspective to the impact of context, the aesthetic perspective relates largely to the form of the group. This is influenced by recent views about analytic groups, particularly Cortesao's (1991) 'aesthetic equilibrium' and Rance's (1992) 'aesthetic transformation', theories that are in turn linked to Bollas' concept of the transformational object and Winnicott's views about transitional space, play, and creativity.

The aesthetic perspective emphasises the achievement of form, contour, harmony, and cohesiveness in the group, both as objective attributes of the group and as the subjective, felt experience of the group. I suggest that it is a valuable part of an integrative group analytic approach in that it draws together aspects of the group that concern: the processing of fragments of experience into coherent patterns; the unfolding of the group as a narrative that brings together a variety of personal narratives; the creative expression of imagination and fantasy as giving shape to the group space; the experience of pleasure in the group, not only in moments of play, humour and affection, but in the opportunity to share in the process of flux and change in a holding environment; and the transformational potential of the group, producing moments of insight, wisdom, and beauty.

I would hypothesise that many people who are attracted to groups, including therapists and patients, are intuitively responding to the potential for an aesthetic experience of this sort. For this reason, too, I suggest that the aesthetic perspective, which is implicit in much existing group analysis, be focused and highlighted. I also believe this to be a valuable aspect of group analysis as a psychotherapy for the future. In a society in which natural communities are breaking down and communication is increasingly mechanised and canalised, people will need and seek the sort of opportunities for creative sharing that group analysis can offer.

The main task of the therapist from this perspective, I suggest, is to step back from technique, from the strictures of practice, and to let the group dream, imagine, play. But it also requires attention to the aesthetic dimension in an active way, helping to weave together the themes and images of the group into a coherent whole.

The anti-group has a core function here. In a general way, it provides the mode of experience that paradoxically generates the creative impulse. More specifically, however, the aesthetic dimension is itself constituted by the interplay of opposites. There is no beauty without ugliness, no harmony without disharmony, no truth without semblance. In a recent commentary on the link between group analysis and the artistic process, I made the following points:

> I believe that art is meaningless without some confrontation with the dark side; similarly, that the group experience is incomplete and likely to be superficial without such recognition. Holding together the constructive and the destructive potential is a major requirement of the group therapist, as I believe it is in the artistic process.... Sometimes the tension between the two is very great, even unbearable, but usually there comes a point of reconciliation, of synthesis, and a new form emerges. I believe this is also what happens in the group. At every moment the dialogue forms and reforms itself and within this, creative and destructive forms emerge side by side. Eventually, an understanding, an insight, a change, is achieved. Openness to this process is the creative gift of the group analyst to the group – and the gift of the group to the analyst.
> (Nitsun 1995b, p. 99)

References

Adorno, T.W. (1966) *Negative Dialektik*. Frankfurt: Suhrkamp. English translation *Negative Dialectics*. London: Routledge and Kegan Paul.
Agazarian, Y.M. (1989) 'Group-as-a-whole: systems theory and practice', *Group*, 13: 131–53.
Agazarian, Y.M. (1994) 'The phases of group development and the systems-centred group', in Schermer, V.L. and Pines, M. (eds) *Ring of Fire*. London: Routledge.
Agazarian, Y.M. and Peters, R. (1981) *The Visible and Invisible Group*. London: Routledge and Kegan Paul.
Amati Sas, S. (1992) 'Ambiguity as the route to shame', *International Journal of Psycho-Analysis*, 73: 329–41.
Anthony, E.J. (1983) 'The group-analytic circle and its ambient network', in Pines, M. (eds) *The Evolution of Group Analysis*. London: Routledge and Kegan Paul.
Anzieu, D. (1984) *The Group and the Unconscious*. London: Routledge and Kegan Paul.
Anzieu, D. (1989) *The Skin Ego*. London: Karnac.
Anzieu, D. (1990) *Psychic Envelopes*. London: Karnac.
Ashbach, C. and Schermer, V.L. (1987) *Object Relations, the Self, and the Group*. London: Routledge and Kegan Paul.
Bacal, H.A. (1985) 'Object relations in the group from the perspective of self psychology', *International Journal of Group Psychotherapy*, 35: 483–501.
Bakhtin, M. (1981) *The Dialogue Imagination: Four Essays by M.M. Bakhtin*, trans. C. Emerson and M. Holquist. Austin: Texas University Press.
Balint, M. (1968) *The Basic Fault: Therapeutic Aspects of Regression*. London: Tavistock.
Barnett, B. (1993) ' "Partisans in an Uncertain World: The Psychoanalysis of Engagement" by Paul Hoggett' (review), *International Journal of Psycho-Analysis*, 74, 3: 633–6.
Bateson, G. (1972) *Steps to an Ecology of Mind*. New York: Ballantyne.
Battegay, R. (1976) 'Concept of narcissistic group self', *Group Analysis*, 9: 217–20.

Beck, A.P. (1981) 'A study of group phase development and emergent leadership', *Group*, 5: 48–54.
Beck, A.P. (1983) 'A process analysis of group development', *Group*, 7: 19–26.
Becker, E. (1975) *The Denial of Death*. New York: The Free Press.
Behr, H.L. (1995a) 'The integration of theory and practice', in Sharpe, M. (ed.) *The Third Eye: Supervision of Analytic Groups*. London: Routledge.
Behr, H.L. (1995b) 'What's in a word?', *Dialogue, Newsletter of the IGA*, 28: 13.
Bennis, W.G. and Shephard, H.A. (1956) 'A theory of group development', *Human Relations*, 9: 415–37.
Bentovim, A., Barnes, G.C. and Cooklin, A. (eds) (1982) *Family Therapy: Complementary Frameworks of Theory and Practice*. London: Academic Press, Grune and Stratton.
Berenstein, I. (1987) 'Analysis terminable and interminable, fifty years on', *International Journal of Psycho-Analysis*, 68: 21–35.
Berger, B. and Berger, P.L. (1984) *The War over the Family: Capturing the Middle Ground*. Harmondsworth: Penguin.
Bergmann, M. (1988) 'On the fate of the intrapsychic image of the psychoanalyst after termination of the analysis', *Psychoanalytic Study of the Child*, 43: 137–43.
Bick, E. (1968) 'The experience of the skin in early object relations', *International Journal of Psycho-Analysis*, 49: 484–6.
Bion, W.R. (1957) 'Differentiation of the psychotic from the non-psychotic personalities', in *Second Thoughts*. London: Heinemann, 1967.
Bion, W.R. (1959) 'Attacks on linking', in *Second Thoughts*. London: Heinemann, 1967.
Bion, W.R. (1961) *Experiences in Groups*. London: Tavistock.
Bion, W.R. (1962) 'A theory of thinking', in *Second Thoughts*. London: Heinemann, 1967.
Bion, W.R. (1967) *Second Thoughts: Selected Papers on Psychoanalysis*. London: Heinemann.
Bion, W.R. (1970) *Attention and Interpretation: A Scientific Approach to Insight in Psychoanalysis and Groups*. London: Tavistock.
Blackwell, D. (1994) 'The psyche and the system', in Brown, D. and Zinkin, L. (eds) *The Psyche and the Social World: Developments in Group-Analytic Theory*. London: Routledge.
Bohm, D. (1980) *Wholeness and the Implicate Order*. London: Routledge (Ark), 1983.
Bohm, D. (1981) 'On self-deception in the individual, in groups and in society as a whole', in Kellerman, H. (ed.) *Group Cohesion*. New York: Grune and Stratton.
Bollas, C. (1987) *The Shadow of the Object: Psychoanalysis of the Unthought Known*. London: Free Association Books.
Bollas, C. (1987) 'The transformational object', in *The Shadow of the Object*. London: Free Association Books.
Bosse, H. (1985) 'The dynamics of understanding culture: a group-

analytic approach in a non-analytic situation', *Group Analysis*, 18: 199–211.
Bowlby, J. (1977) 'The making and breaking of affectional bonds', *British Journal of Psychiatry*, 130: 201–10, 421–31.
Bowlby, J. (1988) *A Secure Base*. London: Routledge.
Boyd, R.D. (1991) *Personal Transformations in Small Groups: A Jungian Perspective*. London: Routledge.
Bramley, W. (1990) 'Staff sensitivity groups: a conductor's field experiences', *Group Analysis*, 23: 301–16.
Brenner, C. (1971) 'The psychoanalytic concept of aggression', *International Journal of Psycho-Analysis*, 68: 21–35.
Brigham, P.M. (1992) 'Object relations and regression in groups', *International Journal of Group Psychotherapy*, 42: 247–66.
Brown, D. (1985) 'Bion and Foulkes: basic assumptions and beyond', in Pines, M. (ed.) *Bion and Group Psychotherapy*. London: Routledge and Kegan Paul.
Brown, D. (1989) 'A contribution to the understanding of psychosomatic processes in groups', *British Journal of Psychotherapy*, 6: 5–9.
Brown, D. (1991) 'Assessment and selection for groups', in Roberts, J. and Pines, M. (eds) *The Practice of Group Analysis*. London: Routledge.
Brown, D. (1992) 'Transcultural group analysis II. Use and abuse of cultural differences: analysis and ethics', *Group Analysis*, 25, 1: 97–105.
Brown, D. (1994) 'Self development through subjective interaction', in Brown, D. and Zinkin, L. (eds) *The Psyche and the Social World*. London: Routledge.
Brown, D. and Zinkin, L. (eds) (1994) *The Psyche and the Social World: Developments in Group-Analytic Therapy*. London: Routledge.
Chasseguet-Smirgel, J. (1985a) *Creativity and Perversion*. London: Free Association Books.
Chasseguet-Smirgel, J. (1985b) *The Ego Ideal: A Psychoanalytic Essay on the Malady of the Ideal*. London: Free Association Books.
Cheever, J. (1991) *The Journals*. London: Vintage.
Cortesao, E.L. (1991) 'Group analysis and aesthetic equilibrium', *Group Analysis*, 24, 3: 271–7.
Cox, M. and Theilgard, A. (1987) *Mutative Metaphors in Psychotherapy: The Aeolian Mode*. London: Tavistock.
Coyne, J. (1985) 'Towards a theory of frames and reframing: the social nature of frames', *Journal of Marital and Family Therapy*, 11: 337–44.
Craib, I. (1996) 'Trying to make sense of the Anti-Group', *Group Analysis*, in press.
Dell, P.F. and Goolishan, H.A. (1981) 'An evolutionary epistemology for cohesive phenomena', in Kellerman, H. (ed.) *Group Cohesion*. New York: Grune and Stratton.
de Maré, P., Piper, R. and Thompson, S. (1991) *Koinonia: From Hate, through Dialogue, to Culture in the Large Group*. London: Karnac.
Derrida, J. (1976) *Of Grammatology*, trans. G.C. Spivak. Baltimore, MD: Johns Hopkins University Press.

Dews, P. (1987) *Logics of Disintegration: Post-Structuralist Thought and the Claims of Critical Theory*. New York: Verso.
Dicks, B. (1993) 'The group matrix as a holomovement and quantum field', *Group Analysis*, 26: 469–80.
Dies, R.R. (1992) 'Models of group psychotherapy: sifting through confusion', *International Journal of Group Psychotherapy*, 42: 1–17.
Dixon, N.F. (1988) *Our Own Worst Enemy*. London: Futura.
Doyle, R. (1987) *The Commitments*. London: Heinemann.
Durkin, H. (1964) *The Group in Depth*. New York: International Universities Press.
Durkin, J.E. (1981) *Living Groups: Group Psychotherapy and General Systems Theory*. New York: Brunner/Mazel.
Eigen, M. (1985) 'Towards Bion's starting point: catastrophe and death', *International Journal of Psycho-Analysis*, 66: 321–30.
Elias, N. (1939) *The Civilising Process*. Oxford: Blackwell.
Eliot, T.S. (1934) Choruses from 'The Rock', in *Selected Poems*. London: Faber.
Elliott, B. (1994) 'The womb and gender identity', in Brown, D. and Zinkin, L. (eds) *The Psyche and the Social World*. London: Routledge.
Emde, R.N. (1991) 'Positive emotions for psychoanalytic theory: surprises from infancy research and new directions', *Journal of the American Psychoanalytic Association*, 39, Supplement: 5–44.
Fairbairn, W.R.D. (1952) *Psychoanalytic Studies of the Personality*. London: Tavistock.
Foguel, B. (1994) 'The group experienced as mother: early psychic structures in analytic groups', *Group Analysis*, 27: 265–85.
Foucault, M. (1984) 'Care of the self', in *The History of Sexuality: An Introduction*. Harmondsworth: Penguin.
Foulkes, E. (ed.) (1990a) *Selected Papers of S.H. Foulkes*. London: Karnac.
Foulkes, E. (1990b) 'S.H. Foulkes: a brief memoir', in *Selected Papers of S.H. Foulkes*. London: Karnac.
Foulkes, S.H. (1948) *Introduction to Group Analytic Psychotherapy: Studies in the Social Integration of Individuals and Groups*. London: Heinemann.
Foulkes, S.H. (1957) 'Psychoanalytic concepts and object relations theory: comments on a paper by Fairbairn', in Foulkes, E. (ed.) *Selected Papers of S.H. Foulkes*. London: Karnac, 1990.
Foulkes, S.H. (1964a) *Therapeutic Group Analysis*. London: Allen and Unwin; reprinted London: Karnac, 1986.
Foulkes, S.H. (1964b) 'Psychotherapy in the sixties', in *Therapeutic Group Analysis*. London: Karnac, 1986.
Foulkes, S.H. (1968) 'Group dynamic processes and group analysis', in Foulkes, E. (ed.) *Selected Papers of S.H. Foulkes*. London: Karnac, 1990.
Foulkes, S.H. (1969) 'Recollections of my visit to Freud', in Foulkes, E. (ed.) *Selected Papers of S.H. Foulkes*. London: Karnac, 1990.
Foulkes, S.H. (1971) 'The group as matrix of the individual's mental life',

in Foulkes, E. (ed.) *Selected Papers of S.H. Foulkes*. London: Karnac, 1990.
Foulkes, S.H. (1972) 'Oedipus conflict and regression', in Foulkes, E. (ed.) *Selected Papers of S.H. Foulkes*. London: Karnac, 1990.
Foulkes, S.H. (1973) 'Address to the first European workshop', *Group Analysis*, 6: 72–7.
Foulkes, S.H. (1974) 'My philosophy in psychotherapy', in Foulkes, E. (ed.) *Selected Papers of S.H. Foulkes*. London: Karnac, 1990.
Foulkes, S.H. (1975a) *Group Analytic Psychotherapy Methods and Principles*. London: Gordon and Breach; reprinted London: Karnac, 1986.
Foulkes, S.H. (1975b) 'Concerning criticism of inner-object theory', in Foulkes, E. (ed.) *Selected Papers of S.H. Foulkes*. London: Karnac, 1990.
Foulkes, S.H. (1977) 'Notes on the concept of resonance', in Foulkes, E. (ed.) *Selected Papers of S.H. Foulkes*. London: Karnac, 1990.
Foulkes, S.H. and Anthony, E.J. (1965) *Group Psychotherapy: The Psychoanalytic Approach*, 2nd edition. London: Pelican.
Freud, S. (1908) 'On the sexual theories of children', in Vol. 9 of *The Standard Edition of the Complete Psychological Works of Sigmund Freud*, ed. J. Strachey. London: Hogarth Press, 1953–74.
Freud, S. (1913) *Totem and Taboo*. SE 13.
Freud, S. (1920) *Beyond the Pleasure Principle*. SE 18.
Freud, S. (1921) *Group Psychology and the Analysis of the Ego*. SE 18.
Freud, S. (1923) *The Ego and the Id*. SE 19.
Freud, S. (1930) *Civilization and its Discontents*. SE 21.
Freud, S. (1937) 'Analysis terminable and interminable', SE 23.
Fried, K.W. (1979) 'Within and without: the examination of a ubiquitous resistance in group therapy', in Wolberg, L. and Aronson, M. (eds) *Group Therapy*. New York: Stratton.
Frude, N. (1991) *Understanding Family Problems*. Chichester and New York: Wiley.
Gans, J.S. (1989) 'Hostility in group psychotherapy', *International Journal of Group Psychotherapy*, 39, 4: 499–516.
Ganzarain, R. (1992) 'Introduction to object relations group psychotherapy', *International Journal of Group Psychotherapy*, 42: 205–23.
Garland, C. (1982) 'Group analysis: taking the non-problem seriously', *Group Analysis*, 15: 4–14.
Gay, P. (1989) *Freud: A Life for our Time*. London: Papermac.
George, C., Kaplan, N. and Main, M. (1985) *The Berkeley Adult Attachment Interview*, unpublished protocol, Department of Psychology, University of California, Berkeley, CA.
Gfäller, G.R. (1993) ' "Figuration": the contribution of Norbert Elias to group analysis and the contribution of group analysis to the social sciences', *Group Analysis*, 26: 341–56.
Gibbard, G.S. and Hartman, J.J. (1973) 'The significance of utopian fantasies in small groups', *International Journal of Group Psychotherapy*, 23: 125–47.
Glasser, M. (1985) 'The weak spot – some observations on male sexuality', *International Journal of Psycho-Analysis*, 66: 405.

Glatzer, H. (1987) 'Critique of women's groups led by women', *International Journal of Psychotherapy*, 37: 155–8.
Glenn, L. (1987) 'Attachment theory and group analysis: the group matrix as a secure base', *Group Analysis*, 20: 109–17.
Gordon, J. (1991) 'Discussion on J.F. Zender's paper "Projective identification in group psychotherapy"', *Group Analysis*, 24: 120–2.
Gordon, J. (1994) 'Bion's post-experiences in groups thinking on groups: a clinical example of $-k$', in Schermer, V.L. and Pines, M. (eds) *Ring of Fire*. London: Routledge.
Green, L. (1983) 'On fusion and individuation processes in small groups', *International Journal of Group Psychotherapy*, 33: 3–19.
Grinberg, L. (1973) 'Projective identification and projective counteridentification in the dynamics of groups', in Wolberg, L.R. and Schwartz, E.K. (eds) *Group Therapy 1973: An Overview*. New York: Stratton Intercontinental.
Grosskurth, P. (1989) *Melanie Klein*. London: Maresfield.
Grotjahn, M. (1972) 'Learning from dropout patients', *International Journal of Group Psychotherapy*, 22: 287–319.
Guntrip, H. (1961) *Personality Structure and Human Interaction*. London: Hogarth.
Hamilton, J. (1976) 'Some comments about Freud's conceptualization of the death instinct', *International Review of Psycho-Analysis*, 3: 151–64.
Handy, C. (1995) Quoted in Harrison, M., *Visions of Heaven and Hell*. London: Channel 4 Television Publication.
Hargie, O., Saunders, C. and Dickson, D. (1991) *Social Skills in Interpersonal Communication*. London: Routledge.
Harrison, M. (1995) *Visions of Heaven and Hell*. London: Channel 4 Television Publication.
Hartman, J. and Gibbard, G. (1974) 'Anxiety, boundary evolution, and social change', in Gibbard, G., Hartman, J., and Mann, R. (eds) *Analysis of Groups*. San Francisco: Jossey-Bass.
Harwood, I. (1992) 'Group psychotherapy and disorders of the self', *Group Analysis*, 25: 19–26.
Hawkins, D.K. (1986) 'Understanding reactions to group instability in psychotherapy groups', *International Journal of Group Psychotherapy*, 36: 241–59.
Hearst, L.E. (1981) 'The emergence of the mother in the group', *Group Analysis*, 14, 1: 25–32.
Hearst, L. (1993) 'Our historical and cultural cargo and its vicissitudes in group analysis', 17th S.H. Foulkes Annual Lecture, *Group Analysis*, 26: 389–405.
Higgins, R. (1978) *The Seventh Enemy*. London: Pan.
Hillman, J. and Ventura, M. (1993) *We've Had a Hundred Years of Psychotherapy – and the World's Getting Worse*. San Francisco: HarperCollins.
Hinshelwood, R.D. (1994) 'Attacks on the reflective space: containing primitive emotional states', in Schermer, V.L. and Pines, M. (eds) *Ring of Fire*. London: Routledge.

Hirschorn, L. (1988) *The Workplace Within: Psychodynamics of Organisational Life*. Cambridge, MA: MIT Press.
Hoffman, L. (1981) *Foundations of Family Therapy*. New York: Basic Books.
Hoggett, P. (1992) *Partisans in an Uncertain World: The Psychoanalysis of Engagement*. London: Free Association Books.
Hollinger, R. (1994) *Postmodernism and the Social Sciences*. London: Sage.
Hopper, E. (1985) 'The problems of context in group-analytic psychotherapy: a clinical illustration and a brief theoretical discussion', in Pines, M. (ed.) *Bion and Group Psychotherapy*. London: Routledge and Kegan Paul.
Horne, E. (1992) 'Control and leadership in group psychotherapy', *Group Analysis*, 25: 195–205.
Horwitz, L. (1983) 'Projective identification in dyads and groups', *International Journal of Group Psychotherapy*, 33: 259–79.
Hutten, E.H. (1983) 'Meaning and information in the group process', in Pines, M. (ed.) *The Evolution of Group Analysis*. London: Routledge and Kegan Paul.
Inhelder, B. and Piaget, J. (1958) *The Growth of Logical Thinking from Childhood to Adolescence*. New York: Basic Books.
Jacobson, L. (1989) 'The group as an object in the cultural field', *International Journal of Group Psychotherapy*, 39: 475–98.
James, D.C. (1982) 'Transitional phenomena and the matrix in group psychotherapy', in Pines, M. and Rafalson, L. (eds) *The Individual and the Group*. London: Plenum Press.
James, D.C. (1994) ' "Holding" and "containing" in the group and society', in Brown, D. and Zinkin, L. (eds) *The Psyche and the Social World*. London: Routledge.
Jaques, E. (1955) 'Social systems as a defence against persecutory and depressive anxiety', in Klein, M., Heimann, P., and Money-Kyrle, R.E. (eds) *New Directions in Psycho-Analysis*. London: Tavistock.
Johnson, S.M. (1987) *Humanising the Narcissistic Style*. New York: Norton.
Joseph, B. (1982) 'Addiction to near-death', in Feldman, M. and Spillius, E.B. (eds) *Psychic Equilibrium and Psychic Change: Selected Papers of Betty Joseph*. London: Routledge, 1989.
Kaplan, R. (1994) 'The coming anarchy', *Atlantic Monthly*, 273: 44–68.
Karterud, S.W. (1992) 'Reflections on group-analytic research', *Group Analysis*, 125: 353–64.
Kauff, P. (1977) 'The termination process: its relationship to the separation–individuation phase of development', *International Journal of Group Psychotherapy*, 27: 3–18.
Kennard, D. (1991) 'The Fernando Arroyave Memorial Prize Essay: the award committee's choice', *Group Analysis*, 24: 6.
Kennard, D., Roberts, J. and Winter, D. (eds) (1993) *A Workbook of Group Analytic Interventions*. London: Routledge.
Kernberg, O. (1965) 'Notes on countertransference', *Journal of the American Psychoanalytic Association*, 13: 38–56.

Kernberg, O. (1980) *Internal World and External Reality: Object Relations Theory Applied*. New York: Jason Aronson.
Kernberg, O. (1991) 'The psychopathology of hatred', *Journal of the American Psychoanalytic Association*, 39, Supplement: 209-38.
Kibel, H.D. (1989) 'An introduction to the work of Didier Anzieu', *International Journal of Group Psychotherapy*, 39: 531-7.
Kibel, H. (1992) 'Diversity in the practice of inpatient group psychotherapy in North America', *Group Analysis*, 25: 225-45.
King, P. and Steiner, R. (1990) *The Freud-Klein Controversies 1941-45*. London: Tavistock/Routledge.
Klein, M. (1928) 'Early stages of the Oedipus complex', in *Love, Guilt and Reparation and Other Works 1921-1945*. London: Hogarth Press, 1975.
Klein, M. (1946) 'Notes on some schizoid mechanisms', in *The Writings of Melanie Klein*, Vol. 3. London: Hogarth Press, 1985.
Klein, M. (1952) 'Some theoretical conclusions regarding the emotional life of the infant', in *Envy and Gratitude and Other Works 1946-1963*. London: Hogarth Press, 1975.
Klein, M. (1957) 'Envy and gratitude', in *Melanie Klein: Envy and Gratitude and Other Works 1946-1963*. London: Hogarth Press, 1975.
Knauss, W. (1987) 'Trennung und Gewalt im kulturellen Wandel', *Curare*, 10: 117-26.
Knauss, W. and Freund, H. (1985) 'Group-analytic psychotherapy with alcoholic inpatients', *Group Analysis*, 18: 124-30.
Kohut, H. (1971) *The Analysis of the Self*. New York: International Universities Press.
Kohut, H. (1977) *The Restoration of the Self*. Madison, CT: International Universities Press.
Kreeger, L.C. (ed.) (1975) *The Large Group – Dynamics and Therapy*. London: Maresfield Reprints.
Kreeger, L.C. (1992) 'Envy pre-emption in small and large groups', 16th S.H. Foulkes Lecture, *Group Analysis*, 25: 391-412.
Lacan, J. (1977) *Écrits: A Selection*, trans. Alan Sheridan. New York: Norton.
Lacan, J. (1982) 'Intervention on transference', in Mitchell, J. and Rose, J. (eds) *Feminine Sexuality, Jacques Lacan, and the Ecole Freudienne*. New York: Norton.
Laing, R.D. (1976) *The Politics of the Family and Other Essays*. Harmondsworth: Pelican.
Laplanche, J. (1970) *Life and Death in Psychoanalysis*, trans. J. Mehlman. Baltimore, MD: Johns Hopkins University Press, 1976.
Lasch, C. (1979) *The Culture of Narcissism*. New York: Warner.
Layder, D. (1994) *Understanding Social Theory*. London: Sage.
Lear, T. (1991) 'Personal transformations in the group', *Group Analysis*, 24, 4: 441-54.
Le Roy, J. (1994) 'Group analysis and culture', in Brown, D. and Zinkin, L. (eds) *The Psyche and the Social World*. London: Routledge.
Lifton, R.J. (1981) 'Historical and symbolic elements of social cohesion',

in Kellerman, H. (ed.) *Group Cohesion: Theoretical and Clinical Perspectives*. New York: Grune and Stratton.

Main, T.F. (1977) 'The concept of the therapeutic community: variations and vicissitudes', 1st S.H. Foulkes Annual Lecture, *Group Analysis*, 10, Supplement: 1–16.

Malan, D.H., Balfour, F.H.G., Hood, V.G. and Shooter, A.M.N. (1976) 'Group psychotherapy: a long-term follow-up study', *Archives of General Psychiatry*, 33: 1033–4.

Maratos, J. (1987) 'Minde, K. and Minde, R. (1986) "Infant Psychiatry. An Introductory Text Book", book review,' *Group Analysis*, 20: 185.

Maratos, J. (1994) 'Thanatos: does it exist?', *Group Analysis*, 27, 1: 37–49.

Marrone, M. (1994) 'Attachment theory and group analysis', in Brown, D. and Zinkin, L. (eds) *The Psyche and the Social World*. London: Routledge.

Maruyama, M. (1963) 'The second cybernetics: deviation amplifying mutual causal processes', *American Scientist*, 51: 164–79.

Masson, J. (1990) *Against Therapy*. London: Fontana.

Masterson, J. (1981) *The Narcissistic and Borderline Disorders*. New York: Brunner/Mazel.

Maturana, H. (1985) 'Reality: the search for objectivity or the quest for a compelling argument', *Irish Journal of Psychology*, 9: 25–82.

Maturana, H. and Varela, F. (1980) *Autopoeisis and Cognition: The Realisation of the Living*. London: Reid.

Meltzer, D. (1973) *Sexual States of Mind*. Perthshire: Clunie Press.

Mendez, C.L., Coddou, F. and Maturana, H. (1988) 'The bringing forth of pathology', *Irish Journal of Psychology*, 9.

Menzies-Lyth, I. (1959) 'The functioning of social systems as a defence against anxiety', *Human Relations*, 13: 95–121.

Miller, E. and Rice, A.K. (1967) *Systems of Organization*. London: Tavistock.

Modell, A.H. (1976) 'The holding environment and the therapeutic action of psychoanalysis', *Journal of the American Psychoanalytic Association*, 24: 285–307.

Modell, A.H. (1988a) 'On the protection and safety of the therapeutic setting', in Rothstein, A. (ed.) *The Therapeutic Action of Psychodynamic Psychotherapy*. Madison, CT: International Universities Press.

Modell, A.H. (1988b) 'The centrality of the psychoanalytic setting and the changing aim of treatment: a perspective from a theory of object relations', *Psychoanalytic Quarterly*, 52: 577–96.

Mollon, P. (1993) *The Fragile Self: The Structure of Narcissistic Disturbance*. London: Whurr.

Money-Kyrle, R.E. (1961) *Man's Picture of his World: A Psycho-Analytic Study*. London: Duckworth.

Morgan, G. (1986) *Images of Organization*. Beverly Hills, CA, and London: Sage.

Nitsun, M. (1988) 'Early development: linking the individual and the group', *Group Analysis*, 22: 249–60.

Nitsun, M. (1989) ' "Nippets and Imps": the transformational process in

a psychotherapeutic group', unpublished paper, Institute of Group Analysis, London.
Nitsun, M. (1990) 'Sexual abuse as a theme in group-analytic psychotherapy', *Psychoanalytic Psychotherapy*, 5: 21–35.
Nitsun, M. (1991) 'The anti-group: destructive forces in the group and their therapeutic potential', *Group Analysis*, 24, 1: 7–20.
Nitsun, M. (1994) 'The primal scene in group analysis', in Brown, D. and Zinkin, L. (eds) *The Psyche and the Social World*. London: Routledge.
Nitsun, M. (1995a) 'Group analytic supervision in a psychiatric hospital', in Sharpe, M. (ed.) *The Third Eye: Supervision of Analytic Groups*. London: Routledge.
Nitsun, M. (1995b) 'Artist and group facilitator: thoughts on paper by Gillian Recordon', *Group Analysis*, 28, 1: 97–9.
Norcross, J.C. and Goldfried, M.R. (eds) (1992) *Handbook of Psychotherapy Integration*. New York: Basic Books.
O'Connor, N. and Ryan, J. (1993) *Wild Desires and Mistaken Identities: Lesbianism and Psychoanalysis*. London: Virago.
Ogden, T.H. (1980) 'On the nature of schizophrenic conflict', *International Journal of Psycho-Analysis*, 61: 513–33.
Ogden, T.H. (1988) 'On the dialectical structure of experience: some clinical and theoretical implications', *Contemporary Psychoanalysis*, 24: 17–45.
Ogden, T.H. (1989) *The Primitive Edge of Experience*, Northvale, NJ, and London: Jason Aronson.
Ogden, T.H. (1990) *The Matrix of the Mind*. London: Maresfield Library.
Ogden, T.H. (1992a) 'The dialectically constituted/decentred subject of psychoanalysis, I, the Freudian subject', *International Journal of Psycho-Analysis*, 73: 517–26.
Ogden, T.H. (1992b) 'The dialectically constituted/decentred subject of psychoanalysis, II, the contributions of Klein and Winnicott', *International Journal of Psycho-Analysis*, 73: 613–26.
Ormont, L.R. (1984) 'The leader's role in dealing with aggression in groups', *International Journal of Group Psychotherapy*, 34: 553–72.
Perls, S. (1972) *Gestalt Therapy Verbatim*. New York: Bantam.
Petrella, R. (1995) Quoted in Harrison, M., *Visions of Heaven and Hell*. London: Channel 4 Television Publication.
Piaget, J. (1952) *The Origins of Intelligence in the Child*. New York: International Universities Press.
Piaget, J. (1957) *Logic and Psychology*. New York: Basic Books.
Pines, M. (1978) 'Group analytic psychotherapy of the borderline patient', *Group Analysis*, 11: 115–28.
Pines, M. (1982) 'Reflections on mirroring', *Group Analysis*, 15, Supplement: 1–32.
Pines, M. (1983a) (ed.) *The Evolution of Group Analysis*. London: Routledge and Kegan Paul.
Pines, M. (1983b) 'The contribution of S.H. Foulkes to group therapy', in Pines, M. (ed.) *The Evolution of Group Analysis*. London: Routledge and Kegan Paul.

Pines, M. (1986) 'Coherency and its disruption in the development of the self', *British Journal of Psychotherapy*, 2: 180–5.
Pines, M. (1987) 'Shame – what psychoanalysis does and does not say', *Group Analysis*, 20: 16–31.
Pines, M. (1990) 'Group analysis and the corrective emotional experience: is it relevant?', *Psychoanalytic Inquiry*, 10: 389–408.
Pines, M. (1993) 'Interpretation: why, for whom and when', in Kennard, D., Roberts, J., and Winter, D.A. (eds) *A Work Book of Group Analytic Interventions*. London: Routledge.
Pines, M. (1994a) 'The group-as-a-whole', in Brown, D. and Zinkin, L. (eds) *The Psyche and the Social World*. London: Routledge.
Pines, M. (1994b) 'Borderline phenomena in analytic groups', in Schemer, V.L. and Pines, M. (eds) *Ring of Fire*. London: Routledge.
Pines, M. and Schermer, V.L. (1994) 'An editorial introduction: Silence = death', in Schermer, V.L. and Pines, M. (eds) *Ring of Fire*. London: Routledge.
Powell, A. (1993) 'The psychophysical matrix and group analysis', *Group Analysis*, 26: 449–68.
Powell, A. (1994) 'Towards a unifying concept of the group matrix', in Brown, D. and Zinkin, L. (eds) *The Psyche and the Social World*. London: Routledge.
Prodgers, A. (1990) 'The dual nature of the group as mother: the uroboric container', *Group Analysis*, 23, 1: 17–30.
Prodgers, A. (1991) 'Counter transference: the conductor's emotional response within the group setting', *Group Analysis*, 24, 4: 389–407.
Rance, C.K. (1989) 'What has group analysis to offer in the context of organisational consultancy?', *Group Analysis*, 22: 333–43.
Rance, C.K. (1992) 'The aesthetics of group analysis', *Group Analysis*, 25: 171–81.
Raphael-Leff, J. (1984) 'Myths and modes of motherhood', *British Journal of Psychotherapy*, 1: 14–18.
Raphael-Leff, J. (1992) *Pyschological Processes of Childbearing*. London: Chapman and Hall.
Richards, B. (ed.) (1989) *Crises of the Self*. London: Free Association Books.
Richards, B. (1995) 'Psychotherapy and the injuries of class', *British Psychological Society Psychotherapy Section Newsletter*, 17: 21–35.
Ricoeur, P. (1970) *Freud and Philosophy: An Essay on Interpretation*. New Haven, CT: Yale University Press.
Roberts, J. (1983) 'Foulkes' concept of the matrix', *Group Analysis*, 15, 2: 111–26.
Roberts, J. (1991) 'Destructive phases in groups', in Roberts, J. and Pines, M. (eds) *The Practice of Group Analysis*. London: Routledge.
Roberts, J. (1993) 'Intervening to establish and maintain a therapeutic environment', in Kennard, D., Roberts, J., and Winter, D.A. (eds) *A Work Book of Group Analytic Interventions*. London: Routledge.
Roberts, J. and Pines, M. (eds) (1991) *The Practice of Group Analysis*. London: Routledge.

Roberts, J. and Pines, M. (1992) 'Group-analytic psychotherapy', *International Journal of Group Psychotherapy*, 42: 469–94.

Rogers, C. (1987) 'On putting it into words: the balance between projective identification and dialogue in the group', *Group Analysis*, 20: 99–107.

Roitman, M. (1989) 'The concept of projective identification: its use in understanding interpersonal and group processes', *Group Analysis*, 22: 235–48.

Rosenfield, H. (1971) 'A clinical approach to the psycho-analytic theory of the life and death instincts: an investigation into the aggressive aspects of narcissism', *International Journal of Psycho-Analysis*, 52: 169–77.

Rosenthal, L. (1987). *Resolving Resistances in Group Psychotherapy*. New Jersey: Jason Aronson.

Rothe, S. (1989) 'The Frankfurt School: an influence on Foulkes' group analysis', *Group Analysis*, 22, 405–15.

Rothenberg, A. (1971) 'On anger', *American Journal of Psychiatry*, 128, 4: 454–60.

Sandler, J., Dare, C. and Holder, A. (1973) *The Patient and the Analyst: The Basis of the Psychoanalytic Process*. London: Maresfield Reprints.

Scharff, D. (1982) 'Object relations theory and the family', in *The Sexual Relationship: An Object Relations View of Sex and the Family*. Boston, MA, and London: Routledge and Kegan Paul.

Scharff, D. and Scharff, J. (1991) *Object Relations Couple Therapy*. Northvale, NJ: Jason Aronson.

Schermer, V.L. (1985) 'Beyond Bion: the basic assumption states revisited', in Pines, M. (ed.) *Bion and Group Psychotherapy*. London: Routledge and Kegan Paul.

Schermer, V.L. (1994) 'Between theory and practice, light and heat', in Schermer, V.L. and Pines, M. (eds) *Ring of Fire*. London: Routledge.

Schermer, V.L. and Pines, M. (eds) (1994) *Ring of Fire: Primitive Affects and Object Relations in Group Psychotherapy*. London: Routledge.

Schindler, W. (1966) 'The role of the mother in group psychotherapy', *International Journal of Group Psychotherapy*, 16: 198–200.

Schlachet, P. (1986) 'The concept of group space', *International Journal of Group Psychotherapy*, 36: 33–53.

Schlapobersky, J. (1994) 'The language of the group: monologue, dialogue and discourse in group analysis', in Brown, D. and Zinkin, L. (eds) *The Psyche and the Social World*. London: Routledge.

Schlapobersky, J. (1995) 'From the speech of hands to the language of words: the group-analytic approach in forensic psychotherapy', in Cordess, C. and Cox, M. (eds) *Forensic Psychotherapy*. London: Jessica Kingsley.

Schwartz, H.S. (1990) *Narcissistic Process and Organisational Decay: The Theory of the Organisation Ideal*. New York: New York University Press.

Segal, H. (1979) *Klein*. Glasgow: Fontana/Collins.

Segal, H. (1990) *Dream, Phantasy and Art*. London: Tavistock/Routledge.

Segal, H. (1993) 'On the clinical usefulness of the concept of the death instinct', *International Journal of Psycho-Analysis*, 74: 55–62.

Sharpe, M. (1991) 'Death in the practice', in Roberts, J. and Pines, M. (eds) *The Practice of Group Analysis*. London: Routledge.

Sharpe, M. (1995) 'Training of supervisors', in Sharpe, M. (ed.) *The Third Eye: Supervision of Analytic Groups*. London: Routledge.

Simpson, I. (1995) 'Group therapy within the NHS I. We all know about "good enough" but is it safe enough?', *Group Analysis*, 28: 225–37.

Skynner, A.C.R. (1983) 'Group analysis and family therapy', in Pines, M. (ed.) *The Evolution of Group Analysis*. London: Routledge & Kegan Paul.

Skynner, A.C.R. (1984) 'Institutes and how to survive them', 8th S.H. Foulkes Annual Lecture, in Schlapobersky, J. (ed.) *Institutes and How to Survive Them*. London: Methuen, 1989.

Skynner, A.C.R. (1987) *Explorations with Families: Group Analysis and Family Therapy*. London: Methuen.

Skynner, A.C.R. (1988) 'Marriage and personal change', in Schlapobersky, J. (ed.) *Institutes and How to Survive Them: Selected Papers by Robin Skynner*. London: Methuen, 1989.

Skynner, A.C.R. (1989) *Institutes and How to Survive Them: Selected Papers by Robin Skynner*, ed. J. Schlapobersky. London: Methuen.

Slater, P. (1966) *Microcosm*. New York: John Wiley.

Slavson, S.R. (1964) *A Textbook of Analytic Group Psychotherapy*. New York: International Universities Press.

Slochower, J. (1991) 'Variations in the analytic holding environment', *International Journal of Psycho-Analysis*, 72: 709–17.

Smith, K.K. and Berg, D.N. (1988) *Paradoxes of Group Life*. London: Jossey-Bass.

Spero, M. (1986) 'Group drop outs', unpublished theoretical paper, Institute of Group Analysis, London.

Steiner, J. (1993) *Psychic Retreats*. London: Routledge.

Stern, D. (1985) *The Interpersonal World of the Infant*. New York: Basic Books.

Stevenson, B. and Ruscombe-King, G. (1993) 'Corking and uncorking: a reflection on group-analytic treatment for alcoholics', *Group Analysis*, 26: 213–24.

Stokes, A. (1965) *The Invitation to Art*. London: Tavistock.

Stone, W.N. (1992) 'A self psychology perspective on envy in group psychotherapy', *Group Analysis*, 25: 413–31.

Stone, W.N. (1992) 'The place of self-psychology in group psychotherapy: a status report', *International Journal of Group Psychotherapy*, 42: 335–50.

Storr, A. (1968) *Human Aggression*. Harmondsworth: Penguin.

Storr, A. (1972) *The Dynamics of Creation*. London: Secker and Warburg.

Thompson, A.E. (1991) 'Freud's pessimism, the death instinct, and the theme of disintegration in "Analysis terminable and interminable"', *International Review of Psycho-Analysis*, 28, 2: 165–80.

Thyssen, B. (1992) 'Diversity as a group-specific therapeutic factor in group-analytic psychotherapy', *Group Analysis*, 25: 75–86.

Toynbee, A. (1972) *A Study of History*. New York: Oxford University Press.

Tuckman, B. (1966) 'Developmental sequence in small groups', *Psychological Bulletin*, 63: 384–99.

Turquet, P. (1975) 'Threats to identity in the large group', in Kreeger, L. (ed.) *The Large Group – Dynamics and Therapy*. London: Maresfield Reprints.

Tuttman, S. (1991) ' "The anti-group": an historical and ideological breakthrough', *Group Analysis*. 24, 4: 483–4.

Tuttman, S. (1994) 'Therapeutic responses to the expression of aggression by members in groups', in Schermer, V.L. and Pines, M. (eds) *Ring of Fire*. London: Routledge.

Van der Kleij, G. (1983) 'The setting of the group', *Group Analysis*, 16: 75–80.

Watzlawick, P., Weakland, J. and Fisch, R. (1974) *Change: Principles of Problem Formation and Problem Resolution*. New York: Norton.

Webb, R.E., Bushnell, D.B. and Widseth, J.C. (1993) 'Tiresias and the beast: thinking of Lacan, interpretation, and caring', *International Journal of Psycho-Analysis*, 74: 597–612.

Weinhold, B.K. (1991) *Breaking Free of Addictive Family Relationships*. Walpole: Stillpoint.

Welldon, E. (1993) 'Forensic psychotherapy and group analysis', *Group Analysis*, 26: 487–502.

White, W.L. (1988) *Incest in the Organisational Family*. Bloomington, IN: Lighthouse Training Institute.

Williams, M. (1966) 'Limitations, fantasies, and security operations of beginning group psychotherapists', *International Journal of Group Psychotherapy*, 16: 150–62.

Williams, P.R. (1989) *Family Problems*. Oxford: Oxford University Press.

Winnicott, D.W. (1948) 'Reparation in respect of mothers' organized defense against depression', in *Through Paediatrics to Psychoanalysis*. London: Karnac/Institute of Psycho-Analysis, 1992.

Winnicott, D.W. (1949) 'Hate in the countertransference,' in *Through Paediatrics to Psychoanalysis*. London: Karnac/Institute of Psycho-Analysis, 1992.

Winnicott, D. W. (1953) Transitional objects and transitional phenomena', in *Playing and Reality*. London: Pelican, 1974.

Winnicott, D.W. (1960) 'The theory of the parent–infant relationship', in *The Maturational Processes and the Facilitating Environment*. London: Tavistock/Hogarth Press, 1965.

Winnicott, D.W. (1963a) 'Psychiatric disorder in terms of infantile maturational processes', in *The Maturational Processes and the Facilitating Environment*. London: Tavistock/Hogarth Press, 1965.

Winnicott, D.W. (1963b) 'Dependence in infant-care, in child care, and in the psycho-analytic setting', in *The Maturational Processes and the Facilitating Environment*. London: Tavistock/Hogarth Press, 1965.

Winnicott, D.W. (1965a) 'The concept of trauma in relation to the development of the individual within the family', in Winnicott, C., Shepherd, R., and Davis, M. (eds) *Psychoanalytic Explorations*. London: Karnac, 1989.

Winicott, D.W. (1965b) 'Integrative and disruptive factors in family life', in *The Family and Individual Developement*. London: Tavistock.

Winnicott, D.W. (1968) 'The use of an object and relating through identifications', in *Playing and Reality*. London: Pelican, 1974.

Winnicott, D.W. (1971) 'Playing: a theoretical statement', in *Playing and Reality*. London: Pelican, 1974.

Winnicott, D.W. (1975) 'The relationship of a mother to her baby at the beginning', in *The Family and Individual Development*. London: Tavistock.

Wojciechowska, E. (1993) 'The group as transformational object: fusion, transition, transformation', unpublished theoretical paper, Institute of Group Analysis, London.

Wolff, E. (1988) *Treating the Self: Elements of Clinical Self Psychology*. New York and London: Guilford Press.

Wong, N. (1981) 'The application of object-relations theory to an understanding of group cohesion', in Kellerman, H. (ed.) *Group Cohesion*. New York: Grune and Stratton.

Wooster, G. (1983) 'Resistance in groups as developmental difficulty in triangulation', *Group Analysis*, 16: 30–40.

Yalom, I. (1975) *Theory and Technique of Group Psychotherapy*. New York: Basic Books.

Yerushalmi, Y. (1991) *Freud's Moses: Judaism Terminable and Interminable*. New Haven, CT: Yale University Press.

Zender, J.F. (1991) 'Projective identification in group psychotherapy', *Group Analysis*, 24: 117–31.

Zinkin, L. (1983) 'Malignant mirroring', *Group Analysis*, 16: 113–26.

Zinkin, L. (1989) 'The group as container and contained', *Group Analysis*, 22: 227–34.

Zinkin, L. (1994) 'Exchange as a therapeutic factor in group analysis', in Brown, D. and Zinkin, L. (eds) *The Psyche and the Social World*. London: Routledge.

Zulueta, F. de (1993) *From Pain to Violence: The Traumatic Roots of Destruction*. London: Whurr.

Name Index

Adorno, T.W. 71
Agazarian, Y. 1, 52, 59, 61, 288
Amati Sas, S. 110
Anthony, E.J. 13–14, 17, 19, 22, 24–5, 28–30, 181, 227
Anzieu, D. 1, 80, 107, 114, 116, 151, 180, 237
Ashbach, C. 1, 52, 59, 73, 114, 186, 211, 214

Bacal, H.A. 107, 115
Bakhtin, M. 38
Balint, M. 107, 134
Barnett, B. 11
Bateson, G. 288
Battegay, R. 205
Beck, A.P. 52, 59
Becker, E. 115
Behr, H. 174, 195
Bennis, W.G. and Shephard, H.A. 214, 223
Berenstein, I. 37, 149
Berger, B. and Berger P.L. 236
Bergmann, M. 37
Bick, E. 114, 116, 156, 237
Bion, W. 1–2, 8, 10–11, 15, 40, 45–7, 64–9, 71, 86, 107, 109–10, 114, 116, 123, 138, 165, 178, 198, 218, 229, 237, 248, 277, 287
Blackwell, D. 22, 202, 285, 289
Bohm, D. 198, 205
Bollas, C. 107, 118, 194, 210–11, 229, 280, 290
Bosse, H. 23

Bowlby, J. 24, 164, 237
Boyd, R.D. 198
Bramley, W. 92, 255
Brenner, C. 37, 149
Bridger, H. 22
Brigham, P.M. 50, 110, 135, 191
Brown, D. 2, 11, 23, 46, 67–8, 121, 138, 161, 167, 181
Brown, D. and Zinkin, L. 5, 202, 271, 278, 286

Chasseguet-Smirgel, J. 12
Cortesao, E.L. 9, 202, 209–10, 230, 290
Cox, M. and Theilgard, A. 201
Coyne, J. 179

Dell, P.F. and Goolishan, H.A. 52
de Maré, P., Piper, R. and Thompson, S. 11–12, 137, 198, 210, 258, 283, 285
Derrida, J. 277
Dews, P. 70–71, 277
Dicks, B. 9
Dies, R.R. 3–4
Dixon, N.F. 265, 268
Doyle, R. 251
Durkin, H. 69, 288

Elias, N. 155, 160, 232, 283
Elliott, B. 117, 218
Emde, R.N. 121
Empedocles, 39

Fairbairn, W.R.D. 40, 107, 142, 185

Foguel, B. 156
Foucault, M. 288
Foulkes, E. 19
Foulkes, S.H. 2, 6, 8–41, 45–46, 51, 64, 68–9, 71, 109, 117–118, 121–2, 137, 143, 146, 149–50, 155, 161, 163, 174, 180, 184, 191–2, 198–9, 214–16, 218, 229–30, 264, 270–3, 276–7, 280–3, 287, 290
Freud, A. 24
Freud, S. 12, 18, 20, 28, 30–1, 34–5, 37–9, 53, 57, 71–2, 108, 138, 146–7, 149, 203–4, 214, 228, 269
Fried, K.W. 78, 89, 120
Frude, N. 236, 238–9, 240

Gans, J.S. 175, 185, 193–4
Ganzarian, R. 114
Garland, C. 22, 53
Gay, P. 149
Gfäller, G.R. 17, 160
Gibbard, G.S. and Hartman, J.J. 69, 139, 214
Glasser, M. 134
Glatzer, H. 69
Glenn, L. 237
Goldstein, K. 17–18, 25
Gordon, J. 66, 123, 125, 178
Green, L. 69
Grinberg, L. 188
Grosskurth, P. 20
Grotjahn, M. 163
Guntrip, H. 142

Hamilton, J. 37, 149
Handy, C. 263
Hargie, O., Saunders, C. and Dickson, D. 46
Harrison, M. 263
Harwood, I. 26, 107, 115
Hawkins, D.K. 43, 52, 154–5, 176
Hearst, L. 163, 232, 258–9
Hegel, F. 203
Higgins, R. 265
Hillman, J. and Ventura, M. 274
Hinshelwood, R.D. 178
Hirschorn, L. 248–9, 254–5
Hoffman, L. 238

Hoggett, P. 11–14, 233–6, 271
Hollinger, R. 277, 288
Hopper, E. 158
Horne, E. 180
Horwitz, L. 78, 124
Hutten, E.H. 147–8, 151

Inhelder, B. and Piaget, J. 189

Jacobson, L. 7, 63, 107, 197, 212–13, 236, 288
Jacques, E. 248
James, D.C. 63, 106, 123, 154, 211, 238
Johnson, S.M. 260
Jones, E. 18
Joseph, B. 150, 219
Jung, C.G. 26, 41

Kaplan, R. 267
Karterud, S.W. 34, 36, 194, 273
Kauff, P. 60
Kennard, D., Roberts, J.E. and Winter, D. 9, 178, 194
Kernberg, O. 49, 54, 107, 111–12, 143–6, 187
Kibel, H.D. 112, 124
King, P. 20
Klein, M. 20, 40, 63, 68, 107, 124, 129–32, 138–9, 147, 204, 209
Knauss, W. 23
Kohut, H. 24, 115, 260
Kreeger, L. 130–1

Lacan, J. 118, 203–4, 280
Laing, R.D. 236
Laplanche, J. 39
Lasch, C. 260
Layder, D. 258
Lear, T. 197
Le Roy, J. 234, 237, 254, 259
Lifton, R.J. 205

Main, M. 165
Main, T.F. 22
Malan, D.H. 11, 67
Maratos, J. 107, 148–50, 285
Maruyama, M. 199
Masson, J. 274–5

Name Index

Masterson, J. 239
Maturana, H. and Varela, F. 149, 200–2, 208, 230, 289
Meltzer, D. 140–141, 241–242
Mendez, C.L., Coddou, F. and Maturana, H. 165–6
Menzies-Lyth, I. 248
Miller, E. and Rice, A.K. 109
Modell, A.H. 154
Mollon, P. 115
Money-Kyrle, R.E. 266
Morgan, G. 197, 203, 250, 266, 285

Nitsun, M. 36, 45, 59, 77, 80, 115, 138–40, 216, 291
Norcross, J.C. and Goldfried, M.R. 24

O'Connor, N. and Ryan, J. 274
Ogden, T. 118, 122–3, 203–4
Ormont, L. R. 43, 186

Perls, F. 120
Petrella, R. 264
Piaget, J. 189, 202
Pines, M. 17, 25, 27, 32, 47, 49, 69, 111, 115, 121, 179, 181, 232, 280
Powell, A. 22–3, 26, 40–1, 197
Prodgers, A. 9, 69, 187, 192, 194–5, 200, 273, 280

Rance, C.K. 22–3, 197, 209–10, 230, 290
Raphael-Leff, J. 69
Richards, B. 15, 274
Ricoeur, P. 37, 149
Roberts, J. 9, 18, 22, 24, 198, 273, 280
Roberts, J. and Pines, M. 18, 22
Rogers, C. 117, 124, 185
Roitman, M. 124, 191
Rosenfield, H. 125, 151
Rosenthal, L. 185
Rothe, S. 17
Rothenberg, A. 143

Scharff, D. 237
Scharff, D. and Scharff, J. 165

Schermer, V.L. 2, 9, 52, 59, 68, 73, 114, 186, 211, 214, 232, 273
Schermer, V.L. and Pines, M. 232
Schindler, W. 69
Schlachet, P. 22, 63, 211, 228
Schlapobersky, J. 7, 23, 117, 161, 202, 215, 288
Schmideberg, W. 20
Schwartz, H.S. 36, 247–9, 255, 261, 285
Segal, 114, 148, 151, 209
Sharpe, M. 21, 157–8, 290
Simpson, I. 155
Skynner, R. 3–5, 9, 11, 17, 22, 25–7, 22, 235, 237–8, 249–50, 258
Slater, P. 214
Slavson, S.R. 175
Slochower, J. 154
Smith, K.K. and Berg, D.N. 8, 45–6
Spero, M. 171
Steiner, J. 20, 114, 151
Stern, D. 24, 120–1, 280
Stevenson, B. and Ruscombe-King, G. 161
Stokes, A. 209
Stone, W.N. 115, 129, 131
Storr, A. 209, 265

Thompson, A.E. 37–8, 53, 71, 146, 203
Thyssen, B. 50, 161
Toynbee, A. 232
Tuckman, B. 52
Turquet, P. 133, 258
Tuttman, S. 154, 163, 186, 193

Van der Kleij, G. 155

Webb, R.E., Bushnell, D.B. and Widseth, J.C. 203
Weinhold, B.K. 239
Welldon, E. 161
White, W.L. 250
Williams, M. 189, 239
Winnicott, D. 2, 22, 63, 107, 116, 154, 194–6, 204, 208–9, 211–13, 225, 227–8, 237, 240–1, 283, 290
Wojciechowska, E. 210
Wolff, E. 130

Wong, N. 205
Wooster, G. 217

Yalom, I. 10, 24, 51, 115, 155, 161–2, 164, 169, 171–2, 179, 181

Zender, J. F. 124, 191
Zinkin, L. 5, 26, 104, 122, 125, 197, 202, 271, 278, 280, 286
Zulueta, F. de 148, 150, 265

Subject Index

abandonment 60, 85, 136, 163, 170, 207, 212
acting out 29, 30, 44, 56, 99, 117, 129, 193, 208; in wider social sphere 243, 250
addiction to near-death 150, 218–19
aesthetic equilibrium 209, 210, 290
aesthetic transformation 209, 210, 290
aesthetics, of the group 209–10, 229–30, 290–1
aggression 1–2, 37, 40, 41, 43–4, 49, 149, 205; counter-transference and 192–4; in culture 265–8; dealing with 175, 184–6; and death instinct 147; differentiated 185; Foulkes and 15, 20, 30–4, 35, 40, 215, 270, 287; and hatred 143–6; and regression 108, 111; and selection 162–3
alienation 118; social 46, 89
ambiguity of primary task 109–10
anarchy 268
anger 43, 143, 169, 184
anti-group 2–3, 4, 6–8; and aesthetics of group 291; alternation with 'pro-group' 90–1, 204–5, 279, 286; in clinical setting 54–7, illustrations 75–105; conductor's attitude to 59, 175–6; as critical principle 70–2, 104, 273, 278; criticisms of concept 73–4; cultural origins of 14, 259–70; definition of 1, 44–5; degrees of intensity 145–6; determinants 106–52, 279–80; as developmental phenomenon 61–2; implications for group-analytic principles 280–1; indirect expression of 62; latent and manifest 57–9, 60, 87–90, 200, 224, 230; levels of 67–8, 81–3; management of 281–2; origin of the concept 29, 42–4; other theoretical links 64–8; in psychoanalytic milieu 14, 35–6; scope of 273–4; and stages of development of group 59–61; summary of concept 278–9; in wider sphere 232–71, 283–5; *see also under* transformation
anti-libidinal ego/forces 100, 142–3
anxiety, about groups 1, 4, 6, 49, 50, 60, 169, 213, 230; clinical illustrations 76, 77, 78, 80, 85, 87; large groups 12; organisations 248; staff support groups 57; *see also* stranger anxiety; survival anxiety
attachment theory 24, 237
attacks on linking 123, 127, 177–8
attunement 24, 121; failures of 121–2
authority, in group 109, 174, 214–15, 220, 221, 224, 229
autonomy, group 201, 214

Subject Index

autopoesis 200–2, 208, 216, 230, 283, 289

barometric event 214, 223, 229
basic assumption groups 10, 65, 109, 114, 138, 248, 277; as anti-groups 66–8; dependence 65, 67, 177; flight–fight 65, 67, 86, 95; pairing 65, 67, 82, 96, 172
basic fault 107, 134–5
basic law of group dynamics 33, 270, 272
biography, of Foulkes 18–21, 30, 34–5, 270, 273
birth, as traumatic fantasy of group 116–17
bizarre objects 127–8
bonding capacity: and conductor 172; and group selection 164–5, 281
borderline phenomena, in groups 111–12
boundaries 116, 156, 196, 219, 237, 281, 289; in staff support and experiential training groups and organisations 57, 92, 93, 94–5, 96, 98, 101, 249, 257
breaks 53, 56, 79, 189–90, 208, 217, 222

catastrophe 116–17, 134, 212; *see also* trauma
causality, related to determinants of anti-group 107–8, 150, 279
coherence 5, 27, 47, 61, 79, 200
cohesion 2, 7, 43, 47, 69, 110–11, 116, 172, 250, 254, 290; clinical illustrations 90–1, 94, 157, 219; in group analytic milieu 36; pathological (extreme) 205–6, 261–2, 287
Commitments, The, creative and destructive forces in 251–3
communication 275, 277, 280–1; and autopoesis 201–2; failures/difficulties of 56, 82, 83, 108, 117–23, 172, 205, 279; Foulkes' theory 9, 12, 21, 22, 23–4, 40, 117–18, 143, 264, 280

community 12, 291; political conceptions of 259–61, 263–4; virtual 262; and technological advance 262–4, 275, 284; *see also* koinonia
competition 2, 85; in society 253–4, 260; *see also* rivalry
conductor 24, 78, 84–8 *passim*, 135–7, 214, 289; and the anti-group 56, 59, 85–7, 106, 169, 173, 174, 219–20, 226, 229, 282; intervention of 89, 95–6, 102, 175–86, 196, 282; and technical considerations 159, 160, 168, 171, 174; *see also* facilitator; leadership
connecting function of conductor 87, 177–8, 282
consensus 33
constructive forces of group 7, 8, 10, 32, 33, 44, 59; *see also* creation; creativity; 'pro-group'
constructive potential of anti-group 16, 45, 70–2, 104, 153, 273, 278, 291; *see also* dialectics *and under* transformation
constructivism 200, 202
containment 50, 63, 78, 82, 117, 155, 156, 187, 198, 230, 254; conductor as container 106, 191, 196, 282; container–contained 65, 66, 124, 183, 237; group as container 22, 100, 107, 111, 145, 209, 280
contaminating communication 86–7, 121–2, 124–5, 167, 281
context 22, 154–5, 158, 160, 181, 253, 289; anti-group and 54, 76, 103, 105, 106, 232–3; and selection 168
co-operation, in group 87–8, 90
counter-transference 29, 53, 105, 137, 174, 186–96, 216, 282
creation of the group 49, 208–11, 291
creative destruction 2, 283
creativity 22, 147, 211; creative vs. destructive in group 45, 63, 70, 74, 213; *see also* dialectics

Subject Index 313

cult groups 205
culture 232, 258–71, 284; breakdown of established structures 259–61; destructive forces 265–8; and group analysis 15, 232–3, 270–1; linking intra-psychic and social 268–70; politics and the group 259–61; technological change 262–4
culture of the anti-group 232–71, 284
cybernetic model 199–200

death 115, 116, 117; fantasy of 100
death instinct 31, 37, 39, 68, 210, 272; and anti-group 146–52, 279
decentred group 287
deconstructionism 38, 71; and group analysis 27, 184, 276–7, 280, 286; and group therapy 5, 47
defences 40, 110, 111, 145, 185–6; social 248, 254, 255; *see also* denial
defensive agglomeration 145, 184
denial, defence of 105, 150, 273; Bion and 66; of death (Becker) 115; Foulkes and 21, 35, 36
depressive position 63, 107, 139, 204, 205, 209, 255
destructiveness 1–2, 54, 68, 150, 205, 233, 258, 270, 273, 276, 277; in culture 265–8, 271; Foulkes and 8–9, 20, 31–4, 40, 43, 272; vs. constructive/creative 44, 63, 70, 74, *see also* dialectics
developmental stages of the group 59–61, 185; early 59–60, 76–80, 85–6, 87, 115, 156–7; middle/ mature 60
dialectics: tradition of thought 203; perspective of the group 69–70, 91, 197, 202–7, 213, 216, 230–1, 232, 250–1, 280, 283, 286–8; work groups 251–3
dialogue 12, 198, 283
differentiated aggression 185

differentiation 27, 50, 129, 147–8, 214
disillusionment 219, 222
disintegration 38, 71, 72, 147, 271; group 60, 93–8, 150, 205–6, 207, 273
distrust, of groups 1, 4, 6, 55, 60, 230, 243
dreams 23, 83, 218–19
drop-outs 29, 55, 61, 62, 163, 169–71, 176, 200, 208, 289; clinical illustrations 78, 84, 86, 87, 88, 89, 102, 103, 224
dynamic administration 155, 282, 290

ecology of the group 288–90
ego 107, 142
ego psychology 24
empathy 24
Emperor's new clothes phenomenon 26–7
environmental mother/support 103, 107, 116, 154–5, 157, 254, 268–9
envy 2, 29, 65, 123, 129–32, 139, 150, 163, 269; clinical illustrations 91, 99, 104, 126, 220; and envy pre-emption 130, 220, 222; in work group 252
exchange 23, 122, 277, 280, 281
experiential training group 75, 76; clinical illustrations 101–4, 156–7, 158–9, 189–90, 196, 206

facilitator 92–105 *passim*, 129–30; *see also* conductor; leadership of group
false self, group as 78, 89, 120
family 139, 232, 235, 236–47, 270, 284; as anti-group 239–42; cross-sectional and longitudinal view of 242–5; disintegration of 236–7, 239, 241–2, 245; dysfunctional 88, 89, 239, 245, 249–50; healthy 237–8; place of therapy 245–7
family therapy 22, 179, 275
fantasies 58, 59, 67, 68, 69, 100,

107, 109, 143–4, 216; birth 116–17; death 100; about nature of group 80, 109, 114, 130, 222, 229; sexual 112, 128, 138–42
father 182, 217, 228–9; loss of 83, 217–22, 223
fear, of groups 1, 29, 50, 58
figuration 155, 160, 232, 283
fixation to the trauma 146
foundation matrix 51, 89
fragmentation, in groups 80, 84, 91, 111, 127, 142, 190, 200, 205, 267
Frankfurt School 18, 71
free-floating discussion 23, 216
frustration 1, 49, 53, 55, 135–6, 143, 146, 151, 169, 170, 176, 198; cultural 267; in large groups 11, 198

gang, the 125–7, 130, 131, 151, 222–3
Gestalt psychology/therapy 18, 25–6, 275
greed 65, 132
group 1, 133; as act of faith 29, 276; complexity 5–6, 14, 51, 72, 123; composition 48, 105, 161, 289, *see also* selection; emotive power 14; ending 87, 136–7; identity 110, 116, 158, 219; incomplete experience of 53–4; instability/unpredictability 6, 43, 51–3, 54, 72, 91, 94, 123, 176, 182; as mother 64, 68–70, 80, 208, 209, 217, 229; as plural entity 50–1; as public arena 50; and wider culture 232–3
group analysis, place of 276–8
Group Analytic Society 36
group-as-a-whole 25, 26, 33, 47, 94, 136, 206; and anti-group 43, 61, 82–3, 84, 169
group diseases 65, 66, 277
group interpretations 181, 183
group matrix 47, 49, 72, 104, 198, 199, 280; Foulkes and 9, 21–2, 25, 26, 39, 276; and quantum theory 9

group mentality 64–5, 66
group object relation 2, 107, 110, 111, 144–5, 166–7, 195, 212, 279, 281–2; conductor's 188–90, 191; family and 238, 242, 284; negative 169, 170
group psychotherapy 2–16; antagonism of psychoanalysis to 12–14; anti-group perspective 2–3, 6–8; challenge to 274–5; ideological split 8–11, 277; place of group analysis 276–8; status of 3–6, 274
group revolt 214, 223–5
group skin 116
group suicide 79
groups illustrated: Group A: alternation of 'pro-group' and anti-group 90–1, different levels of the anti-group 81–3, envy 130, 131, hostile pairing group 172, primal scene 138–9, 141–2, projective identification 126–7, setting 159–60, the start of a new group 76–80, transformational process 216–31; Group B 129, 145, 163, 167, breakdown of the group 83–5; Group C 121, 124–5, 142, 145, 167, flawed development of group 85–7; Group D 120, 130, 132, 141, manifest and latent anti-group 87–90; Group E: staff support group on a psychiatric ward 94–8; Group F: staff support group in a general hospital 98–101; Group G: an experiental group in a psychotherapy training course 101–4, 129–30, 145, 158–9, 196; Sally's group 127–8, 136–7

hatred 123, 136, 143–6, 184, 185; in the counter-transference 194; degrees of 144; transformation of 11–12, 198
helplessness, conductor's 196
heterogeneous groups 161
holding 66, 237, 282

holding environment 106, 154–5, 195, 196; work groups 253
Holocaust 34, 221
homogeneous groups 161, 163
hostility 2, 29, 43, 49, 60, 66, 73, 94, 103, 206; dealing with 185, 193; positive value of 175

idealisation 105, 193: of Foulkes 36, 41, 194, 273; of the group 7, 12, 69, 139 194, 206, 210, 276, 288, by Foulkes 17, 27–8, 29, 34, 36, 69, 118, 147, 287
idealising self-objects 130
ideological split between Foulkes and Bion 8–11, 277
ideological totalism 205, 262
ideology, group analytic 36
imagery 77, 79, 80, 116–17, 127–8, 216, 217–18, 225–7, 229
impasse, states of 12, 43, 51, 56, 66, 85, 118, 120, 151, 190
individual: and anti-group 43, 58, 61, 62, 68, 81–2, 83, 84, 85, 105, 141, 151, 169; and society 258; vs. group 14, 64, 252
individual psychotherapy 4, 13, 72, 275; preferred to group psychotherapy 4, 55, 78, 82, 119–20, 134–5, 172
individualism, social 260
infancy 121, 154, 211; group as infant 115–16, 154–5, 156, 183, 226–7, 229, in wider culture 268–9; see also group, as mother
instinct theory 39, 146, 147, 203; Eros 39, 68, 147, 148, 150, 210; Thanatos 39, 68, 147, 210; see also death instinct
Institute of Psycho-analysis 19, 20
institutions: anti-group in 101–4, 158–60; social 284; see also culture; family; organisations
integration 7, 11, 26, 33, 38, 147–8, 179, 278; family 241–2; social 271
integrative theoretical perspectives of group analysis 285–91

interpersonal relationships 51–2, 53, 93, 152, 163; as determinant of anti-group 133–7, 279; family 88, 243; organisations 249–50; selection and interpersonal relatedness 164–6; and technological culture 263–4, 275
interpretation 179–83, 185, 257
intra-psychic dimension 66, 93, 110, 152; anti-group as link between intra-psychic and social 54, 268–70
irritation 143

jealousy 131
Jungian approach 26, 41

-k 65, 66, 123
koinonia 11–12, 137, 198, 210, 258

large group 11–12, 108–9, 198, 258; work groups 251–2; see also organisations
leadership of group 190–1; Foulkes and 24–5; Freud and 108–9; transformation of 213–15, 220, 226, 229, 230, 283; see also conductor; facilitator
levels of group functioning 6, 51, 216
life instinct 39, 68, 147, 148, 150, 210
limit setting 193
linking, theories of 107
linking function 87, 177–8, 282
location 184
logics of change 197–8, 199–207, 231, 283
loss 87, 134, 163; and family 237, 238; of father 83, 217–22, 223; and group development 53, 63, 136–7, 170, 207, 218, 221–2, 223

madness, fear of 80, 159–60
malignant mirroring 104, 122, 125, 159, 280
masochism 144
meaning 5, 122, 123
membership of the group:

introduction of new members 60–1, 78, 79, 88–9; suitability for 85, 162–4
Messiah fantasy 82
metaphor: of group 39, 68; the gang as metaphor of anti-group 126
mirroring 23, 54, 80, 106, 111, 123, 125, 130, 160, 188, 280; group as mirror of societal norms 34; malignant 104, 122, 125, 159, 280; in organisations 103–4, 255, 268, 285
misattunement 121–2
mistrust *see* distrust
mother 182, 214, 218; environmental and object mother distinction 154–5, 157; *see also under* group; infancy
mourning 139, 170, 273; of the father 218–19, 229

narcissism 1, 125, 188, 189, 205; cultural 260; and rage 129
National Health Service 54–5, 134, 155, 247, 254; clinical ilustrations 85, 177, 182, 207, 209, 246
nature/nurture 150
negative therapeutic reaction 44, 131, 175, 220
network: global 262–4, 275; group 22, 25, 27, 36, 166
neurobiology, influence on Foulkes 25
Nirvana principle 147
nodal point 32, 68, 264, 276
non-clinical settings 6, 7, 9–10, 23; excessive cohesion 205; *see also* culture; family; organisations; staff support groups
non-dialogic mirroring 280
Northfield Military Experiment 19, 22

object relations theory 123, 131; and group analysis 24, 25, 37, 40, 106–7, 166; and group psychotherapy 114

Oedipus complex 139, 214, 241
omnipotence 66, 288
optimism 10: and pessimism 11, 71, 203, 277; therapeutic 7–8, 32, 36, 42, 118, 149, 270
organisations 23, 43, 232, 247–58: anti-group in 54, 249–58; change 101–4, 158, 160, 253–4, 255, 257, 284; clockwork/ snakepit 247–8, 249, 285; compared to dysfunctional family 249–50; competition/ rivalry in 249, 252, 256, 270; dysfunctional 249, 250; incest in 250; as psychic prison 250, 285; setting 155, 157–60, 196; theory 11; unconscious in 250, 256–7
original sin 150
out-patient groups 55, 56, 77, 85, 118, 170, 177, 182
overt vs. covert expression *see* anti-group, latent and manifest

paradox, of the group 45–54, 66, 74, 176
paradoxical characteristics of group 47–53, 106
paranoid-schizoid position 107, 114, 204, 267
passion for proximity 154, 165–6, 281
pessimism 11, 277, 288; and anti-group 68; corrective 31, 35, 37–8, 71
phenomenology 150; and anti-group 151, 279–80
play 63, 211, 212–13, 216, 225–8, 230, 231, 283, 288, 290
plunging interpretations 180, 183
politics: and the group 259–61, 263–4, 266; and group analysis 15
positive connotation 179
postmodernism 5, 38, 70–1, 278
potential space 211; *see also* transitional space
power, issues of 60, 93, 145, 185, 215, 229
pregnancy, as theme 222

preparation for group therapy 171–3
primal horde 214
primal scene 108, 112, 133, 138–43, 145, 166, 241, 279
primary task for group 109–10
primitive aspects of group 10, 40, 64–7, 68–9, 93, 105, 114; organisations 248; *see also* primal horde; primal scene
professional counter-transference 194
progress 38, 45, 71, 72, 85
'pro-group' 66; alternation with anti-group 90–1, 204–5, 279, 286
projection 40, 49, 61, 76–7, 95, 105, 106, 107, 109, 110, 132, 145, 170
projective identification 40, 66, 80, 91, 105, 110, 111, 138, 145, 150, 158, 183; conductor's 104, 186, 191–2; determinants of anti-group 123–8, 132, 279; in organisations 254
psychic skin 114, 116, 156
psychoanalysis 4, 71–2; antagonism to groups 12–14, 35–6; and group analysis 19–20, 35–41; principles of 131, 149, 203–4, 210
psychotherapy: criticisms of 274–5
psychotic group formations 114

quantum physics 9

rage 89, 123, 143–4, 145, 163, 185, 243, 269
reality 149, 198
reframing 179
regression 38, 54; as determinant of anti-group 108–12; in groups 2, 8, 10, 45, 68, 84, 106, 113, 115, 277
reparation: anti-group and 16, 62–3, 209, 214, 218, 222, 230, 283; and staff development 254–8
repression 142, 150, 163
research 11, 36, 69, 214
resistance 43, 87, 168, 269

resonance, in groups 23–4, 40, 79, 277, 280
responsibility to the external context 290
rivalry 2, 60, 99, 131, 185; in work group 252, 256
roles, in groups 167, 228; conductor's 159, 174–96; leadership 190–1; as voice of anti-group 141

sadism 29, 144, 145
scapegoating 62, 186, 193, 206, 255
scarcity, psychology of 269–70
scientific status, attributed by Foulkes to group analysis 28
selection 85, 161–9, 281–22, 289; context of 168; criteria for 162–7; process of 168–9
self-destruction 8, 31, 149, 150, 151, 207, 272; culture and 265–8; *see also* death instinct; destructiveness
self-psychology 26, 107, 115, 129, 130
setting 30, 59, 155–60, 281; changes in 159–60; organisational 155, 157–60; physical 102, 155, 156–7, 196
sexual fantasies 112, 128, 138–42
sexual tension, in groups 83–5, 141–2, 221, 252
slow-open groups 60–1, 136, 161, 289
socialisation 32, 281
society: Foulkes' view of 15, 32, 33–4, 155, 270–1, 272; change/breakdown in 235–6, 261–2, 275, 278; *see also* culture; family; organisations
sociobiological orientation of Foulkes *see under* society
splitting 40; in culture 266; in groups 61, 70, 97, 110, 125, 127, 130, 138, 200
staff support groups 6, 43, 75, 91–101; in general hospital 98–101; in organisation 255–8,

285; on psychiatric ward 56–7, 93–8
status of group psychotherapy 3–6, 274
stranger, of primal scene 140, 141
stranger anxiety 48, 185; in family 244
structural coupling 201–2, 289
structure in groups 111, 198; lack of 48–9, 111
structure of opposition 70–1
sub-group, and anti-group 43, 58, 61, 67, 82, 83
supervision 99, 103, 104; necessity of 195–6
survival anxiety 113–17, 279
survival of the group 56, 202, 207–8, 288
systems theory 61–2, 199–200, 289

Tavistock approach 11, 181, 248
techniques for handling anti-group 175–86, 282: connecting function 177–8, 282; interpretation 179–83; maintaining group position 176–7, 282; positive connotation/reframing 179, 282; *see also* conductor, interventions of
techno apartheid 264
technological advance/change 253, 261, 262–4, 265, 275, 28
theoretical coherence, lacking in group psychotherapy and group analysis 4–5, 9–10, 26–7; *see also* integrative theoretical perspectives
therapeutic community 22
thinking 65, 122–3
total situation 25, 26
Tower of Babel effect 51, 78, 82
training 6, 43, 192; and conductor's role 190, 194–5; *see also* experiential training group
transcultural group analysis 23
transference 38, 53, 71–2, 105, 128, 135, 137, 195, 216

transformation 22, 26, 66, 70, 76, 271; clinical illustration 216–31; of hate 11–12, 198; potential of anti-group 2, 16, 62–3, 104, 197–215, 282–3; theories of transformation 197–8, 199–207; *see also under* leadership
transformational flux 198, 200, 203, 271, 283
transformational object 209, 210, 211, 228, 283, 290
transitional object 211, 228; group as 63, 211–12, 228, 230
transitional space 22, 63, 211–12, 216, 225, 228, 283, 290
translation 24, 40, 117, 281
transpersonal psychology 41
transposition 285
trauma 56, 107, 116, 134, 163–4; *see also* catastrophe
true self, and false self 120
trust, in the group 29–30, 60, 228

unconscious 64–5, 67, 69, 80, 87, 109, 125, 143, 222; in organisations 250, 256–7; *see also* translation
universality, sense of 24
use of an object 63, 208, 212, 225, 283

valency 165
virtual community 262–4, 275, 284

wholeness: Foulkes' emphasis on 25–6, 36, 39, 40–1, 276, 287; and reparation in organisations 254, 258
womb, group as 117, 130, 218, 229
work 249; and the anti-group 66, 251–3; *see also* organisations; staff support groups
world wars: and aggression 267; influence of World War II on Foulkes 19, 20–1, 34, 41; related to death instinct 149